UNACCEPTABLE

UNACCEPTABLE

Privilege, Deceit & the Making of the
College Admissions Scandal

MELISSA KORN

AND

JENNIFER LEVITZ

PORTFOLIO / PENGUIN

Portfolio / Penguin
An imprint of Penguin Random House LLC
penguinrandomhouse.com

Most Portfolio books are available at a discount when purchased in quantity for sales
promotions or corporate use. Special editions, which include personalized covers, excerpts,
and corporate imprints, can be created when purchased in large quantities. For more
information, please call (212) 572-2232 or e-mail specialmarkets@penguinrandomhouse.
com. Your local bookstore can also assist with discounted bulk purchases using the Penguin
Random House corporate Business-to-Business program. For assistance in locating a
participating retailer, e-mail B2B@penguinrandomhouse.com.

Library of Congress Cataloging-in-Publication Data

Names: Korn, Melissa, author. | Levitz, Jennifer, author.
Title: Unacceptable : privilege, deceit & the making of the
college admissions scandal / Melissa Korn, and Jennifer Levitz.
Description: New York : Portfolio / Penguin, [2020] | Includes bibliographical references.
Identifiers: LCCN 2020017723 (print) | LCCN 2020017724 (ebook) |
ISBN 9780593087725 (hardcover) | ISBN 9780593087732 (ebook)
Subjects: LCSH: Universities and colleges—United States—Admission—Corrupt practices. |
Universities and colleges—United States—Administration.
Classification: LCC LB2351 .K65 2020 (print) |
LCC LB2351 (ebook) | DDC 378.1/61—dc23
LC record available at https://lccn.loc.gov/2020017723
LC ebook record available at https://lccn.loc.gov/2020017724

Printed in the United States of America
1   3   5   7   9   10   8   6   4   2

BOOK DESIGN BY ELLEN CIPRIANO

For my parents, Rich and Amy, who always encouraged me to be curious. And for my daughter, Abby, who continues to ask why.
—Melissa

For Mark, who inspires me with his tenacity and love, and for my mom, Shirley, who taught me to see stories everywhere.
—Jennifer

CONTENTS

AUTHORS' NOTE

THIS BOOK IS THE culmination of more than a year of reporting and writing. We spoke, emailed, and messaged with hundreds of people to piece together the stories here, and also utilized court filings, public information requests, and myriad other records.

Many of the people we interviewed were involved in ongoing legal battles at the time of our discussions. Some still have criminal cases pending. As a result, those who agreed to speak generally asked to do so on the condition that they not be identified.

Because we relied on so many different people and written sources in retelling this narrative, readers should not assume anyone in any particular scene was a source of information or spoke to us at all. We tried to contact everyone who is mentioned in a substantive way.

We have chosen to provide pseudonyms for some of the children of those charged in the criminal cases. Specifically, we have changed the names of young adults who were not named in any court filings or identified publicly by their parents or on their own.

CAST OF CHARACTERS

THE RINGLEADER

- **Rick Singer**, a California college counselor and the admitted mastermind of the scheme

SINGER'S LIEUTENANTS

- **Igor Dvorskiy**, director of West Hollywood College Preparatory School and test-site administrator
- **Martin Fox**, a Houston athletics fixer who connected Singer with other key players
- **Laura Janke**, a former USC assistant women's soccer coach who helped Singer create fake athletic profiles
- **Mark Riddell**, a college entrance exam whiz and proctor who rigged tests for Singer's clients
- **Niki Williams**, a teaching assistant, cheerleading coach, and test-site administrator at Jack Yates High School in Houston

THE PARENTS

- **Marcia and Greg Abbott**, parents who lived (respectively) in Aspen and New York, and who used Singer to rig their daughter's tests
- **Jane Buckingham**, a Beverly Hills trend forecaster who paid to have Singer fraudulently boost the ACT for her son, Jack, a student at Brentwood School
- **Gordon Caplan**, cochairman of law firm Willkie Farr & Gallagher, who lived in Greenwich, Connecticut, and used Singer to cheat and raise his daughter's ACT score
- **Robert Flaxman**, a Beverly Hills developer who used Singer to rig the ACT for his daughter, Emily

- **Mossimo Giannulli and Lori Loughlin**, a married Los Angeles fashion designer and actress who worked with Singer to pitch their daughters, Bella and Olivia, to USC as fake crew team prospects
- **Manuel Henriquez**, the founder of Hercules Capital, a publicly traded finance company; he and his wife, **Elizabeth Henriquez**, worked with Singer to cheat the system for daughters Julia and Megan
- **Doug Hodge**, an executive for bond manager Pimco, based in Newport Beach, California, who used Singer's illicit services for multiple kids
- **Felicity Huffman**, the *Desperate Housewives* actress, who is married to fellow actor William H. Macy and who conspired with Singer to rig the SAT for daughter Sophia
- **Agustin Huneeus Jr.**, part of a Napa Valley wine dynasty, who worked with Singer to present daughter Agustina as a phony water polo recruit
- **Davina and Bruce Isackson**, a Hillsborough, California, couple who used Singer's illegal services for two daughters
- **Michelle Janavs**, a Newport Beach, California, mom and Hot Pockets heiress who engaged with Singer for two daughters, including to rig tests and pitch one as an athlete
- **Elisabeth Kimmel**, a San Diego media executive who hired Singer to work with her son Spencer
- **Marjorie Klapper**, a Menlo Park, California, jewelry designer who used Singer's illicit help for her son
- **Toby Macfarlane**, a Del Mar, California, title insurance executive who used Singer to pass off two children as bogus athletic recruits
- **Bill McGlashan**, a San Francisco–area private equity investor who hired Singer for his son
- **P. J. Sartorio**, the Menlo Park, California, founder of a frozen Mexican food company who turned to Singer to rig a test for his daughter
- **Stephen Semprevivo**, a Los Angeles business executive who used Singer's shady services to help place his son Adam at Georgetown
- **David Sidoo**, a Canadian businessman and former pro football player who paid to have Riddell take tests for two sons, Jake and Ethan

- **Devin Sloane**, a Bel Air water-sector entrepreneur who used Singer's illicit operation for his son, Matteo, then a student at the Buckley School
- **Morrie Tobin**, a Los Angeles investor who didn't know Singer but who bribed Yale women's soccer coach Rudy Meredith to tag his daughter Sydney as a recruit
- **John B. Wilson**, an Atherton, California, private equity investor who retained Singer for his son Sam, a high school water polo player, and for two daughters
- **Robert Zangrillo**, a Miami Beach developer and investor who worked with Singer and his team for a daughter, Amber

THE TROJANS

- **Donna Heinel**, USC associate athletic director who worked with Singer on admissions for athletic recruits
- **Ali Khosroshahin**, former USC women's soccer coach who slotted in Singer's clients as recruits and went on to connect Singer with other coaches
- **Jovan Vavic**, USC's illustrious water polo coach and a longtime contact for Singer

THE OTHER COACHES

- **Michael Center**, head men's tennis coach at the University of Texas at Austin who took one of Singer's clients as a recruit in exchange for cash and money for his program
- **Gordon Ernst**, Georgetown's men's and women's tennis coach who was accused of tagging teens who weren't tennis stars as recruits
- **Rudy Meredith**, who coached Yale's women's soccer team and took payment from Singer and Tobin to flag teens as recruits

THE CURIOUS COUNSELORS

- **Philip "PJ" Petrone**, codirector of college counseling at the private Marymount High School, who wondered why the Giannulli girls were being classified as rowing recruits

- **Julie Taylor-Vaz**, the director of college counseling at Buckley, who raised questions about certain Singer clients and false information submitted to colleges

LAW AND ORDER

- **U.S. District Judge Indira Talwani**, a federal judge in Boston who would sentence eleven parents in the college admissions cases
- **U.S. District Judge Nathaniel M. Gorton**, a federal judge in Boston who handled many of the admissions cases
- **Judge M. Page Kelley**, a federal magistrate judge who handled initial appearances and discovery hearings in the admissions cases
- **Andrew Lelling**, U.S. Attorney for Massachusetts, appointed in December 2017, who oversaw the investigation into Singer's criminal enterprise
- **Eric Rosen**, an assistant U.S. attorney in the economic crimes unit and a top prosecutor on the college admissions cases
- **Steve Frank**, Rosen's boss and chief of the economic crimes unit
- **Donald Heller**, a Sacramento defense attorney who represented Singer

THE CONNECTORS

- **Dana Pump**, a charity founder and basketball fixture who connected Singer to some well-off families and to **Martin Fox**
- **Scott Treibly**, the former college placement adviser at IMG Academy who connected Singer with parents and at least one coach
- **Brian Werdesheim**, founding partner of the Summa Group, a Los Angeles wealth management firm, who introduced Singer to many families
- **Michael Wu**, a Morgan Stanley financial officer who connected Singer with the family of **Yusi Zhao**
- **Qiuxue "Valerie" Yang,** an analytics associate at Summa Group, who introduced the family of **Sherry Guo** to Singer

UNACCEPTABLE

PREFACE

I N 2016, JANE BUCKINGHAM was at her son's soccer game in Brentwood, one of the most exclusive parts of Los Angeles, when another mom turned to her and said something unexpected. "Who'd you hire as a college counselor?"

"Wait," Buckingham said. "Do we have to do that? Now?" Her son Jack was only a sophomore.

"Oh, my God!" her friend replied. "We're already behind."

Jack attended the Brentwood School, set on a stunning campus designed to replicate the medieval hill towns of southern Europe. With annual tuition then approaching $40,000, it had been referred to by *The Hollywood Reporter* as the place "to up your kids' Ivy League odds." But insecurity ran through the school, with parents trading stories about this or that kid who had a 4.5 GPA, was captain of three teams, and inexplicably *got in nowhere.* No parent wanted to become that cautionary tale.

Buckingham, then forty-seven and Pilates-toned with shiny blond hair, was not known for being behind the curve on anything. She lived in Beverly Hills in a stately home with a red-tiled roof, Moorish arches, and ivy clinging to the walls, and she owned a company that advised corporations and nonprofits on how to understand the younger generations. She strode the stage at conventions, lecturing enthusiastically to audiences about "Gen V," the kids and young adults that for a time she dubbed "Gen Viral" for their digital prowess. She authored books, including *The Modern Girl's Guide to Motherhood*. She appeared on *Good Morning America*. She had once been named one of the twenty-five most powerful women in Hollywood by *Elle* magazine.

She was all the more credible because she was raising a teen and tween, Jack and Chloe, herself. As Buckingham's longtime friend Andrea Hutton would put it later: "She felt she had to be the perfect mom. Not just the perfect mom, but the perfect everything."

Yet standing on the sidelines of that soccer game, Buckingham felt anything but. Her dashing husband had recently left after twenty years of marriage, which was heartbreaking and humiliating. Jack's grades had tanked.

So she bit. "Okay," Buckingham said to her friend, "who'd you hire?"

"Rick Singer."

Buckingham wasn't familiar with the name, which had been passed many times before from one parent to another alongside soccer fields and basketball courts, in boardrooms and golf clubs.

ABOUT A DECADE EARLIER, Buckingham had spoken at a marketing panel at the fashionable Sofitel hotel in Beverly Hills, describing the friction under way as a new wave of coddled young people headed into college and the workplace.

They were so fragile that college admissions officers called them "teacups."

But parents in Westside Los Angeles, where Buckingham lived, often were the more high-strung ones. Entertainment industry power brokers and celebrities, lawyers and financiers, jostled to get their children into the private elementary schools considered feeders to a fairly small circle of elite high schools that, in turn, were seen as stepping-stones on the path to distinguished coastal colleges.

The moms and dads approached parenting with the same vigor with which they handled their careers. Insularity warped perspective, making it seem standard practice to pay hundreds of dollars an hour for SAT prep tutors or tens of thousands a year for tuition at private schools. School fundraisers featured performances by Beyoncé and auction items like a sing-along with Neil Sedaka and a luxury villa vacation in Cabo, complete with jet and yacht access.

At circle time for a toddler gym class in the early 2000s, for instance, parents went around introducing themselves and their children at each meeting. At some point during the multiweek session, the teacher suggested the children could try to introduce themselves and their parents. Some kids eagerly engaged, while others were taking longer to open up. Actress Felicity Huffman was there with her daughter Sophia. "This is making me sweat," she whispered to a nearby dad. The two chuckled and bonded.

A fracas once shook Larchmont Charter School in West Hollywood after a staff member there had the gall to start an advanced kindergarten reading group, recalls publicist Alison Graham, who lives in the high-end Hancock Park neighborhood and had a child in the school. Some parents whose children weren't advanced readers erupted. They weren't about to let other kids get further ahead of theirs in *The Cat in the Hat* or *Chicka Chicka Boom Boom*.

"The culture is competitive on every level," says Graham. "There is this mentality that the achievement of your children is a reflection of you as a parent."

Jane Buckingham never wanted her children to suffer the least bit of defeat, according to her brother, Michael Rinzler, who recalled Jack as a little boy struggling with a puzzle one day. "The last piece was almost in, and he just couldn't quite get everything lined up. That's when Jane took her index finger and gave the piece the gentlest of nudges to help it into place. He was happy. She'd saved him from frustration."

Buckingham was the kind of overproviding parent that she hadn't known as a kid. She grew up in New York City as Jane Rinzler, with a psychiatrist father who was an alcoholic and a mother who was a columnist at *Glamour* magazine. When Jane was five, her parents had a bitter split, and then three years later, her mother went to Yale for her law degree, commuting to New Haven.

Buckingham's mother was warm and loving, but busy, and Jane carried adult responsibilities and cares at a young age. She cooked and cleaned. She was told by her school that tuition was overdue, and to remind her mom to pay up. She felt let down. Why was she in charge? She reacted to the instability by working hard, and her drive stood out even at the ultraelite Horace Mann School. She became a published author while still a teenager. The work, *Teens Speak*

Out, based on her research of adolescent attitudes, brought national publicity, even an interview with Oprah, and enough savings that she could pay part of her own tuition at Duke University, where she'd graduate with an English degree in 1990. Her drive only grew when she was twenty-one and her mom died unexpectedly, leaving Buckingham to deal with a host of problems. Her mother had been about a half million dollars in debt and their apartment was being foreclosed upon.

Buckingham decided she would never let her children experience that fundamental scariness of thinking that everything could suddenly fall apart. She was going to be that person everyone counted on. She was never going to be caught without a plan. And a backup plan.

She pushed forward, working in the youth marketing division of an advertising firm and then starting her own youth intelligence firm at age twenty-six. She sold it in 2003 to Creative Artists Agency, a powerhouse representing major Hollywood stars, catapulting her into L.A.-land. She and Marcus Buckingham, a Cambridge-educated Brit, whom she married in 1996, moved to Beverly Hills. Jackson was born in 2001 and Chloe in 2003. Marcus's bestselling books on harnessing one's strengths propelled him onto the leadership speaking circuit, while Jane authored the Modern Girl series and founded another company, the boutique marketing firm Trendera.

Buckingham became one of the most popular and involved moms at the sought-after Center for Early Education, where her kids went. She helped in classrooms, headed committees, threw the big annual fundraiser, and offered up her backyard for charity events, baby showers, even a babysitter's cousin's wedding. She sat on panels at parents' events that drew hundreds of people. She was known as down-to-earth and almost excessively generous. She hated more than anything to have anyone mad at her.

But she could also seem like she was pedaling like crazy to control her image. "Every birthday party was a little bigger, with a few more celebrities," says a friend of Buckingham's. "It sort of felt like she was always climbing to the next rung on the ladder."

In 2010, celebrities and socialites nibbled on mini cupcakes and soaked up city views from the top floor of the members-only Soho House on Sunset

Boulevard in West Hollywood to celebrate Buckingham's newest book, *The Modern Girl's Guide to Sticky Situations*. Buckingham posed for a photo with her friend Huffman, the *Desperate Housewives* actress.

Chloe by her side, Jane signed copies of the book, which covered a multitude of thorny scenarios, including one that would become all too vivid to the children of both women: "One of your parents has done something you can't forgive."

BUCKINGHAM AND HUFFMAN JOINED a wave of media-savvy mothers who were pitching themselves as relatable fonts of family wisdom. They had an appealing message: Enough with trying to be supermom or trying to raise perfect kids. Let things go.

Huffman sold "Good enough mom" mugs on her parenting blog. Buckingham's mantra was to "try to take joy in who my kids ARE not who I want them to be," as she tweeted with the hashtag #mommyanswers. She took a folksy, empathetic tone in her Modern Girl series, which were collections of practical tips and tools she thought people might need but not know. Buckingham had gotten the idea for the books because, after her mother died, she felt at a loss for that kind of advice herself.

She preached authenticity to the point that she gave a tough-love talk to a contestant on *Job or No Job*, a short-lived ABC Family show, who'd told a small fib on her résumé, lying about her home address to make it look more desirable. The show followed recent college graduates who would go on three interviews and then get Buckingham's career advice. Buckingham, in a bright pink dress, stared at the contestant sternly. "When your friends tell you to lie on your résumé, you *100 percent* DO. NOT. DO. IT."

But, each for her own reasons, Huffman and Buckingham would not follow that advice to chill out.

MARCH 12, 2019

Boom boom boom went the thud of fists. Pounding, for minutes on end, on front doors, on the outside walls, at thirteen homes in some of the toniest neighborhoods around Los Angeles.

The time was about 6:00 a.m.

What the hell is that racket?

"FBI! Open up!"

FBI?

Doors swung open. The groggy upper class of L.A. discovered armies of G-men in navy windbreakers on the stoops of their magnificent houses. The agents had brought battering rams for the doors, just in case. Sidearms were drawn.

Holy Christ, is that a shotgun?

Hands flew up in surrender. One woman almost fainted in her Beverly Hills mansion. Some of those arrested were escorted back to bedroom closets and permitted a quick change from pajamas into jeans or sweatpants. What was this about? It was a blur. Handcuffs were cinched before the men and women were guided into the backs of government vehicles, to bob along the hills above Hollywood or cruise down tranquil palm-tree-lined boulevards past the predawn traffic of morning joggers and maids and nannies making their way to work.

Hundreds of agents had fanned out across the country that morning, from Manhattan to Miami, from Houston to Silicon Valley, conducting similar sweeps at dozens more homes. Arrest warrants gave bare details for the raid: conspiracy to commit mail fraud for some; racketeering conspiracy for others.

In Los Angeles, the FBI's unmarked sedans pulled into an underground garage at the ruddy granite Edward R. Roybal Federal Building and U.S. Courthouse as the sun peeked over the horizon. The cars eased into a secured port guarded by deputy U.S. Marshals. A steel door slammed shut, and the stone-faced agents pulled out their prominent passengers, took them up one floor in an elevator, and flipped a switch to buzz through one more secure gate. They had arrived at the United States Marshals Service lockup.

Gloved hands patted the inmates down for weapons and drugs, and then slapped them into leg irons. They were outfitted with "belly chains" around the waist, to which their hands were cuffed—just the way violent criminals and lowlifes are shackled on the TV news.

The processing room was sparsely furnished with a couple of stainless steel tables and a camera in the corner. Next came fingerprints, mug shots, swabs in the mouth for DNA. On the wall hung an ominous poster of an old-timey U.S. Marshal with a long ZZ Top beard, pictured next to a hangman's gallows. Cheery.

The inmates shuffled down a hall with four jail cells on each side. There were no windows and no clocks, like the world's worst casino. Into cells they went. Deputies uncuffed one hand so the inmates could use the not-very-private toilet in the cell or eat their rationed snack: turkey on white bread, a bag of chips, water.

The cells filled quickly, men in one and women in another. They sat, squeezed ass to ass on benches.

Prisoners recognized each other. Eyebrows went up.

"Oh, you, too?"

It began to sink in that many of those in custody moved in similar circles. Buckingham spotted her friend Huffman wearing glasses and her hair in a messy ponytail. And there was Donna Heinel, the tanned athletics administrator from the University of Southern California.

Over in the men's cell, Robert Flaxman, an outgoing Beverly Hills developer, chatted with Mossimo "Moss" Giannulli, a fashion designer married to actress Lori Loughlin, who was on location in Canada but about to be arrested herself. Devin Sloane, an L.A. entrepreneur, slumped on the bench, in no mood to banter. A distinguished periodontist was in scrubs, as if he had been pinched on his way to work. There were two soccer coaches in the cell, a onetime star from USC and one from the University of California, Los Angeles.

Perhaps some knew why they were there, but others weren't sure. And no one quite understood what they all had in common.

Until finally one of the coaches piped up: "Do you all know Rick Singer?"

Mouths fell open. A sense of understanding spread, followed by dread. Together the men moaned as a chorus: *"Fuuuuuuuuuck!"*

Oh yeah, they knew Rick Singer.

1

FUTURE STARS

Kim Miller had a long list of things she'd rather do. Perusing the Arden Fair mall, for one. Spending time with her boyfriend. Anything was more exciting than the heavy gray pages of a college application, for sure.

It was fall 1993, and Miller was sixteen. In upper-middle-class Sacramento, this was what you did at sixteen. You started planning to get into college. Though she was a good student, the prospect scared her. Those little fill-in-the-dot tests were just not her friend. She had already convinced herself she would bomb the SAT. And what would she study? She liked theater and fashion, but "I didn't know what the hell I wanted to do," she recalls.

But then a minor miracle touched down in her life, a force of nature.

Years later, she would still have his business card, imprinted with FUTURE STARS, the royal blue letters in all caps with a star in place of the *A*.

Miller's parents had retained Rick Singer as a private college counselor. She liked him straight off. He was in his early thirties, super fit, energetic, tanned, and conspicuously casual, often in shorts, running shoes, and a windbreaker. He was hired to help her study for the SAT, to weigh her college options, and to complete those intimidating applications.

Singer led strategy sessions at the formal dining room table in her family's pretty Mediterranean-style home on leafy Forty-Sixth Street in East Sacramento. Just as important as nailing the test, he told her, was shaping her image.

"What is going to really make you stand out on paper to these schools?" he would probe. "What are you going to bring to the table, Kim Miller? Who are you? Who is Kim Miller?"

No one had ever talked to Miller like that before. She liked it. His words, his coach-like "you got this, kid" attitude, empowered her. She discovered a growing strength inside, and a new, kick-the-door-down confidence that she could choose who she would be.

Singer knew firsthand about transforming himself.

The sun beat down on Proesel Park in the Chicago suburb of Lincolnwood, Illinois, one summer around 1973 when "Ricky" Singer was a young teenager on the edge of high school. He was a regular at the park, where he ran for miles in a sauna suit, like what boxers wear to shed weight fast. He lived off Diet Coke, raisins, and peanuts for the summer. He encouraged his close friend Cheryl Silver to do laps with him so she could make the tennis team. "Silves," he would say, using her nickname. "Come on, we gotta do this because, don't you want to make the team? You've got to push hard. Watch me. Push hard. Push harder."

Ricky had curly dark hair and a spirited personality that made him popular. He could wallop the ball in Little League. But he was also chubby and by the time he reached his teens, it gnawed at him. He was the heavy kid and he hated being the heavy kid. He wanted to be like everyone else, and at the beginning of high school he set out to make that happen. It wasn't just his physique that bugged him. Ricky seemed to always have something to prove.

He played baseball and football at Niles West High School, a strong public school that propelled most teens to college, with alumni that included future Supreme Court nominee Merrick Garland. Lincolnwood was a comfortable, heavily Jewish suburb that had ballooned in recent decades after the opening of an expressway offering easy access to Chicago. Roomy homes with backyards and double garages dotted tree-lined streets, while less well-off families, like Singer's, lived in townhouses.

His parents married in Los Angeles in 1959, and had Singer the next year in Santa Monica and then a daughter a few years later. They divorced early, and his father moved away and remarried when Rick was nine, building a new family and giving Singer half siblings. His mother also remarried. She and Singer's stepfather were down-to-earth parents and Singer adored his mother. He rarely saw his father, and friends later thought it bothered him, but he didn't talk about it. No one talked about divorce back then.

Kids in Lincolnwood had ways, besides the size of homes, of knowing who had money and who didn't. In wealthier families, the kids got braces, the moms were at after-school activities because they didn't work, and the children went away to overnight camps. Singer and his good friend Silver stayed in town and went to day camps. Now Cheryl Silver Levin, she recalls, "He always wanted more. He always said he was going to have a million-dollar home, be a multi-millionaire with a million-dollar home."

Singer's personality could fill a room. He smiles in his senior yearbook photo, in which he wears a wide seventies-style collared shirt and a big afro, like an extra on the sitcom *Welcome Back, Kotter*. Singer had a notable quality that would only become more pronounced as he got older—and would, one day, make him infamous. He was prone to gross exaggerations, if not outright lies. He didn't win the basketball game by two points, he won by fifty points. If he had a hit in baseball, he didn't just get a line drive, he hammered one out of the park. Animated and fun to be around, Singer got away with the obvious embellishments, which were then harmless. Everyone knew he was fabricating, but they didn't care because they loved him.

He already seemed to know that his ability to command attention was his ticket. His yearbook message said, "I would most like to be remembered for the outstanding personality I have been given, and being able to get along with others."

In late summer 1978, he drove to Tucson with Levin and another friend and they all enrolled in the University of Arizona, but any plan for a typical college life seemed to change fairly quickly. Unlike most of his high school classmates, Singer didn't graduate in four years from a name-brand college. Ironically, he took a somewhat hardscrabble path that he'd build his career helping others to avoid. He joined a fraternity and enjoyed school, but left in fall 1979, mentioning that he was having trouble coming up with the out-of-state tuition. He moved to Dallas, where his father, who had fallen ill, lived. Singer later said he moved to help run his father's vending business, selling candy, soda, and cigarettes, after the old man had a heart attack. The small business employed Singer, his father, and his stepmother, until his father died just a few years later, in 1983, in his late forties.

Singer went to Brookhaven College, a community college in suburban Dallas, where he was featured in the school newspaper for his skill at intramural basketball, and then went to Our Lady of the Lake, a four-year Catholic university in San Antonio, for one year. He then transferred again, enrolling in Trinity University in that city in 1984.

Trinity, a small private liberal arts school, was not well-known outside the region, but it was respected and felt like a school on the rise. It was known for its Division I tennis team, but the Division III baseball and basketball teams also recruited promising student-athletes from other schools in the area, and Singer played on both teams.

Singer was six years out of high school by the time he entered Trinity. The school had plenty of rich preppy kids, Izod and Polo and nice cars bought by Mom and Dad. The other students, many from Texas, had established cliques when Singer arrived as a transfer student. With an afro and beard stubble, Singer looked obviously older and out of place. He was cocky, an outsider, not likely to be seen at the fraternity and sorority parties that dominated weekend social life.

Singer had a part-time campus job at the gym and, at five foot ten, he was one of the very smallest guys on the hoops team. But he had swagger. He was super competitive even during a friendly pickup basketball game. Classmate Grant Scheiner, originally from New York, liked him, but not everyone did.

"I was asking him, 'Why are you this way? If you throw elbows, people aren't going to like you,'" Scheiner recalls. "He says, 'I just want to win.'"

Singer graduated from Trinity in 1986 with degrees in English and physical education. He was almost twenty-six years old. Singer glossed over his circuitous path in education. Years later, in a deposition, he would simply say he went to Trinity, leaving out the other stops.

He almost never returned to Lincolnwood. As his old friend Cheryl Silver Levin put it, "He created a new Ricky."

IN 1987 JOHN RANKIN, then a men's basketball coach at Sierra College in Rocklin, California, needed an assistant coach, and Singer was looking for a new job.

After college, Singer taught English and PE and coached basketball at MacArthur High in San Antonio, but he and the head coach there clashed and he wanted to move up to the next rung. For many up-and-coming coaches, that meant junior college, and California fielded some of the country's most competitive teams. Sierra was a junior college about twenty-five miles outside Sacramento, which tended to live in the shadow of its sophisticated coastal cousin San Francisco and was sometimes derided as "Cowtown": that nondescript place you drive through on the way to Lake Tahoe. Short on Fortune 500 companies, it was a brew of lobbyists and political power brokers at the domed state house, middle-class career bureaucrats, and professionals in law, medicine, or real estate. Some people considered it to be the most Midwestern city in California, but with plenty of sunshine. Not a bad place for a kid who grew up outside Chicago.

Sierra had just come off a stellar season, with a surprise run to the state championships. Rankin was looking for a couple of assistants, and Singer called from Texas.

Singer started working at Sierra College as an assistant coach and adjunct PE instructor. Rankin saw Singer as a great hire. In his view, Singer was a passionate go-getter and "one of the best people I've ever met."

Singer thrived on a jam-packed workload and picked up a second job in Sacramento, leading the boys' basketball team at Encina High School in Sacramento. His day began at 6:00 a.m. and ended near midnight, and he recruited as well, helping Sierra to draw players from outside the region.

Singer's job trying to turn around the struggling Encina High basketball team was short-lived. Ever blunt, he told *The Sacramento Bee* in February 1988 that his players "haven't learned how to score. The kids work hard, but they have never been taught the game." The one outstanding player on the team was "not a jet, he's missing that one engine." Within days, the district fired Singer after reports from parents and referees about his sideline rants and hassling of officials.

Despite Singer's harsh assessments, the players liked Singer and protested his firing by voting 10–0 to boycott the next game. "We feel very strong about this," team captain Willie Martin told the *Bee* at the time. "The only way he could get through to us was by yelling. And occasionally he cussed, but so does every other coach you see. Singer was the best thing we've ever had."

Singer was fired anyway and moved on as he settled into the fabric of Sacramento with his 1989 marriage to Allison Karver, another fitness buff. Then twenty-eight, a hair younger than Singer, she came from a longtime Sacramento family, with a father who worked in sales for a drapery-fabric manufacturer and a mother who had been a hostess at one of the best restaurants in town.

Karver graduated from St. Francis, a Catholic high school, and then from San Diego State University. After college, she returned to Sacramento and married her high school sweetheart, a graduate of Christian Brothers High School, another local Catholic school, in a big wedding. The marriage lasted a few years. Karver played tennis, did triathlons, and had an aerobics studio with her first husband in the early 1980s before going into real estate.

She and Singer, who married in Southern California, were both high-energy people who liked a disciplined lifestyle. Singer rose before dawn to exercise, and at some point, probably scared in part by his father's heart attack at a young age, ate mostly vegetarian.

The couple settled into a ranch-style home near Sacramento State University, where Singer became assistant basketball coach in 1989. The team media guide listed Singer as a "multisport standout" who earned varsity letters in four sports—basketball, baseball, football, and tennis—at Trinity University. Trinity's records showed Singer played only two of those sports, baseball and basketball.

Singer threw himself into the Sacramento State job, traveling around California and other states to recruit, visiting prospects at small colleges and high schools.

"He was the kind of guy who'd give you the shirt off his back to help, he was that generous. He was generous to a fault, even to strangers," recalled fellow assistant coach Ron McKenna, who became close friends with Singer. "And he was a great recruiter when we were at Sac State. He loved to go into places like East Los Angeles to recruit, and he'd get out there and play with prospects."

Don Heller, a lawyer who knew Singer from Sacramento, described Singer's rapport with teen athletes: "In some ways with the kids he was a Pied Piper."

But the Sacramento State post illustrated the pressure and insecure nature of a coach's job. All that work mattered little if the team came up short. The head coach, Singer, and McKenna were all pushed out in 1992 after the team went 4–24 in its first year of Division I competition.

McKenna wasn't too unsettled by the firing, because he'd kept his other job, as a high school guidance counselor, while at Sacramento State. But McKenna felt bad for Singer, who lost his main source of income.

Singer shifted into a new venture. He worked as a substitute teacher for local public schools and, also in 1992, earned a master's degree in school counseling from the University of La Verne. The coaching gig had provided a valuable education. Crisscrossing the country and vying for prospects, Singer built a network of coaches and witnessed firsthand the incredible edge athletes, even just those tapped as walk-ons, can have in college admissions. Most crucially, Singer may have learned college coaches have a weak spot that could be exploited. Many colleges are constantly trying to raise money for athletics, and they put much of that fundraising burden on coaches, who often resent the task and, for lower-profile coaches, their own modest paychecks.

Singer had just the expertise he needed to remake himself yet again.

IN FALL 1993, MARGIE AMOTT was busy organizing Rio Americano High School's first "College Night." Amott was a volunteer in the guidance office at the high-performing public school, where her daughter was a junior. Rio invited the parents and the local Sacramento community to come learn more about the application process, which had changed dramatically since the parents went through it themselves. Most of the scheduled speakers were high school personnel, like an English teacher who planned to talk about writing essays for applications.

Then word got to Amott that someone named Rick Singer wanted to speak—whether it came from Singer or someone who knew him, Amott doesn't recall. Singer introduced himself as a businessman: he worked as a professional private college counselor, whom families could hire to help with the process of preparing to apply to college. Intriguing, Amott thought. That concept was relatively new, and Singer may have been one of the first for-hire college consultants in Sacramento, according to Amott, who later became active in the profession herself.

Singer was only in his early thirties, but he carried himself much older in terms of his ability to project authority. From his past in Lincolnwood, Singer could easily speak to suburban parents who considered college a foregone conclusion. Addressing a couple hundred people in Rio's gymnasium, he came across as earnest and humble, and better than the volunteers who'd organized the night expected. Never a fancy dresser, he wore a collared polo shirt and pants.

"He wasn't dramatically impressive, but he was offering a service none of us had heard of," Amott recalled. "For many parents it was a relief."

Singer had brilliant timing.

In the early 1990s, California was recovering from the recession and grappling with a state budget crisis. A 1992 budget shortfall cut fifty-five counseling positions from the Sacramento City Unified School District. At the same time, the University of California system, among the largest in the nation and a target for many Sacramento teens, had shifted to a more nuanced admissions review process and allowed candidates to apply to multiple campuses under one application. The resulting increase in applications helped drive down overall admit rates on nearly every UC campus.

A gifted networker, Singer became a popular guest right away, going school to school to speak at parents' events. "How're you doing? How are your kids?" he would ask when meeting potential clients. He talked constantly about how guidance counselors were wonderful but overworked. A few counselors began to feel Singer was exploiting the situation to gain clients, and they were skeptical about his grandiose public claims that every top kid in Sacramento worked with him.

Singer didn't come off as particularly polished. He wore tracksuits and had a car packed with files. He stocked shelves with college brochures, alphabetized, at a home office to lend to students. His business, formally incorporated as Future Stars, would charge a flat fee of $1,200 or an hourly rate for specific tasks. He ran radio ads pitching a sort of white-glove operation, even setting up cars, plane tickets, and hotels for college visits.

A few other college counselors popped up in Sacramento in the mid-1990s, but word traveled through parent circles that Singer was a cut above. His currency, in those pre-Google days, was his expertise.

He talked about how applying to certain majors would give a kid a better chance of admission. He also knew schools sought not just ethnic diversity but geographic diversity as well.

"You want a great school, you should apply to Washington University. I happen to know they are looking for kids from California," Singer advised a friend's niece around then. She ended up at the St. Louis school.

IN THE SPRING OF 1993, Kim Miller and her friends stepped into Burr's Fountain, a fifties-style diner and after-school hangout, to find a peer sitting with a man she introduced as her college counselor.

It was the end of Miller's sophomore year at St. Francis Catholic High School, the same place Singer's wife had attended. Miller maintained a 3.5

grade point average and was in the French club and honor society. After classes, she would change out of her school uniform, a light blue and white seersucker pleated skirt, white polo, and navy sweater, and put on sports gear. She ran the 400 meters on the track team and competed on the swim team.

But her home life was complicated. Like many teens, she clashed with her mom. She was the family's built-in babysitter for her sister, Amanda, seven years younger, who was developmentally disabled. Miller put pressure on herself to be an extra-good student for her parents, "because I knew they weren't going to get that from Amanda."

The idea of having an outside adult, who didn't get on her nerves and could help her, was appealing. She approached her mom, an interior designer, and stepfather, who worked in insurance, and asked, "Hey, can we have this guy over?"

Miller's home sat in an affluent enclave one street over from where former president Ronald Reagan had lived as governor. The neighborhood kids, many attending Rio or St. Francis or Jesuit High School, knew one another. College was a huge topic among teens and parents.

"Rick became known as the guy you hire," says Miller, now Kim Perry. "He is going to help you navigate those waters that are so ominous."

Singer showed up at Miller's house for regular hour-long appointments starting in the fall of 1993, her junior year. Mom would write the checks, but the meetings were almost entirely just her and Singer.

He struck Miller as the type of guy who didn't break rules. He would set a typed agenda on the glass-topped dining room table. He might ask her to write a draft of an essay or speak about herself as if in a college interview. At one point, he brought over a video about Southern Methodist University, and the two watched it together. She hung on his advice.

He was cool and charismatic, and she felt like she could confide in him, even telling him she would've preferred him over her actual track coach. "He had this way of convincing you that he knew things, he knew people, and you just trusted him."

Miller's vague goals involved something to do with the performing arts. She had appeared in a school play. Casting calls for commercials never went anywhere. "You want to make a decent living, and not go to Hollywood and starve," Singer told her bluntly. He suggested she could parlay her tenacity, as well as her love for costumes and big events, and her knack for public speaking, into a more stable career.

He dug, asking questions about her childhood, until he seized on an idea. Together, they crafted her brand, which she could recite years later: "I'm a giver. I'm compassionate and empathetic as a result of helping to raise my sister, a person with special needs."

This brand was based in truth and felt authentic to Miller. She later went to UC Davis and worked in fashion design and fundraising, speaking to nonprofits around the country.

Singer had planted that seed.

"You're talking to a sixteen-year-old who is hormonal and moody," she says. "You help them figure out who they are at that point in their life and what makes them a shining star—that is a powerful thing."

SACRAMENTO LAWYER DON HELLER met Singer in the mid-1990s and knew him as a decent guy who legitimately helped Heller's son and other local teens apply to college. Singer was smart, interesting, and certainly scrappy, still throwing elbows when the two played pickup basketball. They hit it off.

Born in the Bronx, Heller was the son of a taxi driver who himself drove a cab while attending Brooklyn Law School. He'd gone on to be an assistant district attorney in Manhattan and later a prominent assistant U.S. attorney in Sacramento.

Heller was known as a fair and tough prosecutor who tossed around profanities. He wrote the 1978 initiative that broadly expanded California's death penalty. He prosecuted Manson Family member Lynette "Squeaky" Fromme for trying to shoot President Gerald Ford. A law clerk once said he was like a "mad dog" after Heller called a major drug dealer, who pushed a particularly vicious strain of heroin, a "merchant of death" at the criminal's sentencing. If the death penalty was an option, Heller volunteered, he would personally throw the switch. From that day, he'd be known as Mad Dog.

Now a criminal defense lawyer, Heller kept busy defending clients on charges ranging from mail fraud to murder. He had evolved as a person and as a lawyer. He became a death penalty opponent, and he saw more nuance in his clients.

He realized most every defendant had likeable qualities, and saw some as good people who had gone astray and fallen prey to universal human flaws.

He would never have a practice, he would tell people, "if not for greed, avarice, and stupidity."

Neither man could have imagined that thirty years later, those traits would draw Singer to Heller again as a client.

COLLEGE COUNSELING could be humdrum, with weekends and evenings driving around, sitting at crumb-covered kitchen tables talking about SAT scores and essays. And Singer wasn't getting rich, or close to that million-dollar home he talked about as a young boy.

He charged prices middle-income families might afford. He and Allison hewed to a careful spending plan for household expenses and extras, budgeting for months for vacations and to adopt a baby boy, who was born in 1996.

In 1998, Scott Hamilton, a project manager in Sacramento, was looking for a more personally fulfilling career and the chance to own his own business. He learned through a business broker that Singer had put Future Stars up for sale.

Singer was making a career change himself. He told Hamilton he'd been offered a job with the Money Store, a national subprime lender based in Sacramento. Singer landed the position after doing college counseling for the children of management at the company. He would be handling recruitment and training at a call center and seemed excited. He'd make more money and work regular daytime hours.

Hamilton took over Singer's database and hauled away boxes of Singer's college brochures. Singer was busy, already working at the Money Store while wrapping up applications for counseling clients.

Allison was sentimental about leaving the business, but it was different for her husband, she told Hamilton.

"Not Rick," she said. "He's ready to move on to the next thing."

Taking over Future Stars, Hamilton got a couple of surprises. Most of

Singer's counseling business looked fairly ordinary, but Hamilton had strange conversations with two families. Both had hired Singer to work with their older kids and were now using Hamilton for younger siblings. Both mentioned that Hamilton seemed different from Singer. One family matter-of-factly said that Singer had essentially written their older child's college essay. And the other said Singer had advised their child, who was white, to list himself as Hispanic on his college application. (The teen had gone ahead and done just that, but the college questioned it, saying there was a discrepancy with how he'd listed himself when taking the SAT.)

Hamilton was bothered to hear about the unethical practices and told the families he didn't plan to operate that way. But he also was struck by how blasé the families sounded as they relayed this information, like this was a practice they'd accepted.

2

TIMING IS EVERYTHING

O N FEBRUARY 1, 2002, the front page of *The Jewish Press* in Omaha, Nebraska, ran a story about how small investors were still feeling the fallout from the collapse of Enron, the energy giant that filed for bankruptcy earlier that winter.

The paper, published by the local Jewish Federation of Omaha, also touted an upcoming evening event with a photo of the featured speaker. His dark hair cut short, Singer wore a crisp white shirt, tie, and bookish glasses. Headlined "Program to Outline '25 Steps to College,'" the article expanded into a preview of tips from Singer. One quote from him read, "Families and students need to understand that the college process is a game."

It had been a busy few years for Singer. After the Money Store folded in Sacramento, he continued on in the telemarketing industry, his initial success in the field landing him a job as an executive vice president at West Corporation, an Omaha-based company that then ran thirty-four call centers in North America. Singer was living in the Huntington Park neighborhood with Allison and their five-year-old son, Bradley, a little boy who, Singer liked to say, already had his sights set on Vanderbilt University. (He would end up at DePaul University.)

And Singer was still dabbling in college counseling. He built on the message he'd started giving in Sacramento a decade earlier, but now transformed his pitch for a generation of parents who'd grown more anxious about getting their kids admitted. Applications were soaring for all types of schools, and the colleges were touting their hyperselectivity. Parents would need to be more sophisticated to get their children into the right schools, and students would need to have a brand to sell themselves beyond their grade point averages and extracurriculars.

Families naturally rushed to Singer, a man who was almost pathologically obsessed with winning.

BOB FRANZESE, THEN THE athletic director of the Jewish Community Center, felt lucky as he arrived for his appointment at the headquarters of West Corporation in downtown Omaha in 2001.

Franzese, then in his late twenties, organized the adult and after-school recreational leagues at the bustling West Omaha community center known as "the J." The sprawling brick complex, with swimming pools, dance and music studios, and meeting rooms, served as a central hub for Omaha's small, tight-knit Jewish community. In the gym, two full-size basketball courts teemed with activity, and parents would watch practices from the indoor running track circling the courts.

A few board members mentioned to Franzese that Singer, then forty-two, had moved to town and wanted to give back. He had coached at the college level and now wanted to volunteer to fill an opening to coach a mediocre middle school basketball team at the Jewish Community Center. Thrilled at the idea of landing a volunteer with such an impressive pedigree, Franzese got in touch. Singer invited him to his office.

Singer was most comfortable around other sports nuts. Though he had a contagious laugh he found small talk, like chatting about politics or movies, a waste of time. But anything connected to sports excited him. He patted Franzese on the back, shook his hand, and welcomed him into his spacious, immaculate office at West's headquarters. Singer arranged for lunch to be catered in his office. The meeting, just to fill a volunteer spot for kids coaching, got more unusual. Singer launched into a General Patton–style aspirational speech about how he wouldn't quit until this team of seventh graders was turned around. He even began scribbling on the whiteboard in his office, outlining his goals, objectives, and strategies.

It was a bit over the top, sure. But to Franzese, it showed Singer as someone who was going to take things seriously.

Singer exploded onto the mild-mannered scene of the JCC's 2001–2 basketball league like he was channeling Bobby Knight, the brilliant but volatile chair-throwing coach from Indiana. A fit and wiry man who would do a thousand crunches a day, Singer was as intense and as focused on crushing the competition as ever. The young JCC basketball team didn't know what hit it.

This was not an elite team by any stretch. Given Omaha's small Jewish community, the JCC's team of middle schoolers was allowed to play in the local Parochial Athletic League, which was made up of teams from local church schools.

Practices, once an hour or so, now ran into two and three hours and featured demanding drills and running exercises. Singer raced along the sideline during games, cursing, barking orders, and chewing out young players who didn't seem to be trying hard enough.

"He would go from zero to one hundred as soon as the ball was in the air," says Franzese. "The kids were scared of him and the parents were half-scared of him."

But Singer's frenetic ways also built confidence and improved basketball skills in a group of kids who hadn't experienced much athletic success. A funny thing happened: This second-rate squad got better. More than better, it began dominating the parochial league to the point that parents on opposing teams raised questions about whether the JCC team technically belonged in the league.

"He was the talk of the town. 'Who is this guy?'" recalls Alex Epstein, who played on the team as a seventh grader. "I think he inspired me to want to get better because he was hard on us."

But with winning came another problem, which would escalate. The more the team won, the more failure became intolerable to Singer.

During games, Singer exploded into full-blown theatrics. He ran up embarrassing leads; he hounded referees about calls and noncalls. He'd start cocky back-and-forths with competing coaches. A couple times Singer was whistled for technical fouls for unsportsmanlike behavior and thrown out fifteen seconds into the game. Singer always needed the last word in a scrap. Epstein remembers Singer challenging a parent from an opposing team to step outside.

Singer showed even then that he was not afraid to find tricks to win. That season, he also briefly ran some practices for Omaha JCC's high-school-aged boys as they prepared for the JCC Maccabi Games, a huge summer sports competition for Jewish teens from around the world. Singer brought in a tall student, suspected by other players to be a ringer from a local Catholic prep school, to play on the Jewish team.

Franzese came to see Singer as a guy who would rather go out in a ball of fire than lose. The final straw came after the JCC middle school team obliterated a Catholic school team by a punishing fifty points. Singer and the opposing coach didn't get along, and at the end Singer got in a final dig. "If you had my team and I had your team," Singer taunted, "I would have still beat you by fifty."

Soon after, Franzese called Singer in for a meeting with him and the JCC's executive director.

"Rick, is there any way you can tone it down and dial it back?" Franzese asked him.

Silence filled the room as Singer considered the idea.

"No," Singer responded. "This is the way I coach."

There were no hard feelings after he dismissed Singer from the volunteer coaching job in Omaha. Franzese went out with him for one last lunch right after that meeting and as quickly as Singer entered his life, he was gone.

Singer was never one to acknowledge shortcomings and in his view, his friends say, he had nothing to be sorry for and no reason to change his approach. If some people didn't like his victory-at-all-costs style, he would find others who did.

And there was no shortage of people who loved a winner.

SINGER'S RESULTS-ORIENTED APPROACH earned him a good reputation in the call-center industry and he was recruited for a new post. He returned with his family to Sacramento in 2002 and took a job as CEO of a different company's overseas call center.

Owned by FirstRing India, it had more than five hundred employees and attracted money from a venture capital fund that was bringing in new leadership, including a new CEO, Singer, to improve performance.

Outsourcing had soared, and the call center, in a building outside Bangalore, ran round-the-clock shifts. Workers in cubicles with soundproofed walls made outbound sales calls for Discover Card and answered calls for companies ranging from American Express to ADT Inc.

Prab Singh, an easygoing U.S.-raised Sikh with a turban and beard, was helping to manage the center when he learned Singer would be his new boss.

Though the call center was set in a modern technology park, leading a business in the fast-growing but poor country came with operational obstacles. No public transportation went to the call center, so managers ran vans back and forth to Bangalore between shifts. The roads were bad and the vans were constantly breaking down, preventing people from getting to work.

Sometimes comical cultural challenges abounded. Managers were judged on performance metrics, including how fast employees dealt with calls. But many Indians have long, complicated names, and trying to relay them to customers would waste valuable seconds, Singh recalls. When managers told employees to pick American names, the workers wound up using the same handful of well-known monikers. That would waste even more time as surprised customers learned they were on the phone with "Tom Cruise" or "Johnny Walker."

Singer came in with a new leadership team, including a vice president of training, a head of client services, and a technology director, and made clear that he was there to whip things into shape.

For his first day on the job, he rented a conference room at the Leela Palace, a five-star luxury hotel in Bangalore, and brought in the top staff. He sat at the head of the table and directed his questions to the group now running the call center.

"How many of you think you're part of the A-team?" Singer asked them.

Worried they'd stumbled into a trick question, Singh and the others didn't know whether to put their hands up or not. Singer quickly answered for them.

"I think all of you have the potential to be on the A-team," he told them. "But right now you're not on it."

The guys he'd brought over, he explained, were the A-team. Singh felt resentful. He knew there were some hard workers in the current group.

Singer then went around the table asking everyone what their education was. Most of the Indian managers had master's degrees, and Singh had a degree in psychology from UCLA. Singer seemed very impressed with those academic pedigrees, asking follow-up questions. But he was silent after some managers from the United States said they hadn't gone to college. One manager with years of call-center experience told Singh he realized then that he had no future under Singer. He was soon shown the door.

"He had this big thing about education," Singh recalls. "That was a sticking point for Rick." Degrees were a sign of having made it—something Singer constantly sought to prove.

Singer made his own credentials clear, and Singh says Singer told him he had a doctorate. Singer had indeed enrolled in a doctoral program at Capella University, a for-profit college, between 1999 and 2002, but he never finished his degree.

Like the basketball players in Omaha, Singh came to see two sides of Singer, who still lived in Sacramento but would visit India for stretches of time each quarter. He realized that Singer was a braggart and a blowhard, and that he had to discount about 30 percent of everything the guy said. But Singer also exuded charisma, confidence, and certainty, and Singh found it alluring just to be around him.

Singer wanted the call-center managers to understand just how tough the phone work could be, and he wanted them to inspire the employees.

"You guys have to get on the phones as well," he told Singh and another top manager.

Singh pushed back: Employees go through months of training. Handling people over the phone wasn't his strong suit. "I suck at it," he told Singer, after getting a string of rejections from potential customers.

"Those are just stats," Singer assured him. "They are going to happen. If you just keep asking, keep going at it, you're going to get somebody."

Singer himself was disciplined and relentlessly efficient. He wore a personal uniform of pressed slacks, polo shirts, and brown loafers and worked long days at the call center when he was there. Worried about getting sick in India, he didn't bother with local cuisine: he chugged Diet Coke and mostly ate Pizza Hut, which by then had expanded into India. No matter how busy his day, he would go back to his hotel at the end and work up to a full-blown sprint on the treadmill before swimming for an hour.

He was so high-energy that Singh remembers being taken aback to see Singer doze off for ten minutes on a flight the two took to Delhi. Singh, a new father, grew tired of the long hours and quit within months of Singer arriving, then moved his family to Italy for a new job. But the two stayed in touch. A year later, in 2003, Singh got an email from Singer, who said he'd done very well for himself financially when the call center had sold. He was back in Sacramento full-time and was onto a new idea that he wanted Singh to be a part of. He planned to launch another college counseling business, but it would be a far grander operation than Future Stars, his first foray in the field.

"Now," says Singh, "his idea was to make this a much bigger thing."

THE MOMENT HAD ARRIVED for an aggressive college counselor. Baby boomers' children were graduating from high school in droves, ratcheting up competition for spots at elite and even formerly middling schools. Just over three million Americans graduated from high school in 2002, an increase of more than 21 percent in just a decade.

Meanwhile, the expansion of the *U.S. News & World Report* college rankings had changed the admissions process dramatically in those ten years. The rankings, launched in 1983 and published annually starting in 1987, helped turn senior year of high school from one where kids were focused on heading to the best college for them, to one where they could be angling for a way to get into the best college, period.

The No. 55 school may actually be a better fit for little Johnny, who thrives in more intimate environments and has a penchant for politics. But the No. 45 school is ten spots better, and therefore will become the goal for some families, no matter that it's three times the size and has stronger engineering than social science programs.

The "Best Colleges" list sparked a cottage industry of rankings breaking down schools by everything from majors to party atmosphere to who operates the most environmentally friendly campus. For the first time, families that previously relied on school tours, input from friends and guidance counselors, and simple personal preference, had hard data on everything from student selectivity to the alumni giving rate. "The understanding of the school gets reduced to someone else's algorithm of what's important," says E. Whitney Soule, now dean of admissions and financial aid at Bowdoin College in Maine, who was previously at Bates College and Connecticut College.

It helped them organize their thinking—shop for schools, optimize outcomes, and, perhaps most crucial for a certain subset of the population, compare themselves to others. While the rankings rated colleges, in essence they also served to rate the students, graduates, and families connected to those schools. Families started to think only a few dozen schools were worth going to; otherwise, their kid was not going to have a great life.

Tara Dowling, now director of college counseling at Rocky Hill Country Day School in East Greenwich, Rhode Island, who has been counseling at private prep schools since the early 1990s, says media focused too intently on the difficulties of getting into college. Nobody was talking about the many colleges where B students were enrolling just fine. Instead, they just focused on "Stanvard," she says, using a mishmash for Stanford and Harvard that became an inside joke among college counselors.

As rankings riveted the country, the process of applying to schools was changing as well. While Mom and Dad may have applied to two or three colleges, hammering out their essays on a typewriter, high schoolers at the turn of the twenty-first century were able to blast out applications digitally to many more schools.

As application numbers rose and acceptance rates fell, families fretted.

Another shift also defined the moment: Well-educated parents with disposable incomes could afford to worry about details like whether Jimmy had practiced piano enough. Obsessing over the little things can be a luxury, and these parents, often younger baby boomers, hovered over their children, teens, and young adults, intervening when things got even the slightest bit tough and earning the moniker "helicopter parents."

Wealthy parents have long tried to leverage influence over their children's education, but now they were more proactive than ever and began to increasingly try to "fix it." They complained about teachers who graded too hard and would show up at schools to take petty complaints to high-ranking administrators.

Dowling saw a disturbing rise of hubris among parents, but also a buildup of something even more striking: parents seemed to be losing trust in their own children.

"When you have done everything for your kid their whole life, you have no faith in their ability to do anything on their own," she says.

It was ultimately a recipe for disaster.

"Americans systematically weakened their children in the 1990s and the early 2000s," says Jonathan Haidt, an NYU professor and coauthor of the book *The Coddling of the American Mind: How Good Intentions and Bad Ideas Are Setting Up a Generation for Failure.* "Children do not become strong if they are protected from setbacks, teasing, exclusion and conflicts."

His view may be a blunt generalization, but it touches on a real shift in Americans' approach to parenting, particularly near the end of high school. College applications for many became a family affair, with parents weighing in on the list of target schools and interview attire, every comma or period scrutinized by a willing editor with the hope of helping to win an acceptance offer.

Emboldened by the moment, Singer sped ahead. He registered a company, CollegeSource, in California in 2004 to his four-bedroom brick home on a tree-lined drive in the desirable American River Drive area of Sacramento. Singer envisioned a sort of networked, mass-counseling model: He would hire representatives, or "coaches," all over the country to work with students on college admissions and test prep, for a fee. The tutor and Singer would split that fee, fifty-fifty.

Singer would maintain his own list of clients and call himself "CEO and master coach."

He increasingly displayed a skill that would become a powerful asset—the ability to draw prominent people into his orbit, giving him gravitas. A consummate networker who now had a long list of corporate contacts, he assembled an impressive advisory board that included Ted Mitchell, then the president of

Occidental College. Mitchell saw his unpaid role on the board as helping a venture "aimed at providing college counseling to low-income students," he would say years later.

Singer enticed Singh to move from Italy back to India, to start a branch of CollegeSource there in 2004. Singh soon came to Sacramento to train under Singer and found him remarkably good at his job. Singer had visited scores of campuses as a basketball coach and he maintained an almost photographic memory of them, from dorms to cafeterias. He gave Singh videos of schools to study as if they were game tapes.

A big part of his appeal was that Singer made house calls rather than have families come to him. People were more comfortable in their homes, and in turn, he could see how they were living. "He just took charge. He would sell his confidence and within an hour that family would be ready to work with him," Singh recalls.

They landed press releases in local Indian papers in 2004, talking up the counseling service. But within months Singer grew frustrated at the pace of growth. He urged Singh to speed things up by going to banks and offering to give free presentations on college admissions to the institutions' "VIP," or ultrawealthy, customers, with the aim of nabbing new counseling clients. Singh did one such seminar but largely resisted and worried service would suffer if he expanded too quickly.

The two amicably split ways, with Singh taking over CollegeSource in India, while Singer focused on more fertile ground back in the United States.

"I understood soon after starting that this is not something that will make you rich," says Singh. "Rick always came across as someone who wanted to be rich."

It wasn't about the fancy car. Other people who knew Singer said money just proved that he'd won.

IN EARLY 2005, Singer said in a local article that he had a dozen coaches, three administrative employees, several part-timers, and around 725 clients nationwide, including in Sacramento, Southern California, New York, Florida, and his native Illinois.

Come hear "nationally acclaimed college advisor Rick Singer from the CollegeSource," touted a newspaper advertisement for "South Florida's College Night," held in 2005 at the private Sagemont School in Weston, Florida. A mom in the audience had become deeply immersed in her son's college process and told Singer she had learned so much, she wished she, too, could guide others as a job. "Well, come work for me," he told her—and she did.

Back in Sacramento, Singer's new business looked different from his 1990s endeavor. When he returned to the profession after his stint in the call-center industry, he ran a much more high-end operation.

Singer drove a Porsche Cayenne, hiked his previous rates, and networked at the high-end Arden Hills Athletic & Social Club. "I don't know what happened," says Hamilton, the local businessman who bought Singer's first counseling business, Future Stars. "When he came back, it just seemed like he said, 'I'm going to take this to the next level.'"

Singer was charging $2,500 a year for juniors and seniors, a fee that stuck out in Sacramento, a government town. And he began to tell families that he really needed to start advising their kids earlier to create the kids' brands, directing their course choices and extracurricular activities. He would charge $1,500 a year for freshmen and $2,000 for sophomores.

College counselors get business largely by referrals, and Singer's name circulated quickly in affluent circles. He sat for interviews. "Thousands turn to college-prep coach," said the headline for an article on Singer in the *Sacramento Business Journal* in 2005. It described how he met Anat Bird, a banker and former Israeli tank commander when he sat next to her on an airplane, inquired about the Hebrew crossword she was doing, and then followed up with an email two hours after the plane landed. "Instant credibility," she said. She hired him to work with three of her children.

Some of Singer's employees thought he was motivated by far more than money. He really seemed to care about some of the kids he worked with and would still be in touch with them years later. "It was a big ego boost for him, getting them in," recalls one employee. "It almost activated the part of his mind that would be jolted in gambling."

In Sacramento, Singer's clients were upper-middle-class parents who themselves may have gotten into a University of California school with B grades and were now freaking out because they were hearing of kids with very strong GPAs being denied. They weren't imagining things. As the applicant pool grew, most UC schools became substantially more selective. Between 1994 and 2002, admit rates of first-time freshmen fell by 32 percentage points at UC Santa Barbara and 23 points at UC San Diego. Both UC Berkeley and UCLA were now admitting less than a quarter of their applicants.

While Singer could come off like a "bullshit artist," as one father put it, he also seemed far savvier than other local college counselors. What made him so appealing to parents was that he gave the impression of having a sophisticated insider's awareness of the culture of admissions. He convinced people that he knew legitimate ways, even if they involved some truth-bending, to work the system.

Singer would launch into a discussion about "yield," or the share of admitted students who actually enroll, saying colleges craved certainty and would look more favorably on students who would definitely attend if accepted. During campus visits, admissions counselors would ask kids if they had made up their mind, and honest kids would answer that they were still deciding.

"Don't tell them you're confused," Singer would advise kids and families. "Say, 'This is my first choice. USC is my whole life.'"

He wasn't wrong. Yield calculations are crucial, as schools that rely on tuition revenue can't afford to fall short on enrollment but those with residential programs can't get too crowded. There are now entire consulting practices devoted to predicting yield and analyzing exactly what financial aid package might push someone from a "maybe" to a sure thing.

Singer also knew of another angle: that teens with diagnosed learning differences could get extra time on college entrance exams, and that it apparently didn't take much to get that designation. He would advise his clients to have their children tested for learning disabilities whether or not they were obviously suffering, because he knew they could then get this advantage and potentially boost their scores on the SAT or ACT, say some Sacramento families who hired him.

And from his years as a coach, Singer was incredibly knowledgeable about athletic programs—which schools were trying to grow their water polo or volleyball teams, for instance. And he would cite names, saying that he knew the coach and could put in a call.

Parents also liked the tough love Singer doled out to the kids, especially the teenage boys. He would press them to do their homework, warn them to stop screwing up. The students listened to him more than they listened to their parents, and he was aggressive in building up the kids' résumés. Whether the student was "saving the world" or a "soccer star," the kid needed a brand and Singer wasn't afraid to stretch the truth. He would make it sound like a student had built dozens of houses for the poor when the teen had just volunteered for a day. He even began selling families internship opportunities to beef up a kid's portfolio of activities. Summers spent as a camp counselor wouldn't cut it anymore. "Internships Plus," as he called it, promised to pair young people with interesting summer jobs for $2,500.

It's not clear how many students Singer actually placed; as with most of his ventures, there was a mix of truth and braggadocio. The website listed a summer 2007 speaker series, promising weekly presentations from local leaders including the former publisher of *The Sacramento Bee*, two property developers, and an executive at a brand marketing agency. Some of those named say they never gave any such talks.

At Rio Americano High School in Sacramento, guidance counselor Jill Newman would let out a big sigh as she walked from the lobby, down a short hall to her office, with parents, kids, and Singer trailing.

"Oh, no," she would think. "What are we in for?"

Her sunny office at the highly regarded public school had a window onto the courtyard, signs with motivational sayings hung on the walls, and a bowl of lollipops and Smarties candy sat on the desk. But the inviting space would quickly grow tense. Newman would sit at her desk, across from the parents. Singer would pull a chair right up to sit alongside the parents.

By the mid- to late-2000s, local high school teachers and guidance counselors were talking about the pushy college counselor who seemed to have an unusual sway over families and an ability to ingratiate himself with school leaders. Singer even managed to secure a role leading a session at a district-wide teacher training day. His presentation was ostensibly about writing letters of recommendation, but the full fifty-five minutes were used for a recruiting pitch for teachers to encourage their students to hire him.

"That really peeved lots of people," recalls Karl Grubaugh, a longtime economics teacher at Granite Bay High School. "It kind of got him on our radar screen that 'Hey, this guy is over the top.'" Singer became a significant presence at Granite Bay around 2004 to 2006 and stuck out because he began to lobby the administration to have kids switched out of certain classes and placed with other teachers. Singer was known for keeping a list of instructors he thought were more likely to give out good grades. The math department in particular grew tired of it, and the issue came to a head one day when a family—including parents, the student, and "an uncle"—called a meeting with an administrator, a guidance counselor, and a teacher and, as Grubaugh recalls, "kind of bashed and berated this teacher semipublicly in this meeting about why their daughter needed to be transferred to a different teacher." After the meeting, it came out that the "uncle" was not a family member at all; he was a Singer employee who passed himself off as a relative.

After that, the head of the math department wrote a stern letter to Singer, copied to the entire faculty, saying Singer and his representatives were not welcome in family meetings.

In the mid-2000s, Newman was in her early thirties, enthusiastic and eager, and knew many families in the district. She had taught elementary school and special education before joining the counseling team at Rio Americano, where Singer would eventually send his own son.

Singer would show up in the guidance office at Rio so often to pressure counselors to change schedules or teachers that once he left the lobby, Rio counselors would call their counterparts at Jesuit High School, a nearby private school where Singer also had clients, to alert them that Singer was coming their way. The favor went both ways.

Schools were uncomfortable having Singer join parent meetings, but he got around that by telling families to say they wanted him there. Newman would find that good working relationships with families deteriorated once Singer entered the picture. Often, Singer would have sold the idea to parents that he could turn around a student's middling record very quickly and get them into a college the family hadn't thought possible.

Newman recalls one high school athlete whose original plan was to go to a community college. He had failed Algebra 1 three times and had other poor grades; Newman worried he wasn't on track to graduate and wanted to put him in a less challenging math class. But in a family meeting, Singer insisted he could get the boy into a four-year college. He would clean up the boy's transcript and get him caught up by having him enroll in three online math classes over the rest of the school year. Newman was flabbergasted—how would the boy do that work on top of an already full day of classes and activities?

"I'm not signing on for this," Newman told Singer and the parents. "This goes against everything that I know to be educationally sound and correct."

"Don't worry about it. We will get him through it," Singer told her.

The student passed those math classes and went to the four-year college. Newman didn't know how it had happened, but she believed something questionable occurred. Years later, Singer would brag about having his employees take online classes for kids to clean up their transcripts.

Newman and her peers suspected Singer went so far as to misrepresent himself to colleges as a staff counselor at local high schools, which would have allowed him to write letters of recommendation to colleges. Rio's guidance office would get mail from colleges, addressed to Singer care of the high school. For the most part, the letters were basic introductory notes, saying they'd enjoyed meeting Singer. Rio's guidance counselors would have to contact the colleges to let them know Singer wasn't on staff.

What struck Newman the most was not just Singer's pushiness, but how parents would acquiesce. Singer may have been a hustler, but he clearly also had willing customers—parents all too eager to buy what he was selling. When Newman pushed back against Singer's ideas, parents would defend him, and she'd feel cut out from the process, as if she'd lost credibility with the families. "That's not what Rick said; we're going with what Rick said," they would say.

Singer told the families what they wanted to hear: "Yes, your kid can do this. Don't pay attention to what the high school counselor says. They don't know."

"It was no wonder," Newman says, "why he had parents falling all over themselves to become clients."

SINGER ACCELERATED HIS BRAVADO around 2007 as he became more successful, similar to how he became more amped up as his youth basketball team won in Nebraska. As he ran on the treadmill at Arden Hills one morning, a skeptical friend on another fitness machine told him he was full of crap. "What can you do with the UC system? The UC has a formula."

"Well, let me give you an example," Singer said. He explained that the UC system gives applicants "points" for certain attributes, such as being the first person in their family to attend college.

"Do you really think they audit these applications if someone says, 'My parents didn't go to college?' No, they have no way of knowing," Singer said.

"What if they get caught?" the friend asked.

Singer didn't miss a beat. "They don't get caught," he said.

3

———

ROAD TO RICHES

D OUG HODGE OVERSAW THE entire Asia-Pacific region for the world's largest bond manager, Pimco. But in early 2008, he had a problem he couldn't solve.

He was living in Tokyo with his wife, younger kids, two dogs, cat, bird, and two newts. His eldest daughter, Peyton, was five thousand miles away, a junior at the Cate School in Carpinteria, California, embarking on the college search process in early 2008. He was constantly on the road, building up and managing operations in Tokyo, Hong Kong, and elsewhere and soon steadying the business as the financial crisis began to rock global markets. His wife, Kylie, had gotten involved in a nonprofit that built schools and helped educate girls in rural Cambodia, keeping her plenty occupied as well.

An only child himself, Hodge loved his brood, then five kids, more than anything. He took pride in their educational achievements and was an involved parent, even serving on the boards of two of his kids' schools. But Peyton was moving into a stage of life further outside his reach.

He mentioned Peyton's impending college search to his longtime friend and California-based colleague Bill Powers, a managing director and portfolio manager. The two had known each other since college, when they were football punters for their respective schools. Both then worked at IBM, then Salomon

Brothers, then moved to Pimco in the early 1990s. (Powers peeled off for a two-year stint at Bear Stearns in 1988.)

Powers had a fix.

"Why don't you meet Rick Singer?" he told Hodge. "He's the best there is."

HODGE, WHO'D RELOCATED TO Tokyo in 2002, had moved up the ranks at Pimco as an account manager and then account executive. His job was to pitch the portfolio products to potential clients, a hybrid between salesman and investing expert, with a CFA earned in 1992 helping to bolster his bona fides.

He was known as a guy who worked really hard, didn't cut corners. A team player and ambitious, he eagerly raised his hand to take the job in Japan when Pimco had almost no reputation out there. Hodge's job was to build that name brand, and he did so quite well.

"He was like the classic good success story going along," says one former colleague. He grew up in Connecticut and went on to Dartmouth, where he was a punter on the football team and member of Alpha Delta, the fraternity that inspired the 1978 movie *Animal House*. Then he was off to IBM marketing for a few years, and he finished up his studies at Harvard Business School, graduating from there in 1984.

He fit right in on the trading floor at Salomon—"one of the guys," says one of the other guys who worked with him there.

Hodge cultivated his image as a gee-whiz-I'm-lucky family man.

He would update his Harvard Business School classmates with humble-brags. "I am firmly ensconced at Pimco, heading up the Asia Pacific business," he wrote in the March 2008 bulletin. "Our family of seven now boasts three teenagers. Yikes! The eldest two are now attending boarding school in California. We are all together for a wonderful two-week Christmas vacation in KohSamui, Thailand. Sell my clothes! I am moving here!" The prior year was a ski trip to Whistler and Christmas in the Seychelles. Before that was a safari in Botswana, and he visited Mumbai for work and vacation. And, a fitness buff, he mentioned having run marathons in New York and Sydney.

Powers had gotten Singer's name from other area parents, and he used the counselor when his daughter was applying to college in 2007. Passing the name along to Hodge was just like handing over a referral for a plumber or nanny, a friendly favor.

Peyton wanted Georgetown. Hodge wanted what would make Peyton happy. Singer's response, by email in early 2008, didn't provide comfort. Singer told Hodge his daughter had a 50 percent chance—at best—of getting into Georgetown on her own.

Peyton certainly could have gotten into a good school. She was named an AP Scholar with Honor in 2009, meaning she earned at least a 3 out of 5 on four or more Advanced Placement exams. She played varsity volleyball and served as a teaching assistant for a sophomore seminar when she was a senior. But her graduating class of sixty-two had plenty of stars, kids coming from across the western United States, South Korea, Taiwan, and Saudi Arabia to settle near Santa Barbara and attend one of the nation's best boarding schools. They'd go on to Northwestern, Columbia, Amherst, and other impressive colleges.

Hodge was a people pleaser, or at least he tried to be. But he had some notable weak spots. He wasn't always known to be a very good listener, charging into meetings with an agenda and undeterred in the face of a chorus of dissent. Hardheaded and tone-deaf, some would say. He had an extreme desire to do good by his family, but also poor judgment. "He tended to lack strategic vision, which made him vulnerable to bad decisions," as an ex-coworker explains.

So when Singer dangled an offer, he bit.

WORKING WITH PEOPLE LIKE Powers and Hodge, Singer had officially broken into elite circles. It was common for parents in the same economic stratosphere to share notes and resources on the admissions process, like they'd earlier passed around recommended wedding photographers and babysitters.

Powers had passed along Singer's name after Singer did a good job helping his daughter, an already strong candidate, prepare her application for USC. In June 2008, Powers had urged James Ward, then head of human resources, to invite Singer to Pimco's Newport Beach headquarters for a presentation on the college admissions process. (Powers has said he doesn't recall making any such introduction, or the company having any such presentations at that time.) Soon after, Singer sought a follow-up lunch with Ward, offering a special partnership in which Singer would provide his services as a perk to Pimco executives. Singer was too aggressive in the pitch and rubbed Ward the wrong way. A tie-up just wasn't going to happen, as far as Ward was concerned.

Singer ignored the brush-off and pasted on his website the false claim that his consulting business worked with Pimco and others in financial services to "utilize the life-coaching model for employees' private wealth management clients and executives as a corporate benefit." (He had spoken there in 2008, and would do so again in 2015, but that was the extent of the relationship.)

Getting wealthy clients—and keeping them amid the 2008 financial crisis—was crucial to Singer's business.

There were plenty of high school students who could benefit from college counseling, and plenty of parents who wanted it, especially now. Families felt their financial footing grow more fragile and wanted to protect their kids from future hardship. More than eight million jobs were lost during the recession and the downturn had particularly walloped people without college degrees.

But the number of families that could afford it, let alone actual tuition once they were accepted to college, in those days was more limited.

Sure, Singer served the wealthier doctors, lawyers, and business owners in the state capital, and he proudly noted that he charged more than other local college counselors. ("It's kind of like the difference between going to Nordstrom and JC Penney," he'd tell a Sacramento student paper at one point.)

But there were only so many people in that top group in Sacramento, where the recession brought 12 percent unemployment, a wave of foreclosures, and "Furlough Fridays" for state workers.

When house prices plummeted in the 2008 crisis, the leveraged middle class experienced substantial losses, while the quick rebound in stock markets would boost wealth at the top, contributing to the largest spike in wealth inequality in postwar American history. Newport Beach, not Sacramento, was where Singer could find the big-money clients.

"Rick would brag about, 'I met this person and that billionaire,' and he really got caught up in this whole world of wealth that never existed in Sacramento," recalls one friend from the Arden Hills gym, describing Singer in the late 2000s. "That is where really he went on the dark side. That is where everything kind of changed."

He exploited fertile ground. "The parents are so whacked out with thinking that the right school gives them bragging rights at cocktail parties," says the workout partner, a Sacramento businessman who got to know Singer well through mutual friends. "Rick was a master at playing this."

The irony, said another person close to Singer, is that he had such a following he could have had a comfortable life doing counseling the legal way.

"None of this would have happened if he wasn't so damn competitive and focused on winning," the friend said.

"I SPOKE TO MY connection at Georgetown and he will work with us," Singer wrote Hodge and his wife in February 2008. "He helped me get two girls in last week."

That connection was Gordon Ernst, Georgetown's head men's and women's tennis coach since 2006. "Gordie," a former tennis and hockey star, connected to Singer through a tennis coach and college counselor at a sports academy in Florida. After telling Hodge that Peyton had a slim chance of getting in based on her academic record, Singer dangled another approach: "There may be an Olympic Sports angle we can use."

Peyton's Georgetown application, submitted in November 2008, said she won a number of U.S. Tennis Association tournaments, though the USTA has no record of her ever playing a match. Peyton got a special Christmas present that year: a letter stating, "The Committee on Admissions has conducted an initial review of your application to the Class of 2013 at the request of Mr. Gordie Ernst, Tennis Coach. I am pleased to report that the Committee has rated your admission as 'likely.'"

Hodge paid Ernst $150,000 for the spot.

By 2009, Hodge was promoted to chief operating officer and relocated back to Newport Beach, California. The brood settled back into West Coast life, buying a $12.2 million house in the guarded and gated Emerald Bay neighborhood of Laguna Beach. Other residents of the community have included Warren Buffett, astronaut Buzz Aldrin, and Las Vegas casino executives. Hodge did well for himself, and for Pimco, in his years as COO. Sitting in an office right by CEO and co-CIO Mohamed El-Erian, he was in the C-suite as total assets under management topped $2 trillion in 2012.

Situated between the Pacific Ocean and the Pacific Coast Highway, with panoramic views of the water, his sun-drenched 6,800-square-foot mansion emblemized sophisticated seaside living, albeit with a look-at-me style. The Hodge house had plenty of room for their growing family—the couple had adopted two children from Morocco in 2009. Kylie, with long blond hair, deep blue eyes, and sun-kissed skin, spoke openly in interviews about how, raised in a Seattle household without any hardship, she was expected to "do it all and be successful." She became a Wall Street trader, then went on to get advanced degrees in psychology.

She founded the nonprofit Global G.L.O.W. (Girls Leading Our World), aimed at educating and empowering teen girls. She came across in interviews like an intellectually enlightened earth mother determined to keep her family grounded and give back to others without such financial fortune. The family donated more than $30 million between 2007 and 2018, mainly to schools and organizations for disadvantaged youth.

The Hodges were a social couple, hosting an impressive Christmas party at their home each year. A bouncy house in the yard and a Santa Claus actor kept kids occupied, while adults gathered upstairs for a feast. Pimco executives were always in attendance. College, of course, was a hot topic at any Newport Beach or Laguna Beach soiree. Whose kids were applying where? Which teens had gotten accepted for early admission? Did anyone know a top college counselor?

Hodge's oldest son, Mason, had enrolled at Thacher School, a boarding school in Ojai, California. He was a good kid, and class president his junior year. When it came time for the college hunt Hodge would go on to work with Singer to land Mason at Georgetown in 2011. This one cost him $175,000, again paid directly to Coach Ernst.

His next daughter, Quinn, went to Sage Hill School, a private high school in Newport Coast. Founded in 2000, the program billed itself as being heavy on community service, the arts, and exposure to people and places outside the Orange County bubble. It immediately drew funding from O.C. heavy hitters, including former America Online executive Steve Johnson; Buy.com founder Scott Blum; and Pimco cofounder Bill Gross.

Sage Hill's honor code was nothing short of lofty for little kids and their parents: "Face challenges with courage and dignity, the community with respect and dedication, and academics with integrity and honesty: Live honorably." To emphasize the importance of maturity and personal responsibility, school administrators even did away with bells signaling the start and end of classes. Students shouldn't need a reminder to go learn, a school administrator explained.

Sage Hill was intended to be a counter to the superficial images broadcast into living rooms via the once popular teen dramas *The O.C.* and *Laguna Beach*, which ran around the same time. "This was not a school just to get your kid into Harvard or Stanford," says Dori Caillouette, one of the school's founders.

And while the school did value personal fit, the attention paid to top colleges could be just as bad there as anywhere else. Marketing material used in 2012 had dozens of dots on a map representing recent graduates' destinations, with oversize logos calling attention to just nine brand-name institutions: places including Harvard, Stanford, the University of Chicago, and Brown.

In 2011, Sage Hill's website featured a group photo of its smiling board of trustees, who were meant to represent the school's mission of raising teens with integrity. There in the back row was Hodge.

The glowing blurb below Hodge's name noted that a daughter would graduate in 2013.

Another college admissions journey was bearing down on the family.

SINGER PUSHED INTO THOSE ultrawealthy and high-profile social networks thanks to people like Powers and Hodge and some good old-fashioned advertising and networking.

He landed a spot as a featured mentor for a prestigious, invite-only camp for high school quarterbacks run by coach Steve Clarkson and Leigh Steinberg, the sports agent credited as the inspiration for the Jerry Maguire movie character. The quarterback academy brought seven top recruits, as well as a bunch of younger kids, to sharpen their leadership skills, boost game know-how, and run drills just steps from the Pacific Ocean.

Singer spent a portion of the 2009 trip holed up in a characterless hotel conference room, a space dominated by a putty-colored oval table. Wearing a white polo shirt and shorts, he advised the kids, as well as their entire families, on college admissions basics, including how to look for the best fit and how to approach standardized tests. Hall of Fame quarterbacks Joe Montana and Warren Moon made appearances. Montana would become a client.

Singer took out ads for his newest company, Edge College & Career Network—which he referred to as "the Key"—in *Westlake Malibu Lifestyle*, claiming space in the magazine alongside pitches for Rolex watches, Tuscan-style residential estates, and Botox treatments. His message warned of kids getting "locked out" of college and showed a distraught teenage boy sitting outside the closed door of a building, head in his hands. "Getting into college today is far more difficult, competitive and expensive than ever before," the ad read, warning that "even a small oversight or mistake in the college admissions process" could throw them off track for admission or an athletic scholarship. It closed, "The Key can help you win the college admissions game!"

Singer also wrote a column in the magazine in mid-2010 relying on the same tropes about "winning at the college admissions game." It got front-cover billing, along with a feature on Wayne Gretzky and his family. Singer wrote about how he'd whipped a high schooler named Brad into top form. In Singer's telling, the teen had too many interests, from athletics to student government. He needed a personal brand.

Singer said in the piece that he and Brad had settled on a "backpack business," orchestrating an intricate plan to have backpacks with the school logo mass-produced by manufacturers in India—with the help of Singer's old telemarketing coworker.

A video advertisement for the Key, uploaded to YouTube in January 2012, strikes a tone somewhere between an after-school special and paid programming for a gadget you didn't know you needed. There's a worried mom in a kitchen extolling the virtues of the Key's advisory services, saying that without the company, "My son would've missed his chance to go to USC." Other scenes also reveal that Singer's company was more than a solo operation. A teen, Amanda, tells one of Singer's coaches her high school counselor said she only needed three years of science in high school. The coach, Brian Hewitt, gently sets her straight and says she'd need four years of every major subject if she wanted to get into top colleges.

"My Key coach helped me find the real me," says one boy, Conti, seated in front of a fireplace and dressed for the occasion in a sharp white polo shirt. "I was so excited to uncover my passions for the internet and communications," he continues, his energy level and demeanor suggesting he's not even the least bit excited. "I can hardly wait to finish my business degree."

Singer even tried his hand at reality TV, answering an open-casting call for a proposed series on admissions consultants being pitched to Bravo around 2011. The show, with a working title of *Chasing Ivy*, was developed in part by Jeff Gaspin, a former president of Bravo and chairman of NBCUniversal's television entertainment unit who said he wanted to highlight the absurdity of just how far some parents would go to land their kids at top colleges. Nothing illegal—just things like sending Junior on a private jet to a third-world country for some community service.

This was, after all, the network that did the wildly successful *Real Housewives* franchise. Each episode would have an arc ending in the admission decision. Great drama either way: crushing defeat or overwhelming joy.

The producers captured one set of parents joyously filming a teen in a ballet performance, with the aim of getting into a performing arts school. The kid was objectively awful. Another time, a counselor left the session and said deadpan to the camera that the client had no shot of admission to a target school. Like all great reality shows, they'd often cut the scenes for comedy and absurdity.

Singer's audition tape had both.

"This is a game—just realize that this is a game," Singer says in his flat Midwestern accent, speaking straight into the camera, wearing a white polo shirt and baby blue cable-knit sweater vest, a small black microphone clipped to the collar. "The things that I see on a daily basis are amazing, what's going on in people's homes across the country."

The sloppily edited reel leaves Singer jumping from sentence to sentence without transition, but his message is clear: it's a war zone out there, and someone like Singer helps keep the peace within families and secure a victory for the kid.

Singer describes how parents would share stories about their kids at Saturday night dinner parties, and then come home more insecure than ever that they were not doing enough. They'd reach out first thing Sunday morning. "My phone rings off the hook," he says. "They're out of control."

Singer makes clear he's dealing with rich kids, dropping how families in Champaign and Miami send their private planes to pick him up for a few hours of meetings before flying him back across the country. But he also briefly tries to dispel any illusions that just donating is a sure bet. "At some schools, giving ten million isn't enough because ten million makes no impact on their school, they want thirty, forty, fifty million."

Singer didn't make the cut for the final presentation used to pitch the show, and Bravo never did pick up the series. Singer would eventually be all over TV—just not in the way he intended.

AROUND 2010, SIRENS WERE going off for Singer's Sacramento peers like Margie Amott, the former high school volunteer who had heard Singer at the speaking gig at a parents' night in the early 1990s. Amott now ran her own college counseling service in Sacramento.

She knew Singer offered a "full service" program—signing students up for testing and completing their online applications—and she started to see that with some families, it had crossed into an outright illicit menu of offerings.

In one case, a Sacramento-area mom came to Amott saying she and her husband had hired Singer for their teenage son, and they were still clients. He'd been helpful, but something was starting to bother the mom. She'd heard buzz around town that Singer wrote essays for kids and did other unethical things.

The woman and her son sat down with Amott, who went online and pulled up the teen's application, which had not yet been submitted to any colleges.

Amott began reading it: The family spoke Spanish at home, it said. The kid wrote a screenplay that made it to TV. And while in real life the teen was an avid fantasy football participant, his application said he'd organized fifty sports teams.

"I think he has me confused with someone else," the teen said. Singer's team had typed exaggerations and falsehoods into the application.

The family decided to pay Singer and tell him they'd chosen to do things on their own, without mentioning the inflated application. If Singer really had all the connections he said he did, they didn't want to be on his bad side.

The family had been surprised about the lies, but Amott wasn't. She also got a disturbing call around the same time from a young man she knew who was working as a tutor. He said Singer had offered him $1,000 to take an online chemistry class for one of Singer's students. He didn't do it. Singer would find someone else—a Harvard graduate living across the country in Florida—who would.

By late 2011, Singer and his wife had homes in Sacramento and Maui, and substantial retirement accounts. And he was quickly turning his college counseling business into a vast criminal enterprise.

4

GOLDEN BOY

O N DECEMBER 2, 2011, Mark Riddell boarded a plane in Tampa, Florida, and left the balmy Gulf Coast to travel more than three thousand miles to Vancouver, Canada.

It certainly wasn't an obvious winter route, but Riddell, twenty-nine, was on a business trip—even if it was one he kept from colleagues at his regular job at IMG Academy, an elite sports boarding school south of Tampa.

At IMG, Riddell prepared students for their SAT and ACT, and he stood out on the campus: Six foot three, he had preppy all-American looks and a loud, fast laugh. He always seemed to be on a mission. He'd shoot the breeze briefly, then push up the center of his glasses with a knuckle and turn serious, listing the ten students he needed to go see. He walked so briskly around campus that people would sometimes wonder if something was wrong.

A few other things stuck out: A Harvard graduate, Riddell seemed a bit underemployed, and even he was talking to his boss about wanting to do more. He could also seem a little too eager to please. There was no reason for him to drive back to campus at night to help students who waited until the last minute to meet a deadline. But he did it constantly.

"You know, Mark, it's as easy as saying 'no,'" his friend and former IMG colleague Jeff DeRuiter remembers telling him. "And I don't think anyone would be upset with you if you said 'no.'"

Riddell said yes to this business trip. The morning after he arrived in Vancouver, he entered an SAT testing center. He had an ID at the ready, to show at the sign-in table or in case a proctor asked for proof he was who he claimed to be. On it was a picture of Riddell, blond and handsome.

And near that, the name: Jake Sidoo.

BRILLIANT YOUNG TEST TAKERS for hire. Rich people willing to pay them. The very month Riddell got on a plane to Vancouver, a well-to-do community on the North Shore of Long Island was grappling with a brazen cheating scheme of its own.

Bernard Kaplan, the principal of Great Neck North High School just outside New York City, had gotten an urgent call from a test prep tutor, asking to see him right away.

Private tutors were common in affluent Great Neck, where Jazz Age mansions had served as F. Scott Fitzgerald's muse for the fictional town of West Egg in *The Great Gatsby*. But this tutor's warning was shocking: a Great Neck student was boasting about having a peer take his SAT for him at a New York City testing site.

Sure enough, the kid's score came back suspiciously high. A concerned Kaplan directed a guidance counselor to look back through SAT scores and flag other ones that looked incongruent with grades. Seven or eight names stuck out. Kaplan called these students into his office, and most fessed up. The crisis escalated. Some parents were crestfallen; others said they'd sue if word got out. Kaplan believed there were real testing-security lapses and alerted local authorities.

By late November 2011, the Nassau County District Attorney's Office had charged twenty students from a handful of area high schools with either paying someone to take their SAT or ACT or taking tests for others. The main "academic gun for hire," as authorities put it, was nineteen-year-old Sam Eshaghoff, a Great Neck North graduate. Over the course of nearly three years, Eshaghoff took the SAT at least fifteen times, using fabricated high school IDs and even standing in for girls with neutral names.

The scam exposed gaping holes in test security. Proctors looked at IDs but had nothing to compare them to, to make sure the kid in front of them was the teen who signed up. Eshaghoff said he'd just walk in, keep his head down, and flash his ID to a proctor, who'd only check that the name on the ID matched one on his roster.

He charged up to $2,500 per test, and once got a $1,100 tip. When he went off to college, he'd fly home on weekends to take tests. Eshaghoff cut a plea deal that included community service and tutoring low-income students.

The money was easy, and he even told himself he was helping poor test takers get a new lease on life. He knew he was doing something wrong, but it was hard to stop, he told *60 Minutes* in 2012.

"I just told myself, 'One last time, one last time, one last time.'"

LIKE ESHAGHOFF, RIDDELL CAME across as the perfect kid. He grew up in Sarasota, Florida, the son of a prominent lawyer and a mom who worked in real estate and was active in local charities.

By about age twelve, his tennis skills landed him on the radar of Nick Bollettieri, who in 1978 had started the famed tennis academy; Andre Agassi, Monica Seles, and other greats trained there. Sports marketing giant IMG Worldwide bought the academy in 1987. Riddell got a partial scholarship to train at IMG, while attending Sarasota High School.

Riddell was so personable with adults that a friend, his doubles partner, recalled him as "every grandparent's dream grandson." The pair won the Florida high school state doubles championship in 2000.

Harvard recruited Riddell to play tennis, and he worked his way into one of the top eight spots on the team. He also joined the Spee Club, a Harvard social club whose members have included John F. Kennedy. Though certainly kind and handsome, the most defining thing about Riddell was his normalcy, recalled a former classmate. He just seemed to have wandered in, well-adjusted and calm and able to smoothly juggle the pressures of academics and competition.

It seemed a direct pipeline ran from Harvard athletics to jobs on Wall Street, and many of Riddell's friends rode it. But after graduating from Harvard in 2004 with a degree in biology, he took a different path. He had talked about becoming a doctor, but instead decided to try professional tennis.

It's not uncommon for college players to give the pro circuit a go, to take part in the travel and have no regrets about not trying. But it's costly. A Harvard coach thought Riddell's family had money and was helping him out. Riddell played in Spain, Israel, Canada, and the United States. Though he accumulated only a few wins and little prize money, and didn't stay on the competitive circuit long, he'd always talk about it as an enriching experience. By 2006, he was back on IMG's campus, where he would oversee college entrance test preparation.

And he had a new colleague.

SINGER HAD EXTENDED HIS counseling operation into South Florida, identifying a market of independent schools in search of extra support for college counseling. CollegeSource, his mass-model operation, offered a solution.

He'd begun to provide college counseling services to the University of Miami Online High School, which was eventually bought by Kaplan Inc. And lots of other private schools were popping up, catering to wealthy parents whose kids needed flexibility while they trained for sports in the Sunshine State.

IMG was expanding from mostly a tennis hotbed into more of a full-fledged sports-focused boarding school with an eye toward getting kids into college, and an ecosystem of consultants rose up around it. "Everybody and their uncle came to the academy," said Greg Breunich, a former IMG executive. "It was a pretty exciting, charismatic environment."

Singer was also exciting and charismatic, Breunich recalls. He seemed to run a pretty straightforward, legitimate business: He had tutors and representatives all over the country who would work with students on college admissions for a fee of $3,500. Half went to the company, and half went to the tutor.

Singer signed a contract with IMG around 2003 and in time employed two IMG regulars to serve as his representatives on campus: Scott Treibly, a popular tennis coach on campus, and Mark Riddell.

IMG would grow far beyond its already impressive tennis identity into six hundred acres of state-of-the-art fields and facilities, including training for baseball, basketball, football, golf, lacrosse, soccer, tennis, and track and field. A "Gatorade Sports Science Institute," dedicated to improving athletic performance, popped up, as did a 150-room hotel for visiting coaches and parents. A guard stood at the entrance of the gated, manicured campus, and gleaming white and glass buildings reflected the hot Florida sun.

The program attracted up-and-coming all-stars, as well as children who weren't as athletic but had money to burn and big dreams. Tuition soared past what New England boarding schools charged, though the school did provide substantial financial aid. One IMG student's family owned a diamond mine in South Africa, while a teen from Bermuda buzzed around on a Lamborghini golf cart. Private jets owned by IMG families lined up at Sarasota's airport.

Some IMG students were Division I recruits, while other families just hoped their children would improve and land on a Division III team. Quite a few families were completely unrealistic about the schools their kids qualified for athletically or academically—though Riddell was known for always having a tactful way of bringing families around to more reasonable goals.

IMG, as it became a more comprehensive college prep boarding school, ended its contract with Singer in 2009 because it was bringing all of its college counseling services in-house. Treibly was named the program's director, while Riddell would handle tutoring and college-test preparation.

Riddell embraced his job at IMG with gusto. He'd get to work before anyone else, looking more Harvard Yard than Florida. Neat as a pin, he wore loafers every day and often had a polo shirt tucked into a pair of shorts with a belt. He ran the SAT and ACT prep classes for year-round students and IMG's summer programs, and he was the person to whom students went if they needed help in a class or wanted to arrange a tutor.

Riddell would spend hours helping students rewrite college essays or, at parents' request, doing tutoring himself. It seemed he was working seven days a week. "He had the patience of a saint," said Richard Odell, then vice president of student affairs at IMG. "He was somebody who would just be giving all the time."

He was organized and communicative and dedicated to the job. But his most notable skill may have been his ability to ace standardized tests.

Andrew Sanderson, an aerospace engineering student at Embry-Riddle Aeronautical University, was floored by Riddell's performance when he interviewed for a test prep job at IMG. Riddell suggested he and Sanderson go into his office and actually take part of a sample SAT. It was just a formality to make sure Sanderson knew what he was doing before IMG hired him. "You'll do fine," Riddell assured him.

Riddell's desk faced the door, with a window to the campus behind him. Two chairs were at a small table. He plopped down an abbreviated sample test, with about fifteen questions, for each of them and handed out pencils. He hadn't seen that sample before, so wanted to try it out as well.

His brow growing damp from nerves, Sanderson began carefully tackling the questions, drawn from the English, writing, and math sections. He felt he was moving along at a pretty normal pace, until he glanced over at Riddell.

Read. Pencil in the answer. Read. Pencil in the answer. No break to think through the answer options. Riddell didn't pause until he got through the practice test, at which point Sanderson had made it through about one-third of the questions. (He still got the job.)

Enrolled at an elite science college, Sanderson was used to being around super-bright people, but Riddell was on another level. It was more than his academic ability. Riddell had been teaching SAT preparation for so long that he had mastered the scoring system, understood how the questions were formatted, and knew how the people preparing the tests wanted students to answer.

Sanderson would run students through practice tests and invariably get stumped, particularly when it came to more-subjective questions that asked students to read a passage and then describe an author's tone or the passage's mood.

He would dash down to Riddell's office and, no matter the subject, Riddell would follow him back to the class and politely and effortlessly spill forth with the correct answer. "It was almost scary," Sanderson recalls. "He could rattle off the answers like it was breathing."

Riddell knew he had a gift, and he would talk about how he felt he was making a real impact in his job by helping get students on the right path, a mediocre test score no longer holding them back. He would occasionally talk about how his Harvard friends were starting to make huge salaries and accumulate toys, but that was all right. He also appreciated that he had the work-life balance to do the private tutoring, outside of IMG, that he really enjoyed.

Riddell seemed to be building a nice life along the Gulf Coast of Florida. He lived near his parents, who were active in the community. In 2010, he married Sandrina Mayela, who was also notably bright. Educated in economics, she worked as a nanny when she first arrived in the United States, then landed a job as a financial analyst for well-known money managers like Raymond James. They played tennis, attended events held by the Harvard Club of Sarasota, and she appeared on local society pages, photographed in a wide-brimmed hat at a charity event with Riddell's mother.

Yet Riddell wasn't entirely satisfied. He'd swing by the office of Odell, the vice president of student affairs, to talk about career goals. He wanted to become an administrator, and eventually lead a private school. Odell found Riddell enthusiastic. But for all his book smarts, Riddell also came across as "pie in the sky" and somewhat naive about the practical steps he would need to take to reach his goals. Odell provided a bit of a reality check. Riddell would need to come up through the ranks, he said, and either get another degree or do more teaching in the classroom, rather than simply tutoring kids.

Riddell wasn't talking only to Odell. He was talking with Rick Singer, about a different line of work.

"Rick probably made him feel like he was worth a million bucks," Odell said.

DAVID SIDOO HAD A heartwarming origin story, as the son of a sawmill worker from Punjab, who made it through college with side jobs and scholarships to become a Canadian professional football player. He gave his football signing bonus to his mother to cover mortgage payments, and later became an investment banker and petroleum company executive. He lived in a thirteen-thousand-square-foot mansion on a waterfront lane known as Vancouver's Billionaire's Row.

A vanity website bearing his name touted his many business honors and philanthropic endeavors. Photos showed him attending opera galas and receiving awards for his good deeds. There was Sidoo awarding a $1,500 scholarship and posing with kids. There was an inspiring quotation: "'To whom much is given, much is expected,' David is often heard to say."

Sidoo seemed to expect a lot—or at least a lot more—from his eldest son, Jake. The teen had already taken the SAT once but earned a mediocre 1460 out of 2400.

Singer had a plan to raise that score, costing Sidoo a cool $100,000.

That December day in Vancouver, the dirty-blond Riddell showed up at the testing site, handed over the fake ID, and went in to take the SAT for the young man from an Indian family.

A year later, he'd take a test for Sidoo's younger son. And he'd keep going.

5

NEWPORT BEACH

Newport Beach, a staggeringly attractive city 430 miles south of Sacramento, is dotted with oceanfront mansions and marinas for private boats. The well-educated, overwhelmingly white population had high ambitions for their kids—and money to support those goals. It turned out to be a brilliant choice for Singer's next move. He bought a five-bedroom, five-and-a-half-bath Mediterranean villa in April 2012, picking up the 5,167-square-foot home for a relatively reasonable $1.55 million.

Ready for a fresh start, Singer chose an area not only close to his sister and half brother, but with far more wealthy potential clients. Singer had split with his wife, Allison, in late 2011 after more than twenty years of marriage, the divorce agreement committing him to providing $6,000 a month in spousal support for a decade. Allison kept physical custody of their son, Bradley. Singer maintained a townhouse in Sacramento to use as a satellite office and place to stay when he visited town.

Singer settled in the Newport Heights neighborhood, a short drive from the ocean. His home sat on a street jammed with other large ones in an eclectic mix of architecture, from boxy and modern to large New England clapboard–style. Parents swarmed the street to pick up kids from the elementary school a block away. Dog walking was a social endeavor.

Singer's hard-core running and swimming routine fit in well in the Orange

County town full of toned workout warriors. The beach helped provide a false veneer of a laid-back atmosphere, but everyone worked hard to maintain that image, and to afford that lifestyle.

The market practically begged for an aggressive college counselor who catered to parents for whom a child's failure was not an option, whether or not the kids actually put in the hard work needed to succeed. Because while many teens were genuinely pursuing activities and opportunities to make themselves as attractive as possible to colleges, others were decidedly not. They spent their downtime in Cannes and Kauai, not building homes for poor people in Los Angeles or Honduras. Or they went skiing while others pulled all-nighters with SAT prep.

And they, or their parents, would only realize around junior year that the status symbol of an elite college acceptance (or even their more middling dream school) might be out of reach through traditional means. Labels, whether Gucci or Prada or Princeton, mattered in Orange County.

Iris Berkley, a college counselor in Newport Beach, saw people walk in looking at the same five schools. She saw the high school parking lots packed with what she observed were some "pretty nice cars they drive at sixteen years old." There was no denying the emphasis being placed on brands.

To obtain those brands, sometimes they went rogue. An academic tutor, Timothy Lance Lai, hatched a plan in 2013 with a group of students at Corona del Mar High School, a few miles from Singer's home, to log in to the school's computer system and change the teens' grades. The fairly elaborate scheme involved a nighttime break-in at the high school, installing key-stroke loggers to capture passwords used to sign into the grading database, and securing advance copies of chemistry and other exams. They'd make small changes to grades, say, a B+ turning into an A–, to limit the chances of anyone noticing a massive shift in GPA.

The whole story had a comical resemblance to one used about twenty years earlier by the character Steve Sanders in the TV show *Beverly Hills, 90210*. (Fun fact: in the same episode in which Sanders sweats a police investigation into the hack, another character, Dylan McKay, faces the aftermath of an accusation that he cheated on his SAT because he scored surprisingly high.)

In the real-life case at Corona del Mar, eleven students were expelled or moved to other schools on their own. The tutor, Lai, eventually pleaded guilty to twenty counts of computer access and fraud, and one of burglary, and was sentenced to a year in jail and five years' probation.

SINGER DESCRIBED THE KEY as "the world's largest private Life Coaching and College Counseling Company," with a presence in eighty-one cities and a track record of mentoring over ninety thousand people. He dropped names of prominent families he worked with through his counseling business, but sometimes also blended fact and fiction.

At one point, he said he'd life-coached around thirty CEOs and twenty-four NBA players. He told one friend that he saw the iPhone a year before it came out, because, according to him, Steve Jobs was a client. "He's naming Steve Jobs, he's naming this and that. 'Wow, it's serious,'" thought a Walnut Creek, California, father who hired Singer for his son. "He knows these people." Singer helped the kid think through things like which math sequence he'd need to take in order to be considered at certain target schools.

The irony is that Singer provided legitimate services and apparently did it quite well. Over the years, he gave regular, aboveboard counseling to children of Joe Montana and Phil Mickelson, and venture capitalist John Doerr of Kleiner Perkins also used Singer for his kids, for test tutoring and run-of-the-mill help on college applications.

A Las Vegas chief executive said he hired Singer in 2012 for his daughter after a recommendation from a trusted friend, Mark Mastrov, the Sacramento Kings co-owner. The Vegas family, who hired Singer for basic counseling services at $7,000 a year, kidded with one another that Singer had such a big head, they needed a bigger front door at home. Yet they were drawn to Singer's confidence and his connections, even if they didn't always know what to believe. They saw him as a rainmaker who could smooth the path for their kids.

He told the family he served as an application reader for three different universities each year, so he had firsthand knowledge of what schools wanted to see. He bandied about names like UCLA, Northwestern, Georgetown, Dartmouth, and Yale. Especially in the UC system, it's not uncommon for admissions offices to hire outside readers to help get through the piles of applications; but if he ever did that, Singer exaggerated his role as a gatekeeper.

He would text college coaches right in front of parents, and seemed to have a direct line to university leaders. There was some truth to that. Singer met with the then president of Chapman University, Jim Doti, twice, in 2005 and 2012, and met for lunch with some in the admissions and enrollment department around 2010.

On one of Singer's trips to Las Vegas, the dad spoke about how the daughter of a friend had been wait-listed at Chapman. Singer asked for the friend's name and called over to Chapman to see where the girl ranked on the list.

The person on the other end reported that the girl's grades had dipped slightly in high school, where colleges typically want to see improvement.

After hanging up, Singer looked the father in the eye and said it just so happened he had a meeting scheduled with the president of the university a few days later. "She's in," he reassured the dad. The girl did get into Chapman, and everyone involved credited Singer.

Or maybe fortuitous timing just made Singer look good. The college shifted the girl from the wait list during the normal time for such movement, and her academic qualifications were in line with those of applicants who get in from the list, according to Chapman. More than one hundred wait-listed candidates got shifted over to the admit pile. Chapman later said it had no record of a get-together between Singer and Doti at that time.

On an evening in late July 2013, Mackin Carroll trudged into an auditorium on UCLA's campus and signed in to begin a weeklong camp that Singer promised would make his college applications shine.

Carroll, a songwriter who wanted to study music in college, was heading into his senior year of high school at Mater Dei High School, a Catholic school a few miles inland from Singer's Newport Beach home. He'd started working with Singer a year earlier, at the recommendation of another counselor who'd helped his older sister.

Singer had been pitching summer enrichment programs for a few years,

first renting space at Loyola Marymount University before moving over to
UCLA. Rich kids could pad their résumés with a real volunteer project highlighting their entrepreneurial skills and good hearts.

Carroll was not impressed with Singer. Then again, he was a teen and
pretty much nobody impressed him. But his mom gobbled up every last word
the counselor offered about the competition for college admissions and how
they needed to play the game. "Tweak your narrative," Singer advised Carroll,
suggesting the teen tell colleges that the September 11 terrorist attacks had influenced his music and moved him to write patriotic ballads. He was six when
the attacks occurred. He declined.

At the summer program, fees from students like Carroll helped cover costs
for the other group of participants, abused and traumatized teens who worked
with the 1736 Family Crisis Center, an L.A.-based nonprofit. Singer didn't offer
too many specifics about the program when he first reached out to the crisis
center, but hinted at opportunities for the teens to develop practical skills. The
kids would stay on campus, eat for free, and learn. The project, identified after
a brainstorming session in the early days of the program: plan and stage a charity run, with proceeds going to 1736.

The 1736 group sent about thirty kids, with senior staffer Tobi Quintiliani
working in the weeks leading up to it with Key employee Mikaela Sanford and Joel
Margulies, a longtime friend and occasional business partner of Singer's. The organizers from 1736 helped dot the days with inspirational speakers. But things
broke down quickly when it came to the actual logistics of the task at hand. The
teens got into small groups, and Carroll was assigned the concert committee—
what that meant, though, was unclear. Carroll and four others sat in a corner
Googling leads on lighting and audio setups from their iPhones. At one point
during the week, Singer snapped at a kid with ADHD. The event never happened.

The highlight, by far, was a day trip to Disneyland. Well, that was the official highlight. Carroll's favorite part was sneaking out to a Postal Service concert at the Greek, a nearby theater. "Fuck this place, this place sucks," Carroll
told himself as he fled. He was proud of himself. Maybe the camp did teach
practical skills—like when to pull the plug on a fruitless venture.

Singer didn't ask to work with the 1736 group again, and Quintiliani would not have said yes if he had asked.

The following year, Singer posted an ad online promising a camp where teens could "build your personal brand, increase your followers and monetize your passions." This camp wasn't any better than the one Carroll had attended. Singer sat the group in a room on the UCLA campus. "Make a Twitter account and start a brand," he told them. The teens stared at one another. They ordered pizza to their dorm. Six bored campers decided to leave early.

SINGER SEEMED TO BE everywhere, all at once. He told one father he traveled more than 320 days a year. He told another counselor he oversaw hundreds of consultants, trained in the proprietary "Key system," and was on the road with his own clients four or five days a week.

Singer created a charity, Key Worldwide Foundation, that claimed credit for work with Atlanta and Houston high school students, a math curriculum for California middle school students, and more good deeds. Some of it appeared true, while other lines were exaggerations.

There was a hint of something else, too, in a banal line about how their work—particularly contributions to university athletic programs—"may help to provide placement to students that may not have access under normal channels."

Neighbor Daniel Darrow said Singer would stop to give advice to his grandsons, and that he came across as "a really sharp guy" who was "all about doing good for people." But he wondered: "How can one guy be doing all these things?"

Singer also continued to coordinate his far-flung network of "coaches," remote workers who helped counsel students at private and online high schools. He connected to one at a college night at a Florida high school, meeting a mom who'd just gone through the process with her own kid and who expressed interest in doing it professionally. He quickly brought her on board, and she worked out of her home. Another he found via a Craigslist ad. He'd had a vendor agreement with Laurel Springs, an online school based out of West Chester, Pennsylvania, since 2007. The counselors charged $500 or $1,000 per student, depending on the student's grade, and split the fee with Singer. It operated like a Tony Robbins organization, where clients sign up for motivational coaching based on his name, then get assigned a stranger as a guide through self-actualization. Singer mostly left his team alone. He didn't have time. The master coach was plenty busy growing his own roster of clients.

ONE SUNDAY EACH MONTH or two, Eric Webb and his son stood in the hallway of a low-slung office building in Champaign, Illinois. It looked like all the other office buildings in the nondescript professional park there, with one difference: it had a steady stream of anxious young adults and parents churning through a conference room on the weekend.

The Webbs were among dozens of middle- and upper-class families in the Peoria and Champaign areas who used Singer.

Hour-long slots broke up the day, Singer in a conference room in his tracksuit or sweats and a college T-shirt, teens taking turns showing him the latest essay draft, more polished résumé, shorter list of target schools.

For the Webbs, the process started in 2012, when Eric saw Singer speak at an event for the Young Presidents Organization, an international business club. The event took place at a hotel near the University of Illinois at Urbana-Champaign. Webb found it to be "a great presentation," and absolutely eye-opening. While his wife had worked in admissions at a few colleges before the couple settled down and had three children, they knew things had changed a lot since she'd had that role, and certainly since they were in school themselves. Webb, a Peoria, Illinois, business executive, considered himself "the type that wanted to give my kids any extra edge that they could have. Legitimately."

Singer wasn't giving away state secrets. He spent the presentation, bouncing and energetic in khakis and a blazer, laying out the critical elements needed to get a kid into a good college these days: good grades across a tough set of classes, high ACT or SAT scores, a strong personal brand. He also mentioned opportunities for candidates who were academically or athletically gifted or musically inclined.

Impressed, Webb paused for a moment after the presentation to meet Singer face-to-face. Two months later, he signed up, agreeing to pay about

$6,000 a year for each of the next three years, to have Singer coach his son and then daughter through the admissions process.

Singer set up an ACT tutor for the son, helped arrange for private campus tours at some North Carolina colleges, and urged him to think about a few other schools besides those on his initial list. Singer showed genuine interest in fit, considering what kind of school the teen wanted, what size, what location. Southern Methodist University wasn't on his radar—until Rick came along.

And he went to bat for the family: the son loved basketball but wasn't good enough to play at the collegiate level; Singer connected him to someone in the athletics department, and helped him land a spot as a volunteer manager of the SMU basketball team. The boy ended up going there, and thrived.

Webb kept Singer on for his middle child as well. The kids got academic scholarships worth more than what he paid for Singer's services, so he felt getting a return on his investment was "a piece of cake."

There was that one thing with the daughter, though.

Singer gave Webb the message that even though the girl had straight As and a good résumé, there were some schools she might not get into. "They're just extremely competitive," the counselor said. "But if you go there through sports you may have a leg up." Made sense, Webb thought. The girl was a cheerleader, and generally athletic. Singer suggested she try rowing.

Webb bought an ergometer, and wanted to see if his daughter's times were at least in the ballpark of competitive. But the teen wasn't interested, so they dropped it. Only later did Webb realize, "Holy shit."

SINGER KEPT EVEN BUSIER back in California, where he made his regular spins through Sacramento, Silicon Valley, Orange County, and Los Angeles.

The next development: making more inroads with coaches and colleges that wanted those affluent families to help boost their bottom lines.

Vince Cuseo was in his office on the northern edge of the Occidental College campus one day in 2012 when he got an email that made him cringe.

Spanish Colonial–style buildings and grand oak and eucalyptus trees dotted Occidental, a small private liberal arts college. It resembled an oasis in the middle of urban Los Angeles. But decades earlier, "Oxy" had made the decision that it didn't want to be an island far removed from the city in which it operated.

The school had opted out of the chase for well-heeled students, not prioritizing athletes, legacies, or donors' kids. It put more money into scholarships for less well-off minorities, so it could better reflect L.A. 's diversity. That came at a cost. The college lagged in the infrastructure and amenities arms race taking root at many colleges, including nearby USC. No lazy rivers or luxury dorms would pop up at Oxy. And its endowment was smaller than it might have been if the school prioritized prestige and wealth. But Occidental had notable attributes, such as a high percentage of working-class students and a strong tradition of activism around social justice issues.

Now Occidental had rejected the academically challenged daughter of a wealthy Southern California family. And Cuseo, the vice president of admissions, had an email from her irritated college counselor, Singer. Cuseo almost never heard directly from a private college counselor.

"Are you kidding?" Singer wrote. He wanted a meeting to talk about helping the girl "find her way to becoming a student at Occidental this fall." Implied in the email was the message that the family would donate to the university: "I think we can create a win-win."

Cuseo felt proud as he typed his reply to Singer: no.

"You are off base," Cuseo wrote. He couldn't help but wonder about Singer: "Has he written to other people and gotten a different kind of response?"

Over the years, Singer would talk freely about how some colleges were much more flexible in letting underqualified kids in if the parents could donate money. He told some friends that Occidental was "dumb" for putting too many barriers between the admissions and development offices.

Barriers kept Singer thinking creatively about ways to give his clients' children an edge.

TRE CONWAY KEPT HEARING about Rick Singer through her boyfriend—Rick's younger half brother, Cliff Singer, who also lived in the L.A. area.

Cliff had dabbled on a different dark side than his brother—sentenced to prison after being caught in 1990 for selling three to seven ounces of cocaine a week over the phone to a man in Dallas, and shipping it via UPS and the U.S. Postal Service. The customer had flipped and was cooperating with federal authorities.

But Cliff had drive and smarts, and he admired his older brother.

Cliff Singer, who'd go on to become a legal businessman, told Conway she just had to meet Rick, who worked in education just like she did. At the time, Conway was a marketing manager at Halstrom Academy, a chain of private, for-profit schools. The three of them met at a Starbucks one day, and Conway quickly found herself agreeing to introduce Singer to Halstrom's top boss.

The Newport Beach–based program had cropped up in California's wealthiest communities and was part of a particular subset of schools that Singer cultivated: growing, pricey programs that didn't offer full college counseling operations, and where deep-pocketed families were eager for extra advice on getting into college. The schools offered yet another shortcut for some students to get ahead in the college-admissions game.

Alternative schools weren't always as rigorous as regular schools. Some inflated grades under pressure from paying parents, in the view of critics including educators, school administrators, and former regulators. Halstrom offered one-on-one instruction for kids, such as actors, athletes, or students with ADHD, who needed extra attention and flexible schedules. But it also drew students who wanted to fix a poor grade at school or boost their GPAs with Advanced Placement or Honors courses in an easier setting.

Singer struck up a short-lived partnership with Halstrom in 2013, agreeing to provide counseling services to the students and refer his own clients there. A match made in heaven, one administrator realized. He was particularly helpful in one aspect. Regular schools didn't always want students taking, say, biology or math elsewhere. "Go throw a huge hissy fit with the school," he would tell parents who wanted to sign up with Halstrom, when the primary school was wary of the plan. In these conversations, he got out word about his services to many parents. He was pitched as the featured speaker for events at Halstrom's Manhattan Beach and Woodland Hills campuses.

Conway watched Singer at the talk in Manhattan Beach. A hell of a salesperson, she thought. Very sure of himself, and very knowledgeable. He offered sound advice and talked about his track record of getting kids into top schools. He made high goals seem possible, if parents followed his advice. The audience hung on every word.

One day, though, Singer told Conway a curious story. He talked about a client who wanted to get a child into an elite East Coast school that represented a real reach for the teen, Conway recalls. Singer seemed sure it would work out.

"How is he going to get in?" Conway asked.

"Through the side door," Singer told her. "Some people go through the back door, I go through the side door."

Conway didn't know what that phrase meant, but it sounded iffy. She didn't ask for more details. She didn't want to know.

Allen Koh, a college counselor himself and head of Cardinal Education in the Bay Area, was also hearing about Singer's growing reputation as "the guy who gets people in," but he couldn't get any specifics. He figured Singer was just getting lucky. Koh offered counseling packages from $20,000 to the high six figures—and up to a million for a customized package.

In 2013, Koh found himself in the San Francisco Peninsula home of a financier. Out back of the gated estate was a tennis court, pool, and waterslide, and expansive bay views. Inside sat the client, his son, and Singer. Parents did sometimes interview multiple college counselors, but it was uncommon to hire two. The father explained the game plan: Singer was to be the "strategist," and Koh's firm was the "essay support team."

Singer and Koh had creative differences on that essay. The prompt asked the student to describe his greatest challenge—that's a tough question for many teens, and anyone from the fabulously wealthy town of Atherton needed to be careful about whining.

Usually Singer's coaches, reluctant to highlight an applicant's privileged upbringing, might focus on a challenge like getting over a sports injury. This time, Singer gave what struck Koh as obviously misguided advice: write about how friends who went to public school had it so easy, and the teen had to work harder for lesser grades at a top private school in Silicon Valley.

"This is not a winning topic," Koh told the family. "I don't think you need to be a college consultant or rocket scientist to know that's a very unsympathetic stance."

The family didn't back down. They wanted Singer. And they'd paid Koh already, so who was he to argue? Another interaction later gave Koh more pause about his colleague/competitor.

Koh had turned to Singer for help for a different client: a family with a good but not stellar student wouldn't accept Koh's firm assessment that USC was out of reach. The family kept begging, as if that was going to change his answer. But he didn't traffic in false hope.

Still, to satisfy the family Koh thought it worthwhile to at least consider a "development angle," or a donation to USC. And Koh remembered how Singer constantly talked about how he knew how things worked at USC. "Look, you said you're really plugged in at USC," he told Singer over the phone. "What are your thoughts here?"

Koh gave Singer the relevant details about the teen and his academic record. Singer didn't hesitate.

"Oh, this is no problem," he said.

Koh hadn't expected that.

Then Singer explained the way in: a convoluted plan involving a donation to his charity, Key Worldwide, which would then funnel the gift over to USC's athletic department. Singer suggested at least $500,000.

Koh asked a lot of questions, but the answers he got left him more confused. Singer offered nonsensical reasons for why the money should go first to his organization, not straight to USC as most donations did. This bundling wasn't normal, and further, the dollar amount, though hefty, was actually too low to get noticed by university administrators, Koh knew from past experience helping clients get on VIP lists at various schools.

And then there was Singer's insistence that this was a sure bet.

Koh knew a donation—even one with an additional zero at the end—was no guarantee, particularly in this situation. Admissions season was almost upon them, which would raise eyebrows. And the family had no authentic ties of any kind to USC.

Koh didn't imagine anyone was getting bribed, but he knew something wasn't right.

"This is not for us," Koh told the family, and they found a better fit for their son.

But there were plenty more desperate families out there.

6

FIERCE

R EBEKAH HENDERSHOT SAT STUNNED as a teen she was coaching on his college essay went over his draft essay topic: the anguish of growing up poor.

They were meeting in his family home, a mansion.

But his college counselor, Rick Singer, had advised him to focus on that narrative, betting a tale of overcoming hardship would impress admissions officers. So Hendershot, a writer and copy editor who contracted with Singer to help teens shape their essays, sat incredulously as the client, still unsold on this tack himself, used mental and rhetorical gymnastics to concoct a coherent personal statement on his experience with poverty.

Sometimes, Singer himself took a stab at putting together the fictional sob stories himself.

In fall 2013, he drafted an essay for Ethan Sidoo, a Vancouver teen, detailing a harrowing run-in during an internship with an anti-gang-violence group in Los Angeles. Ethan, the dramatic essay said, had endured a holdup.

That went a bit too far even for David Sidoo, the Canadian businessman who paid Singer to have Riddell take the SAT for his two sons. "Can we lessen the interaction with the gangs. Guns . . . ?" Sidoo wrote Singer after seeing a draft. "That's scary stuff."

But he still deferred to Singer's judgment. "Your call you know what they look for."

That he did. Admissions officers, Singer would have known, wanted a standout with a unique backstory, a special talent, a hook. They wanted someone who shone in a sea of applications from fairly well-qualified candidates.

Context had begun to play a new role as colleges committed to holistic admissions reviews, meaning they looked at more than just grades and scores. What obstacles did the applicant overcome? How hard was his or her journey to this place? Was there a tragic death in the family, homelessness, drama? The essay was a crucial place to display such nuance.

The rich and connected—rarely is someone just one, after all—aren't the only applicants with a leg up. Candidates from certain backgrounds and with interesting personal stories, such as dealing with poverty or racial prejudice, can also catch admissions officers' eyes.

Thang Diep, for instance, understood he had something special to share with Harvard when he applied a few years ago. The teen's SAT score didn't look extraordinary by Harvard standards, a 2060 out of 2400 on the old scale. His essay did. The recent Vietnamese immigrant wrote about enduring racial slurs, struggling to learn English, and spending hours reading books aloud with a pencil between his teeth to perfect his pronunciation of unnatural English words.

Admissions officers wrote comments on his application revealing they were impressed by his intellectual curiosity, infectious happiness, and what seemed to be a true commitment to social impact and the arts.

How can upper-middle-class kids compete if they've never had to work part-time to help pay bills, or overhear parents fretting about a major expense? How can someone whose sole brush with adversity entailed a community service trip to Honduras—for which Mom and Dad likely paid thousands of dollars—actually stand out?

And when schools are clamoring to increase racial and ethnic diversity, how can a white kid who grew up comfortable but whose parents can't buy a building (or endow a coach's job) get a fair shake?

At least, that's what some white applicants asked.

One high school sophomore from Naples, Florida, posed the question in an email to a reporter: "Being a Caucasian male, how can I strengthen my application to the point where my ethnicity isn't relevant?"

One father, meanwhile, said in an interview, "The best thing today is to be American Indian or black. Being a white male is like the worst category there is."

That's the category the younger son of Marjorie and Jeff Klapper fell into. The family lived just minutes from Stanford University's pristine campus in a nice neighborhood with streets named after Ivy League schools. Marjorie operated a jewelry shop, while Jeff ran a telecommunications service provider in San Mateo. The teen was a senior at Menlo-Atherton High School, a racially and socioeconomically diverse public school where 90 percent of graduates continued on to some sort of college. It offered classes like Advanced Placement Chinese and Russian history and literature.

Singer and his team helped fill out the boy's college applications, marking the boxes for "African-American" and "Mexican" on at least one. They also indicated the parents had no college education. Marjorie Klapper waffled a bit there, wondering whether the teen would be better off applying as a first-generation candidate or as a legacy to the school her husband had attended.

SOME FAMILIES LOOKED AT the numbers and decided they needed an edge. Acceptance rates continued to tick down at schools, including Stanford (from 12 percent to 5.1 percent between 2005 and 2014) and Vanderbilt (35.3 percent down to 13.1 percent). They fell by half at Duke, Penn, and Claremont McKenna.

Those plummeting numbers stoked panic in high school hallways and the offices of college counselors, and led the next year's seniors to apply to even more schools, just in case. That drove up application volumes, and pushed down the rate of prospects who were admitted. A vicious cycle.

Except for the colleges. They often embraced the surge in interest, even as admissions officers began to vent about all the applications they now had to review. Lower admit rates brought schools an aura of prestige. Though just rejecting more candidates wouldn't alone boost rankings in the U.S. News &

World Report, appearing exclusive helped in other ways—a buzzy reputation meant the pick of the best candidates. Better brand awareness could drive donations, attract high-caliber faculty, and justify campus upgrades.

A shift that had begun in the 1990s ratcheted up to new heights by the 2010s. Admissions had reached a fever pitch. Northeastern University in Boston, for example, dispatched a recruiting team of more than two dozen around the country, visited over a thousand high schools, sent hundreds of thousands of letters and emails to teens. The effort led to a sharp uptick in applications: nearly fifty thousand in 2014, double the number from a decade earlier. Over that period, as the class size remained relatively flat, the school vaulted from an unremarkable triple-digit ranking into the coveted top 50 in the *U.S. News* rankings. It went from a safety school to a hot target in short order.

There was something in the air in enclaves like Brentwood and Bel Air. After dropping their teens off in Porsches, Volvos, or Mercedes SUVs, moms in workout gear might pop into a local coffee shop, where the area near the straws and napkins was blanketed with ads for test prep services and tutoring companies.

They'd wonder, "Does my kid need extra help in chemistry? If the ones at Archer or Crossroads are getting tutored, as the flyer says, mine probably should, too."

Perfectionism, or something close to it, could perhaps be bought, claimed ads touting guaranteed ACT scores and an opportunity to master the test.

Nonfat vanilla latte and low-fat muffin in hand, off they'd go to book an appointment and make sure they weren't left behind.

Parents in this bubble brought on much of the angst themselves, by buying into the idea—and socializing their kids to think—that only a certain small list of selective schools are worth going to, when the country is in fact filled with excellent options. As one mother's lawyer put it, her family had become convinced the children wouldn't get into "the right college" without Singer's help. The schools they coveted hovered further out of reach than ever before, and even safety schools that once had the reputation of admitting anyone with a pulse weren't that way anymore.

The parents aren't all transactional. Some are just busy and a bit over-whelmed, and they want a miracle, says Alexis White, who has owned A-List Admissions and Tutoring since 2003. "It's like going to an OB and saying, 'I'm forty-eight. What are my chances of getting pregnant?'"

Other parents seemed dumbfounded at how dramatically unpredictable it had all gotten since they went to school.

"My kid needs a 3.6 to get into CU Boulder? Are you kidding me?" they'd ask White. "How can it be so impossible to get into USC?" She compared it to real estate: "Twenty years ago, there were certain neighborhoods you'd never set foot in, and are now the hottest neighborhoods. The same is true with col-lege admissions."

Talking about fit—the actual best school for a teen, not just the one that looks best to outsiders—could be "like speaking into the void," says Alexis Brooke Redding, a lecturer at the Harvard Graduate School of Education who has studied achievement culture and written extensively on the pressures of applying to college.

Even at the time Singer was on his rise, the vast majority of Americans were going to colleges that admitted the vast majority of applicants. It's not just community colleges and regional schools, like Eastern Illinois or Western Michigan. Virginia Tech's acceptance rate, for example, topped 72 percent in 2014, and the University of Missouri's flagship campus took nearly 78 percent of those who submitted files. Many hot private schools, like NYU and Baylor, opened the door pretty wide as well—35 percent and 55 percent of applicants got into those schools in 2014. If the mothers and fathers drawn to Singer had broadened their lenses, they would've found many strong schools with far greater admissions odds and plenty of opportunity for postgraduate success.

COLLEGE COUNSELORS, RESEARCHERS, even parents have used the vivid term "blood sport" to describe modern-day admissions. So, how to navigate these murky waters? Manage to nab at least one acceptance letter in what seems like an impossible situation? Identify the hook that'll make a candidate more memorable in a crowded field?

Find an expert and read up.

The Princeton Review's "Best Colleges" guides give information about schools, not necessarily about how to get into them. For that task, families can avail themselves of a niche genre with titles like *What You Don't Know Can Keep You Out of College* and *The College Hook: Packaging Yourself to Win the College Admissions Game.*

Singer self-published a book in 2014, cowritten by the essay coach Hendershot, promising to share fifty secrets to help applicants get into the college of their choice. He called it *Getting In.*

"The competition to get into the best colleges is fierce," he wrote. "Smart students take every advantage they can get."

The thin guidebook put forth some logical advice and recommendations for advantages, such as encouraging teens to take leadership positions in extracurricular clubs and to visit campuses while school is in session. But it also brimmed with contradicting directives and fairly shallow insights. Admissions officers don't care much about the SAT, he wrote. But then again you should buy prep books and hire tutors, because "with their help, these tests are easily beaten."

Kimberly Lord watched as families went to extreme lengths to stand out. While working as a college counselor at an elite private school in Texas, in 2015, "I had a parent who straight up asked me to write a student's essay for him." (She declined.)

Parents would complain the school was supposed to be a "feeder" to certain selective colleges and blame the counseling staff if the kids didn't get in. At one point, parents angry with the counseling staff actually managed to change the school's Wikipedia page to "call us out individually," Lord said. "I was briefly famous on Wikipedia."

Some families turned to outside experts because they just didn't like what the counselors were telling them. Were they saying Jamie should set his sights lower than Princeton because he really wasn't qualified, or because they were gunning for a classmate to get that coveted spot instead?

Others just wanted an insurance policy, proof they'd done everything possible to help their kids.

Lord, who has worked in four private high schools, says outside college counselors only accelerated the angst. "I have described a number of independent college counselors as fearmongers," she says. "That is what they trade in."

The idea that there are secrets to know, ways to win, helped fuel a burgeoning industry. The Independent Educational Consultants Association had a little under 600 members in 2007, and more than 1,400 by 2015, soon after Singer published his book. Private college counselors gained a reputation for catering to wealthy, high-maintenance clients, but many actually made a living working with professional and middle-class families; their average all-in fee in 2015 hovered around $4,600. Those families wanted help figuring out which schools to even look at, as well as guidance on course selection, extracurricular pathways, and test prep.

But experts weren't the only ones giving advice. In the late 2000s, two-thirds of independent college counselors were retired school counselors. Then, around 2014, psychologists, teachers, lawyers, and others entered the field in droves. And some who did have relevant experience had worked at a high school counseling office or college admissions office for only a few years before making the switch.

A good number got into the profession after helping their own kids navigate the way into MIT or Dartmouth, and then deciding they had expertise to share. Others took continuing education courses and earned certificates in college counseling at UCLA and elsewhere. ("Just because you survived cancer," one counselor—who does have more credentials—explained bitterly, "doesn't mean you're an oncologist.") A few industry groups offer training and best practices to college counselors, but membership is voluntary, and nobody needs a license to actually practice.

No wonder so many people joined the ranks of counseling, with its extremely low barrier to entry and potentially lucrative upside.

Some families sought even more of an edge by starting the college prep process earlier.

Many high schools still held off on formal college counseling until winter of eleventh grade, hoping to tamp down the frenzy. Private schools offered plenty of academic advising, but some parents wanted more explicit direction, down to which freshman math class a kid should take to stand a chance at Stanford three years later.

Guys like Allen Koh, the Bay Area college counselor who shared at least one client with Singer, would say a bad ninth-grade year could destroy a kid's chance of getting into a good college. He'd often take on clients starting in middle school, and even went on vacation with families to get to know the teens better.

These moms and dads were successful in their own right and had grown accustomed to getting what they wanted. They attacked parenting the same way: Have a plan. Identify the target. Score.

Betsy Brown Braun, a parenting expert in Beverly Hills, would field questions about the best nursery school to get into the best elementary school, to feed into the best high school that'll get the kid into Harvard or Yale later. "I can't tell you how often parents will say to me, 'What do I need to do to get in?' And I say that your child is who is going to get in."

THE PRESSURE, THE STRIVING, the expectation of perfection. It all took its toll on high school students.

Some, like the Corona del Mar students who worked with Timothy Lance Lai, turned to cheating. Stuyvesant High School in New York City seemed to have an epidemic. And the Buckley School in Los Angeles, where many families circulated Singer's name, faced its own outbreak as well.

The March 20, 2015, issue of *The Student Voice*, the school paper, had a two-page spread on students' unseemly shortcuts. "Not only does cheating hurt the students who do cheat, but cheating also hurts the students who do not cheat," wrote sophomore Ben Semprevivo. "Due to the growing number of people who cheat, scoring curves are altered, therefore putting those who do not cheat at a disadvantage."

It was contagious, he warned. "With the growing level of cheating, many students who do not cheat feel pressured to cheat in order to compete with those who do."

Ben's family would eventually know too well the dangers of cheating.

But all things considered, cheating wasn't the biggest concern when it came to the high-stakes world of high school. Palo Alto teemed with tech start-ups and venture capital firms and more millionaires than anyone could track. Parents had graduated from college, and grad school, and gotten PhDs to boot. They had no doubt their kids would, too.

That achievement-focused environment, where sleep came second to school-work, led teens to buckle. A cluster of suicides shook Henry M. Gunn High School in 2009, then another started there and at Palo Alto High School in late 2014. In total, nine incoming, current, or recent high school students took their lives. A junior at Palo Alto High School begged for change as she gave a vivid, searing description of her peers' mental state in a March 2015 opinion piece in *Palo Alto Online.*

"We are not teenagers. We are lifeless bodies in a system that breeds competition, hatred, and discourages teamwork and genuine learning. We lack sincere passion. We are sick," wrote Carolyn Walworth, who served as a student representative on the school district's board. "We, as a community, have completely lost sight of what it means to learn and receive an education." She called for change, punishments for teachers who violate homework policies, and a rethink of how they teach. "It is time we wake up to the reality that Palo Alto students teeter on the verge of mental exhaustion every single day. It is time to realize that we work our students to death."

Just as the *U.S. News* rankings helped fuel the admissions frenzy that kicked into high gear in the 2000s and 2010s, social media turned receiving acceptance letters into a public spectacle. YouTube videos went viral, capturing teens clicking on links to their decision notices with bated breath, with moms, dads, and siblings peeking over their shoulders, a messy bed or kitchen table in the background. They'd start reading, "Congratulations! You've been invited to join the Class of . . ." and begin screaming at a pitch only dogs can hear.

Of course seventeen-year-olds want to livestream their moments of joy. For teens of the 2010s, it didn't happen unless it was online. But a calculus lurked beneath the ritual: Would anyone tune in if the cheers were for a middling state university? Was it worth posting about a regional college that may not have much name recognition?

. . .

COLLEGE COUNSELORS AND FAMILIES spoke of finding a hook for applicants. Being well-rounded didn't cut it—you had to be extraordinary in a particular area.

"Remember, colleges are looking for a certain mix of students—geographically, ethnically, gender-wise, you name it. It's like they're assembling a jigsaw puzzle, one where they begin with the borders and then fill in the middle however they can," Singer wrote in his book. "The students who stand out are the ones who get in."

Standing out for academic success was already becoming nearly impossible. About one-third of public high school graduates around that time took at least one Advanced Placement exam, compared with 19 percent in 2003. And they scored better, too—20 percent earned at least a 3 out of 5, up from 12 percent a decade earlier.

Meanwhile, the Common Application offered up to twelve lines for students to crow about their extracurricular involvement. Those blank spaces served as a finger wag, a nagging sense that high school seniors should even have twelve activities to include.

Admissions officers weren't excited by a load of rigorous high school classes and a decent score on a couple of AP exams. Every applicant seemed to hail from Lake Wobegon, far above average.

It hit wealthy places like Newport Beach, North Shore Chicago suburbs, and the Bay Area especially hard, but these were national phenomena. Around the country, families hired essay experts and tutors for regular classes to try to stand out. They shelled out hundreds of thousands of dollars to send their kids on humanitarian volunteer trips to Guatemala and Rwanda, so they'd be able to write about the life-changing experience of building a house or a well. They hired private violin instructors and tennis coaches. Heck, families whose kids lost at regionals would eventually be able to pay $750, plus travel and lodging expenses, to get their kids entry into the Scripps National Spelling Bee.

Then, they urged Junior to find a favorite college and apply early.

Not everyone can afford the luxury of submitting an application in the binding early-decision cycle. People who commit to a single school can't compare financial aid offers, so they expect to pay out of pocket or have little concern the final bill will be unmanageable. And applicants need to know their guidance counselors have time to write meaningful recommendation letters by November, rather than the regular-round deadline of early January—a tall order at a public school with hundreds of students for every counselor.

One analysis of applications from 2013 and 2014 found 29 percent of students from families making more than $250,000 and who scored in at least the 90th percentile on the ACT or SAT applied early decision, versus about half that rate for those from families earning less than $50,000.

Many schools, including New York University and Johns Hopkins University, offer binding early-decision programs, meaning if someone is admitted they promise to attend. Some others are slightly less restrictive; Princeton, for example, allows early applicants to submit paperwork to state schools and service academies but no other private colleges.

Colleges want certainty, as soon as they can get it, just like teens who fret over their next steps in life. With more applicants applying to more schools, the yield, or the share of admitted students who actually enroll, has become less predictable. So locking in a big share of the class with kids who can't back out is an enticing option for schools.

Dartmouth, Vanderbilt, and Northwestern fill about half their class with early-round applicants. At some schools, early applicants could see admit rates two or even three times as high as those for regular-decision candidates.

Those who can afford to apply early reap tremendous benefits. Those who can afford test prep, personal coaching, and private tutoring do, too. And those whose families can afford to endow a professorship or building on campus are way, way ahead of the pack.

7

THE GRAY AREA

IN NOVEMBER 2013, Alessandra Bouchard, a staffer in Harvard's development office, asked Roger Cheever, a more senior fundraising administrator, to weigh in on an applicant at the request of admissions dean William Fitzsimmons. The applicant wasn't a legacy, but their late grandfather had given about $8.7 million to Harvard over his lifetime.

Cheever responded a day later that much of the donor's art collection would likely go to a museum, not the university, and the family was probably tapped out. "Going forward, I don't see a significant opportunity for further major gifts," he said. He recommended rating the applicant a notch below the most enthusiastic.

For centuries, money has bought access to higher education. At many colleges, even just indicating you can pay full tuition, rather than ask for scholarships, can give you a leg up.

Parents and grandparents understand the game. Even wealthy schools are always in the market for more money, and being able to deliver on a donation could help someone's kin get a closer look from the admissions office. As one of Singer's clients put it, "You put your name on the library, five generations of your family get to go to the university of your choice." So really, what's the difference? Where's the line between legitimate gift and shady bribe? And how much power does a donation have, anyway?

Twenty thousand dollars, probably not so much. Millions, maybe.

The pull of particular dollar figures is unclear, and that's likely intentional. Elite colleges discuss the relationships between their development offices and admissions offices delicately, preferring to dangle the hope of special consideration rather than flatly say money buys a path in. Quid pro quo arrangements are frowned upon. They go against schools' public claims about rewarding students' exceptional hard work through a fair, holistic, merit-based review of applications.

Years later, Singer would explain the various entry points. "There is a front door getting in where a student just does it on their own; and then there's a back door where people go to institutional advancement and they make large donations but they are not guaranteed in; and then I created a side door that guaranteed families to get in," he said. "So that was what made it very attractive to so many families is I created a guarantee."

Singer focused on what he called the side door to get clients into colleges. That entryway on the side was a fancy way of referring to bribery and cheating. But the back door sat wide open, with special privileges given to families of major donors, celebrities, children of alums, and other groups deemed to be of particular importance to the institution.

Singer regularly blurred the line between the side door and back door. They might have been right next to each other, in his mind, maybe even shared a threshold. As he said in a 2014 email to one parent, "Ok side door is not improper nor is back door both are how all schools fund their special programs or needs." The main difference, he explained, was the back door cost more. The side door was just about giving a donation to a more modest program, where a still substantial but markedly smaller gift would have outsize impact. The music department, for example, or an under-the-radar athletics team.

He told one father the side door at Harvard or Stanford would cost $1.2 million—bargains compared to the $45 million and $50 million, respectively, expected if you wanted to get in the back door. "And they're getting it. That's the crazy thing," he told the father. "They're getting it from the Bay Area and from New York."

. . .

JARED KUSHNER IS PERHAPS the best known example of a "back door" deal, as Daniel Golden detailed in his 2006 book *The Price of Admission*. The son of a real estate magnate turned convicted felon, and son-in-law of President Donald Trump, Kushner was a mediocre high school student at best, with test scores below Ivy League standards.

His father, Charles, pledged $2.5 million to Harvard in 1998, around the time Jared was starting the college admissions process at the Frisch School in New Jersey. The gift was to come in annual installments of $250,000, and Harvard's former president said it was intended for scholarships. "Frisch officials were surprised when he applied to Harvard—and dismayed when he was admitted," Golden wrote in the book, which shattered any illusion of meritocracy in admissions.

A spokeswoman for Kushner Companies later said "the allegation" that Charles Kushner's gift to Harvard was related to Jared's admission "is and always has been false." The parents, Charles and Seryl Kushner, "are enormously generous and have donated over 100 million dollars to universities, hospitals and other charitable causes," she said.

The conversations about how money mattered could be just as explicit a few years later. In June 2013 David Ellwood, dean of the Harvard Kennedy School, sent Fitzsimmons an email praising the admissions dean for considering some applicants who, presumably, offered connections of great import to the graduate public policy program. "My Hero," the subject line read.

"Once again you have done wonders," Ellwood wrote, adding that he was "simply thrilled about all the folks you were able to admit." They were "big wins": one had already committed to a building, and another promised major money for fellowships.

A 2014 lawsuit against Harvard laid bare many of the ugly truths about preferential treatment in college admissions. The suit was filed by Students for Fair Admissions, a nonprofit that said it represented Asian Americans who didn't get into the school because, they alleged, Harvard discriminated based on their race and held them to a higher standard than other applicants. The case would go to trial in fall 2018, with a federal judge ruling nearly a year later in favor of Harvard. (Her decision has been appealed.) Court filings and sworn testimony proved enlightening and, to many, troubling.

A recruited-athlete flag is nearly a guarantee for admission. A Duke economist's statistical analysis of six years of Harvard University admissions data—nearly 167,000 applicants—found recruited athletes were admitted 86 percent of the time, compared to 6 percent for nonrecruits. For Harvard, which like all members of the Ivy League does not award athletic scholarships, the "athlete" label is "not so much a message as it is essentially a command," said plaintiffs' attorneys at the 2018 trial.

Other groups got special treatment, too. Legacies—the children of alumni—stood a nearly 34 percent chance of getting in. And then there were the mysterious people on the dean's interest list, applicants who were flagged to Fitzsimmons, the admissions head, by the development office or others throughout the year.

When Fitzsimmons was asked at the trial if admitting the children and relatives of large donors mattered, he responded, "It is important for the long-term strength of the institution that we have the resources we need."

Harvard men's tennis coach David Fish emailed Fitzsimmons in October 2014, thanking the admissions dean for meeting with a recruit. Over the prior four years the recruit's family had given about $1.1 million, including funding for two full professorships. They had family ties to Harvard, but much of the "clan" ended up at Penn, Fish notes. They wanted him up in Cambridge, "thus we rolled out the red carpet."

Fish wrote that the teen hadn't always been a serious contender for the team. "A year ago, there was no way that I could have offered [the recruit a] spot on our roster with a straight face." But the kid improved markedly, moving up in the ranks and playing doubles with another strong tennis player who was being recruited to Harvard. So Fish asked Fitzsimmons to flag the boy for a "likely" letter when they reviewed the early-admission application that fall.

Fitzsimmons replied that it was "perfectly appropriate" to consider the boy for a likely.

· · ·

IN MAY 2014, a worried mother called UCLA and asked if there was any chance they'd reconsider her daughter for admission. She was still willing to pay, the mom said. She understood she'd need to give around $100,000, no problem.

The mother had hired Singer in August 2013, paying him $6,000 for counseling services. He told her he could help the daughter get into UCLA, but the family should be prepared to pony up a sizable donation. Some would go to the school, some to coaches, she was told. "If someone helps you, it would be good of you to help them back," Singer explained to her. Consider it "a show of appreciation."

The girl played high school tennis, so in October 2013 Singer introduced her to UCLA tennis coach Billy Martin and his assistant, Grant Chen. Martin had known Singer for a decade and told the mother that the college counselor had helped him find many student-athletes over the years. Martin was even the point person who helped UCLA secure a $30,000 donation directly from Singer in 2008. Martin also knew Scott Treibly, who worked for Singer at IMG and went on to run his own counseling company.

Singer had mentioned the family was well-off and could support UCLA, Martin later said, but there was no discussion of exact figures.

The women's tennis roster was already full, so Martin's assistant, Chen, made an introduction to Brandon Brooks, who coached the highly regarded UCLA water polo team. The daughter met Brooks in December, and even though she had no experience in the sport, Brooks said she seemed like she could help the team, as a player or manager. Singer offered his advice: tell Brooks you could be a player for the sake of admissions, attend practice, and then take on the manager role. "I have a friend . . . that can create a profile if needed for polo."

The girl fired off a thank-you note to Brooks, who forwarded it on to Chen. Then Chen got cracking drafting a commitment letter, planning to ask the family to agree to gifting $20,000 a year over four years. Chen liked to be "proactive" and "run with it," he later told school officials, and understood fundraising was part of his job.

Singer sent the mother a text in December: "Everything is all set," he wrote. "She will be presented at the January admissions meeting, and there is no question she will be approved without a second thought. HAPPY HOLIDAYS!!!" During a second review, though, someone in the athletic department's compliance group realized the girl didn't actually have experience as a water polo player. She was rejected.

That prompted the mother's call to UCLA. Her comment that Singer implied a donation would be expected in exchange for admission launched a formal investigation by UCLA's compliance office. Turned out, Chen wasn't new to finagling admission offers for mediocre athletes with deep pockets.

The investigation found that Chen had pursued a similar approach the year before, that time for a young woman from Brentwood who was flagged as a prospect for UCLA's track and field program. The same day she was coded by the track and field director as a recruit—which that person said they did at the request of someone in the development office—Chen got sample pledge forms for $80,000 and $100,000. He soon confirmed the family had committed to giving $25,000 a year for four years.

The contribution was clearly a quid pro quo, the school determined. The coach expected her to be a manager, not a runner, and coaches weren't supposed to flag managers as recruits.

Chen's involvement in both those cases led UCLA to review tennis recruits, too, to see if there was any fishy connection between admissions of middling players whose families made donations. There was. Between 2004 and 2014, families of "a relatively high percentage" of men's tennis recruits whose talent was characterized as "limited" donated significant amounts to the tennis program. At least two of those recruits had used Singer.

According to the school's investigative report, completed by the head of the compliance office and passed along to other high-level officials, it all "suggested a pattern of admissions actions that were influenced by the expectation that the family would likely contribute to the program."

Fact pattern found. Eyebrows raised. Then lowered.

UCLA determined that while some coaches did violate school policy, none of those tennis recruiting situations were particularly egregious, since they were at least minimally talented athletes and the donations didn't actually arrive too close to the kids' admission. After issuing its report, the school instituted a new policy requiring that they wait until student-athletes were enrolled before accepting donations from their families.

THE UNIVERSITY OF TEXAS at Austin admissions official was in a bind. This applicant was wholly unqualified—"so bad for so many reasons," the administrator would say—yet there was little choice but to extend an offer. The president of the university wanted it done. And so it was.

The situation reflected a concern that applicants with ties to legislators or other influential people were getting preferential treatment at the flagship campus. It led to an internal probe, and when that was deemed insufficient, investigations company Kroll took over the job.

In its 2015 report summarizing its review of admissions at UT Austin, Kroll didn't find any quid pro quo exchanges or things that veered into illegal territory, but what was happening still didn't seem entirely kosher, the report's authors determined. Existing policies, the company warned, could lead to "affirmative action for the advantaged" as the president, deans, and others flagged prospects of special interest and encouraged or pressured the admissions office to take their recommendations.

Bill Powers, who had been president at the flagship campus since 2006—and is not the same Bill Powers who introduced Doug Hodge to Rick Singer—acknowledged intervening in admissions decisions at the request of regents and others. He said it helped maintain good relationships with important stakeholders, like lawmakers who hold the state's purse strings.

Kroll found seventy-three prospects were admitted to UT Austin's undergraduate program between 2009 and 2014 with SAT scores below 1100 and high school GPAs under 2.9—both significantly lower than the general pool of admitted students. Nearly half came from families with incomes over $200,000.

At the time Kroll was poking around, deans, the president, and a few other people at UT Austin could request that a "hold" be placed on an application file, meaning a rejection decision couldn't be made final until the advocate was notified—and, the implication is, had the chance to challenge the outcome.

Hundreds of applicants received holds each admissions cycle and over the six-year period reviewed by Kroll, those with a hold had a 72 percent admit rate, compared to an overall rate of about 40 percent. Applicants received special consideration, and holds, at the urging of lawmakers and regents, as well as prominent alums, major donors, faculty members, and other university officials.

Powers responded to the report, writing on his *Tower Talk* blog on the school's website, "It is my observation that some similar process exists at virtually every selective university in America, and it does so because it serves the best interests of the institutions."

NORTHWESTERN UNIVERSITY PRESIDENT Morty Schapiro has a similar understanding of the system. "I don't think there's a question whether donor or other institutional reasons play a role in undergraduate admissions decisions at selective privates," he said in an interview in summer 2019. "It's *how* they play a role."

Schapiro, who personally reviews more than five hundred applications each year, says smarts and skills absolutely matter most when he's making recommendations. "It's what the student can contribute inside and outside the classroom. It's not what the student's family can contribute in fundraising. Now, that said, I would be crazy never to think about institutional reasons in admissions."

Schapiro looks over applications tied to major donors, the kids of faculty and staff, local high schoolers, teachers, kids of alumni volunteers, little siblings of his students, and people flagged by former students who now work for Teach for America.

In the 2018–19 admissions cycle, between 400 and 450 of the files Schapiro looked over were already tagged by the admissions office as obvious admits or rejects. He met with Chris Watson, dean of undergraduate admissions, to discuss the other 100 candidates, who were more borderline.

Northwestern officially says endorsements and letters of support rarely affect admissions outcomes. Schapiro says there are usually two to four kids every year he tells Watson he'd really like to admit, but for whom Watson and his team disagree—often when Schapiro thinks someone's senior year grades trump mediocrity earlier in high school. Schapiro ultimately demurs to them, he says, and doesn't "pull rank."

Schapiro, an economist, has focused his academic research on higher-ed financing, student aid, and other topics related to admissions, so he says the special attention he pays to applications is partly due to scholarly interests. He's also a realist. If a distinguished professor has a kid applying, and the kid doesn't get in, he says he'll have to answer for that. And as for children of big donors, "I'd be crazy not to take a close look at the application so I can explain why their child was rejected."

IN LATE OCTOBER 2018, a seventy-something African American woman took the stand in a packed courtroom at the federal courthouse on the Boston waterfront to speak in defense of diversity on campus—and in defense of Harvard's special "tips" for legacies, athletes, families of donors, and other special candidates.

Ruth Simmons wasn't the most obvious champion of such practices. The youngest of twelve children, she spent her early years in a sharecropper's shack on a plantation in Grapeland, Texas. She went to elementary, middle, and high school in a completely segregated part of Houston, then landed at Dillard University for college in the 1960s. A Romance language scholar, she held a number of high-level administrative posts—provost at Spelman College, president at Smith College and Brown University—and had come out of retirement a few years earlier to lead Prairie View A&M University in her native Texas.

Simmons didn't defend explicit donation-in-exchange-for-admission practices when she took the stand in Boston. "You'd never, ever admit a student because their family promises a contribution," she said. That would be "completely inappropriate."

But. But . . .

"But it is certainly possible that there are students who come along whose families can do incredible things for an institution." If they're highly able, Simmons said, "I don't believe that it is problematic to admit those students."

How does a school survive for four hundred years? "It doesn't happen because we sit on our hands and do nothing. It happens because we are constantly looking for help, from as many different corners as we can find it."

THE ONE THING AN applicant has literally no control over—who his or her parents are—can weigh enormously on college admissions. Harvard calls it lineage status, but most other schools refer to these applicants as legacies.

"Without lineage, there would be little case. With it, we'll keep looking," a Harvard admissions officer wrote about an applicant a few decades ago. "Not a great profile but just strong enough #s and grades to get the tip from lineage," wrote another.

Though student populations at colleges have changed dramatically over the past half century, the offspring of graduates from a generation ago still look a lot like their parents: wealthy and overwhelmingly white. More than 20 percent of the University of Notre Dame class that started in fall 2018 had a parent who'd attended the school. At Baylor University, 32 percent did. The practice of giving preference to legacies has its critics, including New York Federal Reserve Bank president William Dudley, who said he doesn't know how the nation's best universities can continue to justify a practice that "only preserves the status quo and constrains economic mobility."

Schools argue that the apple doesn't fall far from the tree, and if Mom and Dad cut it at an elite university, chances are the kids got some of those smarts and will also do well. The children of college graduates also tend to have access to better schools and end up with higher standardized test scores, which can make them appealing candidates in their own right.

In recent years the admit rate for legacies at Georgetown was about double the rate for the overall applicant pool. At Princeton University, legacies got in 30 percent of the time, compared with 7 percent overall for a recent five-year stretch.

But if kids of alums are just as qualified as those without familial ties, why give them special treatment? It can be a tough practice to defend, especially as schools claim they want to diversify their populations more.

Applicants with strong but not outrageous academic profiles—which Harvard tags a 2 on a scale of 1 to 4 (1 being the best)—generally had about a 10 percent chance of getting in, according to a review of six years of admissions data analyzed in the lawsuit against that school. That jumped to a fifty-fifty shot for those who were legacies, who were children of Harvard faculty or staff, or who landed on the dean's interest list.

According to statements from the Harvard trial, as many white kids in special preference categories—athletes, legacies, dean's interest list, and children of Harvard staff and faculty—were admitted over the six-year period as were the combined number of Hispanic and black candidates.

By letting graduates believe their kids stand a better shot of getting in, schools can entice graduates to stay in touch, remain cozy, donate. Duke University's alumni website has a whole page on admissions in its "benefits" section, offering "advice and assistance" to children and grandchildren of graduates. "While alumni affiliation by no means ensures acceptance to Duke, the university values meaningful connection to Duke and its traditions and does note alumni status when reviewing applications." In other words: we've got your back.

8

PLAY BALL

O N THE SOCCER OR lacrosse field I am the one who looks like a boy amongst girls with my hair tied up, arms sleeveless, and blood and bruises from head to toe," Madison Macfarlane wrote in her college essay in 2013. "My parents have a hard time attending my soccer matches because our opponent[s'] parents are always making rude remarks about that number 8 player who plays without a care for her body or anyone else's on the field. It is true that I can be a bit intense."

Madison was a senior at La Jolla Country Day School in San Diego in 2013. She was bright, her college list including schools like NYU, Boston University, and UC Santa Barbara. And she was best known at school not as a striker, midfielder, or defender, but as a particularly wealthy kid in an already affluent area, nice enough and popular enough and fairly stylish. She wasn't the wild one or the funny one or the troublemaker. She played soccer, but she wasn't good enough to be on a college team, let alone be recruited.

She also didn't write the essay: in September of Madison's senior year Singer forwarded to her and her father, Toby, a draft with that dramatic wording, preparing to submit the teen as a soccer recruit at USC. They'd pay $200,000 for the service. With the mom, Christy, providing a photo of Madison playing soccer, Singer pitched the girl as having been a "US Club Soccer All American" her sophomore, junior, and senior years.

Macfarlane was a well-regarded senior executive at a title insurance company. He lived in upscale Del Mar, California, overlooking the Pacific Ocean. In addition to his insurance job, Macfarlane also invested in commercial properties like restaurant buildings. And he was active on the San Diego philanthropy circuit.

Yet he and Christy were making their way through an unsuccessful round of couples counseling, the marriage ultimately doomed. Macfarlane, whose own parents split when he was a kid, didn't want to disappoint his children. He also liked the idea of someone taking the pressure of navigating college admissions off his plate and, after working with a local counselor briefly, had signed up with Singer soon after Madison began her junior year. Macfarlane wanted certainty, and it wouldn't hurt if that certain path led to his beloved alma mater, USC.

"All I could think of was not having to worry about my kids getting into college," Macfarlane later explained.

SINGER'S ILLICIT TACK SOUGHT to exploit the incredible advantage athletes have in admissions. They are considered ideal students: driven, disciplined multitaskers; natural leaders; and team players. It doesn't hurt that when they win they can fill a stadium and keep alums engaged and generous.

College officials speak about their student-athletes in superhuman terms, language not generally trotted out for thespians or computer scientists. "Our sports teams engender pride among our whole community, and I have often said that we bask in their reflected glory, bringing the Yale College community closer together," Yale president Peter Salovey wrote once in a letter to the school community. He went on to explain exactly why there's all that basking: athletes "learn self-discipline, how to work as part of a team, how to subordinate individual ambition to a group accomplishment, and how to be resilient in the face of failure. These skills are important in every area of life, including academics."

Colleges work hard to recruit and enroll these special students, in some cases reviewing their applications on a sort of parallel pathway, separate from the general pool of candidates. Schools say that for recruited-player spots, they really only give an edge to athletes who show commitment and excellent skills to boot. Playing soccer sophomore year isn't enough; admissions officers expect to see an application chock-full of references to the sport—tournament trophies, race times, essays about hours they spent sacrificing social lives and physical health to compete.

But with most sports losing money for schools, why bend over backward to favor athletes at all? Critics say the practice only serves as a sort of affirmative action for wealthy applicants. Elite club programs, camps, and showcases that get teens in front of collegiate coaches easily run into the thousands of dollars. Lift tickets and country club memberships aren't cheap. Then, there's the racial disparity. About 65 percent of all students who participate in NCAA sports are white, higher than the overall student population. For skiing, lacrosse, and field hockey, the proportion of white participants is over 80 percent.

Coaches can hold extraordinary power in the admissions process. Their endorsement that someone is a top recruit, or even a preference for the team, can be enough for an application reader to rubber-stamp an applicant who meets minimum academic requirements.

Even at schools not known as athletic powerhouses, sports skills matter. A 2016 review at Amherst College—a Division III school that doesn't award athletic scholarships and pretty much never sees student-athletes end up in pro sports—found that athletics played a role in the admission of at least 127 students from an entering class of roughly 450. Some were flagged by coaches for excellence, while others were coded as having solid skills and still got in at a much higher rate than the general nonathlete pool with similar academic qualifications.

Here's how athletic recruiting is supposed to work: a coach or the coach's assistants spot a talented player. That sighting could come at the high school state championships or, just as likely these days, through a regional club program or a camp hosted on a college campus. The coaching staff then assembles a list of top picks. For NCAA Division I and Division II programs, that means potential scholarship recipients. Each sport gets a different number of scholarships—thirteen for Division I men's basketball. That's nearly enough for a full roster.

But there are only fourteen scholarship spots in Division I women's soccer, enough financial aid for about half the team. In men's tennis, scholarships don't even cover half the players.

In addition to those scholarship slots, coaches at many schools also get to flag candidates who may be on the bubble, players who could help the team but aren't superstars worth shelling out money to cover tuition, room, and board. Those kids are called "preferred walk-ons."

No matter the sport, the coaching staff determines its top picks and puts the names forward to the admissions office. They're generally delivered via an athletic department liaison, though coaches can have plenty of direct contact with admissions officers as well. At many institutions, the names are accompanied by what's called an athletic profile, something akin to a one-page review of each applicant. The most pertinent information: how much of an athletic standout the student is—race times, national championship tournament results, participation in regional clubs—and whether he or she meets the minimum academic requirements for admission.

The NCAA has fairly low standards for a qualified student-athlete. Teens need to have graduated from high school with at least a 2.3 GPA in core courses. The higher the GPA, the less performance matters on the SAT or ACT. But many schools do expect at least slightly better of their student-athletes. In the Ivy League, student-athletes must stay within a range that doesn't stray too far from the norm of other admitted students' grades and standardized test scores. Each of the eight Ivy League schools has its own academic index average from which players can deviate, and each team average has to remain in that band as well.

In some cases, an athletic department official or the coaching staff has already run its top picks by the admissions office early in the fall, before offering a recruiting spot to the player, just to get a gut check on how tough a sell it may be to land a star player with a C average. "Certainly there are athletes who, the only way they're getting in is because they're super talented at their sport," says Elizabeth Heaton, a former athletics liaison in Penn's admissions office, now vice president at Bright Horizons College Coach, the college counseling operation of Bright Horizons, which runs day cares and provides education advising as a corporate perk to many major companies.

Serious athletes are urged to apply in the early-admission cycle so that coaches can square rosters away quickly. While early-action or more binding early-decision deadlines are generally in November, with acceptance or rejection letters going out around mid-December, athletes at many schools get an early peek at their fate by way of a "likely letter."

Penn says on its admissions website, "These 'likely letters' have the same effect as letters of admission. As long as you maintain your academic and personal record as detailed in your application, we will send a formal admission offer on the appropriate notification date."

THE AUTONOMY COACHES HAVE in setting their rosters and handing out coveted team spots gives them huge influence, particularly considering the value of an acceptance letter at a place like Yale or Georgetown or USC.

Admissions officers at some schools may be expected to review applicants in under eight minutes, so even if they understand the difference between a setter and a middle hitter, they don't have the time to check out how good a potential athletic recruit really is. "I'm not a volleyball expert. The coach is the expert. So if they're telling me, I've got to assume that's what it is," says Jamie Moynihan, a college counselor at Boston-based AcceptU who worked as an admissions officer at two Division I schools between 2008 and 2013. He regularly worked directly with coaches who wanted to flag particular applicants as recruits or preferred walk-ons, and served as a liaison to the athletics office at one school.

In Moynihan's experience, the coach would generally indicate who his top few picks were, for context. "You still need to be admissible to the school, but if you're a recruit . . ." He trails off.

Preferred walk-ons don't have quite the same sway as top recruits, Moynihan says, but "the coach would like to get them in, so I'm going to do what I can to make that happen." If you're a recruit, there's more room for forgiveness. A good basketball player, for example, doesn't need to get straight As. "I understand that student has been playing at a high level, the time commitment," Moynihan explains. "To do that and still maintain Bs is pretty impressive."

For years, Stanford required only the recruiting coach to review a prospect's athletic credentials before sending names to the admissions office, though now another administrator is expected to verify the claims. Heaton, the former Penn admissions officer, doesn't recall being asked or encouraged to do background checks or in any other way verify coaches' claims about athletes. "The assumption was if a coach is advocating for a kid, the coach's job depends on winning. Why would they advocate for a student who wasn't going to contribute?"

SINGER HELPED COACHES SELL his clients as worthy picks. He drafted essays referencing sports and recommended teens send emails to coaches to create a paper trail showing some sort of relationship.

After all, while admissions officers don't pore over highlight reels, they still might get suspicious if an applicant claimed to live and breathe basketball or sailing but never mentioned the sport in their essay or list of extracurricular activities.

As he had done for Madison Macfarlane, Singer provided such material to Julia Henriquez, a senior at the all-girls Notre Dame High School in Belmont, California, in 2015.

Julia was an especially rich kid in an already wealthy area—in college, she'd don Hermès belts and Gucci sneakers to attend parties. Her father, Manuel Henriquez, cofounded and ran Hercules Capital, a publicly traded specialty finance company that provides loans to venture capital and private equity-backed startups. His 2014 compensation package topped $8.2 million, and was nearly $7.9 million in 2015. The family lived in Atherton, a lush, peaceful pocket of Silicon Valley where sprawling houses, hidden behind gates and fences, looked more like they belonged in Greenwich, Connecticut, than in California.

Manuel and his wife, Elizabeth, would ultimately be in deep with Singer, as the counselor helped both Julia and her younger sister, Megan, cheat on their college entrance exams (Julia's SAT subject tests and SAT, and Megan's ACT—twice—and SAT subject tests). They also recommended his services to other families in the area.

The essay Julia submitted to Georgetown indicated not only that it was her top-choice school but that joining one particular activity on the D.C. campus was something she'd always aspired to. "[B]eing a part of Georgetown women's tennis team has always been a dream of mine," the essay read. "For years I have spent three-four hours a day grinding out on and off court workouts with the hopes of becoming successful enough to play college tennis especially at Georgetown. What is most amazing is how quickly I connected with Coach Ernst. He spent time with me while on campus and at several tournaments I played in."

Her application also claimed she played club tennis all four years of high school and held a top-50 ranking in the U.S. Tennis Association junior girls program her sophomore, junior, and senior years, and that she was on the USTA all-academic team the final two years. (As in Peyton Hodge's case, USTA records show no sign that Julia played in any of its tournaments in high school.)

A coach would drool over that résumé, and it scored Julia a "likely letter" that stated she had a better than 95 percent chance of getting in if she maintained her grades. The Henriquez Family Trust then sent $400,000 to Singer's charity.

9

"ISN'T IT A GREAT DAY
TO BE A TROJAN!"

ON AN UNCHARACTERISTICALLY GRAY DAY in October 2010, C. L. "Max" Nikias stood beneath a red tent, draped in black academic regalia and a sparkling gold necklace bearing the University of Southern California medallion.

"Good morning, everyone!" He beamed. "Wow."

The bespectacled, Cyprus-born electrical engineer was formally taking the baton as the eleventh president of USC and delivering his inaugural speech in a park adorned with flowers and flags in USC cardinal and gold. Nikias welcomed the Trojan Family, the affectionate nickname for USC students and alums. He expressed gratitude to the board and search committee, and to his predecessor, Steven Sample, who'd been credited with USC's dramatic rise in the late 1990s and early 2000s. He thanked his wife, Niki, with whom he'd come to the United States more than thirty years earlier.

"Niki and I believe that, when you have been given so much, you have a debt to repay," he said, his left hand bopping as if he were a conductor marking each momentous word with a beat. "Working together to take USC higher, to the undisputed mountaintop, will be our payment on the debt."

The undisputed mountaintop. An animated Nikias would repeat some version of this lofty ambition many times throughout his speech. His message was unmistakable: though USC could now hold its own among its venerated rivals, it hadn't yet gotten the credit it deserved.

USC, outside of its film program, had been derided a generation earlier as the "University of Spoiled Children," the safety school for wealthy teens who couldn't get into UCLA. Stanford's marching band snidely spelled USC's average SAT score with just three digits in 1987.

USC had since dramatically improved the academic caliber of its students and shifted under Sample into a hot destination for faculty, philanthropists, research funds, and bright kids. Yet a we've-still-got-something-to-prove vibe dominated Nikias's speech. The newly anointed leader occasionally tapped his fist on the podium for emphasis as he drew on the classics, calling for USC to embark on an epic journey akin to the founding of Rome.

He didn't want the school to be described as "up-and-coming" anymore. It was time to become "undisputedly one of the most elite and influential institutions in the world." USC must rise to a place where "there is no doubt, there is no argument" that it belongs in the pantheon of world-class education.

He pledged to represent USC to powerful decision-makers in the California statehouse and Washington, D.C. He'd integrate the riches of Los Angeles into the campus experience and share the school's expertise with its neighbors. He predicted USC could become no less than a "new Rome in higher education." He'd work to establish Trojans as the premier network of leaders across the Pacific Rim. He'd woo top faculty and students, turning USC into an intellectual giant of the twenty-first century. He'd raise money, and he'd do it relentlessly.

Troy was ascending.

"My own commitment to you," he said, "is to run the next marathon at a sprinter's pace."

William Tierney, a professor and the founding director of USC's Pullias Center for Higher Education who'd been at the university since 1994, grew worried when he heard that aggrandizing line. A university should be an environment of reflection and reasoned debate, not one of racing to achieve a certain status. Tierney, a marathon runner himself, approached Nikias after the speech to share his concern. He said the analogy was foolish; no one can sustain that kind of speed.

Nikias laughed and responded, "We have to."

"What's happened," Tierney said years later, "is the result of trying to run a marathon at a 10K pace."

WARM AND LIKEABLE, NIKIAS had risen through the ranks from engineering school dean to provost, and then president, at USC in part because of his fundraising prowess. As the new president, Nikias wasted little time, pushing past skeptics and fundraising experts to pursue a fundraising goal of $6 billion. When first announced in 2011, Nikias's Campaign for USC—also grandly called Fas Regna Trojae ("The Destined Reign of Troy" in Latin)—was the largest fundraising campaign in the history of higher education.

Now Nikias, nicknamed the "$6 billion man" at USC, worked around the clock raising money as USC further cemented itself in the California psyche as a luxury brand, with almost cult-like status among aspirational and status-minded parents. The name adorned license plate holders, sweatshirts, and banners foisted outside homes during football season. Membership in the Trojan Family club often passed down through generations, an inherited passion. Many just called it "SC." USC's board of trustees was like a hot social group, with billionaire real estate developers, industrial and media tycoons, and a sports team owner. Alums held top posts at Salesforce, Walt Disney Animation Studios, and NBCUniversal.

To the north of the school, in the community of La Cañada Flintridge, crowds would erupt into cheers at the annual Fiesta Days celebration in May when a Trojan warrior paraded a white horse named Traveler, USC's mascot, down Foothill Boulevard.

The university's acceptance rate had declined sharply, making entry to the cool-kids' club more of a crapshoot. While 75 percent of applicants for the 1987 entering class made the cut, by 2011 the admit rate was just 23 percent. USC even surpassed UCLA in the U.S. News & World Report rankings in 2010. By 2014, applications topped 50,000; the school admitted about 9,400 and enrolled one-third that number.

As a college counselor at the prestigious Harvard-Westlake School in Los Angeles until 2015, Tamar Adegbile saw parents contorting themselves over the school. "People will crawl through glass to get there," she says.

Desperate parents and a college hungry for cash. Rick Singer took notice. He'd have a ready answer when parents asked whether their kids were qualified for USC. As one dad put it in an email, his son "would go there in a heartbeat!!"

"No," Singer answered, the son wasn't qualified, "but I can try to work a deal."

A FEW MONTHS BEFORE Nikias formally took the helm at USC, he'd announced a masterful appointment: Pat Haden would leave his job in private equity and become the university's new athletic director. The genial fifty-seven-year-old Haden exuded SoCal cool, steering a golf cart around the sunny campus, dressed in a tie while also sporting shades and a cardinal-and-gold cap with an interlocking *SC*.

Long before he was hired to that role, Haden was an absolute legend at USC, the stuff of "My Hero" papers written by local schoolchildren. A Rhodes scholar and a quarterback who led USC to two national football championships in the 1970s, he was prominent in Southern California sports and business worlds. After six years with the National Football League's Los Angeles Rams, he became a sports broadcaster and a partner in a private equity firm cofounded by former L.A. mayor Richard Riordan.

Nikias tasked Haden, a longtime USC trustee, with righting a wayward ship that for years had been plagued by scandals, including illicit payments to football star Reggie Bush and basketball player O. J. Mayo. The NCAA sanctioned the university in June 2010, after a four-year investigation determined Bush and his family got hotel stays, a home, and other gifts while he was technically still an amateur student-athlete. USC offered up its own sanctions after Mayo was accused of taking payments from an agent, via a coach, while at the school. The NCAA cited USC for a lack of institutional control over its athletic programs.

USC doubled its athletic compliance staff while Haden was athletic director, and he said he didn't want that "compliance culture" to keep sports from thriving. "We must do what we have to do without dampening the competitive spirit. You don't want to be so compliant that all you're doing is saying 'no' to everything," he said.

One thing was certain: USC welcomed money, especially in the push to raise $6 billion.

The university was an early adopter of a decentralized budget model that made smaller units, like the film school and engineering program, responsible for their own costs—and able to keep most of the money they generated. More centralized schools doled out money to various departments. Responsibility-centered management, as some called it, came with opportunity, but also pressure.

Non-moneymaking centers, like the library, were motivated to try to raise funds on their own. Athletics was in the same boat, on a much larger scale, needing to make sure it could cover its own costs. At that point only football and basketball were making money. But all coaches wanted bigger staff, the coolest equipment, travel to the best tournaments. The university couldn't pay for everything.

Haden, incredibly skilled at making asks for investments from his private equity days, spent at least a third of his time as USC's athletic director on development-related tasks. "You need to always be out on the fundraising trail and really kind of developing new revenue streams, new ways of approaching people," Haden said in a 2011 video filmed in Heritage Hall, a three-level brick-and-concrete colonnaded paean to USC's athletic glory that, fittingly, sat in the center of its campus. "We always have to feed the beast through development."

One of Haden's major goals was to endow all USC's athletic scholarships, about 250 in total, at a cost of about $1 million apiece, so they could be funded in perpetuity. In 2012 he announced a $300 million fundraising drive, dubbed the Heritage Initiative, for scholarships, as well as amenities including suites at the Galen Center sporting arena and the construction of the new Merle Norman Stadium—a palm-tree-ringed beach volleyball facility that would be named for the late cosmetics entrepreneur (a donor's great-aunt) and feature courts with sand from the U.S. Olympic Training Center.

The Heritage Initiative launched with the dedication of the John McKay

Center, a $70 million athletic and academic training hub complete with hydro-therapy pools and a nutrition center.

Troy kept rising. At breakneck speed, USC began sprucing up its grounds, with more than eighty projects in 2014 alone. People joked that cranes and construction on campus were as USC as cardinal and gold. Donations had fu-eled USC's new bioscience center, adding 190,000 square feet of labs and of-fices. A new building was going up for dance enthusiasts.

The $35 million renovation of Heritage Hall turned the two-story main lobby into a Hall of Champions museum centered around a scowling Trojan warrior statue with his fists in the air. The modern building included a sports performance center, broadcast studio, and virtual indoor golf driving range. Every inch seemed to be for sale. Naming rights had even been given to an ele-vator, where a plaque noted that a ride from one floor to the next had been "uplifted" by a particular generous family.

In the most ambitious project of all, USC also broke ground in 2014 on the fifteen-acre "USC Village," a $700 million project featuring housing for up to 2,700 students as well as a Trader Joe's, Abercrombie & Fitch, and 150-foot clock tower in a historic architectural style. "A fantasia of just-add-water heri-tage, equal parts Disneyland and Hogwarts," wrote the *Los Angeles Times* ar-chitecture critic.

The "slow creep" of Collegiate Gothic architecture, with its regal towers and spires, across USC, the critic noted, was sending a message: "USC is gear-ing up to compete with the Ivy League."

USC was now a place where the rich wanted to send their kids. Fourteen percent of students in Nikias's early years as president came from families with income in the top 1 percent, while 63 percent came from those in the top quin-tile. Only 4.9 percent came from the bottom quintile.

Campus commerce acknowledged the well-heeled. USC's bookstore had cases of pricey sunglasses, including $300 ones by Versace, and sold $30 Kiehl's conditioner. The off-campus Lorenzo student housing complex, which opened in 2013 for 3,600 students, mostly from USC, was built to resemble St. Mark's Square in Venice. It advertised lavish amenities (think concierge, Pilates and yoga, four resort-style pools with cabanas, and each room equipped with a forty-six-inch flat-screen television) and featured dancing Bellagio-style fountains.

With a constant eye on that $6 billion goal, various members of USC's administration might pay attention to an applicant's track record of donating, or ability to make future gifts. Athletic officials sent wish lists to the admissions office, detailing prospects they wanted to be accepted and making notes like: "father is surgeon," "250,000 signed pledge," "$100,000 dive tower," and "$15 mil."

Staffers routinely bantered and debated via email about particular prospects and their families' wealth and influence, with different departments jockeying over who would get the bounty from a big donor.

In 2014, for instance, reps from USC's business school and athletics were tangling over who had dibs on a water polo walk-on whose family was a "high level prospect with 1-5M potential." Business school fundraisers said they would be happy to explore "carving out a piece" of the initial gift for athletics. "There is plenty of room with this family for everyone to 'win' here, in my opinion," one said in an email.

Athletics wasn't backing down. One administrator offered to that department's fundraising head, "If this is not working out the way you planned, I can have Admissions pull the approval."

"Really sucks," he responded later that night. "Don't pull we will guilt them."

THE BACK DOOR AT USC seemed wide open.

"It is so, um, commercial," one outrageously rich Bay Area dad observed to Singer. "It's very clear to me that if they sense that I'm gonna write a check, they're gonna do what they can do to get me in." Singer agreed. It was why, he said, "USC's become the power."

Loaded and high-profile moms and dads regularly reported back to Singer that the university had reached out about setting up a special tour or interview, or discussing opportunities for the parents to financially support particular programs.

After Doug Hodge made a donation to USC in 2015, he and his wife were invited to a private dinner at the president's house. At that event, he was offered the opportunity to watch a USC football game from the president's private box. A USC spokeswoman would later say, "both tuition and philanthropy are essential to providing scholarships, programs, services and financial support to our students."

And while it was hard not to notice all the USC buildings, rooms, and bricks dedicated to benefactors who may have had a kid or grandkid entering the college search process, Singer also advised clients, truthfully, that donations didn't completely guarantee admission. The school had other competing interests as well, like diversifying its student body and continuing to improve standardized test scores. People would try to butter up the admissions department, sprinkling emails with ass-kissing lines like "Your job is a tough one and you perform it incredibly," or "The University is fortunate to have you captaining the ship," or, everyone's favorite, "You look thinner."

USC's admit rate was sliding lower and lower, and getting in was tougher even for the well-connected. Was it really worth it to shell out all that money for a maybe?

That made the promise of a sure-thing admission, even before an application was filed, and for a lower price than the market rate of high-six-figure or seven-figure checks, particularly appealing.

10

TAG, YOU'RE IN

S EVENTEEN MILES SOUTH OF San Francisco, John B. Wilson had all the trappings of the good life. The Harvard MBA was a licensed pilot, skied all over the world, and did business from Dubai and Amsterdam. Married with three children, he was president of Staples Inc.'s European division, after having been an executive vice president of the Gap and a partner at Bain & Company.

Singer often drew clients for whom the truth, as good as it was, may not have felt like quite enough. WBUR, Boston's National Public Radio news station, concluded that Wilson's résumé, later posted on LinkedIn, made fishy claims about his business record, including exaggerating financial performance during the time he was an active executive. Wilson's lawyer said the news story accurately quotes securities filings, but that the filings didn't adequately measure his impact over a longer period of engagement with the company.

Maybe unsurprisingly, Wilson also may have been willing to puff up the achievements of his son Sam, a water polo player at the private Menlo School in Atherton. Six feet tall with a huge smile, Sam was known as a hard worker in the pool and a generous teammate.

Sam grew up in Hillsborough, among the wealthiest towns in the nation, a place where debate at town hall meetings included whether a new wave of homes twenty thousand square feet or greater fit into an area of not-as-enormous mansions. The enclave overlooking San Mateo was reminiscent of the Italian countryside, dotted with villas on winding roads. John's wife, Leslie, volunteered for the Hillsborough Beautification Foundation, and he spoke out at town hall in an effort to protect the community's image. (One stated concern was whether a neighbor's tennis court would be adequately set back, like Wilson's own tennis court.)

They donated to the Menlo School and hosted team dinners at their home: a thirteen-thousand-square-foot Tudor outfitted with a waterslide reported to be the longest of its kind west of the Mississippi.

In February 2013, Sam's junior year, his dad emailed Singer about options for the side door.

"Jovan," Singer replied, "is giving me 1 boys slot."

Singer knew USC intimately by now, given his client base's inherent—and inherited—affinity for the school. He'd even managed to set up a 2007 meeting between then university president Sample and a wealthy client. He understood the push for ethnic diversity; he could reel off the general-ed requirements for the engineering program; and he informed parents about the "Trojan Transfer," a program in which students could move to campus after earning decent grades at another college first.

Singer had connected in late 2007 to Jovan Vavic, USC's illustrious water polo coach, describing himself, Vavic's lawyer would say later, as a former Berkeley basketball coach turned college counselor. Singer referred to the coach as "my guy."

Vavic, tanned with tousled sandy-blond hair, resembled an aging laid-back surfer, but that was deceptive. He screamed at players in his thick eastern European accent and once kicked a container filled with exercise balls so hard he seriously injured a toe. He had taken USC's men's team to a history-making six consecutive national championships between 2008 and 2013 and would be named "National Coach of the Year" fifteen times in his sport. The yellow game ball from his first USC national victory, as co-coach, was encased in glass and displayed in Heritage Hall.

Originally, all the "side door" athletes Singer got into USC were players, though not top recruits. Singer maintained a relationship with Vavic to get other kids into USC down the road, and the government alleged the alliance ventured into illegal quid pro quos. Vavic's lawyer later said there was pressure to raise money for the program, and even to meet with prospective donors whose children were interested in athletics.

Singer told John Wilson the good news in fall 2013: no payment was required until the admissions office gave Sam a nod. But, Singer said, Vavic wanted him to "embellish" the teen's profile more. (Though Vavic did tell Singer in an email that the boy's profile "needs to be a good résumé," the coach's lawyer later said Vavic never requested anyone falsify materials, and that he insisted students he recommended be qualified.) Sam was a very good water polo player at Menlo and could have played college somewhere. It wouldn't be outlandish for him to land at USC, but it would be a stretch.

Singer got to work and sent the fabricated profile to Vavic. Among the fibs was that Sam had captained his high school team starting his sophomore year.

With Vavic's wildly positive endorsement, USC admitted Sam as a water polo recruit in early 2014. "Thanks again for making this happen!" Wilson wrote to Singer.

Throughout the process, Wilson expressed a concern to Singer: Would teammates know his son was a "bench warmer side door person"? Wilson wanted him to at least be able to scrimmage with the team, but Singer said the approach would not require Sam to actually "get in the pool." Sam just needed to be on the roster for a bit and "frankly after the 1st semester he can move on." Sam was listed on USC's water polo roster only as a freshman. He sent a note to Vavic after the fall term, saying his grades had suffered because of the time commitment and he wanted to be careful after having a few concussions.

USC athletics staff expressed puzzlement over Wilson's contribution, which one employee described as the "mysterious $100,000 cashier check for water polo." Overall, Vavic's water polo program would get a total of $250,000 from Singer's foundation and clients.

Vavic also received money for his kids' private school payments, the government would later say. (Singer's charity listed a 2015 donation of nearly

$38,000 to Loyola High School in L.A. Vavic's lawyer said the charity gave water polo scholarships to the coach's boys.)

Wilson's lawyer would later say the payment to USC was an aboveboard donation, not a quid pro quo.

VAVIC WASN'T SINGER'S ONLY connection at USC; he had a few other secret weapons, ultimately even more powerful.

Intense and tanned, with bright green eyes, Ali Khosroshahin was hard to miss as the coach of USC's women's soccer team. He was a fireball, a loud alpha type on the field, but more introspective off. He also motivated many players, who stayed in touch long after being on his teams. "Khos" had jumped to USC from a coaching job at Cal State Fullerton in 2007, bringing with him Laura Janke as an assistant coach.

Janke had been following Khosroshahin for years. He was an influential figure in her life, first as a coach at Fullerton, then as her boss. Janke, in her twenties, was calm and reliable, and Ali leaned on her to handle a lot of the organizational tasks of his teams. She also coached kids' club soccer on the side and had seasons plotted out nine months in advance. Parents felt she really cared about the kids and their development.

They ran an intense program, instituting 5:30 a.m. practices and chants of "So what? Get over it!" USC won its first NCAA women's soccer championship in 2007, their first year as coaches.

A testament to Khosroshahin's big win was engraved on a tall display in Heritage Hall. He gave an NCAA championship windbreaker to his father, a longtime educator and Iranian immigrant who'd envisioned a more conventional career for his son but was sure proud now. But by 2011, Khosroshahin, then forty-two, was in a more precarious position as the team's leader. The team had its first losing season since 2001.

He also worried that Haden, his boss, held a grudge for a clash many years earlier. Khosroshahin coached Haden's son in youth soccer and benched him for coming to a match without his cleats, even though his dad had driven a considerable distance to watch him play. Haden still occasionally ribbed Khosroshahin about it, but the coach thought some tension remained.

The losses kept mounting. Khosroshahin told people he didn't think USC was going to renew his contract. Singer, meanwhile, had approached Khosroshahin several times about doing the side door, telling Khosroshahin to talk to Vavic about how it all worked.

In fall 2012, in his second straight losing season, Khosroshahin agreed to designate one of Singer's clients as a recruit in return for a bribe, and the illicit relationship grew. Singer gave a total of $350,000 to a legitimate private soccer camp that Khosroshahin and Janke ran for side income, in exchange for tagging four teens—including a daughter of former Pimco chief Doug Hodge and the daughter of Toby Macfarlane in San Diego—as fake recruits.

USC fired Khosroshahin in 2013 after a third losing season and soon canned Janke as well. Khosroshahin was so upset he gave away trash bags full of his USC-logoed clothes. He threw himself into raising his newborn daughter and struggled to land another good college coaching job.

Though no longer such a direct conduit to the USC admissions office, he kept working with Singer, now acting as a broker who connected the counselor to other coaches willing to take payments in exchange for admission slots. Khosroshahin would admit to earning $75,000 for three successful connections, including introducing Singer to coaches from Yale and UCLA and a former USC coach who later went to Wake Forest.

Janke got a job coaching at a private school, and leading a club soccer team, and briefly partnered with Khosroshahin again to run a business talking to parents of soccer players about the recruiting process. By then a married mother, Janke also started working with Singer in a new capacity. "Would you be willing to put the profiles together for pay?" Singer asked Janke in an email at one point, referring to some kids he wanted to pass off as fake recruits. She replied two days later, agreeing. Janke earned more than $134,000 from Singer in exchange for flagging his clients as recruits and, by 2015, writing up their fake athletic profiles herself.

IN 2015, THE USC ATHLETICS department hit its $300 million fundraising target, the first program to meet its goal in the big $6 billion campaign and well ahead of schedule. Haden called it a "significant milestone" but hardly the end, and he pushed to raise more for the department's endowment and upgrading facilities. (That $300 million number would grow to nearly $750 million.) There was a lot to celebrate around that time, including the firm belief that USC was running a clean operation when it came to recruiting. The expanded compliance team was causing headaches for some coaches, but that was, in the grand scheme of things, a good thing. It meant the NCAA couldn't hit them with more sanctions.

Problem was, the system still had kinks.

Back in 2011, Haden had made a pivotal decision to give more responsibility to a longtime USC athletic department coordinator named Donna Heinel.

Heinel was around fifty, with spiky blond hair and a Philadelphia accent. A former all-American swimmer at Springfield College, she'd coached swimming and water polo at the University of Massachusetts before moving to USC. Haden promoted her to the position of senior woman administrator, a role developed by the NCAA to increase female leadership in college sports. She would also be handling day-to-day oversight of athlete admissions and eligibility.

Heinel may have already used her USC ties to earn outside income. She'd launched a side business by 2008 called Clear the Clearinghouse, working with another USC athletics administrator to offer workshops to coaches, guidance counselors, and other administrators on topics tied to the athletic recruiting process. The presentations, held at USC, at one point cost $100 per person. She'd travel to school districts, too, charging up to $2,700 for each of those events. She offered subscription services costing up to $700 a year.

The workshops were a bit odd because many schools, including USC, offered versions of them as a public service for little or no cost. Even if it wasn't against the rules for Heinel to be running these for-profit seminars, and USC officials were aware of the business, it didn't look great.

Heinel would admit she had a bit of a hard shell. Participating at one point in a USC panel discussion on lesbian, gay, bisexual, and transgender athletes, she described herself as a "loner for mostly all of my life." She'd been estranged from her parents for more than two years after a bad experience coming out to them. They later reconciled when her sister got cancer, but Heinel had been shaped by that painful strain with her parents.

"I've just kind of been, 'I do what I want to do, when I want to do it,'" she said.

Haden had a great deal of trust in Heinel. And she admired Haden, a proud father of a gay son. Early on, he'd invited Heinel and her partner to travel with him to Hawaii for a USC game, a shift for Heinel, who had often kept her home life separate. She now talked more at work about her partner, a special education administrator, and their two young children.

Singer had worked to make inroads to both Heinel and Haden. In 2015, he'd asked a client to introduce him to Haden. The emailed introduction was enthusiastic, calling Singer "one of the top college counselors and a great guy" and noting that he'd advised many families with whom Haden was familiar. Haden's associate athletic director thought the meeting might be a decent idea, not because of Singer but because the man who extended the invite had valuable connections. At the time, Haden and the associate athletic director were trying to sell luxury suites being built as part of the renovation of the Los Angeles Memorial Coliseum, home to USC's football team.

Singer, the client, Haden, and his associate director met for coffee that June in a quiet room at the clubhouse of the exclusive Los Angeles Country Club. It ended up being a ten-minute meeting that mostly consisted of Singer pitching himself as someone who worked with wealthy families and could steer more to USC. "You guys are pretty great, but I think there is a pipeline of other kids out there that could make USC even greater," he said. Haden and his deputy left thinking Singer was a name-dropper.

Singer tried further to get a line of communication open with Haden, at one point seeking help getting the daughter of a client from Texas into USC. But Haden wrote to Heinel in a July 2015 email that he had a "red flag" up about Singer, noting the consultant's connection to the sometimes-shady AAU youth basketball circuit. He told her to "do some homework."

Also in July 2015, the dean of undergraduate admissions raised a flag. He and Heinel had spoken earlier that day, and he wanted to close the loop. "I don't know anything about this Singer guy," he wrote in an email, "except to steer clear!"

It's possible Heinel had one set of rules for herself and another for her coaches. She wielded immense power over recruiting decisions. Some of the coaches saw her as an unbending stickler, unreasonably strict on recruiting. Former USC director of track and field Ron Allice called her "tough as nails." She'd nix some really strong prospective athletes, he said, if all the *t*'s weren't perfectly crossed. "She played hardball with us," he said.

This power worked for Singer. "Everybody has to go through her," Singer would say.

His approach at USC became highly organized and systematic at every step, starting with the phony profiles. Singer talked about meeting with Heinel in her office to get guidance on how to do the profiles. At times, Heinel would weigh in, providing handwritten edits.

Throughout the year, Heinel met with a small subgroup of admissions officers assigned specifically to review athlete applicants. Coaches gave their lists to her. She passed them on to the admissions subcommittee—the dean and two assistants—and pitched them hard. She successfully sold a teen who didn't participate in track and field as an elite pole vaulter, nonathletes as no less than national or even global stars, and a five-foot-five kid as a six-one basketball player, although her lawyer later said there was no evidence she personally saw that teen.

Singer was at least a semiregular presence at USC, where he knew a number of coaches. He had outright approached at least one of them about the side door, right on campus, and attended meetings in the main sports administration building. It's no surprise he would come to know Heinel. At some point, the government would later say, she formed her own partnership with Singer, and used that as a form of institutionalized fundraising for athletics. Singer's clients would pay more than $1.3 million to USC accounts controlled by Heinel between 2014 and 2018. She, in turn, facilitated the entry of more than two dozen teens into USC by presenting them as recruited players, even when they sometimes didn't even play the sport. (Heinel's lawyer later said the administrator at all times did the job that was expected of her by USC.)

Singer later said he hid the alliance from others at USC, including Haden, the athletic director.

Heinel or someone who reported to her presented applicants to the admissions department, which was at the same time busy trying to sift through tens of thousands of applications.

As Singer himself once explained it to a father, "Admissions just needs something to work with to show he is an athlete. They do not follow up after Donna presents."

William Tierney, the founding director of USC's Pullias Center for Higher Education, later said he believed that fundraising pressures contributed to the rigged system in USC athletics. "When there is an ethos to do whatever you can to get money, you do whatever you can to get money." But John "J.K." McKay, an associate athletic director at USC from 2010 to 2016, says Haden repeatedly said "no quid pro quos." "The phrase 'no quid pro quo' came up a lot," he recalls.

Haden left as athletics director in 2016, and the incoming director, Lynn Swann—a USC and NFL football legend in his own right—continued to give Heinel great power, apparently with little to no oversight. Heinel's financial relationship with Singer went beyond USC fundraising. Singer would later begin to pay her $20,000 a month in a consulting retainer.

Eventually, USC would start to get suspicious of a number of supposedly top-notch athletic recruits with questionable résumés.

USC officials would get someone to investigate. They'd appoint Heinel.

11

THE COACH

THE NIGHT OF JUNE 22, 2015, Michael Center told his wife and sons he was going out to meet a friend for a bit, but would be back soon.

The Texas summer air hung heavy as he got into his Chevy Traverse and headed down the hill from his house in Austin's Northwest Hills neighborhood, across I-35, and over the Colorado River toward Austin Bergstrom International Airport, about twenty miles away.

Center had just wrapped his fifteenth season as head men's tennis coach at the University of Texas at Austin. By many accounts it was a cushy job. Spend hours outdoors, mentor young adults, participate in a sport that you love at a school that's revered. He made a comfortable living, too, a nearly $200,000 salary plus more for running summer training camps.

But dissatisfaction and frustration had been gnawing at Center.

Tournaments kept him on the road often, away from his boys, who were on the cusp of their teenage years. And while he gave the job so much, it was hard to get noticed at an institution where football was king. He clashed with the new athletic director, who'd started in 2013. Atop his laundry list of perceived indignities: UT Austin had razed his outdoor courts, without a clear plan to replace them. He even lamented about how he'd been tasked with scaring up the money for new facilities himself.

So when Rick Singer told him he deserved some additional income for all his hard work, it resonated. Yes, yes, he did. He'd earned it.

Center arrived at the airport. Singer got into the car, and they drove off to a nearby hotel.

CENTER WAS KNOWN AS conscientious, a rule follower. He asked for special written permission once from his university to spend a day volunteering at a friend's charity tennis clinic for adults. He'd redo a parking job if even one tire was touching a white line, pulling back out and shifting over a few inches till it was perfect. Around fifty, with two kids and a wife, he lived about as far away from the edge as one could get.

A player turned coach at the University of Kansas, Center spent two years in the 1990s as a stockbroker at Paine Webber in Menlo Park, California, before coming back to the courts as head coach at Texas Christian University in 1998. He moved to Austin in 2000.

Intense, competitive, and emotional, he took losses hard. He held his athletes to a high standard, but also celebrated wins and earned their respect. Center ran a consistently good, if not outstanding, team. He racked up NCAA championship tournament appearances every year, occasionally advancing to the round of sixteen and even once to the finals. He'd earned accolades as Big 12 Coach of the Year four times and regularly landed bonuses for his team's athletic and academic success.

Yet by late 2014, Center felt like he was just barely hanging on.

His team became a crew of vagabonds after the tennis courts were demolished in spring 2014 to make room for a new medical school. The school had identified a few potential replacement sites, but nothing firm. And money didn't seem forthcoming after UT Austin had just paid another university millions to hire away its football coach.

For the 2014–15 season, the team hopped around to practice and compete at a country club on the edge of town, public courts, the university's weathered and worn intramural courts, and an indoor facility out near Lake Travis, a half hour drive from campus.

Not everyone understood why Center seemed quite so put-upon by the circumstances. To Center, the logistics were untenable, and he was growing increasingly distressed about what it could all mean for recruiting: it might be hard to lure prospects if they remained without regular courts for long.

Center could see area programs like Southern Methodist University opening dazzling new facilities. If this situation kept up for long, he believed, the tennis program would lurch into a downward spiral.

THE JOB DESCRIPTION FOR head men's tennis coach when Center took the role in 2000 said he'd need to encourage "alumni support, student support, faculty support, continuance of national recognition and generation of maximum revenue to assist the Department in reaching its financial goals."

His performance evaluations in 2010 and 2011 referenced his awareness of fundraising needs and his support for capital projects.

But the football program had thrown off so much cash, it could, along with basketball and baseball, support all the nonrevenue sports. The major athletic conferences report hundreds of millions of dollars in revenue each year thanks to dedicated TV networks, corporate sponsorships, and, of course, ticket sales, almost all connected to just a few sports.

That wealth gap was especially visible in terms of salaries. UT Austin football coach Charlie Strong earned a $5 million salary in the 2014–15 season, and basketball coach Rick Barnes earned more than $2.6 million. Center's salary was just a fraction of those figures, though at $200,000 it still well surpassed those of many other coaches in nonrevenue sports.

The model of relying on football to make ends meet elsewhere was upended as the athletic department stared down a multimillion-dollar deficit by the time Steve Patterson took over as athletic director in November 2013. He made it clear to nonrevenue sports, like tennis, they needed to carry more of their own weight.

"Quite frankly the coaches were spoiled," Patterson recalls. They were well taken care of and hadn't been asked to do all that much until now.

The marching order rankled some coaches, including Center. What did he know about big-dollar fundraising? Was this really part of his job now, on top of coaching and recruiting and coordinating tournaments?

The site agreed upon for the replacement tennis facility was a parcel of unlevel land holding a parking lot and an old warehouse near the baseball, softball, and soccer fields, and the project price tag crept up from $15 million toward $20 million.

The athletic department helped by identifying prospective donors and arranging some meetings, but Center still bristled at his new job responsibility. Everything now felt like a slight.

Fifteen hundred miles east of UT Austin, Gordon Ernst was well entrenched on the Georgetown University campus, perched overlooking the Potomac River.

Gordie, as he was known, had headed both the men's and the women's tennis programs there since 2006, and he earned just about $65,000 a year from the elite university for his toils.

He'd vent and even joke about the pay, as well as some of the other offenses visited upon his sport. (Nobody eagerly awaited a late-night pep rally to kick off the Georgetown tennis season like they did for Hoya hoops.)

Still, Ernst stayed. "There's something about this place. Something about Georgetown that makes it worth it," he told a friend. In its own way, being Georgetown's tennis coach carried prestige. The school is the marquee name among colleges dotting the nation's capital. He gave tennis lessons to Michelle Obama, and to her daughters, Malia and Sasha. He taught children of ambassadors and professors. When tennis pro Anna Kournikova came to town, Ernst held a children's tennis clinic with her.

In a city known for its buttoned-up, workaholic nature, Ernst could be refreshing: he would let his acerbic wit fly, leading people to just shake their heads and laugh.

Georgetown represented another rung in Ernst's success story, one that made him a local hero back home in Rhode Island. He grew up in middle-class Cranston, the son of a teacher and a local tennis and hockey coach so popular that local public courts would be named after him.

A youth hockey and tennis phenom, he'd been called "the golden boy of Rhode Island high school sports." He passed up a chance to play professional hockey right out of high school and instead went on to play both hockey and tennis at Brown University.

After graduation, he played on the pro tennis circuit before parlaying his Ivy League degree into a Wall Street job with Lehman Brothers. But he missed the thrill of sports competition and grew ever more miserable sitting at a desk.

Ernst started coaching tennis at Northwestern, then took a post at the University of Pennsylvania, and later became executive director of a youth tennis program in Martha's Vineyard before heading to Georgetown.

Ernst might have risen to the 1 percent on his own if he'd stayed on Wall Street. But now he'd immersed himself in the world of coaching a country club sport, where a quirky rule generally holds true: the coaches themselves are on very unequal financial footing compared with those around them, including alums and parents of players, or those who want to be players.

Fundraising only upped his engagement with the more affluent.

The president of the Hoya Netters Club, Georgetown's tennis alumni group, said in a newsletter that the new coach had secured major gifts from parents of current student-athletes. "We need these dollars to help our program increase its resources," the Netters Club president wrote, "but we also need to prove to the university that we are serious about seeing our teams succeed."

Ernst kept an eye out for players with talent—and with money. And he saw nothing wrong with that. Teens from wealthy families were a prime way to get financial support for a nonrevenue program.

How to find those moneyed athletes? College coaches would rely on a variety of sources. They might get tips from contacts at prep schools or from private college consultants who work with moneyed families.

At least as early as 2007, Ernst made a pivotal contact: meeting college counselor Rick Singer through a connection at IMG.

Targeting rich tennis players came with its challenges. Some team members thought Ernst could seem jealous of the wealthy athletes. How could a coach not get a little bitter, if he made a beer salary but had champagne taste?

Also, parents who donated wanted their kids to play. And the children weren't always that good.

Singer's "side door" brilliantly eliminated any pesky parents requesting more prominent spots for their kids. Singer would direct money to coaches, who'd use their sway to get the teens admitted as phony walk-ons. Nobody, not even the parents, expected these kids to appear on the courts.

Coaches, in turn, used the money for their programs or, in some cases, took it for themselves.

While coaches of nonrevenue sports may have whined about their salaries, they had that one particularly useful perk: minimal oversight of recruiting and major influence with the admissions office.

Ernst started taking payments from Singer or others as far back as 2007, and he would be listed at times as an independent contractor, paid six figures, on Singer's foundation's annual tax documents. In exchange, Ernst tagged as recruits at least a dozen applicants, some of whom didn't play competitive tennis. The government would say he also took in revenue from parents outside Singer's client base and solicited a $220,000 bribe from one father, who paid via check, cash, and school tuition payments for Ernst's daughters.

Over time, Ernst began to keep pace with the wealthy parents around him. He and his wife bought a five-bedroom classic Colonial in Chevy Chase, Maryland, for nearly $1.6 million in 2012, and a condo on Cape Cod for $530,000 in 2015. They had a membership at the Chevy Chase Club, which bills itself as the "Queen of Clubs."

A LAS VEGAS BUSINESSMAN was visiting Georgetown's picturesque campus on a visit back to his alma mater when it hit him hard: he desperately wanted his son to go there, too.

The father called Singer and asked the counselor, who had advised the boy's older sister and was now doing the same for him, about the odds of the kid getting in.

Singer didn't hesitate. Sure, he said. A $400,000 donation to the tennis team, and the businessman's son would have an almost certain in at Georgetown.

The dad didn't flinch. Why would he? The offer seemed like just a regular play in the college game, a somewhat gray but still completely legal area: large donations that could potentially give the benefactor's family an extra edge in admissions.

He recalled from his own Georgetown tennis days that money for travel had been an issue, and he could help. And the boy wasn't entirely unqualified to play. Win-win, he thought.

Singer offered to set up a meeting for the father with Ernst for that same day. A quick call, and the father soon shook hands with Ernst in his office in the athletic center.

They exchanged pleasantries, and Ernst gabbed a bit about his sports background, his tennis and hockey days, coming off as a bit cocky. Ernst asked about the son, and the father stressed that he'd be a good addition to the team. It all seemed aboveboard.

Then he asked: How, specifically, would his donation help the team? Scholarships? Travel?

Ernst looked confused, and stopped to confirm that the father had talked to Rick Singer. He realized the dad was missing some information, and then he explained how the money would be used. "Well, a tennis coach has to eat."

Stunned, the father stood up, shook Ernst's hand, and made a quick exit.

In a phone call a few minutes later, Singer blurred the line between bribe and donation.

"Rick, I don't understand. I thought this was going to the program," the father said, still flummoxed.

Singer said it was.

"No, it is going to Gordon," the father responded, referring to the coach.

"Yeah, that supports the program."

Not quite. It supports Ernst, and the father wasn't willing to make such a direct payment in exchange for a possible admission edge.

Still, others did play ball with Singer, even if their kids didn't play tennis.

Ernst would earn more than $2.7 million from Singer just between 2012 and 2018, easing the pain of that pathetic $65,000 salary Georgetown offered.

THE HIGH SCHOOL AND collegiate tennis circuit was fairly tight. Many knew Martin Fox, a gregarious gadfly who had valuable contacts not only in tennis but in the cozy worlds of youth and college basketball.

Fox ran a Houston tennis academy and was an informal fixer and concierge to athletes from a variety of sports, driving people around, setting up travel, and so forth. Word spread and he eventually gained a perch as a power broker in Houston's youth sports, organizing college tournaments and becoming an entrenched figure in youth basketball.

His currency: relationships.

That fueled his local rise to fame, said Sonny Vaccaro, a veteran consultant to the likes of Nike, Adidas, and Reebok.

Fox was considered a hustler, but also "really, really smart," Vaccaro said in an interview. "He had the ability to put kids together with lots of different situations. Martin is the man who knew the way to get through the jigsaw puzzle." A honey-voiced North Carolina native, Fox was a slender six feet with graying hair and piercing blue eyes. He was social and chatty and well versed in his preferred sports. He was enthusiastically photographed alongside Kobe Bryant and Magic Johnson, Kentucky's John Calipari, and Louisville's Rick Pitino.

He made a good beer buddy, but usually had some angle, recalls one long-time tennis coach. "He was always moving and shaking, there was always a deal going on," the coach says.

Just the type of person Rick Singer would need.

Fox had a slippery side, for sure. Ironic, considering that he'd graduated from college with a degree in criminal justice. In 2005, he was charged with felony theft, accused of working with a Continental Airlines employee and someone with whom he ran a travel agency to buy tickets a few weeks in advance of a flight date, then have them changed to a more imminent date, without paying the higher price for last-minute fares. The scheme ran between 1999 and 2000. Fox turned state's witness and was given a deferred adjudication where, if he kept out of trouble for two years, the case would be dismissed.

And his name came up in an NCAA corruption trial accusing assistant basketball coaches of taking bribes and making payments to players and high school prospects in exchange for steering the talented youngsters to particular business managers and financial advisers. He wasn't charged, but one central witness in the case said Fox wired him $40,000, which then went to an assistant coach, to hand over to a high school prospect.

Few seemed to know exactly how Fox earned a living, but no matter his title, Fox's deep Rolodex came in handy for Singer. Singer met Fox through an old youth camp and junior college coaching friend, Dana Pump, who himself was well-known in basketball circles. Pump and his brother ran tournaments and camps, connecting college coaches and players. Fox hung out at UT Austin a fair bit, knew the basketball coaching staff, and had even coached some tennis players whom Center ended up recruiting.

So when Singer came calling in fall 2014, looking for help with a client, Fox delivered.

Singer's client was Chris Schaepe, a Silicon Valley venture capitalist who had hired the counselor to help his son navigate the college admissions process, which included applying to UT Austin. The teen, who attended the small, prestigious Woodside Priory School, was more of a supervisor than a player when it came to athletics: though he played tennis his freshman year, his UT Austin application also listed him as a manager of his high school basketball and football teams. He wanted to continue on as a team manager in college, too.

Could Fox help? Fox knew Michael Center, the UT Austin tennis coach, from the tennis circuit and just being a Texas sports . . . well, whatever he was. He introduced Singer to Center, explaining the college counselor had a teen boy who wanted to go to UT Austin and be manager of the basketball team. But he couldn't be recruited for that role, so could he maybe get slotted into tennis?

Singer sent the boy's transcript and application essays to Fox in November 2014. Two days later, Fox passed it on to Center.

Center confirmed receipt of the material, then noted about the teen, "looks like he goes to very high end school." That was intriguing. Center was, after all, looking for ways to fund the new tennis facility. He urged Fox to call him after Thanksgiving so they could discuss further.

The next month, Center emailed the teen's application material to an athletics department official, in order to code him as a student-athlete.

With a nudge from Fox that spring, Center flagged the Schaepe boy as an athletic recruit, which would give him a big edge in getting admitted. UT Austin admitted the teen and awarded Schaepe's son a small scholarship to cover his books. The Schaepes returned to the school a formal letter of intent for the teen to join the tennis team.

They also donated stock valued at $625,000 to Singer's charity, Key World-wide Foundation. A representative for the family, which would not be criminally charged, later said such gifts were in line with their regular charitable involvement in youth and educational programs. The representative also said the intent was for the son to join as a manager, not a player. But letters of intent exist only for players, and the athletic director and a financial aid person need to sign off on the paperwork before it's reviewed by compliance. When he got to campus, the boy returned the scholarship money and started a job as a manager of the basketball team.

Center knew it was an unusual situation, but he didn't think it was a crime. He'd heard of other coaches around the country adding to their rosters kids who weren't really college-level athletes.

In exchange for his services, Singer sent Fox $100,000 from his charity.

He had told Center somewhere around $100,000 would be coming his way, for UT Austin, the exact division of funds to be determined. In April and June, Singer gave Center two checks—for $25,000 and $15,000—made out to Texas Athletics.

But as they discussed the finances, Singer hit on one of Center's pain points—that festering wound of resentment at a program that he felt just didn't seem to respect him.

You deserve some of this money.

That spring, Singer withdrew $60,000 from his account, in six separate transactions, to avoid raising suspicion. Then he got on a plane bound for Austin.

Center, on a warm summer night, made a decision that would change the direction of his life. After he told his family he was headed out for a bit, he picked up Singer at the airport and drove him to the nondescript airport hotel, over near the Starbucks on I-71.

When they arrived, Rick Singer handed over a bag stuffed with $60,000 in hundred-dollar bills and then jumped out of the car. Center drove home.

By 5:30 the next morning, Singer was en route back to California.

12

TEST DAY

FINALLY. EMILY FLAXMAN HAD gone through hell in high school but was coming out the other side. She said she wanted to go to college.

Relief washed over her father, Beverly Hills real estate developer Robert Flaxman.

It had been a trying few years for Emily and for Flaxman, a divorced dad raising two teenagers. He'd honestly wondered if his daughter would live to graduate from high school.

Flaxman, a fit, youthful-looking sixty-year-old, had a generous new-money style. He'd left his home at age seventeen after a clash with his stepfather. He went to community college, then attended USC but dropped out after three semesters when he couldn't pay tuition. He'd been a trained chiropractor for five years before finding his calling in real estate, leading Crown Realty & Development and building luxury resorts and large commercial projects. Outwardly, life looked extraordinary. He drove a Rolls-Royce, maintained an address in Beverly Hills, and dated a Playboy bunny. And his Laguna Beach home, in a gated community, had a movie theater, walk-in wine cellar, and saltwater spa.

He showered money on family and friends. He would take fifteen people on vacation to the Tuscan coast or the Caribbean. And he had another clear role in his family: the rich guy who could write a check to fix things. He employed relatives and provided financial support for even distant kin.

But money doesn't inoculate families from the scourge of substance abuse, or the pain of a hurting child.

Emily had flowing sandy-blond hair, with a touch of ginger, and a sprinkling of freckles across her nose. She was thoughtful and bright and made her family laugh by creatively negotiating, like many teens, to get out of her chores. She'd played soccer and loved surfing, Cheetos, and buying secondhand clothes online. She'd also fallen into personal turmoil. Her grades tumbled and she started missing school.

Flaxman sent her to Montana Academy, a $9,300-per-month therapeutic boarding school on a ranch, nestled in a secluded valley and surrounded by mountains. Intense supervision. No social media; limited phone use. Family therapy. And a focus on getting better.

Glimmers of progress shone through. As Emily headed into her senior year in late summer 2016, she talked about her future with hope. Her older brother had just begun his freshman year at the University of San Diego, and she expressed an interest in a four-year college, too. Her treatment team at school voiced optimism. Everyone agreed the worst thing for Emily would be to graduate without having a sense of purpose and a routine to embrace. No one wanted to see her return home aimless and fall back into self-destructive old patterns.

Flaxman reconnected with Rick Singer, whom he had hired to provide college counseling to his son a year earlier. Where, Flaxman asked, could he realistically expect Emily to go?

The response, Flaxman's lawyer would later say, was more than a little discouraging. Singer referenced Emily's unattractive academic history. And a diploma from a therapeutic school didn't exactly scream of promise to an admissions office. Flaxman's stomach sank.

Unless, Singer continued, Emily boosted her ACT score substantially.

She'd taken the test earlier in the year, but had become so anxious she couldn't finish. She scored a 20 out of 36, placing her in the 51st percentile.

Singer said he could arrange for a higher score. But the plan, should Flaxman agree to it, involved sending Emily two thousand miles away, to Houston.

By the time he talked to Flaxman, Singer's testing scheme had changed. In the past, Mark Riddell, his exam guru, used fake IDs to stand in for students on exam day. But the tall, conspicuously handsome Riddell, now thirty-four, no longer easily passed for an adolescent, and he certainly couldn't stand in for all of Singer's clients.

The testing agencies that sponsor the SAT and ACT had also beefed up safeguards, including requiring students to submit photos during registration that would be included on a photo admission ticket, and checked against photo IDs on-site. Proctors would receive extra training to help identify cheaters.

The enhanced measures emerged from the bust of the 2011 SAT cheating ring on Long Island, where students were paying others to take the tests for them. "We have closed the loopholes," Nassau County district attorney Kathleen Rice said at a news conference. "Going forward, it's going to be very difficult for someone to pay someone or have someone take the test for them."

Not all the loopholes.

For at least four years, until federal authorities thwarted the scheme in 2015, a group of Chinese nationals participated in a Pittsburgh-based ring in which they charged fees to take college and graduate school entrance exams for others. Doctored or forged passports helped them slip into the exams.

And even after the old switcheroo became tougher, other strategies emerged. Chinese and South Korean test prep companies exploited the College Board's tendency to recycle questions from U.S. tests on exams given on later dates overseas. Leaked exams would be scanned and sold for clients to memorize.

Singer also found a new way to outwit the testing agencies: work with supervisors at the testing centers.

Each year, on designated days, some four million students file into official testing locations, typically at schools, to take the ACT or SAT. The test agencies each run about four thousand active test centers on a typical Saturday test date.

They rely on an army of contractors, often local school employees, to oversee the exams, including lining up staff to check IDs, administer the tests, and collect materials afterward.

That all meant Singer's clients now had to actually show up to take their exams. But if Singer paid off site supervisors, he could slip in Riddell as a proctor, allowing him to feed answers to the test takers or review their exam sheets after the fact.

As Singer put it, "the only way that the scheme could work was if I controlled the proctor and the site coordinator."

To make inroads at potential testing locations, Singer zeroed in on people who might be interested in the cash.

JACK YATES HIGH SCHOOL elicited immense pride in the Third Ward, a historically African American neighborhood just southeast of downtown Houston. The Yates boys' basketball team smashed state and national records and gained fans and critics for blowout victories.

Yates stood out in a city humming with young hoops talent. And an ecosystem of consultants, coaches, and hangers-on nurtured and exploited that talent. That world included Martin Fox, the basketball power broker who had also coordinated Singer's UT Austin deal. Fox got to know people at Yates, including Niki Williams, a well-liked teaching assistant and cheerleading coach.

Williams, outgoing and then forty-one years old, earned an annual salary just over $25,000. She also had a side gig as a paid administrator for the ACT and SAT at the high school.

By 2015, Singer was paying Fox, who, the government says, paid Williams to allow Riddell into the testing center. (Williams later denied any wrongdoing.)

That year, Singer's clients started rolling into this obscure Houston school, enough that he said they were referred to as "the outta-state kids."

Yates became one of Singer's preferred cheating locations. "I own two schools," he would tell parents.

The other was much closer to Singer's home in Southern California.

BY THE MID-2010S, West Hollywood College Preparatory School in Los Angeles was struggling, no doubt about it.

The tiny nonprofit school, founded in 2000 by Ukrainian immigrant Dr. Elina Dvorskaya and originally named Dvorsky College Preparatory School, drew children from the eastern European and former Soviet refugee community that had settled near the bright lights of L.A. The school promised to keep some traditions from the home country alive, with teachers speaking Russian and language and culture courses and clubs. The founder, Dvorskaya, an elegantly dressed woman with an authoritarian bearing, served as more of a figurehead headmaster.

Igor Dvorskiy, the founder's middle-aged son, served as the school's director and was committed to helping his mother's dream. A father of three with a polite, businesslike demeanor, he worked nonstop running the school. It drew a small, loyal following, but it was a losing battle. The campus, if you could call it that, bore little resemblance to the over-the-top private school compounds dotting Westside L.A. Situated on a busy corner, Dvorsky College Prep rented space on a busy corner, in a dreary building that also housed a synagogue. The school wing was a bland beige block-style masonry building with a whiff of early-1980s government architecture. Quarters were tight and teachers were not well compensated, and paychecks sometimes arrived late.

By 2017, the school had changed its name to West Hollywood College Preparatory School to appeal to a more mainstream clientele, but it still sometimes operated at a loss. Enrollment for the entire K–12 program had fallen to forty-two students, from seventy-three two years earlier.

A new moneymaker came up. That March, Dvorskiy, a contracted test administrator for the SAT and ACT, began taking bribes from Singer, putting the earnings back into the school.

SINGER HAD HIS CORRUPT testing locales, but he also needed a gambit to get the kids there.

The vast majority of high school students, after all, take the SAT or ACT in their local schools on a weekday or Saturday, surrounded by peers.

So Singer exploited a huge loophole: the ease with which teens can secure special designations giving them flexibility over how and where they take college entrance exams.

Across the country, a skyrocketing number of high school students were getting special test-taking accommodations, such as private rooms or more time to take the test, for disabilities like anxiety or ADHD.

This coincided with a notable shift. In the past, teens who got special testing arrangements essentially had an asterisk next to their name when they applied to college, but advocates for the disabled sued. So in 2003, the College Board, the SAT's administrator, stopped notifying colleges if a test taker had received special conditions. The ACT agency also doesn't tell colleges anymore.

Some school personnel sounded warnings. "It's the right thing to do, but it's going to have very negative ramifications," Brad MacGowan, a guidance counselor at Newton North High School, in a high-end Boston suburb, told *The New York Times* as the change took hold. "In a perfect world, if students really need extended time to do as well as they can on a test, they should not have it flagged. But it's that flag, that asterisk, that helps cut down on abuse. This will open the floodgates to families that think they can beat the system by buying a diagnosis, and getting their kid extra time."

He was right. Requests to the College Board for such special accommodations ticked up, and they jumped 200 percent just between the 2010–11 and 2017–18 years. Over that same time frame the number of test takers increased by 25 percent. And students in affluent areas were way more likely than students elsewhere to get the fastest-growing type of these special allowances, a *Wall Street Journal* analysis of data from nine thousand public schools found.

For Singer, these accommodations were the key to his ruse.

Students who could get 100 percent extra time to take the test didn't have to take it at their school, they didn't have to take it with everyone else, and they could take it over multiple days. Which all meant Riddell could work his magic with little notice.

Parents showed up at high schools with letters from psychologists or doctors saying their teens had a learning disability and needed extra time on tests. Many kids had legitimate issues, but others received dubious diagnoses. In wealthier areas, parents were more likely to be able to pay for an outside evaluation if a school wouldn't. The exams could run $5,000 to $10,000 in the Los Angeles area. High schools, reluctant to accuse families of lying, sent the requests to the College Board, the sponsor of the SAT. The College Board approved 94 percent of the requests. The ACT didn't disclose the percentage it approved.

Singer made the entire process even easier. He had long been very adept at navigating the testing agencies. (He'd once crafted a phony tutoring invoice for a teen whose high SAT score was flagged as suspicious by the testing agency.) Now he had his own list of go-to doctors who could write just the letters parents needed to join the cheating ruse.

One day, for instance, Singer informed a psychologist via email that a client's daughter "needs testing for 100 percent time with multiple days."

"I'm gonna talk to our psychologist," he told another father. "We may have to send her to you, or you to her, so that she can get the testing done."

Extra time on tests. Rotten test sites. The brilliant proctor who got scores on demand. It all came together in one fantastically choreographed production on the weekends of the test.

Mom and Dad, often trying to keep the kids from knowing about the plot, would explain to the kid that they didn't want the teen missing two days of school, or maybe it would be a good time to visit that college campus out of state, and oh darn, I guess we need to find another place for you to take your test, to justify the travel. They'd send Singer's charity between $15,000 and $75,000 for the rigged tests and fly or drive to Houston or L.A. Riddell would fly in from Tampa for whirlwind trips usually lasting less than forty-eight hours.

Early on a Saturday, the students would enter either Jack Yates High or West Hollywood Prep, where Riddell would meet them. Armed with their No. 2 pencils, the students would begin to take their tests, following special instructions. Singer's game plan even included a way to deal with the Scantron sheets, the machine-readable paper on which students typically fill in bubbles to test questions: He told kids to write their answers on separate sheets of paper, to avoid mistakes on the grid of dots. He really had them do it so Riddell could bubble in the correct answers later, without having to first erase all those wrong bubbles.

The teens wrote their own essays in their own handwriting, but the rest of the test was generally not their own work. The kids often thought that they took the test themselves, but their parents, Riddell, and the site coordinator knew otherwise.

In some instances, the kids were also in on the game, with Riddell feeding them answers during the exam. In those cases, he'd recommend each kid answer different questions wrong, so as not to rouse suspicions.

Students left after their exams—often long before the extended-time period was up—allowing Riddell a few hours to make his fixes. The site coordinator, Williams or Dvorskiy, would sign the paperwork saying the test had been administered properly, and would send the exams to the ACT or SAT.

And then, as Singer described it, "between 11 and 17 days later, the student would get their score, and it would be a magnificent score."

WILLIAMS EARNED $5,000 DIRECTLY from Singer, and some more through a middleman. Dvorskiy, at West Hollywood College Preparatory School, was paid nearly $200,000 for the scheme, which took place there on eleven occasions involving twenty kids. Riddell would go on to earn upwards of $200,000 crisscrossing the country to rig dozens of tests in Texas and California, as well as in Canada and elsewhere.

As more and more parents signed on to the con, the twisted testing operation fell into a frenzied routine, with complex logistics and lies. The families endured nettlesome travel logistics to get to Houston or West Hollywood. "We got on the last flight out of Aspen last night," one mom told Singer after arriving in L.A.

Riddell's colleagues at IMG Academy in Florida were occasionally curious about Riddell's weekend travel. He explained at one point he was "being flown to the LA area to do tutoring for one of his very high-profile clients." Riddell fudged enough tests at West Hollywood Prep that Dvorskiy at times wrote that the exams had been proctored by someone else, even when Riddell did it. No one apparently wanted the testing agencies to wonder why kids were coming in from all over the country to this tiny school to take tests proctored by the same person.

Repeat customers requested Riddell for subsequent tests. "Alright, she loves the guy," one mom told Singer. "She said he was so sweet."

Riddell got so jammed up, Singer hired a second corrupt proctor, from San Jose, to handle tests on dates when Riddell was already booked.

Some moms and dads were such regulars they could hardly keep their shenanigans straight.

One mother mused with Singer how they'd rigged her daughter's ACT twice, as well as her SAT subject tests, which are the College Board's standardized tests on individual subjects.

But which tests did they fix? It was all running together.

"It was like math B or II or whatever you call it," the mom told Singer. "And then she also did Spanish, some Spanish and some English or history or something. Shit, I don't remember."

Parents had to juggle the cover stories they delivered to their kids with ones given to the schools, about why the tests had to be taken elsewhere, at times in Texas in the dead heat of summer. Singer recommended claiming family commitments, like a wedding or bar mitzvah.

In September 2016, Elizabeth Henriquez emailed a guidance counselor at her younger daughter's school. While the older girl, Julia, attended Notre Dame High School, Megan went to Sacred Heart Schools, a Catholic institution that sat on a sprawling, stunning campus in their hometown of Atherton.

Megan wanted to take the ACT on October 22, but they had to be in Houston.

"Through connections there, we have been able to secure a site and a proctor," the mom wrote.

"No worries," the counselor responded.

Elizabeth and her husband, Manuel, the finance CEO, had already used Riddell to rig a test for their older daughter, Julia, a year earlier. In that case, Singer had actually customized a cheating plan by having Riddell charm his way into proctoring the test in a private room at the girl's high school. Riddell sat next to Julia to help feed her answers, and later said he'd gloated with the girl and her mother about getting away with cheating.

This time the Henriquez family was headed to what Singer dubbed his "Houston Test Center." Rather than pay for this one, Manuel agreed to endorse another Singer client at Northeastern, where he was on a governing board. Still, Singer and his team would get at least $450,000 from the family for their various services.

Flaxman, the Beverly Hills developer, was weighing sending his daughter to that very same subverted spot on the same day. While the Henriquez family was aiming for schools like Georgetown and Northwestern, Flaxman set his sights lower. He just wanted Emily to get into any decent four-year college, so she could stay on the straight and narrow after graduating from the Montana boarding school.

Singer, of course, had leveled with Flaxman in August that Emily made a poor candidate, unless she boosted her modest ACT score of 20 out of 36.

Flaxman was on the fence. Emily took the test again on her own that September, and came out feeling better than the first time. She actually finished the test, Flaxman wrote Singer.

But the scores weren't back yet and the time to apply to college fast approached. What if Emily didn't do much better than 20, a score Singer said simply wouldn't cut it?

Flaxman wanted an insurance policy, and he decided to buy it from Singer. He registered Emily to take the ACT a third time and switched the location to Houston. He gave a phony story: they would be down there anyway, visiting schools.

Flaxman, a street-smart businessman, knew the ACT trick he was ponying up $75,000 for was far from kosher. He would later get emotional as he recalled his wrong turn: Many parents have kids in distress. He had no more right than them to break the law. But at that moment, he felt desperate and out of good options, and his main goal was just to get this test done.

And, he told himself, at least Emily wouldn't know.

EMILY AND HER DAD spoke on the phone right away after her test in Houston. Flaxman listened, stunned and furious.

Emily described to her dad how she'd taken the exam alongside Megan Henriquez and Riddell, who'd helped them answer questions. Riddell, it turned out, had even encouraged them to get different ones wrong, to avoid raising any red flags.

Singer had assured Flaxman, as he did many parents, that his daughter would never find out about the cheating. In most cases, Riddell waited until after the kids left to clean up the tests. But on this day, Riddell had changed the plan, evidently to save time.

Flaxman thought about calling Singer and laying into him. He thought he had been lied to. But he didn't want to do anything to jeopardize Emily getting her score. She was almost over the finish line after a long struggle.

"Don't say anything," he told his daughter. "Move forward."

The rigged ACT got her a score of 28, her best yet and in the 89th percentile, higher than that second September attempt, which came back as a 24. She got into the University of San Francisco and began there in 2017.

Flaxman thought they could put it all behind them.

13

THE ERG

O LIVIA JADE GIANNULLI'S MORNING routine through much of high school looked something like this: tumble out of bed; throw on a gray pleated skirt with a tiny white anchor embroidered on the hem, white polo, and sweater or sweatshirt; spread peanut butter and banana on toast or cook up a few eggs; and head to school about a tenth of a mile away.

She didn't bother much with makeup for Marymount High School, a Catholic girls' school that, like her family's nine-thousand-square-foot Mediterranean manse, backed onto the ritzy Bel-Air Country Club golf course.

Her life revolved around her YouTube channel, which she'd launched at the beginning of high school, in August 2014, and which by September 2017 had one million subscribers. The vlog offered makeup tips, fashion advice, "week-in-my-life" compilations, and Q&As in which Olivia would answer followers' questions about friends, her skin care routine, clothes, even who she'd want to play her in a movie (Jennifer Lawrence, at least at one point). Her sister Isabella, a year older, made regular appearances to offer a heavy dose of sarcasm and snark. And there were cameos by her father, designer Mossimo Giannulli, and a bit more often her mother, actress Lori Loughlin.

As college crept closer, she worked with an essay coach. One early draft focused on how Olivia grew into the role of being a brand ambassador for

Sephora and other companies, and what it meant to her to have gained such fame and influence. Olivia aspired to have her own makeup line.

Another essay referenced her YouTube channel.

Neither mentioned rowing.

But when it came time to apply for college, Olivia did the same thing her older sister had done a year earlier. She sat down on an erg in the family's home gym, back straight, arms outstretched holding the T-bar, knees bent, ready for her close-up.

THE ATHLETIC PROFILES SINGER and his team created worked in part thanks to Singer's deep tentacles inside USC, where the system was ripe for corruption. But the opportunity for him to slide young women, in particular, into secondary sports also came from structural weaknesses that went far beyond USC.

A 1972 statute prohibiting sex discrimination in educational programs, known as Title IX, has dramatically influenced how schools divvy up roster spots and made it easier for women of middling athletic talent to get labeled as recruits. Institutions with football programs can have upwards of 100 men on those teams. So to maintain equitable opportunity, they may have built really, really big women's rowing programs.

The average women's crew team at NCAA Division I schools is about 63 people, quite a bit larger than the average men's squad. At the University of Michigan and Clemson University, women's rosters have topped 100. At the University of Wisconsin, it's over 170.

High school rowers are recruited, though it's not as high-profile a process as for football. Coaches also post advertisements around campus seeking out former volleyball and basketball players with an athletic build, as well as women of smaller stature who can sit as the coxswain, the player who yells orders to the rest of the team. They sign up, they train in the fall, and as long as they stay through the first competition, they count as athletes. Many do drop off by the time the serious spring season gets under way and they realize what a grind the early-morning practice schedule and trips to regattas can be.

Singer described his approach as a benign hack.

He gave one Las Vegas teen his tried-and-true line: there was an admissions "front door," where applicants got in the regular way; a "back door," where families made big donations to increase their odds; and a "side door"—a sure-thing strategy he had invented. College coaches had excess walk-on spots that could go unused each year, the teen recalls him saying, and he matched clients to those spots. The students wouldn't have to play, he explained, and no harm resulted because the "spot would go to waste" otherwise.

OLIVIA AND BELLA'S MOM and dad never went to college. Giannulli told a story about using his college fund to start his first fashion line. Loughlin acted in the CBS drama *The Edge of Night*, then landed a role on *Full House* beginning in 1988. They wanted a more traditional path for their girls, part of the reason they sent them to a school where 2017 graduates had a 100 percent acceptance rate at four-year colleges.

Marymount features beautiful Spanish Mission–style buildings on a tranquil five-and-a-half-acre campus overlooking Sunset Boulevard. With a religious statue and prayer garden out front, it bills itself as an institution "with the core purpose of educating and empowering young women to live lives of consequence as ethical leaders with a global perspective and an unshakable commitment to the common good." Alumnae include Kim Kardashian and actress Mariska Hargitay.

Advising started freshman year, focusing on academics and helping students find their passion. Sophomore year they began talking about fit, and junior year they dove deep into what they actually wanted to get out of college—a reminder that the process really just begins, rather than ends, with an acceptance letter.

But lots of other families at Marymount and other top area schools were using outside experts.

The Giannulli family hired Singer in summer 2015, using his team for college counseling and tutoring. In April 2016, Giannulli wrote Singer—copying Loughlin—asking for some face time after Singer's upcoming session with Olivia and Bella to "make sure we have a roadmap for success" to get Bella "into a school other than ASU!"

Singer responded, "If you want [U]SC I have the game plan ready to go into motion. Call me to discuss." Singer told Giannulli that July that Bella's grades hovered around the low end of what would get her into USC. No need to retake the SAT—just keep up her grades and stay focused and she was within reach.

There were other plans under way, too, besides just making sure Bella kept buckling down. Later that summer Singer asked Giannulli for a photo of Bella on an ergometer "in workout clothes like a real athlete" and Giannulli obliged. Singer said he would pitch her to USC as a coxswain.

The family could have taken the more traditional route for deep-pocketed moms and dads—getting on the radar of fundraising officials in hopes of getting preferential treatment (but not necessarily a guarantee). USC's development office had even contacted Giannulli, offering to arrange a customized tour for Bella and to "flag her application." He told his wife he blew them off.

After talking to Singer, they were pursuing a path through Donna Heinel: make a donation, get flagged as a walk-on athlete, and walk on into school. They'd later say he told them he'd done it many times, it was legitimate, they weren't taking a spot from someone else, and they'd be helping out USC's crew team financially. They also said that he told them it wasn't a problem the girls didn't row, and if anyone asked, they could say they stepped down to concentrate on academics.

They'd later, after months of proclaiming their innocence, plead guilty to fraud conspiracy and acknowledge under oath that they knew Singer would falsely present the girls as experienced coxswains; they also agreed in court that they hid the arrangement from a high school counselor.

But they continued to maintain to others that they'd been led to believe this was done many times, that the girls weren't taking a spot from someone else, and they'd be helping out USC's crew team financially. They also said that Singer told them if anyone asked, they could say they stepped down to concentrate on academics.

Singer would describe the conversations as being less innocuous. He would tell authorities that Loughlin and Giannulli concealed the circumstances of the admissions from people because the girls were not real recruits and that they also understood the money "was part of the deal and had to be paid in order to get the girls into USC."

. . .

ONE OF THE REASONS Singer's scheme was so successful was that he knew
how the legitimate recruiting system worked. Just getting invited by a coach for
a campus visit didn't mean a high schooler was a sure contender, and race times
from senior-year spring weren't very meaningful because schools had already
locked in their teams. Most important, he knew how much autonomy coaches
had in deciding who could be flagged as recruits and how little policing there
was once those lists were created.

Late morning one cloudy Friday in October 2016, he found himself sitting
in a small office suite on L Street in Washington, D.C., not far from the George
Washington University campus.

By now, Singer's growing reputation as an authority on admissions led him
to be selected as an expert witness for Sidwell Friends, the private school of
choice for the Nixon, Clinton, and Obama families, among other D.C. bigwigs.

Sidwell had been sued by a former student's family alleging it had sabo-
taged their daughter's college applications and retaliated when they called into
question a math grade. She wasn't admitted to any of the dozen-plus schools to
which she applied, as a strong student and runner, though she did get into Penn
after a gap year. (The court found in favor of the school.)

The school landed on Singer through a recommendation from its law firm,
Gordon & Rees, which in turn was chosen by Sidwell Friends' insurance company. The goal was for Singer to make clear the girl wasn't a stellar candidate,
and Sidwell didn't have to actively torpedo her chances. He was a combative
expert witness.

"There are certain things that I want to remember, and certain things I
don't," he said in answer to a question about his past experience testifying in
civil cases, unable or unwilling to recall who hired him, when, or on what spe-
cific topics he had been retained.

One could argue Sidwell Friends and its legal team got ripped off, considering he said he was paid $300 an hour and spent forty or more hours preparing
his twenty-eight-page expert report and testimony for the deposition. Singer
didn't bother to include his résumé in his expert report and gave vague answers

when asked about his qualifications. He interrupted and talked over the attorney. He was unaware that the girl served as president of her school's physics club and African society, received academic commendations, worked part-time, and was involved in a number of other activities, according to deposition testimony. He disregarded the difference between an A– and an A for the sake of calculating the girl's GPA.

With coaches on his side, Singer had never really needed to pay attention to how realistic the purported race times were for his clients. He wrote in his report that the standard time for a walk-on women's 400-meter runner at Harvard was 48.53 seconds, nearly a second faster than what won the 2016 Rio Olympics.

But still, beneath the bluster, Singer showed a fundamental understanding of the athletic recruiting process and a key point: he noted it was likely harder to get into a top college as a nonathlete than as an athlete.

Forget about community service and recommendation letters, he said that October day. Coaches would have really only cared about the girl's running times, SAT, and GPA.

Was she recruitable for schools like Caltech, Columbia, or Princeton? "No." An invitation from Columbia's track coach "shows a little interest," but nothing more, he said dismissively. And a note from the Brown University track coach indicates just "some interest."

Singer's characteristic blunt assessment that the kid wasn't special actually made sense since many athletes invited by coaches for official campus visits don't get formally tagged as recruits. The coaches just want to get a better look at them, but could decide the player isn't a great fit, doesn't look as good in person as on tape, or doesn't have the grades to get an admissions endorsement.

Singer also said the girl's dedication to track, roughly eight hours a week, didn't indicate she was ready to compete at the collegiate level. When Singer helped gussy up his own clients' athletic profiles, the finished product would list commitments of four hours a day, or twenty hours a week, or even, in one case, forty-four hours a week for a particular season.

TWO WEEKS AFTER SINGER laid out his understanding of athletic recruiting in Washington, Heinel met with the athletic admissions subcommittee in Los

Angeles to present Bella Giannulli's application. The photo of her on the erg didn't make it to the admissions team, as Janke, the former USC coach and expert profile producer, had swapped out an image of someone else actually on a boat to go with Bella's athletic profile.

The profile included claims that she'd gone to the Head of the Charles, scored gold in the San Diego Crew Classic, and participated in training programs at the University of Washington and Oklahoma.

An endorsement on Bella's application file called her an "earnest, outspoken, incredibly positive-minded coxswain." It also said that her family could pay the full cost of attendance.

She was conditionally admitted to USC on October 27, 2016, and two days later Singer emailed Giannulli, asking him to send $50,000 to Heinel, care of USC Athletics. Giannulli said he asked his business manager to FedEx the check.

Bella was in, and the family could get back to their whirlwind regular lives.

Loughlin was working on the latest season of *Fuller House*, the Netflix reboot of her famed sitcom. She held lead roles in two Hallmark Channel staple series, *When Calls the Heart* and *Garage Sale Mysteries*. And she and Bella had spent much of June in Vancouver filming *Every Christmas Has a Story*, a Hallmark holiday movie and Bella's acting debut.

Loughlin told Al Roker on the *Today* show that November that she was hoping the project would deter Bella from pursuing an acting career. "I wanted to show her the reality of going away and being on a set for three weeks and what that was and maybe she wouldn't like it. And, of course that backfired because she loved it more than ever."

MATTEO SLOANE, another Bel Air teen, was grinding his way through high school.

He didn't have a great freshman year at the Buckley School, a well-regarded private school in Los Angeles's Sherman Oaks section whose upper school tuition topped $40,000 a year.

It jolted him. Buckley had plenty of college counselors, and they made it clear to him and his friends, even in the ninth grade, how competitive the college admissions process was going to be. "You need to work," they told Matteo.

So he did. He enrolled in Advanced Placement classes and some days would get home exhausted from soccer practice and then stay up until 2:00 a.m. to study.

He became a fixture on the honor roll. Along with playing sports through junior year, he served as vice president of Buckley's diversity club. He gave a presentation at a local conference on "the responsibility of privilege." He worked with teachers on his writing, getting on "the college essay train," as he put it. He even spent the summer before junior year at a leadership camp on the Yale University campus, becoming excited about studying environmental science, and envisioning for himself a future shaping environmental policy to tackle global climate change.

Matteo was sociable and friendly, slightly built and handsome, with olive skin and deep dimples framing his mouth like parentheses. His big grin, SoCal speaking cadence, and passion for surfing belied an uncommon maturity and depth of thought. He had a worldly perspective for a teen, having lived in Italy and spent time in India. In addition to English, he spoke Spanish and Italian fluently.

High school had been a pressure cooker, but he was proud of his record.

"I always knew I could do it and I did it," he recalled in an interview.

MATTEO IS THE ELDEST of Devin and Cristina Sloane's four kids, who lived in an elegant, gated Spanish-style home up a windy street in the hills of Bel Air, where stately mansions hide behind gates and tall hedges.

After college, Devin Sloane started developing and operating service centers with car washes, gas stations, and convenience stores all clustered together. The family moved to Italy for eight years, beginning in 2005, and Sloane moved up the ranks at his father-in-law's oil and gas company there.

Upon his return to the United States, he switched gears to focus on a company that invested in water recycling and treatment systems and provided project management for major water infrastructure systems. His brother Lance was a Hollywood producer, and Sloane himself helped produce a film that won accolades at Sundance.

Sloane saw himself in Matteo and vowed to protect the boy and give him some of the guidance he felt he didn't get growing up. He was the take-charge type that felt he needed to do everything himself to have it done right. Sloane admitted later that he tried "too vigorously to solve problems that hadn't yet arisen."

Given all the support Buckley offered, Matteo was surprised to see his dad add another college counselor to the mix. He was still only a sophomore, after all. But Matteo didn't fight it. All the adults were too involved in their kids' accomplishments. That was just the way it was at places like Buckley.

"It's honestly, like, kind of gross that they're trying to live their kids' lives," he says. "It doesn't give kids the breathing room they need to grow and develop into their own person."

He included his parents among those who could have loosened their grip.

"I accepted the reality that my parents were way too invested," he recalls. "In hindsight, that is why I didn't push back as much as I probably should have."

In 2016, Rick Singer began coming by on Sunday evenings, usually after a swim at a local pool, and set up tutors for Matteo as well.

He was friendly, nice as could be to Matteo and a bit of a suck-up to his dad. Singer would ask where Matteo was interested in going. The teen had a range of schools, including UC Santa Cruz, Santa Clara University, and Loyola Marymount in California, and Georgetown further afield.

"I didn't want to go to the school with the best acceptance rate," he says, "I didn't care about that at all. I just wanted to go to a good school where I fit in and would have a good balance between social life and academics and kind of develop into my own person."

Matteo says Singer pressed him toward USC, stressing that it was a terrific school nearby, which his mom would appreciate. Sloane said Singer tapped into Cristina's anxiety about Matteo leaving home, moving so far away. Of course, plenty of West Coast schools fit the bill of keeping Matteo close to home, and Matteo himself suggested a number of them. But Singer's wealthy clients were focused on certain prestigious names, with USC chief among them. USC was an appealing target for Singer, too, since he could use his connections there to get kids admitted, and further run up his wins.

Matteo fell in love with the school after a campus visit. But a perceived problem dampened the excitement. USC had gotten much more competitive. Matteo was a good applicant, multilingual with strong grades and test scores. But Sloane's lawyer would later say the dad came to believe, after talking to Singer, that there was a huge pool of applicants just like Matteo and that his son needed to be even more interesting, with perhaps another hobby on his résumé.

In June 2017 Sloane visited Amazon.com to buy water polo gear, including a ball, a Speedo swimsuit, a padded swim cap, and a vinyl Italian flag decal for the cap.

Later that month he posed Matteo for photos in the family swimming pool, wearing the new items and holding the ball.

He gave some sort of vague reason to Matteo why they needed to do this little photo shoot. Matteo was annoyed but went along. The pair had the type of relationship where if his dad asked, Matteo followed orders. Sloane sent the pictures to a graphic designer, to create an action shot.

"Wow! You nailed it!!!" he wrote to the designer who cropped the image.

The designer didn't nail it. Matteo looked like he was standing in the shallow end of a pool, water up to about his waist, with his right arm, chest, and stomach exposed above the water.

"Does this work??" Sloane asked Singer.

"Yes but a little high out of the water—no one gets that high," Singer responded.

Time for some more Photoshopping, with the designer complaining the effort had been a "beast." The second version of the picture had Matteo mostly submerged.

"Hope this works," Sloane told Singer.

"Perfect," was the response.

The plan went further than making Matteo more well-rounded or interesting.

Laura Janke, by then a key lieutenant in Singer's operation, churned out an athletic profile saying Matteo was a perimeter player who competed for the Italian junior national team and the L.A. Water Polo Club team. Sloane didn't tell his son about the plan, and Singer's team submitted the final application, a person close to the family said.

Heinel successfully pitched Matteo to the athletic subcommittee on November 2, 2017.

In exchange, Sloane sent a $50,000 check to Heinel, payable to USC Women's Athletics, and agreed to pay $200,000 to Singer's charity when Matteo got his official admission letter the following March. Singer later posted on his website a testimonial from Devin Sloane. It includes a photo of Matteo, in a USC sweatshirt, on the USC campus. The message on the testimonial thanks Singer for making a dream come true.

Whose dream?

In April 2017, Giannulli emailed Singer a note with the subject line, "Trojan happiness."

"I wanted to thank you again for your great work with Isabella, she is very excited and both Lori and I are very appreciative of your efforts and end result!" he gushed, copying Loughlin.

Giannulli also sent the $200,000 invoice from Key Worldwide, Singer's charity, to his financial adviser, writing, "Good news," Bella was in at USC. "Bad is I had to work the system."

Singer asked if the couple had similar needs for Olivia.

"Yes Olivia as well," Giannulli replied.

"Yes USC for Olivia!" Loughlin added.

Olivia, who transferred into Marymount her sophomore year, had ditched organized sports years earlier, despite participating in track, volleyball, and other athletic endeavors as a kid, and even maneuvering her stuffed animals to have team meetings and discuss imaginary soccer plays. She told her online audience that she doubted she could survive the Hunger Games. "I'd be like, 'Where's my lipstick?!'"

Olivia's in-home cardio days focused on intervals on the treadmill. She favored organized workout classes, particularly cycling and Pilates, over time in her home gym. While still in high school, she had a personal trainer whose other clients included Courtney Cox, Julianne Moore, and David Duchovny.

She made no secret of her distaste for academic life. She hated physics and bemoaned homework. "My favorite subject is free period because I don't have to do anything," she said at one point. Another time she was asked via Snapchat how she balanced high school with her YouTube channel.

"Psh, you don't," Bella interjects, chuckling, as the pair sit on an overstuffed gray love seat.

"You've just got to learn to just put YouTube before school because school is *so* not important," Olivia says, her eye twinkling as Bella gets more agitated.

She wasn't entirely flaky about school. In her senior yearbook, Olivia told her parents, "I am so grateful you both forced me to finish high school despite all the times I said I did not want to." But her real interest and talent lay in influencing her huge number of YouTube followers. She sat in front of a camera, applying creams and cleansers, talking through each step of the beauty regimen. She showcased "hauls" of new products, trying on endless outfits in front of a mirror.

Hundreds of thousands of people tuned in to watch her eat pizza, review her Christmas gifts, detail her daily diet. Comments rolled in and she regularly spent time on videos answering viewers' questions. Olivia's videos had become such staples of American teen life that they would make an appearance in the opening scenes of the movie *Eighth Grade*.

The summer before her senior year, in 2017, Singer asked Janke to craft an athletic profile for Olivia. He emailed Giannulli and Loughlin around the same time, asking for some details about Olivia and indicating she'd be listed as a coxswain who worked with the L.A. Marina Club team.

Singer asked for an action picture. He asked again, four days later. "If we want USC I will need a transcript, test scores and picture on the ERG," he wrote the couple.

"Moss will get this done," Loughlin replied. "We are back in town on Monday."

HER FIRST DAY OF senior year, Olivia started recording a video while still in bed, her hair uncombed.

"I like . . . refuse to believe this is happening," she whispers, her voice still hoarse with sleep. "Noo-o-o." She collapses back into the white pillows.

On campus, Olivia declares, "I've gone to one class and I already want to die."

She finds solace back home after school, the beginnings of a smile forming on her lips as she records from the gleaming white kitchen.

"I know that I complain about school. I mean, who actually enjoys going to school? If you do, very jealous. But I also feel the need to say that for all of us that like to complain about school, because I get how much it sucks, we have to remember how lucky we are to have an education and how many people would kill to have a good education."

She continues, "So as much as I hate it, I still hate it but I'm grateful that I get to be educated. Even though I hate it, you know?"

The video was viewed more than a million times.

HEINEL PRESENTED OLIVIA TO the athletic admissions subcommittee around November 2, 2017, and she was conditionally admitted. The fabricated rowing résumé said she'd won medals at the San Diego Crew Classic and regional championships and was "highly talented and has been successful in both men's and women's boats." It also said her sister was on the team roster and served as a coxswain for one of their boats.

"CONGRATULATIONS!!!" Singer wrote in an email to Giannulli and Loughlin a few weeks later.

Loughlin was thrilled. "This is wonderful news!" she wrote, adding a high-five emoji.

Giannulli sent a $50,000 check, made payable to Galen Center Gift—USC, and agreed to send another $200,000 to Singer's charity when Olivia received her official acceptance the following spring.

As her older sister had done, Olivia was admitted as a walk-on coxswain, with no plan to join the team.

14

DO IT ALL FOR THE KIDS

B RIAN WERDESHEIM SAT ON a stool, a plain white background and crisp blue-gray suit highlighting his tanned, friendly face.

He looked a bit sweaty, which was out of character for Werdesheim, the charming founding partner of the Summa Group, a wealth management division within big financial firm Oppenheimer & Co. But he was at a film shoot for his new pet project, at an L.A. warehouse on an insanely hot summer day.

With the camera running and a tiny microphone clipped to his sport coat, Werdesheim, who was in his early fifties, began to describe his wealth management firm's charitable arm, the Summa Children's Foundation. His group had started it in 2005 to raise money for Southern California organizations focused on health, social, and educational issues.

Names of beneficiaries flashed on the screen as Werdesheim narrated: An overnight summer camp for impoverished youth. A child-abuse resource center. An arts and athletics program for families affected by chronic illness.

"Ones that with our help we could really move the needle," Werdesheim explained. They'd thrown big galas in big ballrooms with big names in attendance, he continued, as snapshots of smiling VIPs like Kris and Bruce Jenner, Michael Bolton, and famed USC and pro football coach Pete Carroll appeared.

"Fast-forward to today, it's 2017," he said with a smile.

The nonprofit had a new name, the Banyan Foundation, and an entirely new direction: it would train high school students in philanthropy, empowering them to do the work—research and pick the causes, and even make presentations to raise funds.

And it also had a new board.

"I'm very pleased," he said, "to share with everybody that Rick Singer is a board member of the Banyan Foundation."

The video soon cut to Singer, sitting in front of a row of windows in a Los Angeles skyscraper, having shot his segment on a different day.

"I'm exceptionally blessed and excited to be a part of the Banyan Foundation," Singer said, dressed up for the occasion, for him, in a gray sweater over a white collared shirt.

He was helping the kids. And by aligning himself with a handsome, personable wealth manager who had a long list of high-net-worth clients, ran a foundation, and sat on the board of a prestigious private school, Singer was also helping himself.

WERDESHEIM, WHO'D GRADUATED FROM USC and landed a job at Oppenheimer, had built a full life. His wife, Janelle, an interior decorator, had designed their Studio City home, which was featured in *Ventura Boulevard* magazine. He buzzed around in a luxury SUV with a skiing bumper sticker, a sports nut and cool dad to two children who attended the Buckley School, where Werdesheim had joined the board of trustees. He stayed close to his alma mater, serving a three-year term on the advisory council for an entrepreneurial program at USC's Marshall School of Business.

At Oppenheimer, Werdesheim helped build the Summa Group into a twelve-person team that would grow to north of $2 billion in assets under management over the next few years, with clients hailing from L.A. entertainment, athletic, and business circles.

Werdesheim knew what kept his high-end clients up at night, and it wasn't just investment returns. These patrons had enjoyed professional success and maintained equally high standards for other parts of their lives. They wanted a firm that could tend to issues around their health, their philanthropy, their business succession plans, and, crucially, their college planning for their kids.

Summa, like other firms, wanted to know it could refer clients to specialists in these areas.

Some L.A. financial advisers, including Werdesheim, were talking about the need for college counselors at a dinner years earlier, when an attendee mentioned he'd used someone in Sacramento: Rick Singer, who still lived in the state capital at the time. A few months later, Singer met with Werdesheim, and a mutually beneficial professional relationship sprouted.

Wealth advisers, at Summa and elsewhere, used Singer to talk to parents about the basics of the college preparation process, and what was bound to be a very stressful time in their lives. Singer would use the word "coach" to sell himself as someone who could navigate the road from high school to higher education.

An adviser at Goldman Sachs subsidiary Ayco referred a client. Singer delivered his admissions talks to members of the Young Presidents Organization (now known as YPO), employees at Pimco, and hundreds or even thousands of families in places like Nebraska and Florida over the years. And he addressed clients at a Freestone Capital event on the top floor of a Seattle skyscraper.

Werdesheim would become one of Singer's most fruitful links to wealthy L.A.-area families.

SUMMA WOULD INVITE CLIENTS and prospective clients to the events, sometimes held at Oppenheimer Tower, a glass-fronted skyscraper on Wilshire Boulevard.

Werdesheim would open with remarks praising Singer. Good-looking and polished, he contrasted sharply against Singer, who'd bound into the presentation dressed down and carrying a backpack, ready to hook his computer up to a big screen and start the show.

One movie studio lawyer got an unexpected invitation in the mail in fall 2015 from Summa.

"Getting into College is not a secret . . . *It's a Science*," said the invite, which announced a series of two-hour presentations. "Guest Speaker, Rick Singer of The Key."

The lawyer's daughter was only a freshman, but you couldn't start preparing too early for the family's goal of Stanford. At the event, Singer walked around the room in slacks and a collared shirt, speaking loudly and going right up to people who asked questions. He mentioned prominent clients and reeled off tips.

The mom noticed Singer and Summa's symbiotic relationship: Copies of Singer's admissions guide, *Getting In*, were available to attendees. A Summa representative warmly introduced Singer while also touting Summa's services.

She jotted down some of his tips: Listing a zillion extracurriculars shows breadth, not depth or commitment. Top-tier schools choose borderline candidates if they have high SAT subject test scores or standout personal statements and recommendations. Bring a sweatshirt to the test—the room is often cold. Motioning to a PowerPoint, Singer noted that people overlook Washington University in St. Louis and Williams College in Williamstown, Massachusetts, and warned about town-gown tensions in New Haven, Connecticut, home to Yale. He emphasized the growing allure of USC.

At events, Singer would typically show a scene from the 2002 movie *Orange County*. The plot centers on a smart high school student who applies only to Stanford, and then gets rejected when his guidance counselor accidentally submits the wrong transcript. One mistake could derail years of hard work and aspirations.

Parents would start to sweat and shift in their chairs and a number would rush the podium to get a minute with Singer after his presentation.

Singer grew used to these high-stress audiences. A few years later, he'd present for yet another group of current and prospective Summa clients at the luxury Hotel Bel-Air. That evening had a hefty title: "Demystifying Healthcare & College Admission in Uncertain and Challenging Times: How to Be Proactive in Gaining Access to Game Changing Guidance and Expertise for You and Your Family."

Werdesheim could have aligned himself with more pedigreed college counselors, but they could be boring, and Singer had a good track record. Singer's slightly eccentric and unvarnished persona, so single-minded that he didn't have time for stylish haircuts or fancy clothes, added to his appeal.

Werdesheim was a glass-half-full type who saw the best in people. He seemed genuinely impressed with Singer, and how Singer spoke with confidence and conviction. Also appealing: Singer would say that to be successful, kids needed to be happy. That was a crucial message for these audiences, who could put almost intolerable stress on their kids.

And Summa was hearing great feedback from people who hired Singer. The firm kept using him, seeing no reason to vet the claims Singer made at events, such as that he was an application reader for two different colleges each year.

Werdesheim also praised Singer in the Banyan Foundation launch video, repeating his vastly inflated line that he'd advised more than seventy thousand families worldwide.

"He has a skill set that plays in perfectly to what we're doing," Werdesheim said, including "tremendous experience in the area of philanthropy."

SINGER OF COURSE HAD many ways to spread the word about his business. He had a large, legitimate counseling operation, and contracted with test prep tutors and essay coaches around the country to work with clients, for a sizable but not outrageous fee, who wanted nothing more than a little guidance, editing, and math drills to make their way to a good college. They'd be perfectly content landing at schools like Texas Christian University and Seattle University.

But another group of ambitious parents was not willing to lower its sights, and among them, he continued to find a particularly lucrative customer base. He could make money, save the day, and, probably most crucially, satisfy his innate need to win when he successfully delivered on these deals.

Singer's illicit acts involved greed and stupidity, his lawyer, Don Heller, would later write, but he was also the "enabling protagonist" for affluent parents "beset by conceit and arrogance."

Singer often connected with many of these wealthy parents (both the ones who hired him legitimately and the ones willing to go further) in the same way: social connections and references from others. One especially fruitful approach was immersing himself in the world of charities, toward which many of those target parents gravitated.

Singer talked to a friend, an attorney, who helped him prepare the paperwork for his own charity, and in December 2012 he established the Key

Worldwide Foundation as a nonprofit public benefit corporation, registering it as a charity the following March. Singer would say years later that the purpose was to help disadvantaged kids, but that he then thought it could be a vehicle to accept bribe payments from parents to get their kids into college. He'd portray it as a win for all: the parent could write the payment off on their taxes as a donation, and he could help people.

The foundation's mission statement read, "Our contributions to major athletic university programs may help to provide placement to students that may not have access under normal channels."

Just the sort of innocuous statement describing any charity helping underprivileged students gain access to higher education. But in this case it had a double meaning.

It was the perfect cover, really. The foundation let Singer pay off coaches in what seemed like a kind act. He funded college sports and youth club teams.

More important, he provided a place for parents to funnel their payments for illicit activities. The foundation allowed both Singer and his clients to live a sort of double life: generous on the surface, but watching their own backs. With the charity, their money and reputations stayed squeaky clean.

One father later said he did think he was helping disadvantaged kids by giving money to the foundation. However, he admitted, "I also knew that my daughter would be getting some kind of help that was outside the rules. I didn't know exactly how, and, frankly, I didn't want to know."

In May 2016, soon after Julia Henriquez was admitted to Georgetown with fraudulent SAT scores and a fabricated essay about tennis, the Henriquez Family Trust contributed $400,000 to Key Worldwide Foundation. A few days after the funds went through, Singer's team sent a donation receipt to the benefactors, Bay Area couple Manuel and Elizabeth Henriquez.

The receipt stated that the gift would "allow us to move forward with our plans to provide educational and self-enrichment programs to disadvantaged youth." It also said "no goods or services were exchanged" for the money. In other words, the Henriquez family got nothing out of it, other than a warm, fuzzy feeling in their hearts for helping the less fortunate.

Such receipts would be sent to many parents over the years, as they donated $15,000 or $75,000 or $200,000 to the Key Worldwide Foundation as payment for Singer's help cheating on tests or slotting their kids into college as athletic recruits. The money would then be distributed to coaches, test proctors, and others as payment for their services.

Most of the parents were eager to make the payments under cover of charity or as a business expense. When one mother was hashing out details with Singer to cheat on her son's ACT, she exclaimed, "Oh, even better!" when she learned she could get a write-off. Singer told a father that he could make his payment to the foundation as a donation for a write-off, or get an invoice as a business consulting fee from Singer's for-profit company, the Key, so the dad could write that off as a business expense.

Another parent forwarded a $200,000 Key Worldwide Foundation invoice to his bookkeeper, referring to it as "the last college 'donation'" for his daughter. He asked, "Can't I write this off?"

Still, some parents recoiled at the prospect of writing off private college counseling.

Dan Larson was initially intrigued when he heard Singer speak to swim team parents at the Arden Hills Athletic & Social Club in Sacramento in 2012. Larson had a daughter, a competitive swimmer who was bright but not a good test taker. Singer had already told him how he was an insider at a ton of impressive schools.

After the presentation to the swim team group, Larson met with Singer privately to discuss tutoring for the daughter.

Singer casually ran through his program. Doctors he knew would diagnose Larson's daughter with anxiety, awarding accommodations that would then let her take her test with Singer's proctor. Larson thought this sounded odd enough, but then Singer mentioned the price would be a $15,000 tax-deductible donation to Key Worldwide Foundation, with "more of a donation" if she needed more help.

Huh? How does someone write off tutoring on their taxes? Larson, who ran his own business coaching sales teams, had questions for Singer: Why was a nonprofit being used for services that were clearly for profit?

Singer grew vague, and Larson said he'd explore some other options. He never did sign up for Singer's services, and Singer never pitched him again. "I think he realized that I would have been a pain in the ass," Larson says.

IN LOS ANGELES, SINGER made deep ties in the often incestuous charity world, where rainmakers sat on one another's boards or donated to each other's worthy causes. Teaming up with Singer made great sense. He knew wealthy, generous families and could refer them to the charities. And if fundraisers could dangle a valuable asset like a recommendation for a college counselor while courting benefactors, all the better.

Dana Pump, who had met Singer years earlier through basketball coaching, knew this well.

He and his brother, David, had founded the Harold & Carole Pump Foundation, which raised millions for cancer research and treatment and threw an annual banquet that drew A-list actors, sports legends, and recording moguls. "When you're dealing with high-net-worth people, and you're going to ask them for money—you take care of anyone's child, and you've got a layup," he once told *Entrepreneur* magazine.

Many donors were nervous about helping their kids through the college application process. Pump considered Singer to be an extremely knowledgeable, experienced college counselor and connected him to around ten families for legitimate counseling. The families he referred seemed satisfied with Singer's services. (It would emerge later that Singer found an illicit client in one of those introductions. Philip Esformes, a Miami businessman, used Singer to pitch his daughter as a soccer recruit to USC. Esformes was ultimately in legal trouble for much more egregious activities, including a massive health-care fraud scheme.)

The referral path went both ways. Singer told Pump one day: "I've got a well-to-do guy for you." He introduced Pump to David Sidoo, the former football player and petroleum executive from Vancouver, not mentioning that he had rigged the SAT scores for Sidoo's sons. Pump pursued Sidoo for a donation, successfully.

Pump also got the Key Worldwide Foundation to make a legitimate donation to his wife's charity, the Ladylike Foundation, which mentors under-privileged women.

For Werdesheim, Singer would be a known and respected name on the board of Summa Group's new education-related charity. The foundation guided high school students in doing philanthropic work, with adults as mentors. The teens chose themes each year, like nutrition and teen mental health, assessed local charities to see where they could have the most impact, and got involved by making grants and learning more about where the money goes.

Banyan drew big-name donors including hedge fund investor Stanley Druckenmiller and comedy writer and actor Seth MacFarlane in 2017. Singer's company also gave money, though on a much smaller scale.

Singer joined the Banyan board with the warning that he might not have much time to commit to the charity. Sure enough, he attended only one meeting, but maintained the title and its accompanying reputational perks.

The board seat meant Singer would gain greater proximity to L.A. private school circles. Early participants included the daughter of Adam Bass, the CEO of a law firm and fellow Buckley School trustee who hired Singer. Some of the teens attended tony schools like Brentwood and Campbell Hall, while others were from disadvantaged homes and were referred by the Fulfillment Fund, a charity that provided mentorship and college guidance for low-income students. Werdesheim served on that group's board, where other donors included Singer client Devin Sloane and Singer's own foundation.

MEANWHILE, SINGER'S KEY WORLDWIDE Foundation had exploded. The organization went from recording $451,600 in grants and contributions in 2013 to $900,000 in 2014, $1.98 million in 2015, and $3.74 million in 2016.

According to tax documents the group filed, and a Sacramento accountant signed off on, the foundation was doing substantial work supporting poor kids and those in need of a little extra guidance.

The group said that in 2013 it funded 1,400 adults and kids from the Crips and Bloods gangs to play basketball "and develop consensus building programs to stop gang violence and create better communication through sports for 40 weeks." It also reported donations to Generation W, a nonprofit founded by

Donna Orender, a former pro basketball player and WNBA official with whom Singer formed a short-lived company in Florida called the Opportunity Engine.

There were also five- and six-figure donations to USC water polo and soccer. At first glance, benign. Not so much after knowing the connections between Singer and the coaches.

Princeville Enterprises—led by UCLA men's soccer coach Jorge Salcedo as CEO—received a $100,000 donation in 2016, tax forms say. The charity also put money into other for-profit companies, including a chain of Mexican restaurants where Singer's brother, Cliff, was for a time an executive.

It's hard to know exactly how much good work the charity really did. A tutoring program did exist in Oakland, California, at one point. And Singer did put on that weeklong camp at UCLA with kids from the 1736 Family Crisis Center, though tax paperwork exaggerated the scope of his relationship with them.

In 2015, the foundation said it spent $287,000 "developing and researching student placement process at eastern US Tier One Universities, and the average cost per student." A few pages later in that same document, Key Worldwide says it paid Gordon Ernst, the Georgetown tennis coach, $287,000 as an independent contractor, listing no description of services. And in 2016, the foundation gave him $825,000 for "consulting."

Singer would later say parents gave to the charity knowing the payments were for side deals to get kids into college, and they were only pretending to donate to help needy kids.

Singer's bookkeeper, Steven Masera—listed as treasurer of the foundation on tax documents—was generally the one responsible for making sure parents came through on their promised donations, and distributing receipts for those gifts after. In July 2016 he sent an invoice for $250,000 to Davina Isackson, who with her husband, Bruce, had paid Singer to get their older daughter into USC as a soccer recruit.

There had been a paperwork snafu at that school, though, and she was directed to the regular applicant pool. So Singer worked some backroom magic, connecting to the UCLA soccer coach to secure the teen a spot there late in the cycle.

A few days after getting the invoice, Bruce emailed Singer directly. "Per our discussion can you please send me an email confirming that if [our daughter] is not admitted to UCLA as a freshman for the Fall 2016 class that The Key Worldwide Foundation will refund our $250,000 gift."

Singer duly confirmed. "Your donation of $250,000 to The Key Worldwide Foundation supporting educational initiatives we have created to help those who need it the most will be returned," if the girl's admission was reversed from a more informal emailed offer she'd already gotten from the school.

Another father was similarly explicit about the purpose of the money going to the foundation. When his bookkeeper emailed to ask why they'd gotten a text message with bank info for the Key Worldwide Foundation, he responded, "It's a 500k donation I am going to make this year. Tax write off and help getting into colleges."

All the while, Singer and his team churned out those donation receipts confirming "no goods or services were exchanged" for the money.

15

———

THE TARGET

WHEN THE OTHER MOM at Jack Buckingham's soccer game in 2016 mentioned college counselors, Jane Buckingham swung into action.

She got Singer's contact information, and then a second reference from another friend. She called both Singer and the other recommended expert, a hot L.A. counselor named Danny Ruderman, known for steering the eventual founder of Snapchat into Stanford.

Ruderman was very busy and required clients to come to his office for sessions. Singer had an opening, and he made house calls.

She chose Singer.

Buckingham was at a turning point in her life. Her husband, Marcus, moved out in early 2016, a month before their twentieth anniversary. Buckingham had been proud of her marriage, and she felt crushed when it ended. Friend Kaye Kramer saw "a new Jane," one who seemed self-doubting. "Her entire life revolves around the kids and her need to be loved poured into them."

Chloe, twelve at the time, followed after her mom, a precocious go-getter. As a little girl, she ran to the TV cameras that came to the Buckingham home to film the family. Chloe would have 700,000 Instagram followers by age fourteen and would become a social media influencer and digital network star. Her college essay would write itself someday.

Jack, at fourteen, was private, preferring his mother never even mention his name in public, and he had more subtle gifts. Tall and skinny enough to hide behind a lamppost, he had a sweet, toothy grin and a deepening voice offset by a still high-pitched giggle. He played soccer and baseball, though there was no thought of him playing in college someday. He stood out for his passion for sports statistics. He'd even researched the history of mascots.

Jack didn't exhibit much ambition yet, but he was kind and impressed others as having an innate sense of right and wrong and the rare willingness to make waves when he saw an injustice. This was a kid who as a small boy spoke out on an airplane when his father leaned forward to close the window that was situated partially next to the seat in front of them, where a man was sitting.

"Don't do that, Dad, that's his!" Jack had shouted. He didn't want his father, or anyone, getting anything that belonged fairly to someone else.

THE FIRST DAY SINGER came to Buckingham's house, Jack didn't want to meet with him. He didn't understand why he needed a college counselor. But then they sat down and Singer started talking about basketball, and stats, which team was trading which player. Jack seemed to like him.

"Jack, we're going to get those grades up, right?" Singer asked him. "What can you commit to?"

It seemed the answer to Buckingham's prayers. Singer was going to get Jack to focus. Buckingham could stop nagging him, which had been a source of conflict. Singer was going to run this process. Life was about to get easier.

One reason Singer worked so well for successful clients like Buckingham was that he set targets and left no doubt he'd reach them.

Singer was triggered by goals; they were like drugs to him. He was in many ways still the kid who lived on nuts and raisins and ran all summer so he could shed the nickname "Fatman Singer" before high school.

"He's super, super intense," says Rene Vercoe, who met Singer on a flight from L.A. to Seattle. "The kind that gets up at 4:30 a.m. to go running before work."

Singer mentioned to Vercoe that his son, who lived in Sacramento, was really into video games, "which drove him nuts." Singer was into constant self-improvement, and extremely well read. He avoided alcohol and ate a mostly plant-based diet, although he occasionally splurged on veal parmesan. What some saw as bluntness, others saw as an appealing directness.

He networked constantly, but it was mostly business—his drive was astonishing.

When many of his neighbors were settling in for an evening of TV and a glass of wine, Singer was at the city-run Marian Bergeson Aquatic Center at Corona del Mar High School swimming so hard he sometimes got his name on the leaderboard for the most laps. At the gym, he resembled a wrestler in training, a hooded sweatshirt over his head while doing crunches.

Vercoe, who exchanged cards with Singer and stayed in touch, found him helpful and generous with his time, particularly if you came to him with some sort of objective he could grasp on to. She was trying to figure out her next steps when they met. She was newly divorced, with an empty nest, and had sold her travel business. Singer drew out her story, and six months after they met, he called, saying he knew someone who needed an assistant and she would be perfect.

Vercoe soon found herself living in the guest house of a mansion in the Bay Area, helping to homeschool the children of Mark Mastrov, a part owner of the Sacramento Kings basketball team who'd also founded the 24 Hour Fitness chain of gyms. She held the job from 2013 to 2016. In her view, Singer was an insightful guy who helped her think outside the box and find opportunities she hadn't even thought of. "Rick was a connector," she said.

SINGER RAN FROM HOUSE to house across Orange County and Los Angeles. He would also travel to the Bay Area, sometimes sleeping overnight in his Mercedes van as he packed in appointments.

The stratosphere of affluence could still shock. Once, a client told him to mark his calendar for the man's birthday party the following July.

"I rented out Versailles."

As in, the royal palace in France.

"Oh, my God," Singer said. "You're crazy."

Singer would respond to emails at all hours of the day and night. "He was addicted to the hectic lifestyle and the adrenaline of it," says a former employee.

Some clients got on his nerves, checking in constantly for reassurance.

Sure, their children might do fine at a lesser school, but they also knew a name-brand school could open doors. "A great school is part of a person's narrative," says the Las Vegas father who hired Singer. "You get asked all the time where you went to school."

The scariest part for these moms and dads was the uncertainty, the father says. "Parents want a quick fix. This is on parents, too."

At times, Singer seemed like just another frustrated college counselor trying to get choosy families to look beyond ivy-covered East Coast campuses or the hot California school of the moment.

"Well, Atlanta's not redneck," he shot back at one father, who'd turned his nose up at Georgia Tech, calling the southern locale a bit hickish. "Atlanta's very, very hip."

The same client also struck down Singer's suggestion of Yale as "way too liberal."

And there were those who delegated *everything* to Singer yet were still a headache on the few occasions they did need to be involved. They canceled appointments at the last minute, or needed nagging to send information or pay bills of a few thousand dollars. A millionaire developer hired Singer's employee to take online classes, including one called "Fitness Fundamentals 2," so the developer's daughter had enough credits to finish high school. But his invoice was way past due, and Singer threatened to suspend work for the girl if it wasn't "handled ASAP."

In one case, a wealthy mother said she expected a discount on a $3,000 invoice from Singer. She'd hired his team to take online classes for her son—already a student at Georgetown—and was underwhelmed with the service when the stand-in earned just a C grade. She complained that the experience had been "a nightmare." Singer retorted that there'd be no discount, since the process was "a nightmare for all."

The former employee was never entirely clear about how Singer figured out who'd go further than legitimate counseling. Some were direct about their aims, according to the employee, likely just asking Singer, "Who can I pay?"

Others may have just given a "vibe," the employee says, that indicated they were set on a certain outcome and wouldn't be disabused of their goal.

The employee concludes, "Some of these parents were very successful and couldn't deal with the fact they had average kids."

Bari Norman, a former admissions officer at Barnard College and Columbia University who cofounded Expert Admissions, a private college counseling service in Manhattan, has seen the outsize aspirations. "The college process is the first time where they've heard the word 'no,'" she said. "They can't wrap their brains around it."

Or Singer's clients could have been seeking the college admissions version of a "black edge," explains one test prep tutor. The hedge fund term describes inside information, a sure-bet way to get ahead that likely lands on the wrong side of any legal line.

A FEW MILES AWAY from the Buckinghams, Los Angeles business executive Stephen Semprevivo also started helping his son, Adam, plan for college the way a number of his peers did: begin early and hire Singer.

The Semprevivos lived in a fabulous gated Tuscan villa, with a waterfall infinity pool, multiple balconies, and panoramic canyon views on one of Bel Air's most desirable streets.

They hired Singer in 2014, when Adam was fifteen, after meeting the college counselor through longtime family friends Mark and Renee Paul, a Beverly Hills couple who themselves had been referred to Singer by another family at their own son's private high school.

Semprevivo was in his late forties at the time and specialized in growing middle-market and start-up companies. He was tall and lean and resembled the actor J. K. Simmons. He coached baseball, basketball, and soccer when his two boys were young, and was proud that Adam was often the best player.

Adam had a lot to live up to when it came to his dad. Semprevivo had been a brilliant student who took summer science classes at Harvard while still a sophomore in high school, in upscale Ridgewood, New Jersey. Stellar grades at

Ridgewood High, where he also played sports, propelled him to Harvard University, where he majored in biochemistry.

His Harvard experience demonstrated how the right school could open doors. After college, Semprevivo sorted through his alumni directories to find a job. He later went back to Harvard for his MBA.

Boards and managers brought in Semprevivo to expand operations or turn around a business in crisis. He was a data-driven problem solver, the cool head focused on efficiency and delivering results. That same quest for continuous improvement spilled into his parenting. He attended every school conference, sports activity, and recital. He posted new words on a "dictionary board" in the kitchen, for the family to review at dinner.

Semprevivo had long envisioned that Adam would go to a well-known school, perhaps USC, Georgetown, or maybe Cornell. Adam was smart and capable. He took part in student government and made the honor roll, along with playing basketball. He even transferred from Buckley to another area private school, Campbell Hall Episcopal School, for a more competitive athletic experience. But he also struggled with depression and self-doubts.

Semprevivo didn't totally get it. He wished his son was better able to compartmentalize like he could, and find a "constructive distraction" to his internal struggles. He decided a clear path to a top college would give his son a needed confidence boost.

Singer spoke Semprevivo's language, of productivity and measurable results, when he began to work with the family. Singer talked about building a Google Doc of information, collecting an array of data, and formulating action plans built around Adam's future. Regular appointments and SAT tutoring, arranged by Singer at hourly rates of up to $300, commenced.

The focused attention brought results. With tutoring, Adam's SAT score jumped from the 83rd percentile, with which the teen had been disappointed, to the 92nd. Singer helped Adam get summer jobs with a local congresswoman and a Boston state representative.

In early 2015, Singer developed a long list of colleges that met Adam's criteria—medium-to-large, a strong business program, and a "rah rah" atmosphere—from Vanderbilt to DePaul to the University of California, Berkeley.

That March, Adam's younger brother, Ben, wrote for his school paper about the dangers of classmates trying to take academic shortcuts. "With the growing level of cheating, many students who do not cheat feel pressured to cheat in order to compete with those who do." He seemed outraged and frustrated by the vicious cycle of cutting corners.

Adam got mixed signals about what would constitute success in the eyes of his parents. Semprevivo said he and his wife, Rita, regularly told Adam he would be successful no matter where he went, and that "it's what you do and how you do it that counts." Yet Semprevivo also acknowledged "pushing hard for the best possible school on the list."

Adam got into the University of Indiana early, but that was just a safety school.

He had been deliberating between Vanderbilt and Georgetown as his top picks, according to an email he sent to Singer on a Saturday morning in August 2015, when he was heading into his senior year at Campbell Hall. Singer put both schools under the most ambitious category, "a stretch," along with nine others. There were also more than two dozen schools ranked as "safer" or "more of a reach."

In his email, Adam asked Singer how a degree from Georgetown's McDonough School of Business would compare with a marketing degree from Vanderbilt, in terms of getting attention from corporate recruiters. Adam also wanted to know if it would be difficult to gain admission directly into Georgetown's undergraduate business school.

Singer replied minutes later, saying Georgetown might offer more opportunities because of its Washington, D.C., location, and he added that the university's degree was "more widely accepted nationally." Vanderbilt had a good reputation, he said, "but not to the same level."

He wrote that Adam might have to apply first to Georgetown's regular undergraduate program, and get good grades in economics and calculus before moving over to the business school.

Singer's comments seemed reasonable.

It was possible, of course, Singer was more enthusiastic about Georgetown because he had an "in" there, a connection in tennis coach Gordon Ernst. And it was also possible the Semprevivos weren't going to settle for anything less than a stretch school.

Adam seemed encouraged by Singer's answer, writing, "Ok, thanks. I'm going to go with Georgetown as my number one and Vanderbilt as my number two."

What had until now looked like a typical college search turned into anything but. Eight days after that email exchange, Singer sent Semprevivo, his wife, and his son an email with an attached note that Adam was instructed to send to Ernst.

The note, written by Singer, pretending to be Adam, was filled with lies, portraying Adam as a devoted tennis player and intimating that he and Ernst had been in touch.

"I have played very well with terrific success in Doubles this summer and played quite well in singles, too," the email said. "I am looking forward to having a chance to play for you."

Adam emailed it to Ernst later that day, along with his high school grades and SAT scores. Ernst forwarded it to a member of the Georgetown admissions staff, who replied, "looks fine."

That October, Singer sent the Semprevivos a final draft of the activity essay for Georgetown, directing his employee to use the prose when she submitted Adam's application. "When I walk into a room," it said, "people will normally look up and make a comment about my height—I'm 6'5—and ask me if I play basketball. With a smile, I nod my head, but also insist that the sport I put my most energy into is tennis." The piece detailed Adam's unorthodox training regimen, and how a focus on footwork helped him find literal and figurative balance. (His applications to other schools, including the University of Michigan and Tulane, didn't suggest any tennis activity.)

Adam would have to wait months for a formal acceptance letter, but he was labeled a "likely" admit, essentially a sure thing.

Meanwhile, Singer made the following notation, indicating the price of the bribe, $400,000 in his email account: "Semprevivo 400 Gtown."

Years later, speaking to a psychologist, Semprevivo's voice cracked and his eyes flooded as he claimed he was spun by Singer: "I just lost confidence, I lost confidence in Adam, I let Singer make me feel that Adam couldn't do it."

Singer, he said, "worked me over and got me to do and believe things I am ashamed of and deeply regret."

But Semprevivo hadn't sat idly through Singer's scheme. He participated in a plan to include an essay for Georgetown in which the teen lied that tennis was his passion. And his son's formal application to Georgetown was packed with phony tennis accolades and bogus credentials, such as the claim he'd played all four years of high school and excelled in singles and doubles.

Rather than seducing Semprevivo, had Singer simply tapped into his hunger for prestige?

Semprevivo's lawyer would call Semprevivo a "target" for Singer. True—in the sense that Singer seemed to know his customers.

"In the world of successful businessmen and professionals, many who were in fact the parents of the prep-school students in Southern California, an elite university for their child represented the Holy Grail," the lawyer argued.

Adam went to Georgetown in 2016. His GPA topped 3.0, but he also continued to struggle with anxiety in his first year.

Semprevivo said his goal was to ease his son's inner turmoil. He would only make things worse.

16

SEDUCTION

O N A PICTURE-PERFECT DAY at the end of August 2017, Felicity Huff-man sat with her laptop in her red-trimmed Craftsman-style home in the Hollywood Hills.

She huddled with Singer to discuss the prospects of her older daughter, Sophia. Ever the eager student, Huffman typed notes:

- "Control the outcome of the SAT—15 grand"
- "get a proctor in the room with her and she gets the answers she needs to get[.] At the end of the test—the proctor is making sure."
- "75 grand guy will make the scores perfect."

Huffman had what seemed like a storybook life: wildly successful career with movie roles and television series like *Desperate Housewives* and *American Crime*; a decades-long, loving marriage to fellow actor William H. Macy; and two humble, kind, well-adjusted children. Sophia was interested in the perform-ing arts, and Georgia was an equestrian with a passion for politics.

They regularly ate dinner together and played "rose and thorn," in which everyone shares the highlight (rose) and lowlight (thorn) of their days. Huff-man created elaborate spooky scenes for Halloween and engineered full-family

games of capture the flag. Macy played the ukulele. They took regular vacations to Colorado.

Yet motherhood bewildered Huffman. She loved her daughters fiercely
and enjoyed spending time with them, but struggled to feel like she was good
enough, held herself up against other moms, and even fretted over how to plan
family vacations that were both as relaxing and as enriching as she believed
they ought to be.

"I found mothering my two children frightening, alienating, lonely and
relentlessly difficult," she wrote on her parenting blog, *What The Flicka?*

Huffman had launched *What The Flicka?* several years earlier, aiming for
it to be a sort of virtual kitchen counter where moms traded tips and vented
their frustrations. *Forbes* described it as one of the top one hundred blogs for
women. The site sold mommy-themed memorabilia with sassy slogans like
"Resting mom face," and "Make your own damn sandwich."

She came across as vulnerable and honest in her columns, advising parents
to empower their children by letting them stumble and do things for themselves. But, she admitted, "It's hard to let them fail."

THE WEBSITE WAS AN opportunity for Huffman to keep appealing to fans
who related to her *Desperate Housewives* character, and it also represented an
extension of her years-long search for input from people she deemed better
equipped at this whole parenting thing.

For six years starting in 2012, Huffman and Macy met with Wendy Mogel,
a psychologist and bestselling author who spoke about "raising self-reliant, less
defiant, appreciative children in a nervous world" and was revered in some L.A.
circles. Huffman once went to Mogel in a tizzy about planning summer vacations.

"I sat down in her office and poured out my plans, objectives and fears for
the summer, and also my inadequacies as the person in charge," she recalled.

Mogel was impressed by Huffman and came to see her as an unusually
sensible, grounded, anti-helicopter, and anti-snowplow mother.

Macy sometimes doubted Huffman's reliance on outside experts in parenting. "She's struggled to find the balance between what the experts say, and her common sense," he later said.

Yet Huffman felt justified after Sophia, by age four, had difficulty with puzzles and melted down because of a clothing tag or grass touching her bare feet.

The nursery school's advice, to get the girl into occupational therapy, made a world of difference. And when Sophia was struggling in school a few years later, Huffman again sought medical help, landing an ADHD diagnosis from a neuropsychologist at age eight. She started getting extra time on tests when she was eleven.

As college loomed on the horizon for Sophia, it seemed natural Huffman would turn to her friends or others for advice.

SOPHIA WAS A SOPHOMORE at the Los Angeles County High School for the Arts, a public school requiring auditions for entry. The family loved the school, though mothers of previous graduates warned Huffman the counseling office there was stretched thin.

Money could be tight at LACHSA, as the school is known, with a theater technical director collecting bottles to recycle in order to afford basics like masking tape. Huffman and Macy donated, hosted fundraisers, worked the refreshment stand at shows, and cleaned bathrooms.

Singer came highly recommended by multiple other parents, and Huffman hired the counselor in 2016 for Sophia. Singer also began advising Georgia, even meeting with administrators at her all-girls private school, Westridge School in Pasadena, when the younger girl was a sophomore.

He provided tutors for Sophia and began to assess her odds of admission at particular colleges. Huffman would later say he painted a grim outlook within months of starting to work with her: Sophia faced stiff competition at many schools, against others with ties far stronger than just having Hollywood royalty for parents. There were athletes, legacies, kids whose last names adorned the library and dorms, she recalled him saying. Although a school reported a 10 percent admissions rate, she recalled him saying, that didn't mean Sophia stood a one-in-ten chance of getting in. For her, a girl with no such ties and very poor marks in math, it was more like one in thirty or one in fifty.

Singer had already recommended that Sophia receive twice-a-week math tutoring. But, Huffman later said, Singer warned it wasn't enough.

A person close to Singer said the counselor truly thought the college admissions process was broken, from an overreliance on test scores to cryptic admissions policies. He didn't break it, but he felt he had some creative ideas to get around it.

Singer was also highly emotionally intelligent, which might have made him good at pinpointing, then exploiting, parents' fears with a brew of charm and manipulation.

He seemed to realize many well-heeled clients had a particular, deep-down nagging worry. It might be that their kid was a poor test taker. Or they hungered for bragging rights. Or had an irrational fear that life wouldn't work well for their children if they were shut out of the most prestigious schools.

He would then deliver the bad news: parents were not in nearly as good shape as they thought when it came to getting a child into college. He might grow curt and dismissive when parents questioned his judgment, and turn the questions on them: Why were they questioning an expert? Didn't they want what was best for their child?

He let them know he had surefire strategies for admittance and contacts at admissions offices. He never begged for business. He sat back and let his words sink in.

To parents, his message was clear: you can try this on your own, without me, but good luck with that.

AT THE MEETING AT Huffman's Los Angeles home on August 28, 2017, Huffman's lawyer would later say, Singer laid out several problems: regardless of talent, Sophia needed to boost her SAT score if she stood any chance of being admitted to a top performing-arts college; the teen would need to hit a score of 1250, or ideally 1350, to have a shot. It's unclear why Singer would have said that. He may not have known much about performing arts programs, or he may have simply been building up to his illegal proposal by setting the bar unnecessarily high.

That Huffman took this target as gospel spoke to how much she leaned on

Singer for even the most basic information that she could have found elsewhere herself. Several of Sophia's classmates were applying to—and ultimately accepted at—schools on Sophia's college list with SAT scores in the 1100s. Juilliard's website notes that it doesn't even require most applicants to submit standardized test scores.

But Huffman had come to rely too heavily on Singer as a main source of guidance.

"I felt an urgency which built to a sense of panic that there was this huge obstacle in the way that needed to be fixed for my daughter's sake," Huffman later said.

As Sophia began her crucial junior year that September, regular (for Hollywood) events distracted the family: pre- and post-Emmy parties and dinners, as Huffman and Macy were nominated for the TV awards, she for *American Crime* and he for the role of Frank Gallagher in the Showtime hit *Shameless*.

Then it was back to reality, and the looming SAT.

Huffman was still mulling over Singer's shady offer from late August, to "control the outcome of the SAT." She adopted Singer's legal recommendation, to sign Sophia up with a different math tutor for the start of her junior year.

Bit by bit, it began to fall into place.

On October 16, Huffman got word that the College Board had approved a request by Sophia's neuropsychologist for the girl to get 100 percent extra time on the SAT. The clinician had reassessed Sophia in June, before Singer floated his scheme.

"Hurray!" Huffman wrote, as she forwarded the good news to Singer and a LACHSA counselor.

Huffman knew the extra time could help Sophia by allowing her to focus, and to take needed medications during the exam. She also knew the accommodation gave Sophia flexibility on *where* she took the test. It let the crux of Singer's plan kick into action: having Sophia take the test at a West Hollywood testing center meant Riddell could fix her wrong answers.

On October 17, the same day Macy's episode of *Finding Your Roots* aired on PBS, Huffman texted Singer. She had convinced herself she was just giving her daughter a fair shot so that, as Singer explained it, the girl could focus on her grades and audition and not worry about the test.

She told Singer she wanted Sophia to take the test in December, at his test site. He needed to know: "Are we doing this on her own or with my help."

"With your help," Huffman replied.

THERE WAS A WRINKLE: LACHSA wanted Sophia to take the SAT at the school. The high school counselor wrote Huffman, instructing her to register Sophia for a Monday and Tuesday in early December. The counselor herself would proctor the test.

Huffman forwarded the email to Singer with a note: "Ruh Ro!"

They figured out a ruse. Huffman would tell the guidance counselor she didn't want Sophia missing school, so they'd arrange to take the test over a weekend elsewhere.

Huffman seemed untroubled, at least on the surface.

She and Macy visited their old stomping grounds in New York, posting pictures from Central Park and raving about a Broadway show.

On December 1, Riddell flew to L.A. The next morning, Huffman drove Sophia the three miles toward the West Hollywood College Preparatory School. Out the private cul-de-sac, down the hill with panoramic L.A. skyline views, past that hairpin turn and lush eucalyptus, sycamore, and oak trees. Soon the car passed a lively commercial district with yoga studios, ramen restaurants, fro-yo shops, hotels, and movie billboards.

Sophia asked if they could have a treat after the test, get some ice cream to celebrate.

Huffman agreed, but her head was spinning. Her moral compass briefly righted itself even as her GPS was pointing her to the corrupt test site. She knew what she was doing was wrong.

"Turn around, turn around, just turn around," she told herself. She didn't.

Sophia entered the modest private school and, after she emerged, Riddell went to work fixing her answers. She would receive a 1420 on the SAT.

On December 4, promoting merchandise for *Shameless*—the proceeds of which would go to Sophia's high school—Macy tweeted as his character, the deadbeat dad Frank Gallagher, "Best gift you can give your kids is neglect– prepares them for the future."

In February 2018, Huffman made out a check to the Key Worldwide Foundation for $15,000, payment for the test-cheating services under the cover of a charitable donation.

The same month, students at the Brentwood School, where Jack Buckingham went, were sounding the signal. The adults were off the rails. "If you would please stop asking about college every time I see you, maybe I can stop stressing out," a student wrote that February in *The Flyer*, the high school newspaper.

The admissions process could hold valuable life lessons about accepting limitations, advocating for oneself, and learning life is not always fair.

But parents sold their kids short, not always trusting they could handle failure.

"I think probably some people do view college admissions as a referendum on their parenting," says Tom Hudnut, a former longtime head of Harvard-Westlake School, another elite L.A. private school.

Since the *U.S. News & World Report* rankings launched, he says, "There has been a culture-wide neurosis bordering on obsession with where a student gets in. This has infected not only students themselves but to a greater extent in many instances, their parents."

The kids generally survived rejection better than their parents, even when turned away from their dream schools. They bounced back, he says, "while their parents donned metaphoric sackcloth and ashes" in despair. The parents often "had no faith in their children's resilience."

Singer provided legitimate services for Jack Buckingham, including arranging for test prep tutors, for more than a year. Jack didn't love all the extra studying, but his hard work paid off.

He took the ACT twice on his own in winter and spring 2018, his junior year, and scored in the 92nd and 94th percentile. Jack's GPA hovered around 3.3 or 3.4, a solid B student, but Jane Buckingham later said Singer had indicated that wasn't good enough.

Jack, a bit laid-back, thought any number of schools on his list would work. It wasn't hard to imagine him thriving wherever he went, given his two brilliant, well-connected parents. Buckingham herself had always told her kids they'd end up fine, that she didn't care if they went on to make money. As long as they were kind, that would make her happy as a mom.

But when it came down to it, Buckingham was now worried Jack would come up short, and it would be her fault. The fear was that the acrimonious divorce had heaped stress on Jack and caused him to stumble at school. "I needed to make myself feel like a better mother," Buckingham would later say.

Jack had loved Southern Methodist University the minute he saw it, and Buckingham liked it, too. The Texas institution had grown popular among middling kids from L.A. private schools, and it had a strong business program, smallish student body, and spirited environment. It checked all the boxes, and even had a program in sports management, Jack's passion. SMU accepted around half of applicants aiming to be first-year students.

But USC had also moved up Jack's list. He was torn about leaving L.A., having assumed the role of the little man of the house since the divorce.

Jane was conflicted. Jack would experience new things if he went out of state. On the other hand, Jack was a kid who did his best when he felt comfortable and safe, so maybe being close by was the right thing?

USC was a stretch for Jack. Buckingham, along with Singer, talked about having him attend a community college for a time and then transfer to USC. That was a fairly common entry point for USC. In fall 2018, the university accepted 1,448 undergraduate transfer students, nearly half from community colleges. But Buckingham would have felt like she had failed Jack if he went to a community college.

At some point, Singer went to Jane with an offer. He had this thing. He had some guides who could help Jack through the ACT at one of his testing sites. He could help get Jack's scores up. Something around the 99th percentile could outweigh his Bs in a way a score in the 94th percentile couldn't do.

Buckingham didn't let herself think much about it. She knew that this was cheating, even if she wasn't picturing a federal crime. She told no one. But it also seemed like a straightforward way to solve a problem. Singer was going to help make this better. She knew it was wrong but not *that* wrong, right? Jack would just get into the schools he was supposed to get into if she and Marcus had been better parents. If this was something she could do to make up for that, she should do it, right?

IN SUMMER 2018, JACK BUCKINGHAM was enjoying the last stretch of freedom before his senior year, when he would buckle down and apply to college.

He and his best friend, a classmate at the Brentwood School, had just started an amateur podcast about all things basketball.

"Hello, everyone! Welcome to the first episode of the *BasketPod* podcast," the buddy said in the show, posted to Twitter on July 12. "I'm gonna be talking to my *best* friend Jack Buckingham."

Top of mind was LeBron James signing a deal with the Los Angeles Lakers. "Jack. *What. Are. You* . . . feeling about that, bro?"

As usual, Jack offered a thoughtful take. Maybe LeBron was moving to L.A. not to win a title, but because he wanted a nice place to raise his family.

The young hosts would get so excited that they yelled into their mics now and then. They were, they wrote in an intro posted online, "just two 17 year old guys trying to have some fun."

On July 12, the same day the basketball podcast went live, Buckingham spoke twice on the phone with Singer.

"I know this is craziness," she told Singer. "I know it is."

SINGER AND BUCKINGHAM'S INTRICATE plan involved sending Jack to Texas in July 2018, following the same scheme as Huffman's daughter, only at a corrupt testing site in Houston.

Singer and Buckingham discussed the desired rigged score ahead of time, a 34 out of a possible score of 36 on the ACT. But the machinations hit a snag just two days before the weekend test approached.

Jack had been supposed to get sinus surgery the week after the test, but he was sick and there was no way he should be getting on a plane, the doctor said. Houston, they had a problem.

Buckingham raised another idea with Singer.

"So my question is," she mused on the phone with Singer on July 12, "there is no way for him to not go and it still to be done, I assume?" Later that day, Singer called back to okay the unusual plan: Jack could stay home and Riddell could take the entire ACT in Houston, in his place. Of course it was worse, but one could rationalize: by not traveling to the corrupt test site, maybe Jack would be less involved in the scam.

To allay concerns about tipping off the testing agency, Singer asked Buckingham to send him a sample of Jack's handwriting. This was necessary, he explained, because Jack had already taken the ACT on his own.

Buckingham was about to take Jack to the doctor's office and offered to send it along from the waiting room. Jack, then seventeen, was a trusting and believing kid, and a sick kid at the time. Suddenly there were so many moving parts around his ACT. The doctor, not knowing the test in Houston was a fraud, talked about writing a note for Jack to reschedule it. Maybe Jack could take it online, the doctor ventured, not knowing ACTs weren't taken online. So it wasn't that strange when Buckingham told the boy she needed a handwriting sample.

"To whom it may concern, this provides an example of my current writing style. Thank you for your attention," Jack wrote in a cramped chicken scratch.

Buckingham snapped a photo of her son's handwriting sample and attached it to an email: "Good luck with this," she wrote to Singer.

The next day, while Jack was in L.A., Riddell was in Houston, nearly acing the ACT for the teen and signing Jack's name.

But sometimes it's impossible to tell just one lie. Things spiraled out of control. Jane was determined to keep Jack in the dark.

She asked Singer to send a copy of the ACT so she could give it to Jack at home. She'd tell her son she'd gotten permission to proctor his test.

She sat him down at home in the small room where he and Chloe did their homework, and gave him the test. She monitored the room, timed the test, and took it away when time was up. She even put it in an envelope and sent it to Singer, as if going through the motions made it easier to digest.

On July 18 Buckingham wired part of her $50,000 payment for the bogus ACT score to Singer. When Jack's ACT results arrived, he saw a score of 35 out of a possible 36, and sounded proud when he called to tell his father.

Living with the secret wasn't easy. Jane got nervous that November when Marcus left her a cryptic note: "I just found out what you did and I'm so upset I can't talk about it."

She expressed her worries to Singer on the phone, noting, "the only kind of shady thing that I've done is the whole Jack thing." Singer assured her he hadn't mentioned the scheme to her ex. (It turned out Marcus had thought Jane blocked him one day from being able to call or text Chloe. Jane would say Chloe's phone was broken.)

Huffman's older daughter, Sophia, was in the thick of applications that fall as well. And Huffman was in knots over the lie. Singer reassured her she'd done the right thing using Riddell to boost Sophia's score. That way, the teen could focus on her auditions.

At the same time, Singer was providing an SAT tutor to Georgia, Huffman's younger daughter. But Huffman had given Sophia an edge. She wondered: Was it unfair to not do the same for Georgia, too?

17

NAME YOUR PRICE

I N 2016, HULIN GUO met a woman at a networking event at the Peninsula Hotel in Beverly Hills. The encounter would change the course not necessarily of his life, but certainly of his daughter's.

Qiuxue Yang was an analytics associate at Summa Group, the Oppenheimer wealth management firm where Rick Singer had made inroads years earlier. Guo wasn't a Summa client, but he was a wealthy businessman from China, and a relatively new transplant to the United States.

Yang, who went by Valerie, had come to the United States from China to attend college, graduating from Purdue University and then earning a master's at UCLA. At Summa, she did mutual fund research and, as her bio stated plainly, was "a great resource and connection" for Chinese-speaking clients. And prospective clients.

Yang began courting Guo. She invited him to a vintage jewelry auction and to a presentation on investment projects at the Beverly Wilshire Hotel. She provided translation services at the events. She asked about his family.

Guo opened up a bit, mentioning that his daughter Sherry attended a nearby private school.

Yang kept in touch. In early November 2017, she called Guo to again describe the opportunities a relationship with Summa could provide. She had one tip in particular, related to Guo's daughter. She knew an extraordinary college counseling expert who had assisted dozens of prominent Oppenheimer clients.

Sherry Guo, a senior at JSerra Catholic High School, had already completed some applications. But another bit of guidance couldn't hurt, Guo figured.

Yang emailed Rick Singer to get the ball rolling.

SHERRY GUO HAD MOVED to the United States from China in her late teens and lived in a tan two-story home in a quiet subdivision in Irvine, an Orange County city that had become a magnet for well-to-do Asian families seeking the American dream.

Sherry taught herself English after arriving in the United States in 2014 and attended JSerra, a private school where about 10 percent of students come from overseas and a large share aspire to play sports in college. A scrolling list on JSerra's homepage shows seniors' next stops: Notre Dame. Duke. Stanford. UCLA. And other usual suspects.

Sherry won regional accolades for her photography, comics, mixed media and digital art, and the principal of the 1,200-student high school knew her as "super talented" and an "unbelievable artist." She flourished in the classroom, too, becoming a student officer for the JSerra chapter of the National Honor Society.

But when it came to applying to college, her family was a bit out of its element.

BACK IN CHINA, it seemed everyone was in a tizzy about getting into a U.S. college.

Television news crews swarmed the school of a student who'd gotten into Harvard. At another school, teachers surrounded a student headed to an Ivy League school, angling for photos with the new local luminary. Countless businesses and secondary schools adopted the names of elite U.S. schools to confer prestige on their operations: Harvard Beauty School. Harvard Kindergarten.

Some observers traced the obsession with the most elite U.S. schools to the 2000 publication of *Harvard Girl Liu Yiting: A Character Training Record*, a book written by a Chinese couple and detailing the child-rearing techniques they used to springboard their daughter into the famous school known in Chinese as "Ha Fu." (Among the character-building exercises they tried: having their daughter hold ice cubes for long stretches.) The bestseller became a parenting bible and led to a whole new genre, with titles like *How We Got Our Child into Yale* and *You Too Can Go to Harvard: Secrets of Getting into Famous U.S. Universities.*

"Reading it during middle school was the first time I'd ever heard of such a place as *Ha Fu* and other 'Ivy League' universities," Zara Zhang, who made it to Harvard, wrote while at the university in 2015. "It helped me realize that if I aspire to receive the best education in the world, the United States is the place to be."

The infatuation grew as wealth exploded across the country. China had more than a million millionaires by 2013, and the high-net-worth families had plenty of ideas on how to spend their money. Gucci belts and Burberry coats with plaid popped collars proved they'd made it, and the same went for college as parents sought to heap privileges on their only children.

The number of students from China enrolled at U.S. colleges would soar to roughly 370,000 by the 2018–19 academic year, up nearly sixfold over fifteen years.

For a long time, a degree from any U.S. school served as a mark of distinction when young professionals moved back to China and looked for jobs. But by 2014, when some of China's own universities cracked the top 50 in the *Times Higher Education* world rankings, a bachelor's from Wichita State wasn't so sexy anymore.

Chinese families faced a particular challenge: they didn't understand what schools were looking for.

In China, results of the standardized test known as the *gaokao* drove college admissions. American and English universities looked at other things, like extracurriculars, essays about leadership skills. Terms like "liberal arts" and "holistic admissions" baffled.

Never fear, college counselors are here!

An army of consultants established themselves in Beijing and Shanghai and smaller cities, promising to help families navigate American admissions.

Many were U.S. educated and had decided their experience made them completely qualified to guide others as well.

They made it seem like everyone had a chance of getting into Harvard. In reality, almost nobody did.

Tomer Rothschild, who with his wife runs the Beijing-based Elite Scholars of China, estimates that just about two hundred freshmen from China end up at the eight Ivy League schools each year, the largest share at Cornell and Penn. They need superb English-language skills, stellar grades, and extraordinary test scores (think SATs over 1530) to even stand a shot at the brand-name programs.

Plenty of counselors were aboveboard, such as former admissions officers and staffers at American- or British-style schools in China. Their list of recommended schools would probably include some public universities and programs with more modest reputations. But they faced stiff competition from advisers making appealing but outlandish promises.

College consultants in China often used a pricing structure that differed from that in the United States. They might charge a modest amount up front, then reap a hefty bonus for entry to a top-choice school, and a still sizable payment for entry into a second-tier school. In those instances, the initial fee could be $5,000, followed by another $10,000 or $20,000 for a successful admission, depending on the prestige of the target school as measured by *U.S. News & World Report* rankings. (Those balloon payments could go as high as $150,000 for certain consultants.)

Alternatively, consultants might charge an initial sky-high sum, say $100,000, but offer parents a reassuring guarantee: a partial refund, often around 80 percent, if their kid didn't get into that top school.

Either way, the final price ended up between $15,000 to $25,000.

Many families had only a rudimentary understanding of which colleges were best. They looked for the top 5 or 50 on the *U.S. News* list. Terms like "campus culture" didn't really enter the conversation, unless the college counselor forced them in.

Parents also were a little fuzzy on how exactly the kid got in. Was it enough if families could cover tuition? Would it help if they dangled an extra payment or a donation? These were moms and dads who came of age in China in the 1980s, when they needed to know people to get what they wanted. Though independence was growing, this generation thought maybe that was still the way it worked.

Counselors would make clear that clients couldn't walk into an admissions office and hand over $1 million checks. They were strangers with no ties to the campus. U.S. colleges were supposed to report the source of major international funds to the U.S. Department of Education and fully understand where the money was coming from.

Okay, so a direct payment in exchange for admission wasn't kosher. What else might work?

ON A MARCH MORNING in 2015, Dr. Gerald Chow took the witness stand in a courtroom at the U.S. District Courthouse in Boston.

Early questions politely posed to Chow by a federal prosecutor revealed a successful family man, retired dentist, and part owner of a family-run jewelry chain in Hong Kong.

He was there to testify against educational consultant Mark Zimny. The trial didn't get much attention at the time. But it hinted at just how much control—and money—some families in Asia were willing to give to U.S. intermediaries in the hopes of winning admission to elite American schools.

Prosecutors said Zimny defrauded the Chows of $782,000 by persuading them to make donations to specific schools, through him—and then not passing along the money to their intended destinations.

The Chows wanted their sons to attend U.S. boarding schools and then prestigious U.S. colleges, and felt they needed help.

"The U.S. educational system, we totally unfamiliar with," Chow said, in stilted English.

Zimny sat at the defendant's table in a blue suit with a white shirt and purple tie. A former visiting assistant professor at Harvard, Zimny said he ran a business helping Asian students get into top U.S. boarding schools and colleges. He touted his connections to admissions offices and explained that since

U.S. schools were "prejudiced towards Asian applicants," the families needed to pay donations, and the money would have to go through established intermediaries like him, Chow testified.

Chow hired Zimny, and a written plan prepared for one of the sons described the end goal: Harvard.

Zimny did provide some legitimate services. He helped the teens land at respected New England prep schools. And he essentially became their paid guardian in the United States, attending school conferences, even picking up birthday cakes.

The arrangement blew up when the director for the school one son attended visited Hong Kong in 2009 on a fundraising tour. Chow wondered if she'd gotten the money he'd already donated, via Zimny. She said no.

A jury found Zimny guilty of scamming the Chows and in September 2015, a judge sentenced Zimny to sixty-three months in prison. He said at his sentencing that he was proud of his work for the Chows, but failed to properly manage expectations and accounts. (One of the people who wrote the judge on Zimny's behalf at sentencing was Jared Kushner, who'd gotten to know him at Harvard.) The government shut down Zimny, but he was hardly the only person capitalizing on the naivete and eagerness of college-bound families from China. A far more polished industry, the financial services sector, had moved full steam ahead into this space.

SINGER MADE THE ROUNDS at investment banks, even landing for a time on an official referral list for Morgan Stanley advisers.

"It was like he had the magic elixir that would get your kid into school," recalled Betsy Brown Braun, the parenting expert, who spoke with him at an event for another wealth management firm in Seattle.

But what drew Singer's attention now was a niche within that financial services world: advisers who catered to wealthy Chinese families.

The advisers' services included managing assets across borders, guiding on real estate investments, and more concierge-style duties, such as connecting clients to art buyers, divorce lawyers, and accountants. They would keep contact lists of experts across various fields.

Winnie Sun, who runs an Irvine, California, firm, had even helped clients sift through doggy day care options and negotiate a deal on a BMW. "Anytime something starts with a dollar sign, you can start with us first," she said.

Increasingly, clients wanted advice on how to pay for prestigious U.S. colleges—and how to get their kids into them.

MICHAEL WU HAD WORKED since 2015 at a Morgan Stanley office in the Pasadena Towers, a pair of gleaming tan marble office buildings in that city's business district. Off the elegant lobby sat a branch of China Eastern Airlines and a number of Chinese-speaking customers bustled about. Wu served ultra-high-net-worth international clients, particularly from East Asia.

Arcadia, a nearby community, drew the nickname the "Chinese Beverly Hills." Reading material in the lobby of Morgan Stanley's office included a local paper and a coffee table book about China.

Though Singer had been on a referral list the company passed around, he was off it by 2015. Wu learned of Singer from the manager of the Pasadena complex, who told him the counselor was "vetted" and had presented to high-level Morgan Stanley employees.

So when one client who had a daughter preparing for college asked for a suggestion, Wu recommended Singer.

The girl, Yusi Zhao, attended boarding school in the U.K. while her father, pharmaceutical billionaire Tao Zhao, and the rest of the family lived outside Beijing. Ultraluxury cars—Bentley, Ferrari, and others—sat parked by the house. Nearby test prep companies and admissions consultants advertised all sorts of promises in Mandarin, like a Chinese version of Brentwood. A storefront tutoring business posted a list of successful admissions: Yale and Brown for college, Andover and Groton for boarding school.

"Some people think, 'Didn't you get into Stanford because your family is rich?'" Yusi said in a video recorded before going to college in summer 2017, her version of the inspirational "how I got in" books so popular among striving Chinese families.

No, that wasn't it, she said. "I tested into Stanford through my own hard work."

That, and some of Singer's secret sauce.

Singer had tried to get Yusi tagged as a sailing recruit at Stanford, but it was too late in the cycle by the time he contacted the coach, John Vandemoer. Stanford still admitted Yusi, whose application referenced fake sailing accolades.

The Zhao family sent Singer's foundation $6.5 million in April 2017, which, the mother later said through a lawyer, was intended to be a donation to Stanford for things like academic staff salaries, scholarships, athletics, and financial aid. "The donation is in the same nature as those that many affluent parents have been doing openly to prestigious universities," she explained in a statement.

Michael Wu, the Morgan Stanley middleman, would later claim he was tricked, too. He'd say he thought the money would go from Singer's foundation to Stanford for those same benevolent purposes.

As Yusi Zhao navigated her first term at Stanford in Palo Alto, Sherry Guo prepped her own college applications in Irvine, four hundred miles south. Her art portfolio, high grades, and test scores certainly made her a strong candidate.

Sherry's family got to work boosting her already good odds.

Yang from Summa Group emailed Singer that November to say Sherry's father wanted to make a "donation" to "one of those top schools" for his daughter's application. A day after, Singer sent Rudy Meredith, the Yale women's soccer coach, Sherry's résumé and personal statement as she'd prepared them. They included links to her art portfolio, but he assured Meredith that he'd swap out those references in exchange for lines about soccer.

Within a week, Singer had sent Meredith an athletic profile describing Sherry as, among other things, cocaptain of a prominent Southern California club team. She actually didn't play competitive soccer. Meredith flagged Sherry as a recruit. In return, he received a $400,000 check from Singer's charity around New Year's Day.

Sherry's family paid Singer and his charity $1.2 million over the following spring and summer. Their lawyer, Jim Spertus, later said they felt comfortable making the donation after having met with Summa Group's Werdesheim, who they said vouched for Singer. Spertus said Sherry had wanted to go to Columbia or Oxford, but that Singer insisted Yale was the only option; the lawyer also said Singer claimed he was on Oxford's board, and knew the school would reject her.

Coming from China, where there was little free choice in selecting schools, Spertus said, maybe that line didn't seem so strange to Sherry.

She got ready to go to Yale as a soccer recruit, asking JSerra in June how to register with the NCAA clearinghouse, as all recruited athletes are required to do. It was a little strange, her principal recalled. But the registrar sent along the paperwork.

Sherry faked an injury over the summer to explain her absence from Yale's team.

18

"ONE TEAM, ONE PLAN, ONE GOAL, ONE STANFORD"

THE TWENTY-MINUTE DRIVE BETWEEN the boathouse and his house near campus provided Stanford sailing coach John Vandemoer time to unwind.

Most evenings he'd pull out of the Arrillaga Family Rowing and Sailing Center in his Volvo wagon and wind through the sprawling Redwood City, California, office park behind which the facility was tucked.

Stanford was his dream job and he often thought about how he could improve his team. He could run through logistics for the coming week's regatta and, of course, he could mull over fundraising, not any coach's favorite part of the job. His team always needed something, be it sails and ropes or uniforms or a place to stay when they traveled. And sailing wasn't exactly football—colleges weren't throwing big money at the sport.

But the drive was his time to stop thinking about all that. Vandemoer preferred to listen to the news or classic rock, with Van Morrison in heavy rotation, as he prepared to shift from his job as a coach to his job as a dad once he arrived back home.

He also might chat on the phone. Vandemoer was easy to reach, his phone number right there on Stanford's athletic department website. So it didn't strike him as odd when his cell lit up one day in 2016 with an unrecognized number.

What was strange: what the guy on the other end of the line said. Vandemoer had never heard anything like it.

. . .

VANDEMOER, THEN IN HIS late thirties, had been head sailing coach at Stanford since 2008, and he felt extraordinarily lucky to be there. He'd risen up fast, from leading the Chicago Yacht Club after graduating from Hobart and William Smith Colleges with a geology degree, to a spot as an assistant at national powerhouse St. Mary's College of Maryland. Then he headed the team at the U.S. Naval Academy for two years before moving west.

Under Vandemoer, Stanford sailing had rocketed from a pretty good program to one of the very best in the country. It had swept its conference in coed, women's, and team events every single year since 2010, and pretty consistently placed among the top ten at the national level.

Vandemoer was at ease on the water, having grown up on Cape Cod. He never quite outgrew his boyish looks, with a friendly round face, slightly crooked smile, and shock of dark hair, and preferred sneakers and a fleece vest over oxfords and a suit. He hiked and played plenty of sports. But sailing had been his real passion since childhood, when his pediatrician offered to sponsor him for a program at the Hyannis Yacht Club. Vandemoer showed real skill, but also an impressive focus on safety and the little details and rules of the game. "Competent and caring," the pediatrician later recalled.

He sprouted into something of an overgrown Boy Scout, trusting and loyal—maybe to a fault.

Sailing is largely self-regulated; eagle-eyed umpires aren't out in the water, watching over competitors and calling out rules violations. If a sailor runs afoul of regulations, say, by bumping into another boat, the sailor's expected to own up and take a 720, or make two complete turns with the boat, as a penalty.

Vandemoer headed up the appeals committee for the Inter-Collegiate Sailing Association for a number of years and was known for delivering the right rulings, even if they weren't always what the sailors wanted.

His former sailors recalled other teams aggressively involving umpires, and lodging complaints to overturn unfavorable rulings. Vandemoer urged his players to avoid close calls, anything that could even be construed as improper sailing etiquette, even when nobody else could see.

Vandemoer fostered a reputation at Stanford as a thoughtful coach who cared just as much about imparting life lessons as about winning. His team chanted their motto before every competition: "One team, one plan, one goal, one Stanford."

Vandemoer would allow students to miss a string of practices for an internship—and then welcome them back to the team.

He'd married Molly O'Bryan, who sailed at the University of Hawaii and ran a youth program right near the Stanford boathouse. She kept sailing competitively, too, winning a world title in 2011 and representing the United States in the London Olympics in 2012.

They had a son in 2016 and Vandemoer often spent his off hours on the floor at his home, playing with the boy and, two years later, his baby sister. It was in many ways a charmed life. His neighbors were professors and Stanford coaches—head coaches for most teams, assistants for football and basketball.

The job had some perks, like access to university housing and child care, and a car stipend. His salary sat at the high end of the range for collegiate sailing coaches, but still was a fraction of what the football and basketball coaches made. So he earned extra money teaching privately and taking on contract jobs running youth competitions.

The primary money pressures, though, probably related to his team's budget. Like other coaches, Vandemoer felt his job description required him to raise money for his program. (Stanford says fundraising is an ancillary element of a coach's job.)

Fortunately, he had taken the Stanford job after construction was completed on the new boathouse, a pink and tan stone structure with gleaming mirrored glass that the sailing team shared with rowers. And the team had gotten a new fleet of boats just in time for his first year.

But boats needed to be maintained and they wore down after eight years, max. They could be sold off for maybe 50 percent of their original price, but at $8,000 to $10,000 apiece, replacing the equipment still meant a serious undertaking. Travel expenses added up, too, bringing ten players cross-country nearly every weekend, nearly the whole school year. And then there were salaries for one or two assistant coaches.

Vandemoer liked to get to know the parents of his sailors, and hosted an annual weekend-long event with a parent-child race and banquet for seniors. Some parents did offer financial support for the program. But gifts also came from alums, or from sailing enthusiasts in the Bay Area.

Along with fundraising, Vandemoer had another challenge: filling out the roster itself. He needed athletic men and women willing to spend weekends away from campus and persist through a long season that ran through the fall and again all spring. And they needed to be damn bright, too.

"I was never the smartest guy in the room," Vandemoer would later say. "I felt so fortunate to work with student-athletes that were just so creative, just extremely intelligent people. It was a challenge for me."

USC was tough to get into. Georgetown, extremely hard. Stanford, though, was in a different stratosphere.

Just 4.7 percent of applicants for the fall 2017 entering class made the cut, 2,085 out of more than 44,000 who tried. By fall 2018, the admit rate was below 4.4 percent.

The perfect weather and stunning campus were just part of the draw. Stanford sat a few miles from the venture capital firms of Sand Hill Road, where investors looked for the next Facebook or Uber. The engineering and computer science departments were among the best in the nation, and the faculty had an embarrassment of Nobel laureates and MacArthur geniuses. Bay Area companies clamored to be brought in on classroom projects. And the football team was pretty darn good.

You needed to be close to perfect to gain entry to all that. Ninety-six percent of the fall 2018 entering class stood in the top 10 percent of their high school class; everyone was in the top 25 percent. Median SAT scores were between 1420 and 1570 out of 1600, and median ACT scores ranged from 32 to 35.

The odds, of course, rose for those who got the "pink envelopes" that tagged them as applicants who could bolster Stanford's athletic programs. The admissions office historically screened prospective athletic recruits before giving an athletic director a formal all-clear to have coaches mail out an application with a bright pink return envelope that, when mailed back, made clear to admissions this kid was from a particular pool of candidates. Now the process is digital.

Collegiate sailing doesn't offer scholarships, which actually gave Vandemoer a bit more flexibility than some other coaches. He could tag someone as a recruit without tying up any particular funds. Some college sailing rosters could grow to around thirty students, even though only nine or ten were needed for any given competition. Women always outnumbered men, as schools sought to even out athlete numbers for Title IX needs, and because races were either coed or all women.

Though successful sailors can ascend to the Olympic program, as Vandemoer's wife, Molly, had done, they really don't have much chance to make a living by racing. So college competition was it for these kids, lowering the stakes and upping the appeal of potentially more exciting activities outside the sport. "They were in it for something they loved," Vandemoer later explained. "But at the end of the day it was about their degree or grad school or their first IPO or whatever else was going to happen next." Attrition was inevitable.

Sure, Vandemoer signed up youth champions and Olympic hopefuls. And he got good prospects from club teams, including ones he coached. But he could also get creative to fill his roster. Some sailing coaches considered soccer or field hockey players, gymnasts, anyone who was a good athlete and had, as Old Dominion University sailing coach and Inter-Collegiate Sailing Association president Mitch Brindley put it, "some ability to tolerate misery." Not unlike what could happen in rowing.

Vandemoer would willingly sign on someone who'd just picked up the sport recently and seemed to have promise, or who had limited race experience because regattas were just so expensive. If he saw someone who was "hungry for it," as he put it, that helped when he sat down to decide who to recruit. "That's who you want, someone who's going to want to earn it every day."

THESE FUNDRAISING AND RECRUITING pressures made Vandemoer's ears perk up when he got that call on the way back from the boathouse in late 2016.

Rick Singer introduced himself as a recruiter, who helped college coaches find talent. He was referred to Vandemoer by another Stanford coach and seemed interested in learning more about sailing and understanding Vandemoer's particular recruiting challenges. He had a tennis background but wanted to expand into helping coaches in other sports, and fostered a deep network of athletic kids. Oh, and their families were interested in donating to the sporting programs that took their kids.

Vandemoer had never been contacted by a third-party recruiter before. Sure, it happened all the time in other sports. But not sailing.

Singer happened to be in the Bay Area and asked if he could swing by and chat in person the next day.

Vandemoer agreed.

Singer also approached six other Stanford coaches about potential recruits over the years, but, according to the school, none bit.

He and Vandemoer spoke in the coach's glass-walled office on the second floor of an athletics administration building on campus. The conversation flowed easily. Singer struck Vandemoer as respectful and "really engaging." They talked about the skill set needed to be a strong sailor. Technical skills mattered, but so did an eagerness to learn, comfort on the water, and a strong yet agile physique that could fit in a fairly cramped boat. Candidates with these fundamental attributes could always learn the nuts and bolts of sailing.

Vandemoer had spitballed for years with other coaches about improving the recruiting pipeline by creating some sort of secure database onto which players could upload stats and academic qualifications. Sailing didn't have a formal clearinghouse for young athletes who wished to put their names in the prospect pool. Vandemoer thought that was hurting the sport.

"If I could take the development piece and get recruits at the same time that I thought were going to help my team, I thought that was a no-brainer," Vandemoer later said of what Singer seemed to be pitching. "Now obviously that was too good to be true."

Jim Langley, a fundraising specialist, puts it like this: A coach has no background in raising money, no expertise in making an ask. Getting donations for equipment can be a daunting prospect. And then a white knight strides in, this one wearing a tracksuit. "Some glib fellow approaches you waving large sums of money," Langley says. "In the mind of some, it's tempting."

During that first face-to-face meeting in 2016, Singer said he had a particular athlete in mind, a girl who went to boarding school in the U.K. Singer had met her family by way of a financial adviser at Morgan Stanley. Her name was Yusi Zhao.

Singer's team built the girl a fake athletic profile, and he explained to Vandemoer that he'd ensure a donation went to the sailing program if she was admitted.

Vandemoer couldn't help—it was too late in the admissions cycle for athletic recruits—but the girl still got in as a regular applicant. Her stellar sailing record helped her land the spot, prosecutors would later say.

Singer's charity sent Stanford $500,000, care of Vandemoer, after the university admitted the girl.

The sum exceeded most of Singer's payments to coaches, and would go a long way toward paying for an assistant coach's salary and for uniforms and equipment, but it still paled next to Singer's take: Key Worldwide Foundation got a $6.5 million payment from the teen's parents.

Singer then moved along to the next prospect, a teen boy with another fabricated athletic profile. Singer asked if Vandemoer could support him, too—even though he really hadn't done much to support the first one. He said there'd be the "same outcome for both sides"—a cool half million dollars for the program—if Vandemoer flagged the kid as a recruit. He did so, but the "sailor" didn't complete his Stanford application and opted to go to Brown instead. The following May, Singer sent Vandemoer's sailing program $110,000 for the effort anyway.

In August 2018, Singer tried for one more. This Las Vegas teen had minimal sailing experience, if any. Vandemoer agreed to extend athlete-applicant status to her, too, and discussed with Singer the prospect of a $500,000 gift to the sailing team.

Vandemoer wrote to university officials in support of the girl, going off the bio Singer and his team had made up. She was "an athlete from other sports who converted late to sailing. She has the potential to be a really athletic crew for us. She lives in Las Vegas during the year and commutes to Newport Beach to sail."

That teen ended up not applying to Stanford and instead went to Vanderbilt, but Singer still sent $160,000 to "Stanford Sailing John Vandemoer" as a consolation and deposit on a future student.

19

THE SECRET'S OUT

A GUSTIN HUNEEUS JR. NEEDED to know: "Is Bill McGlashan doin' any of this shit?"

Huneeus, who ran Huneeus Vintners, a Napa Valley wine dynasty started by his father, had been a high-maintenance client for Singer: demanding, cocky, and concerned that other, wealthier clients were getting more attention.

And now here Huneeus was on the phone with Singer in late August 2018, demanding intel on others in his parent group—chief among them McGlashan, the founder of the $13.2 billion growth and $3 billion social impact investment arm of private equity firm TPG Capital in San Francisco.

Singer was pissed. It was part of his business model, of course, that many clients were going to know one another. Word-of-mouth referrals were his life-blood.

Robert Zangrillo, a Miami developer and investor, introduced Singer to Robert Flaxman, a Beverly Hills developer, in 2015, the same year that Atherton mom Elizabeth Henriquez passed his name to Davina Isackson. Isackson lived a few houses down from fellow Singer client Marci Palatella and her family, on a steep, curvy street in the hills above San Mateo. And Marjorie Klapper introduced Singer to the Sartorios, who lived a couple miles away at the end of a quiet cul-de-sac not far from Stanford.

But too much scuttlebutt could torpedo Singer's lucrative side hustle. For all his bluster and flexibility with facts, Singer ran a disciplined enterprise.

He relied on parents to adhere to finely honed talking points to fend off high school counselors or college admissions officers who might question, for instance, why a student in the Bay Area was flying to L.A. to take the SAT, or why a nonathlete was suddenly being recruited for a university crew team. They had to make sure the few teens who were in on the illicit plans didn't go chatting to friends about it.

Overly talkative parents or extremely curious school officials could ruin everything—and almost had in the past.

McGLASHAN AND HUNEEUS BOTH had kids in the class of 2019 at Marin Academy, a $45,000-a-year high school in San Rafael, north of San Francisco.

Just coming out of Marin Academy put the teens light-years ahead of most. Situated in one of the wealthiest counties in the United States, the prep school has almost limitless resources. The student-to-faculty ratio is nine to one. Students can participate in a two-year research program where they submit papers to peer-reviewed scientific journals. Still, as Marin Academy admits only 20 percent of applicants and doesn't calculate class rank or award A+ grades, it can be hard to stand out from the crowd of overachievers.

McGlashan's eldest son, Kyle, played lacrosse for part of high school, and Huneeus's second girl, Agustina, was just an ordinary water polo player.

McGlashan was a star of the in crowd. He sat on Marin Academy's board of trustees and was a leading voice on ethical investing.

He had plenty of relationships on which to draw for help guiding his son into college. He launched TPG Rise, the social impact fund, with U2 front man Bono and Jeffrey Skoll, a former president of eBay. McGlashan was a regular at Davos, his three-day stubble of beard growth suggesting a casualness that almost undermined his meticulous rundown of investment priorities and use of words like "colinear."

Though McGlashan tried not to talk much about the college process with Huneeus, he'd intimated to the other dad that he was on the up-and-up when it came to helping Kyle into college after hiring Singer in spring 2017.

Huneeus was suspicious. After all, by that August phone call with Singer, Huneeus was decidedly not on the up-and-up when it came to getting Agustina into college. He'd met Singer through a college friend, and the counselor made monthly home visits to talk about essays, tutoring, and other standard college prep matters. He'd been on the slippery side of Singer's business for months, driven there, he would later admit, by his own ego.

Huneeus was well-known in the wine world, a boldface name in trade publications and chair of the prestigious annual Auction Napa Valley, which raises millions for local charities. Huneeus was a devoted dad, making his four daughters breakfast daily, attending school conferences and activities, and often getting home for dinner, where the family went around the table sharing "two goods and a bad" about their day.

But he also may have had a chip on his shoulder, insecure about appearing as if he owed his success to his parents, Chilean immigrants who'd started the portfolio of wine companies decades earlier. Huneeus was painfully aware that, in his words, he drafted behind with the privilege of sharing his father's name.

He even implied to Singer that connections to a higher-up had helped him get into college. "I became brilliant later in life," joked Huneeus, who attended UC Berkeley and Northwestern's business school.

He told a Marin Academy counselor in fall 2017 that his daughter would not take the PSAT, which the school required, because she was profoundly distracted by recent fires near the family's Napa Valley vineyards. This ensured that the artificially high score on the SAT later wouldn't raise eyebrows.

A few months later, securing special testing arrangements, Huneeus told the high school counseling office that Agustina would be taking the SAT in L.A. because of a "long standing commitment."

That, of course, allowed him to transfer Agustina's test to the West Hollywood school where Singer had bribed the site administrator to let in Riddell, the corrupt proctor, who would fix the girl's wrong answers. Huneeus paid $50,000 for the service and, with a boost from Riddell, she got a score of 1380 out of a possible 1600, in the 96th percentile nationally. Huneeus complained that it wasn't high enough.

Now, in 2018, he was in talks with Singer to spend another $250,000 to falsely pitch the girl as a water polo recruit to USC.

Singer had told him the daughter stood no shot of getting into USC on her own, and likely couldn't get an offer at any of the top six University of California campuses. Maybe University of San Diego or University of Washington. No way on Barnard.

Huneeus was getting too talkative to others outside the need-to-know circle, emerging as a possible weak link in Singer's refined system of secrecy.

Huneeus gossiped to Singer about how McGlashan had portrayed himself as taking the high road: "He laid it out and he said, 'Look, I'm gonna push, I'm gonna prod, I'm gonna use my relationships, but I'm not gonna go and pay to get my kid in.'"

Huneeus didn't buy it. His continued angst over his place in the social hierarchy was not uncommon, and this illustrated why Singer thought he had plenty of demand for his illegal business. And his chattiness revealed a fundamental flaw in the scheme, too.

"Is he just talking a clean game with me and helping his kid or not?" Huneeus demanded Singer tell him. " 'Cause he makes me feel guilty."

McGLASHAN LOOKED LEGIT. The family used Singer for traditional college counseling like talking through the pros and cons of various schools and tutoring.

Kyle had a form of dyslexia and, a few years before working with Singer, obtained accommodations regarding where he took tests and how long he got to take them. After the family hired Singer, the son asked the neuropsychologist for even more time, "double time."

That allowed McGlashan to move Kyle's ACT to Los Angeles, to the West Hollywood school where Riddell could serve as a proctor.

That was looking a little less legit, though McGlashan's legal team would say it was moved to better fit the boy's schedule, so he could take the test before his school's final exams.

The two flew down in a private plane from the Bay Area for a December 2017 test date; McGlashan had asked his assistant to book a stay for the night before the exam at the Waldorf Astoria in Beverly Hills, with a dinner reservation at the rooftop restaurant.

Kyle was supposed to have two days to take the exam, and Igor Dvorskiy even wrote into his file that the test took more than seven hours, over two days. McGlashan's flight home left at 3:21 that first afternoon. Riddell later admitted to correcting the boy's exam answers after the ACT test. He posted a score of 34.

The following summer, Singer let McGlashan know that Huneeus had been digging for information.

"He was pushing hard, like, 'You gotta tell me what they're doing,'" Singer told McGlashan. "And I said, 'Listen, that's their situation and you know Bill's very connected, and you need to discuss it with Bill, not discuss it with me.'"

That was what McGlashan wanted to hear. He and Huneeus both knew the other was in touch with Singer, but that was as far as McGlashan wanted it to go. He already had the impression the guy was ham-handed when it came to subtlety, maybe even a threat.

McGlashan told Singer about how Huneeus had been pressing him for intel as well, but McGlashan hadn't bitten, telling the other dad, "Look, you gotta make your own call what you want to do."

Apparently, Huneeus was telling another family about the "side door" approach, trying to take their temperature on how legitimate a path it was.

"That worries me," Singer replied, adding that he had given Huneeus similar advice, telling him, "Listen, you are in a very competitive environment. You gotta keep what you do to yourself."

"Yup, yup," McGlashan agreed.

"It will blow up on you, no matter who you think you know, it doesn't matter," Singer warned.

OVER THE YEARS, SINGER had a number of much closer calls that almost brought the whole thing crashing down. Ultimately, he was saved by a few things: inertia, idiocy, and an innate trust by admissions officials and guidance counselors that nobody would ever even cook up a scheme as brazen as his.

Around the same time Singer was warning McGlashan to get Huneeus under control, Spencer Kimmel was gearing up to start his freshman year at USC. He attended an early orientation session that July with his father, and even got a chance to meet his adviser as he started plotting out what classes he might take.

That encounter threw Spencer, a pale boy whose freckled face looked younger than his eighteen years. Not because he was worried about a math prerequisite or concerned he'd end up with 8:00 a.m. classes. Rather, he was stumped by a question about sports.

"Oh, so you're a track athlete?" the adviser asked.

"No," Spencer replied. "No, I'm not."

"It has it down that you're a track athlete," the USC adviser pushed.

Unbeknownst to him, Spencer had been admitted as a pole vaulter, with a fake athletic profile featuring a photo of some other athlete and claiming Spencer was a three-year varsity athlete and a top competitor in California.

Spencer wasn't a pole vaulter. He'd cocaptained the Ultimate Frisbee team at the Bishop's School in La Jolla, a ritzy part of San Diego, and had been part of the school's mock trial team.

"Oh, okay, well, I have to look into that," the adviser said.

Elisabeth Kimmel, born Meyer, was a Harvard Law School alumna, and her husband was a former San Diego deputy district attorney. The couple's fortune came from Elisabeth's family's ownership of KFMB television and radio stations in San Diego. The Meyer family's Midwest Television sold the stations in early 2018 for $325 million. They had paid Singer's charity $200,000 for his work with Spencer, and $50,000 to USC, the checks coming from her family's own charitable foundation. They had also sent $275,000 in 2013, after their daughter got into Georgetown as a purported tennis player.

Spencer's parents relayed details of the awkward meeting to Singer a day after, uncertain how to keep the boy in the dark about the circumstances surrounding his admission to the university. Spencer continued to get messages about his athletic obligations. The adviser sent him an email a week after their first meeting, explaining the need to schedule classes around practices.

Kimmel forwarded it to Singer, who passed it along to Donna Heinel.

"I will take care of tmw," Heinel replied.

Crisis averted. If the USC track coach had been asked whether Kimmel was actually part of the program, or someone called his high school to learn more about his participation on the team there, the jig could've been up.

Singer was still safe, for the time being.

OCCASIONALLY, UNIVERSITY OFFICIALS have caught falsehoods. Even more rarely, admissions officers are the ones who find the lies, and more unlikely still is it for those lies to lead to criminal charges. It's almost an accident when that happens, given how much trust, and how little verification, there is in the college admissions system.

Yale once uncovered a scam only because of a messy split between a student and his ex-boyfriend.

The ex told a Yale administrator he knew Akash Maharaj had lied about his age and identity on his transfer application, and school officials began to dig deeper.

Officials tried to verify his age, but couldn't. They found that the dates he claimed to have attended Columbia, from which he transferred, didn't make sense or match what Columbia had on record, and his transcript and recommendation letter he'd submitted were falsified. The paperwork also didn't mention NYU or St. John's University, other schools he had attended.

Maharaj pleaded guilty to larceny in 2008.

Around the time Yale booted Maharaj in 2007, Harvard admitted Adam Wheeler. He said he was a sophomore transfer from the Massachusetts Institute of Technology who'd earned near-perfect marks at Phillips Academy in Andover, Massachusetts; taken sixteen AP exams; and scored a perfect 1600 on the SAT and 800s on five SAT subject tests.

He was a stellar student at Harvard. But in 2009, administrators stumbled on myriad whoppers he told when he applied for Rhodes and Fulbright scholarships. They recognized his essay was plagiarized and summoned him for questioning. They then investigated, and everything began to unravel.

Wheeler had been a fine student at a public high school in Delaware. He didn't attend MIT, but rather had gone to Bowdoin College (using cribbed Harvard admission essays for those earlier applications) before being suspended for academic dishonesty. He copied writings from Harvard's own professors for his transfer application, and his recommendation letters were bogus. The source for much of his prose was a book of "successful" personal statements that had earned past applicants offers of admission to Harvard, published by the student newspaper. He also pulled from admissions guides like *Rock Hard Apps*.

A quick Google search and basic familiarity with the course requirements and grading methods at the various schools—too many courses listed one year, conflicting lines about where he was, when—should've busted Wheeler's plan a few times over. But nobody caught on until after he was already admitted. Rather than stick around for his punishment, Wheeler left Harvard and applied for transfer to yet more prestigious schools. Stanford admitted him, before learning of his legal troubles and lies.

Wheeler was charged in 2010 with multiple counts of larceny and identity fraud related to his admission to Harvard and the thousands of dollars in grants and awards won under false pretenses. He took a plea, got ten years of probation, and had to pay back the more than $45,000 he'd gotten from Harvard, then violated his probation by claiming on an internship application that he'd studied at Harvard.

BY LATE 2017, BELLA GIANNULLI was well into her first semester at USC, where she'd gotten in as a walk-on on the crew team, though she didn't participate in the sport. Her parents, Lori Loughlin and Mossimo Giannulli, were working with Singer to get her younger sister there as a coxswain as well.

But first they needed to get past Philip "PJ" Petrone, the codirector of college counseling at the private Marymount High School. A handsome Long Island, New York, native with a megawatt smile, he had years of experience with the college entrance process, having joined Marymount in 2012 after a decade in the admissions offices of schools including the University of Rhode Island and Whitman College.

Petrone, who worked out of a small office on the second floor, was affable and rules oriented and active in professional-development activities. An excellent listener, he diligently went above and beyond helping students with their college selection. He also had a quiet nature, and it would be easy to see how some parents thought he could be bullied.

And no doubt some of the parents got irritated after meeting with Petrone about their kids' futures. Petrone was a realist, and he'd be honest when he thought a particular college was a stretch or not the right fit.

Petrone had already had some questions about Bella's USC admission.

He had been on a routine call with someone from USC admissions back in March 2017 to go over a list of Marymount students who had applied that year. When the rep got to Bella, he mentioned the teen was flagged as a crew recruit. That was news to Petrone. He told the rep that he didn't know anything about her involvement in the sport, and doubted the claim. Then they moved on to another student, he wrote in notes summarizing the call at the time. Petrone tried to be thorough with his families, but could be a little more hands-off with those who hired outside advisers. Those who used private counselors could also put people like Petrone in a bind—colleges would call them to check on a candidate, but they'd be in the dark regarding what a kid had actually submitted.

Now, eight months later, Petrone was learning that the younger Giannulli girl, Olivia, was also aiming to become part of the Trojan Family crew team.

Again he had questions. Did Olivia really participate in crew? And come to think of it, did Bella? He worried their applications contained false information.

Marymount's senior class was only about one hundred girls, so Petrone generally knew who played what sports, and who was on track to keep playing in college. Olivia lived on social media. Wouldn't crew have been part of her online identity?

Word got back to Loughlin that Petrone was poking around, and she went to Singer for advice. It was mid-December 2017, and USC's subcommittee for athletic admissions had already conditionally approved Olivia as a crew recruit, but she wasn't officially in yet. She still needed to complete her formal application, and they didn't need any Marymount employee gumming up the works.

Loughlin asked Singer how they might finish that application without calling attention to "our little friend" at Marymount, meaning Petrone.

A Key employee would take care of it, Singer reassured her. His team submitted the applications, to USC and elsewhere, on Olivia's behalf.

Singer was aided by the gaping holes in the system, the assumption that kids are generally telling the truth on their applications, as well as the lack of time admissions officers have to question much of anything. High school counselors, especially those at pricey private schools, had little incentive to piss off overbearing but financially generous parents. What good would it do for a high school to have fewer kids land at top colleges? When Singer ran into wary counselors, they were often stopped by scripted lies, closed loops of information, and a lack of curiosity.

AROUND THE SAME TIME Petrone was wondering why the Giannulli girls had suddenly blossomed into college crew recruits, in late 2017, another curious onlooker was raising similar questions seven miles away at the private Buckley School.

Julie Taylor-Vaz, the director of college counseling, had spent time in Stanford's admissions office and had been at Buckley since 2012. She was known as soft-spoken but firm, an honorable "straight shooter," says Jon Reider, who worked with her in the admissions office at Stanford decades earlier, when Taylor-Vaz specialized in outreach to black applicants.

He remembered a time they were taking part in a big group discussion with other admissions counselors at a conference. Reider was apparently dominating the conversation. Rather than talk behind his back, Taylor-Vaz came over and just bluntly told him to his face he was talking too much and drowning out other people and viewpoints. It stung, but he was grateful for the feedback.

"She wasn't afraid to call me out," he said. "She had a backbone."

She would need it at Buckley, where parents didn't hesitate to go over the heads of staff to complain. A longtime Buckley football coach, for instance, said he expected prominent parents to make noise to administrators about his coaching style.

Taylor-Vaz confronted a strange situation in December 2017, when she spoke to a Tulane University admissions officer about a particular Buckley student. The student sounded intriguing to Tulane: an African American girl who'd be the first in her family to attend college.

Problem was, the application belonged to Lizzie Bass, who was known differently at Buckley. She was white. Her parents didn't just graduate from college; both had law degrees. Her father, Adam, had been a trustee at Buckley; was head of Buchalter, a well-regarded West Coast law firm; and had been an executive at Ameriquest Mortgage.

Buckley called the other universities where Lizzie had applied—Georgetown, Loyola Marymount, and a few University of California campuses—to see what version of the résumé they had gotten. Turned out that in the girl's Georgetown application she was an award-winning tennis phenom, one of the best in the state of California. All had received inaccurate information.

The Bass family blamed their college counselor, Rick Singer. They said one of his employees must've added those fabrications without their permission or knowledge. In fact, they said, the family didn't even know the log-in credentials for the girl's applications.

The family claimed they only learned of the lies when, as they described it, Singer told the teen to mention tennis if Georgetown happened to call. She'd refused, they said; they then uncovered more fibs and reached out to colleges to correct the record.

She ultimately got into Berkeley.

Georgetown put its tennis coach, Ernst, on leave at the end of 2017 and launched an investigation. The school found "irregularities" in the credentials and claims of two of Ernst's past recruits, both of whom were Singer clients. (It was clearly a cursory investigation; prosecutors say Ernst took bribes on at least a dozen fake athletes.)

Ernst made a nice soft landing at the University of Rhode Island.

MOSSIMO GIANNULLI WAS ALSO bearing down on PJ Petrone, the Marymount college counselor, who was still a potential obstacle weeks after Olivia received her formal acceptance letter to USC in March 2018. The girl was in— why fuss now?

On April 12, Petrone got a call from the front desk that Giannulli was downstairs and wanted to talk to him. This was unusual. Giannulli and Loughlin rarely visited Petrone.

Petrone went down to meet the father and tried to engage in polite chitchat as they headed up to the office: Had Giannulli walked or driven over?

"What does it matter?" Giannulli replied curtly.

Petrone responded that he was just making conversation.

"Let's not," Giannulli said.

Giannulli's confidence can come across to some as arrogance; he's known as someone who is used to getting what he wants.

Clearly agitated, he started in. What was Petrone telling USC? Why was this guy trying to ruin opportunities for his daughters?

His tone made Petrone nervous, and the counselor couldn't hide his discomfort. Petrone tried to explain that he had no knowledge of Olivia being a rower, but he was never trying to stand in her way.

Giannulli asked: Did Petrone know who his daughter was? And reminded the counselor he "knows lots of people." The exchange grew so heated that their voices carried down the hall and one of Petrone's colleagues came over to shut the door.

A person close to Giannulli said he recalled some details of the meeting, and what Giannulli told Petrone, differently.

In any case, Petrone seemed to stand down, sending a reassuring email to Giannulli that same day.

He recapped the meeting in a tone that an employee might use after being chastised for upsetting an important customer, to let Giannulli know he was providing an update on the status of Olivia's admission to USC.

"First and foremost, they have no intention of rescinding [her] admission and were surprised to hear that was even a concern for you and your family," he said, adding that Giannulli could confirm that with USC's senior assistant director of admissions. He had relayed to that admissions official that Giannulli had come to Marymount that morning and confirmed Olivia was a coxswain.

The language of that note was telling. Petrone didn't say *he* confirmed it, just that Giannulli did. He still had his suspicions and reached out to USC to relay details about the exchange with Giannulli. He also contacted others at Marymount to look for records of Olivia's or Bella's involvement in crew. There were none.

OVER AT BUCKLEY, DEVIN SLOANE would also run into probing guidance counselors. USC had admitted his son Matteo as a water polo recruit around the same time it let in Olivia, from Marymount, as a supposed prospect for the Trojan crew team.

That was a bit tricky because USC and Buckley had a close relationship. The university's admissions director had personally visited the high school in early 2018, giving a talk on admissions to parents in the wake of a recent grade-changing scandal. (A former head of school, James Busby, was accused of having raised marks for some trustees' kids—including Bass's daughter, who in June 2017 had a math grade changed to a B– from a C+. An investigation found Busby didn't go outside his authority in making the changes, for five students over five years, including for some without board ties. But families likely fretted college admissions offices would see Buckley on the transcript and assume As weren't earned the right way. Busby resigned in March 2018.)

That rapport between the high school and college led to things nearly unraveling for Sloane.

On April Fool's Day 2018, a guidance counselor emailed Sloane to get the final list of which schools had admitted Matteo. Sloane wrote Singer: What should they do?

Singer said there was no point pretending USC wasn't on the table, relaying that the Buckley counselor had already called USC and was questioning why Matteo was being recruited as a water polo player, when his high school didn't even have a team. Sloane grew indignant that Buckley would dare question his integrity and call USC to challenge his son's application. "The more I think about this, it is outrageous! They have no business or legal right," he told Singer.

Heinel put an end to the queries about Matteo. She told the admissions director that while there was no water polo team at Buckley, Matteo participated in a local club and traveled internationally with an Italian youth team during the summers. In fact, she said, the teen participated in tournaments in Greece, Serbia, and Portugal. His parents must have money since he was able to travel so extensively during the summer, she told the admissions director. "He is small but he has a long torso but short strong legs plus he is fast which helps him win the draws to start play after goals are scored. He is an attack perimeter player."

The admissions director thanked her for her assessment and said he'd pass a version of it back to Buckley "to assure them we're looking at this stuff" because "they seemed unusually skeptical."

Singer sent Sloane six suggested talking points to use in case Buckley continued its questions, including lines describing a friendship with "Jovan Vavic and Lisa his wife" and one about how Vavic "needs practice players and great teammates plus he knows we are a generous family."

Heinel had gotten Singer and his clients over this hump, but in a voice mail, she told Singer to get his act together and keep the families in line and on point.

They couldn't have "the parents getting angry and creating any type of disturbance" or "yelling at counselors," she said. "That'll shut everything," she said. "That'll shut everything down."

SLOANE ALSO HAD TO face an awkward conversation with USC's development office in summer 2018, soon before Matteo was set to begin school there. The office had reached out, likely wanting to cement a relationship with a new donor. Fundraising staffers there noticed his $50,000 gift to women's athletics, via Heinel.

A USC senior vice president had already contacted Sloane at least once and now an "underling" wanted to know the genesis behind Sloane's donation to the women's athletics program—after all, he didn't have a daughter in the program.

Sloane invoked his dead mother, who had been an ice skater, as the reason he made the donation.

Singer was impressed. "That's great," he told Sloane, hearing the story later. "You are slick."

20

ON THIRD BASE

WHEN LAURA JANKE CRAFTED the athletic profile for Spencer Kimmel, the San Diego son of media executive Elisabeth Kimmel, she wasn't sure what sport to put down.

"Pole vaulter," Singer had replied. "Find pole vaulter pics."

That sport requires strength, foot speed, agility, and a large dose of courage. Spencer didn't necessarily have those attributes. But Jancen Power, a student from the West Texas ranching town of Water Valley (pop. 120), did. Two years earlier, in 2015, Jancen, then a high school junior, had placed sixth in his division as a pole vaulter at the Texas state championships.

Sixth place left him disappointed. Jancen threw himself into his training the next year, long days turning into late nights. He overcame a bad hand injury. He practiced around his volunteer gig, feeding and shearing sheep. His father, a chiropractor, and his mother, a children's minister, paid for a coach, and twice a week Jancen drove himself ninety miles each way for the lessons. His mom always told him, "Character is more important than the accolades."

In May 2016, his senior year, his tenacity paid off at the state championships at the University of Texas at Austin. His entire family made the nearly four-hour drive, and it seemed like half the town came, too, cheering, "Go, Wildcats!"

Jancen cleared fourteen feet, winning gold, upsetting the prior year's top athletes, and beating out competitors from thirty-four schools in his division.

A picture of him clearing the bar, determination etched on his face, leg muscles bulging, was featured prominently on the sports page in *The San Angelo Standard-Times*. Coming from a high school with around eighty students makes it hard to draw notice and get a college sports scholarship. Most students at Water Valley High School go on to Angelo State University, twenty-one miles away.

Jancen secured a walk-on spot on the track team at Abilene Christian University. An academic scholarship helped with tuition, and he waited tables part-time at a steakhouse. His family was "working hard and paying cash" to cover the rest, as his mother put it.

That news photo of Jancen's best day as a high school athlete, a day that represented the prize for months of disciplined training, stayed on the internet long after the local paper was in the trash. It was still there on the web in 2017 when Kimmel worked with Singer to get her son into USC and when Singer directed Janke to turn the boy into a pole vaulter.

And with a few clicks, Jancen's years of sweat and sacrifice were stolen.

At selective schools like USC, admissions is a zero-sum game—as Singer told many parents. If one kid gets in, another is rejected.

The wreckage left behind by Singer's scheme included actual teens who lost spots, as well as accomplished students who had their accomplishments co-opted to plump up the portfolios of others.

Jancen didn't have USC in his sights. Nobody from around there thought about a private college in California with a sticker price over $70,000 a year.

And that's part of the problem. The affluent young beneficiaries of Singer's lies were already on a path to success long before they were wrapped up in illegal machinations. Some, like Spencer Kimmel, didn't seem to know what their parents were up to. But others were brought into the loop.

In fall 2018, Singer met with his high-maintenance client Agustin Huneeus and the vintner's daughter Agustina. They were discussing her college plans, but a comment she made stopped the chat short.

"When will I know about USC," Agustina asked, "assuming we do this water polo thing?"

Singer glanced at the father with a look that said, should I respond?

Huneeus signaled to Singer: go ahead and answer. Singer explained that the teen, then a senior at Marin Academy, should be accepted soon.

Huneeus jumped in with a warning for his daughter. "We're not going to say this to anyone," he told her, adding that she needed to have a "keep-your-trap-shut mentality."

The irony is that Agustina didn't need Singer's subterfuge. She likely would have fared well on her own. Her world was already expansive; beyond participating in water polo, she traveled internationally with her family and had spent a semester of high school in Spain, improving her skills as a bilingual speaker. Her family's Tahoe-area ski retreat was featured in *Dwell* magazine. Her older sister had gone off to Yale.

And her family had influence. Her father had been in talks with someone important who seemed poised to write her a strong USC recommendation—something this person did for only one applicant a year. Even Singer acknowledged her chances would increase significantly with that sort of backing.

And Agustina's grandfather had recently pledged to pay for half a building at Berkeley, something in the $5 million or $10 million range, Huneeus told Singer. That offered some promise, too, no?

In addition, she had huge advantages just by virtue of where she attended school. As at many elite private schools, an entire apparatus swung into motion at Marin Academy to manage the college search process, helping students choose the right classes and summer programs, research campuses, complete forms, prepare for tests, and meet deadlines.

Marin Academy families so vigorously traveled the nation visiting campuses that the school used to feature sample itineraries on its website.

Families barely had to leave the campus to get face time with college gatekeepers. Admissions officers from throughout the country swarmed the school to woo students and their parents directly.

Marin Academy's counselors did an admirable job of presenting families with options for every type of student. The school calendar featured visits from more than one hundred college representatives in the fall 2018 semester alone, the list ranging from Dartmouth (New Hampshire) to Wagner College (New York) to UC Santa Cruz closer to home.

· · ·

AGUSTINA HUNEEUS PLAYED ON Marin Academy's water polo team, but wasn't a real college prospect.

"You understand that [my daughter] is not worthy to be on that team," Huneeus had flatly told Singer about USC.

Yet that November, Donna Heinel endorsed Agustina before the USC sub-committee that votes on admitting student-athletes. They gave their stamp of approval and sent Agustina a conditional acceptance letter that all but guaranteed a final offer.

Somewhere, an actual student-athlete who applied to USC was denied that same glorious letter. The subcommittee, of course, didn't have an unlimited number of spots to fill. In the same academic year it approved Agustina, the panel rejected several student-athletes, including legitimate water polo players.

Agustina was able to slip in, though, thanks in part due to fabricated athletic credentials, which identified her as a "3-year Varsity Letter winner" in water polo and "Team MVP 2017."

The profile also included a dynamic action shot of a young female water polo player. Singer had urged Agustina to send a picture of herself, but after being nudged a number of times she still hadn't done so. So Singer turned to plan B, and the internet.

"You can't tell it's not her," he had assured Huneeus.

THE GIRL IN THAT remarkable shot was Shannon Whetzel, a standout goal-keeper for the water polo team at the public Ukiah High School, about a hundred miles north of Marin Academy. *The Press Democrat*, the daily newspaper in Santa Rosa, California, had run the picture of Shannon soaring out of the water to try to block a shot a few years earlier, back when she was a junior.

Shannon was known as uncommonly polite and diligent, a strong student who racked up the record for most saves in Ukiah High history and dreamed of playing water polo in college. But few student-athletes from Ukiah go on to play at the collegiate level, given the competition for spots and the tough time local kids had getting noticed by coaches.

Shannon played water polo for Santa Rosa Junior College, and later transferred to a different community college, hoping to make her way eventually to a four-year college.

Her path, with twists and turns, was common in working-class Ukiah. Though Ukiah High played water polo against Marin Academy, the two schools couldn't be more different.

The staff at Ukiah pounded one idea into their students: you can all rise to a place of success by sacrifice and hard work. Trade jobs and public service jobs such as firefighting were respected options for graduates, but they could also get to college, even the highly celebrated ones, if they put in the effort.

Still, what gnawed at Ukiah High principal Gordon Oslund was that a baffling "game" had flourished around college admissions, with players including SAT tutors and private consultants, and his students didn't even know the game existed or how to access it. The gap between haves and have-nots was growing, and his kids were on the losing side.

College-bound Ukiah High teens had to piece together patchworks of support: parents, teachers, public workshops on how to fill out the Free Application for Federal Student Aid to pay for higher education. Ukiah High's counseling office helped, but five guidance counselors handled 1,600 students, a ratio of one to more than three hundred.

A small percentage of Ukiah teens retained third-party college counselors, and almost no one hired the private test tutors or took the pricey prep courses that had become a given in affluent areas.

Maggie Flaherty, who would graduate in 2017 and become a local standout by earning a spot at Dartmouth College, relied on unpaid labor from teachers, and Maggie and her friends went to the local coffee shop with their SAT study guides to cram together.

One of the high school's biggest challenges was just making students aware of opportunities. Ukiah did its best, arranging field trips to area colleges, including UC Berkeley, Sonoma State University, and the local community college.

But Oslund wished colleges did more outreach to the young talent pool in places like Ukiah, where he saw bright students who had interesting lives that extended "well beyond the rigid AP track." Not many admissions officers swung by to court teens from Ukiah High. There wasn't a critical mass of prospects. They didn't have a track record there. It was too inconvenient.

And Oslund knew most of his students couldn't afford to tour colleges; local families often visited schools only after getting accepted. Those travel restrictions slammed shut the door on lots of kids who may otherwise have been considered, he worried, since schools tracked things like who showed up for a campus visit. Demonstrated interest, as it's called, served as a way for schools to get a sense of whether an admit would really enroll.

It seemed unfair to Oslund. He wondered, about colleges: "Are you gauging the level of interest, or are you gauging the level of resources?"

Fear of student debt, and even just paying for books and dorms, loomed large among Ukiah High students. So about 60 percent started their higher education at the local community college, often with plans to transfer to a Cal State or UC school later. Others went to the community college because they had been rejected out of high school by a UC school, and they simply didn't see private schools as viable options. Ukiah counselors encouraged kids to try for scholarships, but the price tags were still daunting, particularly for middle-income families who wouldn't qualify for significant need-based aid.

As one local teen, Lexie Garrett, put it: "Oh no way could I ever pay for that."

Lexie got a little help from her dad, a former firefighter, but mainly handled her college application on her own. Yep, just one. The teen, who wrote for the school newspaper, interned at a preschool, and worked part-time at a local gym, planned to attend nearby Mendocino College, and hoped to eventually transfer to a four-year school, to become a child psychologist.

The Ukiah High water polo star Shannon Whetzel was still plugging her way through community college, studying ecology, when Singer needed to create a phony athletic profile for Agustina. Shannon's long, light brown hair was conveniently covered by a swim cap. Singer pulled her photo off the internet and used it to pitch Agustina as a water polo recruit.

"You were plagiarizing a life," Oslund, Ukiah High's principal, said later, expressing what he thought of the Huneeus family and Singer. "These kids are trying so hard to make it to the next rung and you can just walk in and take it."

21

USE THE ODDS
TO YOUR ADVANTAGE

S OON AFTER THE 2016 season ended, Coach Rudy Meredith stood in Ray Tompkins House, a handsome Gothic-style stone building at Yale University named for a college football star of the 1880s.

The three-story building sat near the western edge of Yale's three-hundred-year-old campus, next to a gymnasium known as the "Cathedral of Sweat" for its resemblance to a house of worship. Meredith's sermon wasn't quite so reverential, though his tone was solemn. A handful of athletic department staff were also there to witness Meredith's address to his team, the Yale women's soccer squad. Downcast, he spoke haltingly as he confessed to undermining the trust of his players. Abusing his power. Putting himself before others, without considering the damage to the team.

Meredith had been exposed for asking his players to edit, proofread, research, and even write his papers in an online master's program at Ohio University. By this time, he had been at Yale for more than twenty years and was the winningest coach in the school's history, even if the team hadn't made any NCAA tournament appearances in years.

He probably felt more comfortable with a soccer ball than with a book, having been diagnosed with learning disabilities while at junior college. He was open about his academic challenges and made clear he felt out of place in Yale's hallowed halls, at least intellectually. The kids were whip smart, and even his assistant coaches at times had more certifications and credentials than he did. So Meredith had signed up for a master's in recreation and sport sciences in 2016.

"It would be really great if you could help me out with this," he'd casually suggest to injured players, a few months into his stint as a grad student. Benchwarmers on the soccer team soon became the coach's research assistants and ghostwriters.

Someone finally revolted and reported him to the athletic department. An anonymous complaint was also sent to Yale president Peter Salovey, and the HR office investigated, interviewing Meredith and some players. Eventually he came clean.

Now, he stood sheepish and emotional in front of his team, seeming genuinely distraught by the whole thing. His intention wasn't to cheat, he said, he just needed help. He didn't know how to do the kind of research the program required. He admitted his wrongs, begged for forgiveness, and promised to do better.

None of the players likely knew at the time that Meredith had something else—something much more egregious—to be sorry for.

Meredith, charming, handsome, and fit, had an illustrious start to his career and everything fell into place, professionally and personally. After playing for Southern Connecticut State University, he joined the Yale coaching staff as an assistant in 1992. He coached local youth teams in his spare time and married Eva Bergsten, then an assistant coach at the University of Hartford, after meeting her at a match between the two schools. (She'd go on to become head women's coach at Wesleyan University.)

Meredith ascended to the top spot at Yale by 1995 and earned his one hundredth career win in 2004, leading the Bulldogs to the NCAA tournament in 2002, 2004, and 2005. That third year the Yale squad won a record fifteen games, secured its first solo Ivy League title, and went all the way to the third round of the tournament. Not bad for a team that doesn't offer athletic scholarships.

Meredith was also a bit of a star when he coached for the Connecticut Football Club, a soccer program for high school players.

"If you had asked any CFC player who they wanted their coach to be, they would have said: 'Rudy!'" recalled one teen who played for Meredith in 2012. "He was the main attraction."

But over at Yale, the luster was fading. Coaching is the ultimate what-have-you-done-for-me-lately business, and Meredith was in a slump. After that 2005 peak, the team hobbled along with mediocre records.

By 2015, though he hit his two hundredth win, players felt Meredith was just mailing it in. He didn't bother much with skill drills or dissecting the errors from the latest game. He ran abbreviated practices that included minimal cardio training and often just turned into eleven-on-eleven scrimmages.

As one player from around this time put it, her "soccer intelligence kind of ended when I got to Yale."

Meredith meant well, players roundly believed. But he hadn't kept up as game plans became more sophisticated and collegiate programs more professional. He started to lose the respect of some of his players.

He was flighty, disorganized. His ideas were all over the map and strategies seemed pulled together on a whim. He'd see some stats about scoring in the English Premier League and suddenly change something fundamental, like the way Yale took shots on goal.

Before games, Meredith would deliver his version of *Friday Night Lights*–style motivational speeches, but they often came off as goofy and irrelevant. He once drew a picture of oatmeal on the whiteboard, describing his valiant quest to find the breakfast food for a past team on an away trip. One player thought: "I could see Rudy coaching eight-year-old kids."

Meredith did connect to certain players, pushing them to work harder and improve.

He seemed secure in his post despite his team's frustrations. He enjoyed a close relationship with Thomas Beckett, the athletic director for almost Meredith's entire tenure, which meant players' complaints to administrators always seemed to make their way back to the coach.

When Yale expanded its class size by 15 percent, Meredith saw a potential opportunity: more recruitment slots. As of 2013, the university handed out recruited-student-athlete tags to no more than 180 prospects. Meredith said in 2015 that he had between five and seven of those, but having more would provide a bigger margin for error, reducing worry about injuries or players who end up a poor fit. It would also deprive rivals of talent.

"If I have seven spots, I will recruit seven kids," he told the *Yale Daily News* that November. "If I only had six spots, that [seventh] kid is going to go play for another Ivy League [school], and we will probably end up playing against that very good player."

His team slogan, slapped onto the back of players' T-shirts, fit that sentiment: *använd oddsen till din fördel*, or, translated from Swedish, "use the odds to your advantage."

More recruiting spots could strengthen his squad. They could also help hide a fake.

Meredith had connected to Rick Singer via Ali Khosroshahin, who'd run USC's women's soccer squad and had strong connections in the small world of soccer coaches. A key conduit, Khosroshahin introduced Singer to others who could be persuaded to sell admission spots that nobody really paid attention to.

By spring 2015, Meredith had begun taking payments from Singer in exchange for flagging applicants as recruited soccer stars. Singer directed $250,000 from Key Worldwide Foundation to Yale Summer Time Sports in 2015, with an address on the Ivy League campus. That group didn't exist. What did exist was Summertime Sports LLC, a company Meredith owned that ran summer soccer camps and other clinics and was registered to his white Colonial-style home in Madison, Connecticut, near the Long Island Sound.

When Meredith confessed his academic dishonesty to his team after the 2016 season, he shared nothing about his far more illicit side venture—which went beyond just his involvement with Singer.

In summer 2017, less than a year after his team apology, Meredith approached the Los Angeles father of a rising high school junior with an enticing offer: I'll make your kid a recruit, for a fee.

MEREDITH MIGHT HAVE BEEN the first to acknowledge his heart wasn't fully on the soccer pitch anymore. As his reputation dimmed at Yale, he was fortifying his status as a top player in pickleball, a court sport that was gaining popularity nationwide. (Think tennis, with paddles and Wiffle balls rather than racquets and fuzzy yellow orbs.) He'd taken it up years earlier, a natural extension of a longtime tennis hobby and a way to feed his fierce competitive streak.

There was "a tennis Rudy, a soccer Rudy, a pickleball Rudy," in the view of Chigozie Offor, who met Meredith in their collegiate soccer days and stayed in touch after moving to Florida for law school. They had regular dates to play—tennis, basketball, anything with a winner and loser—when they visited one another. "He would just rip you on the tennis court, on the soccer field. But outside he would give you the shirt off his back."

Meredith made the rounds up and down the Eastern Seaboard during the soccer off-season, earning pickleball accolades and trophies, and even helping to run clinics at a Connecticut racquet club.

He and Eva bought a place for $125,000 in Fernandina Beach, Florida, at the northeastern tip of the state, in summer 2017 and planned a massive rebuild.

And then came another event that seemed to distract him even more: the shocking death of his longtime friend and assistant coach Fritz Rodriguez, in September 2017. They'd been roommates and teammates at Southern Connecticut State. Rodriguez became Meredith's assistant in 1995 and held that role through 2012. "He was the one that tried to keep me organized," Meredith told the *Yale Daily News* upon Rodriguez's death. "We were like an odd couple and he balanced me out."

Meredith told a friend around that time that he felt ready to move on from the school, and relocate more permanently to Florida, maybe continue coaching soccer at a lesser level and give more energy to pickleball.

Other things kept him occupied, too: he was working with Singer to "recruit" a Chinese girl who attended high school in California. Her forte was art; she didn't play soccer. But that wasn't a problem.

And then there was that deal he had going with that L.A. dad who wanted his daughter to attend Yale.

In some ways they seemed like the perfect crimes. Who was going to tell? Not Singer, who was in deeper than Meredith. And parents sure wouldn't want anyone to know they had paid a bribe. Right?

22

QUEEN FOR A DAY

In February 2018, federal agents wielding a search warrant descended on a seven-bedroom French-château-style mansion in Los Angeles's posh Hancock Park neighborhood.

The $6 million house, built in 1927, was near perfection: boxy, pristinely pruned shrubs, palms, and mature trees framing a tasteful taupe dwelling on a prime corner lot. Fountains. A reflecting pool. Chimneys dotted the roof, unnecessary in L.A. but still lovely to look at.

The family that lived inside—Morrie Tobin, his wife, Gale, and some of their six children—looked close to perfect, too. Ivy League bona fides for the parents and older kids; résumés that referenced top Canadian finance firms.

Tobin was a hockey star who'd been the most popular boy in his high school in Montreal. At age fifty-five, he still kept his compact frame in shape, completing the same sixty-five-minute swimming workout every afternoon at the palm-tree-fringed outdoor saltwater pool at a club near his house.

Tobin had a perennial tan, a thick mop of dark hair, and a broad, slightly knobby nose that hinted at past clashes on the ice. He was talkative and could be charming, a born salesman with a talent for schmoozing.

As a high school classmate recalled, "Every guy wanted to be Morrie Tobin. I wanted to be Morrie Tobin."

To some people, Tobin came off as a stereotypical Canadian who didn't flaunt his wealth, at least by Westside L.A. standards. He once offered up his Lake Placid, New York, vacation home to someone he worked with, refusing payment by explaining the house was otherwise just sitting empty. Tobin's family would make an evening out of grabbing dinner from the Kogi Korean BBQ taco truck, a roving vehicle that served up some of L.A. 's most popular street food.

But some saw a striver fixated on status symbols. Tobin seemed particularly adept at working into conversations, even introductory ones, that his was an Ivy League family: He had gone to Yale as a hockey player (though he wouldn't mention that he actually left Yale and finished at the University of Vermont). One of Tobin's daughters had already graduated from Yale, two more were enrolled, and a fourth had gone to the University of Pennsylvania, following in the footsteps of their mother.

Tobin didn't see himself as image conscious, but as a father who was extremely proud of his kids.

Tobin grew up in Côte-Saint-Luc, a suburb of Montreal, and graduated from a Montreal high school, then attended the Northwood School, a private boarding school in Lake Placid.

He and Gale initially settled in Toronto and started their large family. She worked as a lawyer with the real estate division of Scotiabank while Tobin became known as a banker and investor. They bought a beautiful multimillion-dollar home in a historic neighborhood, though they publicly tangled with neighbors after applying for a variance to expand it by 70 percent, to eleven thousand square feet. "A shocking disregard for history and taste," a neighbor huffed.

He eventually moved his family to L.A., a fresh start. An old pal said he lost touch with Tobin, and that some other classmates had no luck trying to get him to come back for a high school reunion. "The feeling was that he had burned a lot of bridges," recalled Montreal criminal lawyer Lloyd Fischler, a high school friend. Tobin disputed that assessment.

The Tobins enrolled their daughters at the Marlborough School, a ritzy and academically rigorous all-girls school where annual tuition now tops $40,000 and purple banners outside extol virtues like "honor" and "excellence."

Marlborough had educated the children of Hollywood stars and political big-wigs and regularly propelled students to Stanford and the Ivies.

THAT FACADE OF BEING a successful family, upwardly mobile from an al-ready high perch, was all about to blow up that February 2018 as agents combed Tobin's home for financial records, documents, and other evidence linking him to a scam to defraud investors of millions of dollars.

The U.S. Securities and Exchange Commission, as well as the U.S. Attor-ney's Office for the District of Massachusetts, was probing a classic pump-and-dump investment scheme, in which the conspirators artificially inflated the prices of stocks so they could sell them at a profit before they crashed.

Authorities suspected the fraud involved a motley crew of a few lawyers and an asset manager with the nickname "Rocket" who helped hide the fact that Tobin held large stakes in the companies. (Owning more than 5 percent of any public firm came with disclosure requirements, which put trades under more intense scrutiny.)

In 2017, the SEC had come across some irregular trading in a penny stock, Environmental Packaging Technologies, which made specialized shipping con-tainers. The probe pointed investigators to a sprawling global scheme that in-volved, among others, lawyers in Miami and Switzerland, a company that took payment for writing promotional material about near-worthless stocks to entice investors, and the British founder of a Swiss brokerage firm. And Morrie Tobin.

Tobin wasn't necessarily the most interesting character in the crew, but he was at the center. For years, the group had coordinated stock purchases, merg-ers, and stock sales on his behalf, while hiding the fact that he, along with an-other person in California, really controlled the vast majority of the stock. He generated $3.6 million in proceeds from boosting two stock listings with mas-sive promotional campaigns and then secretly dumping shares. It wasn't a par-ticularly elegant crime. One glossy mailer distributed to thousands of people touted a stock with the line: "Could be Perfectly Positioned To Put Up To 1,118% In Your Pocket!"

Once they were caught, the government said, the group launched a cover-up, including replacing names on paperwork and backdating client letters.

Some who knew Tobin well weren't that surprised. Even friends described the middle-aged dad as a hustler, almost as if it were a term of endearment. He was in finance, something to do with investing, but they said his exact role always seemed nebulous.

"He was spinning a lot of things in the air," recalled one mom who knew him through their kids.

To friends, he seemed tough and street-smart, yet a bit dense at times, too.

At the pool, even swimmers who liked Tobin wouldn't do laps near him because he was all over the place, kicking into other lanes. He would apologize, and blame an old hockey injury for messing up his stroke, and then do it again. "A bull in a china shop," one swimmer sighed one day.

SYDNEY TOBIN, THE YOUNGEST DAUGHTER, was part of a circle of wealthy kids who socialized with boys from the nearby Brentwood School and ditched a class trip to Hawaii to visit one classmate's family's private island.

She participated in class discussions and was considered smart, like her big sisters. Tobin said she used to come home from soccer practice and then stay up until 3:00 a.m. doing homework. Several times in 2017 and 2018, she even alerted school administrators to a problem she saw: her peers at Marlborough and elsewhere were paying a West L.A. psychiatrist to falsely say they had learning disabilities and needed extra time for standardized tests.

But Sydney also went on to be tagged "most likely to get a PhD without ever leaving bed."

Some people recalled Tobin trying to clear obstacles away for Sydney. Nessim Lagnado, a Marlborough science teacher, had Sydney in his eighth-grade Exploring Science class. Lagnado helped administer a placement test that decided which girls would advance to accelerated chemistry the next year. According to Lagnado, Tobin lobbied him to put Sydney in the class, even though Lagnado thought she wasn't ready for it. Tobin denied the account, saying Sydney was put in the chemistry class because she deserved to be in it.

Outside of Marlborough, Sydney participated in the ultracompetitive Southern California youth soccer club scene.

L.A. club soccer draws affluent families, and the politics and pressure around the sport could eclipse even the craziness of the private schools. Pitting one club's offer against another. Negotiating for starting spots. Scholarships for seven-year-olds. By high school, Sydney played for L.A. Premier FC, with talented teammates ultimately recruited to top programs in the UC system, Oregon State, and Davidson.

Year-round play and tournaments took families to North Carolina, Las Vegas, and even Europe, and moms and dads easily shelled out $5,000 a year, or up to $15,000 for the more elite clubs. Parents eager to get their kids extra playing time (and therefore extra exposure to college scouts) might pay $100 an hour for private lessons from coaches. College coaches at times got verbal commits from players as early as freshman and sophomore years of high school.

At Yale, the process was led by an assistant coach, but Rudy Meredith would jump in to close the deal. A charismatic salesman, he won over parents and prospects who visited campus with his excitement about the program.

He gave the same line to many: get a golden ticket. There are only so many spots on a roster, he'd say, putting the number at roughly six at each school. "If you get any of them, one of them, it's a golden ticket."

Earning one of those golden tickets the traditional way was a brutal exercise, involving endless hours of travel to tournaments and showcases and clinics and camps.

A niche industry had even risen up to market millions of high school athletes. Companies offered an array of services, some costing hundreds or thousands of dollars, to help families identify target schools and teams, create highlight reels, and decide on optimal tournaments to attend.

One parent whose daughter played on the L.A. Premier club team with Sydney felt "chewed up and spat out by the process." The girl met with coaches but fell short and ended up without a Division I offer. Another teen on the Southern California circuit had more conversations with adult men about her soccer game than she did dates with boys her own age.

Tobin's girls were stellar athletes. He said Meredith had recruited one of Sydney's older sisters and was doing the same for her.

At some point before Sydney's junior year, Tobin met with Meredith to discuss "where he was in recruiting" the girl. Tobin would later say that he was confident Sydney could get into Yale on her own merits.

But his behavior at the time didn't indicate that confidence. It's unclear what Meredith told Tobin about Sydney's chances, but the coach may have made it seem to be less than a sure thing. Because Meredith was able to solicit Tobin for a bribe.

Sydney was seen as good but not a star player. So in September 2017, near the start of her junior year, her teammates and classmates were fairly surprised to see her post a picture on Instagram, clad in shorts and a Yale sweatshirt. "So excited to say that i have committed to play soccer at yale," she wrote, two blue hearts accompanying the caption.

SOON AFTER THE FEDS traipsed through his house in early 2018, Tobin was on a flight back east. He walked into the John Joseph Moakley United States Courthouse in Boston, took an elevator to the ninth floor, to the office of the U.S. District Attorney for Massachusetts, and was ushered into a conference room.

He was there to negotiate what is referred to as a "Queen for a Day" proffer agreement, in which a witness tells prosecutors everything he knows about a crime in return for some limited legal protections. It's a typical path for white-collar defendants nabbed for fraud, particularly those, like Tobin, who are facing a potential prison term. If the information is good enough, prosecutors might make the person a cooperator and encourage leniency.

They only offer such arrangements if they think the individual has really good intel on others involved in the scheme, ideally the ringleaders. Tobin was almost like a franchisee of this larger operation, and the feds hoped he could help catch the bigger fish. Prosecutors believed Roger Knox, the guy known as "Rocket" who coordinated stock sales for Tobin's team, was doing the same for more than fifty public companies.

Prosecutors set firm rules for the proffers: Tobin would need to be totally open about anything that might make him a less than superb witness or trustworthy source for the feds to rely on.

Among those meeting with Tobin was Eric Rosen, an assistant U.S. attorney in the economic crimes unit.

Rosen, in his late thirties, had degrees from Harvard and Columbia. But he wasn't boastful and maintained an understated style: He reminded some colleagues of the TV detective Columbo. He had an impish grin, sported slightly worn suits and didn't care, and could sit quietly through meetings before blurting out something brilliant.

Rosen, who'd spent years interviewing hucksters and drug dealers, was well practiced in how to get the good stuff. Make the person comfortable, get the person talking, and never react too enthusiastically to anything the person reveals. He was known for finding the witnesses and evidence that no one else had thought of.

To get that carrot of a lighter sentence, Tobin needed to share with prosecutors dirt about the sprawling pump-and-dump scheme and its various tentacles, and help the government nab other players. He also needed to expose every secret, every wart, every detail that could be used to discredit him and the case at trial.

Authorities had Tobin's financial records at their fingertips, and they had a question: What was up with those payments, moving from Tobin in L.A. to Meredith in Connecticut?

Tobin came clean. He explained that he'd been engaged in a bribery scheme with Rudy Meredith and had been paying off the coach since the previous summer.

At a moment like that, a savvy prosecutor will maintain a poker face and calmly say something like, "Wait, let me understand." Then he'll listen as it comes pouring out.

Rosen played it cool in the proffer that March. But as soon as the meeting ended, he trotted down the hall to alert his boss, Steve Frank, chief of the economic crimes unit. This had just gotten much bigger than any securities fraud case.

Rosen didn't waste a minute if he had a hot lead. "He's like a dog with a bone," says Conor Lamb, who was an assistant U.S. attorney for the Western District of Pennsylvania when Rosen was a prosecutor in that office, before coming to Boston.

Lamb, who would go on to become a U.S. congressman representing a western Pennsylvania district, had just come out of the Marine Corps and was used to being around very hardworking, disciplined people. The two clicked.

After graduating from Harvard and then Columbia Law School, Rosen worked as an assistant district attorney in Manhattan and then clerked for a federal judge in the Southern District of New York before jumping to the private firm of Richards Kibbe & Orbe, where he became a point person on complex securities cases.

When his wife landed a medical residency spot in Pittsburgh, he could've stayed in lucrative private practice. But government service had an allure, and he became a federal prosecutor there, focused on drug cases, navigating gritty distributors, informants, and wiretaps.

His peers saw him as notably tenacious with an unusual ability to laugh at himself. Rosen cycled to the office in a suit, even in the winter, and always seemed itching to dive in, despite whatever misadventure he'd had on the way in.

"He'd have a scrape on his face and arm, and be covered in snow and ice, and already be talking about a case," Lamb recalls. "I mean, he was just determined."

Around 2015, he came to U.S. Attorney David Hickton and said he was leaving Pittsburgh. Rosen and his wife wanted to move to Boston to be near relatives and for her career as a doctor. Hickton picked up the phone and called Carmen Ortiz, then U.S. Attorney for Massachusetts. "I'm going to do you the biggest favor," he told her, as he referred Rosen to her.

In Boston, Rosen handled drug cases, then moved to financial crimes. There, he built the same stellar reputation: super smart and insightful, while never trying to be the smoothest guy in the place. He donned an old-school phone headset that left his hair tousled, and he'd walk into court wrangling an unwieldy stack of papers. Instead of biking to work, he now ran there.

Like Rosen, Steve Frank, the head of the economic crimes unit, was known for being ferociously smart and intense, with a good sense of humor, mostly dry. But he was more polished, with impeccable suits and shiny shoes and never a hair out of place.

He'd cut his teeth as a financial journalist at *The Wall Street Journal* and on the air at CNBC. He was astonishingly cool and confident, even as a cub reporter. One colleague remembered Frank's first front-page story; rather than break into a cold sweat or go drink heavily to calm his nerves, as many others do in that situation, he agreed to grab a burger and then, casually, called in to the desk to check on edits.

Former journalism colleagues recall him often chasing the ungettable story and actually landing it. There was no room for fluff in an interview with Frank. He was cordial, even nice, but made it clear he was well prepared and had a job to do.

A notable moment came in October 1999, on the day famed homemaking maven Martha Stewart took her company public and celebrated by serving fresh-squeezed orange juice and scones outside the New York Stock Exchange. By the end of the day, the share price of Martha Stewart Living Omnimedia had doubled, making her an instant billionaire on paper.

She appeared on CNBC to talk about the big day, and after some banter about how much piecrust a billion would buy, a host introduced Steve Frank, "who has some questions about your prospectus."

Stewart was beholden to shareholders now, and Frank, then only in his midtwenties, questioned her as if he were their advocate.

"I'm tempted to ask about recipes for jack-o'-lantern sugar cookies, but I'm going to actually stick to business," he opened.

Then he dug in: The company revolved around Stewart. What would happen if she got hit by a bus?

Her generic answer, about how hundreds of employees shared the same vision, led to more questions.

What about overexposure, he asked. "Is there a risk that viewers perhaps could have their fill, if that's imaginable, of Martha Stewart?"

He questioned the appropriateness of her company paying her rent for properties she owned. (She said the properties were laboratories for her work.) And how about her control of 96 percent of the voting shares of the company: "Are you responsible to anyone?" (She explained that she had that control because "my name, which I cherish, is on every single thing we do.")

His questions were prescient; the brand took a hit after Stewart was convicted of a felony in 2004.

Frank was on a fairly flashy career path, and *Wall Street Journal* colleagues thought he could have had any beat he wanted. It had bothered him as a journalist to report on obvious wrongdoing but not be able to do more than expose it. His longtime dream was to be a prosecutor and he left journalism to attend Harvard Law. He then went to clerk for a federal appellate judge, and on to a job at the white-shoe law firm Cravath, Swaine & Moore.

While in private practice, Frank married his best friend from college, Adam Berger. They had met as freshmen at Harvard—when neither was out of the closet. Frank said his husband had a calming effect on him, a helpful counter to his intensity.

Frank was an assistant U.S. attorney for the Eastern District of New York for four years before moving to Boston in 2012. Now he could ask the same hard questions he'd asked as a reporter, but he could dig even deeper to find out what went wrong, with the power of things like subpoenas behind him. And everyone would call him back. (He remained proud of his journalistic work and had framed pictures of early front-page stories hanging in his Boston office.)

Frank, though confident, was all too aware of the mistakes that can sink a case. He kept a Nerf gun, a gift from his rabbi, on his office windowsill to remind him. The memento came after Frank's ill-fated first trial as a prosecutor. Police had mistakenly destroyed the gun involved in the crime, so Frank was left with no evidence. The case crumbled. He'd do everything to avoid that kind of outcome again.

At almost exactly the same time that Rosen and Frank were starting to figure out that at least one parent and one coach might be in cahoots to rig admissions, another inquisitive mind was poking around, three thousand miles away.

In March 2018, someone emailed USC senior associate athletic director Donna Heinel with concerns about some walk-on players.

"Hi Donna," they wrote. "Here are a couple students whose high schools were quite surprised to hear they were being admitted as athletic recruits."

Among the students: Olivia Giannulli, whose apparent ascent to USC as a crew team member had seemed odd to the college counselor at Marymount.

The email's author also noted that Bella, the older sister who got into USC as a coxswain a year earlier, wasn't on the USC team roster. And they asked about tennis and baseball players who, it seemed, weren't exactly MVPs of their high school programs.

Heinel responded a day later. There was an explanation for everyone: A new coaching staff excused one. Nonsense high school sports politics cleared another. Crisis averted. For now.

AFTER THE MARATHON MEETING with Boston prosecutors, Tobin headed back to California, as a government cooperator. He'd been instructed by government handlers on how to play it cool while pulling more information out of Meredith.

In a series of phone calls, he and Meredith went over their still-evolving plan to exchange money for a recruitment spot at Yale for Sydney. The two had agreed on a bribe, something in the six-figure range, but were still negotiating the price.

Then on April 12 came the capstone meeting, the sting.

Tobin, at the government's direction, traveled to Boston from L.A., while Meredith came up from New Haven, supposedly to finalize the bribe to tag Sydney for the following year's admissions cycle.

It was an odd meeting spot, a $400-a-night hotel overlooking duck boats and tourist trolleys, a stone's throw from the New England Aquarium and buzzing with families and convention-goers.

The Long Wharf, a redbrick Marriott property, had been built in the early 1980s to resemble a cruise ship: long and low, and you could peer down from railings along the hallways to see the atrium and central meeting spots. The place was tourist central, with a Starbucks in the lobby and guests' waists occasionally accessorized by fanny packs from another era.

It was also where feds occasionally took snitches to help nab other criminals and occasionally run prostitution sweeps, so it was possible to spot some cops or a guy in cuffs on the way to the breakfast buffet.

The hidden video cameras, installed with court authorization, were rolling that April day when Meredith and Tobin finally agreed on a $450,000 price for the deal covering Sydney. Tobin handed over another $2,000 in cash as partial payment, as instructed by feds.

Then Meredith mentioned a name: Rick Singer.

Who? Rosen and the team, watching the video, noted the new player. *Let's look into him.*

As often happens in fraud cases, clues beget more clues, and an early tip turns out to be only half a loaf.

Rosen's team pulled Meredith's bank records and saw he'd gotten about $860,000 from this guy, Singer, in the years prior. They still didn't know what else Singer had done.

Six days after the Boston meeting with Tobin, Meredith got a $4,000 wire transfer from an account he thought was Tobin's. It actually came from the FBI.

The feds confronted him and he agreed to cooperate. Then he went down to Naples, Florida, to play at the US Open Pickleball Championships.

23

THE WIRE

R UDY MEREDITH CALLED Rick Singer around lunchtime on July 28.
"Rudy commissioner," Singer greeted him.

"What's up man?"

The banter flowed between the pair, who had been in one another's orbit for about five years now. Both were hypercompetitive exercise freaks in their fifties. Singer would threaten to whip Meredith in pickleball, while Meredith would joke about being a wingman who could help Singer find a fit, energetic girlfriend.

And, of course, both dabbled in the dark side of college admissions by hawking walk-on slots on sports teams to desperate and loaded parents.

"I'm in London," Singer said. "Working."

"You in London. Can you stay in one spot?"

"I can't because the posse will come after me."

Singer kept the joke running. He was a busy guy who couldn't get any rest. Everybody wanted something from him.

"I got people always chasing me, big boy."

People were chasing Singer, all right. Including Meredith, who had become a government cooperator.

The feds would carefully transcribe and label that call: "12:38:20 Incoming call to Rick SINGER from RUDY MEREDITH. Session 3706."

.   .   .

THE GRAVITAS HITS VISITORS right away in the contemporary ten-story red-brick and granite John Joseph Moakley United States Courthouse, with its sky-lit rotunda, carved inscriptions about justice, and glass back wall offering dramatic views of the harbor and downtown Boston.

A medley of high-profile defendants have played starring roles at 1 Court-house Way, from Richard C. Reid, a.k.a. the "Shoe Bomber," who pleaded guilty here, to mobster James "Whitey" Bulger, who got sentenced to life in prison here, to Boston Marathon bomber Dzhokhar Tsarnaev, who heard his death penalty verdict in one of the building's courtrooms.

Now the resplendent structure was home to a burgeoning probe into a little-known college admissions counselor based three thousand miles away in Newport Beach, California.

The U.S. Attorney's Office for the District of Massachusetts, headquar-tered on the courthouse's ninth floor, is one of the largest in the country. Glass doors open to a well-appointed sitting area that smells of leather. A Depart-ment of Justice seal dominates the blue carpet, and an end table in the recep-tion area holds a book, *A Patriot's A to Z of America*, with the name "Lelling" scribbled in blue ink on the inside cover.

President Trump had only appointed Massachusetts U.S. Attorney An-drew Lelling in December 2017, but Lelling had a long track record of unspool-ing criminal enterprises. The son of a Bronx dentist, he graduated from the public Binghamton University and then went on to the University of Pennsyl-vania Law School.

Lelling left global law firm Goodwin Procter to work for the Justice De-partment's Civil Rights Division in Washington soon after the September 11 terrorist attacks, then spent nearly fifteen years as a federal prosecutor han-dling immigration, fraud, and international drug trafficking investigations. A fit, serious-looking guy with a bald head and short-cropped beard, it wasn't hard to imagine Lelling staring down a kingpin.

In his late forties, Lelling was known as a likeable, skilled trial lawyer with a sharp wit and an ample ego, not unlike many prosecutors who stand up and represent the United States in court. He didn't hang out much for after-work drinks, instead heading home to his family—two kids and his wife, a former prosecutor who was now a state juvenile judge. But you couldn't miss the boisterous and well-caffeinated Lelling at the office, where his phone conversations traveled down the hall. Unlike other "line AUSAs," as workaday federal prosecutors are called, he rarely wore a suit or even a sport coat unless he had to go to court.

Lelling, known as a conservative, had generally drawn bipartisan support in his role as the U.S. Attorney. In the elevated position, he wore a suit every day and worked out of a soundproof office off a long hallway lined with photos of notable past U.S. Attorneys.

Big windows gave Lelling panoramic water views stretching to East Boston and Logan Airport, even a glimpse of the USS *Constitution* on its occasional turnaround trip in Boston Harbor. That soothing view was welcome. If Lelling was doing his job right, he would almost certainly ruffle some feathers.

ONE OF THE MOST POWERFUL—AND controversial—tools that investigators have is a wiretap. Congress passed a law in 1968 allowing it in federal courts, and it was seen as a crucial way to bring down organized crime. It has since been used in an array of crimes, including economic offenses and drug rings. The technology allows them to listen in on calls made by unknowing suspected criminals, catching them planning illegal deals in their own voices. The recorded evidence is extremely compelling to a jury. But it's such an invasion of privacy that courts wield very close control over the process.

Investigators must file applications and affidavits setting out probable cause for why someone's phone should be tapped, showing they've exhausted all other methods of obtaining the needed information. A deputy in the local U.S. Attorney's Office sends the paperwork to the Department of Justice; if endorsed there, it goes to a judge, who grants final approval with intense conditions.

Rosen had seen how effective wiretaps could be from his days prosecuting heroin traffickers in the U.S. Attorney's Office in Pittsburgh. Someone saying

"I'll sell you the heroin" or "We want to pay you to kill this guy" in their own words is just about the best evidence an investigator can get to prove wrongdoing and intent.

RUDY MEREDITH HAD TURNED government cooperator in April. He didn't know much of what was going on outside of his own alliance with Singer, and neither did Boston prosecutors. But they did have a corrupt coach at one of the nation's most selective colleges. They also had a wealthy parent who'd found a way to cheat the system. They knew how valuable a college spot could be, and how hard many kids worked to get them. They wanted to know how deep the rot went.

Rosen and his team planned to deploy Meredith, the Yale coach, to make calls that would lay the foundation for federal authorities to get a wiretap of Singer.

Meredith began making recorded calls to Singer in California. The college counselor quickly revealed that the scam went far beyond a single bribe paid to a single coach for a single parent. He just didn't know he was giving away his secrets. In a May call, for instance, Singer sought Meredith's help enlisting more coaches to sign on to his bribery scheme. Singer had long run a sort of multilevel marketing model, encouraging coaches to bring in their wayward peers. He sometimes even paid a finder's fee for successful matches.

On the call, he advised Meredith on how to make the pitch. Singer ticked off seven elite schools and suggested Meredith relay that Singer was already working at those esteemed places.

"Okay." Meredith played along. "Yeah it definitely would make them feel more comfortable, with all those places."

"Different programs at every school," Singer added.

By June 5, prosecutors had enough material from those Meredith calls to prove the need for a federal court-authorized wiretap of Singer's cell phone. It wasn't carte blanche. They'd have to re-up it every thirty days with lengthy court filings showing the judge that it was still yielding pertinent material. Prosecutors are constantly back and forth with agents, providing significant manpower on the ground level. A shift at a listening post is spent eavesdropping on phone calls, tuning out when the call is obviously unrelated to a crime. After eight hours, the agents can be flat-out exhausted, worn down by boredom. Then the next shift comes in. They listen all day, every day.

And sometimes, they strike gold.

LATE MORNING JUNE 15, Singer took a call from a potential client, a bigwig from New York. A third person on the call—the guy who connected Singer and the prospect—primed the pump a bit, introducing Singer as "the Godfather" as he patched them all together.

Singer's opening line fell flat. "Is this Gordon Gekko of Wall Street?"

"No," came the reply. "It's Gordon Caplan, how are you?"

Caplan wasn't in a joking mood. He apologized to Singer for being so direct, but he wanted to talk about college and his daughter, a ranked tennis player who wanted to keep up the sport in college, maybe even at a Division I program. Federal authorities looking at the transcript later must have been trading high-fives.

From the outside, "Gordie" Caplan appeared unflappable and unstoppable. He exuded cool confidence, with his brisk athletic stride, booming laugh, friendly face, and straightforward manner. It got him far in his field. Willkie Farr & Gallagher, a major global law firm, counted on Caplan, a cochairman and rainmaker there, to navigate high-level corporate negotiations like private equity financing deals, leveraged buyouts, and acquisitions.

He brought the same zeal to his personal life with his wife, Amy, daughter of the late cable and telecommunications entrepreneur Richard Treibick (whose Hamptons estate sold for $35 million in 2014).

Dozens of family photos adorned his New York office. Caplan doted on his two kids: he traveled to tournaments to watch his teenage daughter, a skilled tennis player, and coached his son's flag football team in their hometown of Greenwich, Connecticut.

Now fifty-two, Caplan had checked every box as he rose up the ladder. The son of a successful obstetrician, he'd attended the selective Trinity School in

Manhattan, earned a degree from Cornell, and then graduated near the top of his class at Fordham Law School.

Caplan could use his influence for good. He told administrative staff to work from home if their kids needed them; family came first. He marshaled Willkie's legal forces to go to court to help an Iranian child he heard about through a Fordham Law connection get to the United States for eye surgery during President Trump's 2017 travel ban.

And notably, he championed colleagues and others who didn't have the wealth and pedigree he did. Integrity and hard work, he assured younger associates, would take you further than anything else.

But for all his strengths, Caplan had a weak spot: his own ambitions for his children.

THE CAPLANS HAD ALREADY been approached by an array of private consultants who claimed knowledge about the collegiate recruiting process, and had interviewed at least a half dozen of these counselors. The professionals kept dishing out the same discouraging news: the daughter, who took high school classes online as she traveled for tournaments and training, needed more AP courses, and more standardized tests. Some of these self-appointed experts said she'd only get in by making up some adversity, using a third party to write essays for her, or letting schools know the family could donate to the athletic programs.

The whole system seemed shady to the Caplans. As Amy put it, "Gordon and I panicked."

The couple signed on with Scott Treibly, the former college placement adviser at IMG who'd also been a United States Tennis Association consultant off and on since 2016. Treibly by that time ran his own college counseling firm, and his message wasn't much different. He introduced the family to a longtime contact; Rick Singer could solve all these issues.

Singer seemed slick, but also knowledgeable and legit. He talked about things like stance and the value of having the girl play more doubles tennis. And he clearly had connections—Gordon Ernst spoke favorably of him, and

Singer arranged a tour with Donna Heinel at USC on short notice. Singer had the right résumé. The guy did say he ran a $290 million company and employed nearly 1,300 people worldwide. He also had a sixth sense for knowing when someone wanted an extra push.

On June 15, the court-authorized wiretap intercepted two calls between him and Singer in which Singer essentially laid out his entire menu of illicit add-ons and extras. He was matter-of-fact, like a car salesman walking a customer through the lot: you've got your sunroof here; this little baby's got power steering, automatic locks, and a satellite radio. "What we do is we help the wealthiest families in the U.S. get their kids into school," Singer explained. "They want guarantees, they want this thing done."

He gave a quick primer on his "side door," explaining how that was different from the old "back door" way of giving donations and getting maybe a second look, but certainly no guarantee. He'd done hundreds of side doors, he told Caplan.

Caplan was already familiar with the back door, having endowed scholarships in his late mother's name at Fordham Law and his undergraduate alma mater, Cornell. The idea that a donation to a team could make a kid on the cusp more attractive made sense.

Though Singer called the $750,000 gift to Cornell "diddly dink" as a tool to get noticed by a university, Caplan didn't bite on the side door as Singer ultimately laid it out. (Singer recommended a $1 million payment to Yale's Rudy Meredith.) Whoa, whoa, whoa, Caplan would reply. Wrong sport. Also, where is the check going? He took a pass once Singer explained it went to the coach.

Singer moved along to the testing scheme, with a price of $75,000.

To add to the riches of intercepted evidence, Singer spilled how the scam relied on exploiting an accommodations process that is meant to help kids with disabilities compete fairly. His clients' kids would get tested for learning differences, be granted extended time to take the test, and move their test to one of his corrupt testing sites. Many wealthy families, he said, had figured out the loophole.

"So, most of these kids don't even have issues, but they're getting time," he told Caplan. Singer said Caplan's daughter would need to get tested, too, and would need "to be stupid, not to be as smart as she is" when evaluated by the psychologist Singer would set her up with. That would secure double time on the test. The daughter already got extended time on tests and assignments through her school, so seeking those accommodations for standardized tests didn't seem so strange. How they'd be used, though, was.

Caplan had a lot of questions about the logistics of the exam itself, but Singer reassured him.

"It's the home run of home runs," he told him.

"And it works?"

"Every time," Singer chuckled, eliciting a laugh from Caplan, too.

Six weeks later, Caplan and his daughter flew to L.A. to visit a few college campuses and meet with Singer's recommended psychologist.

AUTHORITIES DIDN'T EVEN HAVE to wait for Singer to dial out in order to catch juicy intel. Many parents walked right into the bait as they called Singer. Every recorded call seemed to shed further light on some corner of Singer's enterprise.

There was Marcia Abbott, of Aspen, asking Singer that June if he could rig SAT subject tests for her daughter. Abbott and her husband, Greg, were satisfied repeat customers, having already hired Singer to artificially boost the girl's ACT to a near-perfect score of 35. Now they wanted to nail those SAT subject tests for literature and math.

One afternoon while driving from Newport Beach to San Diego, Singer pitched a client on the side door, and explained what teens do after they get into college as made-up athletic recruits. "Kid doesn't have to play the sport," Singer said. "Most of the time, kid doesn't even play."

On the phone with Miami real estate investor Robert Zangrillo, and his daughter, Singer discussed how one of his employees was retaking an online art history class for Zangrillo's daughter, to clean up an F. His employees took at least some portion of more than a handful of other classes for the girl, too, including Intro to Environmental Ethics and American Government. She did do some of the work on her own, according to the invoices.

Zangrillo had a question: How about that biology class? Singer's employee, on the call as well, replied that she'd be "happy to assist."

Some clients were so familiar with Singer's menu of options that they talked in shorthand.

Doug Hodge, former CEO of the bond firm Pimco, emerged on a call in August. Hodge had already worked with Singer to get two kids into Georgetown and two more to USC, all as fake athletic recruits. Now he was looking to deal for a fifth kid, with Loyola Marymount University as the target.

"I know how this works," Hodge said. "We don't have to talk in code."

Singer was particularly simpatico with certain clients. He and private equity investor Bill McGlashan would one-up each other about their various enterprises.

"So we're now the largest education investor in the world," McGlashan boasted to Singer.

"We're opening 24 universities in China," Singer countered.

Singer had been hustling. He filled McGlashan in on other recent projects, including an addiction recovery program and a networking site for doctoral students.

"You keep entrepreneuring," McGlashan said. "I love it."

McGlashan and Singer stayed in touch all summer, even discussing potential testing accommodations for McGlashan's two younger children. And they went over the end goal for the oldest son, Kyle: admission to USC's Jimmy Iovine and Andre Young Academy, which specializes in arts, technology, and business.

Things were looking brighter for the teen. He'd become more motivated during his time working with Singer. His grades were up and his internships were going brilliantly. "It's amazing how he's changing," McGlashan said at one point. "I mean it's almost like his frontal lobes grew or something."

But McGlashan, whose academic pedigree included Yale and Stanford just like his own father, was still considering pulling strings to get his son into USC. He'd already arranged a lunch and campus tour with the dean of the Iovine and Young Academy.

McGlashan mulled over his options with Singer. Even working his connections meant he had to "play games," McGlashan pointed out. After all, he'd talked to a friend who said McGlashan would need to join a board and probably donate something in the $1 million to $3 million range to get Kyle into that hot interdisciplinary program. McGlashan worried the boy would feel weird about the whole thing, having his father take a board seat so soon after he got in.

"Okay, so, another way some people have done it, is, I told you I have a side door there," Singer told McGlashan, adding, "you would go through athletics."

That plan, pitching Kyle as a promising athlete without his knowledge for just $250,000 that guaranteed certainty early, sounded appealing. "I would do that in a heartbeat," McGlashan said.

But what sport? "I'm gonna make him a kicker/punter," Singer told McGlashan in a voice-mail message a few weeks later, in August. Marin Academy didn't have a football team, but Singer had a friend who ran a big kicking camp. They could say the teen went there.

A few minutes later, Singer and McGlashan were on the phone, going over the plan.

Singer would need a photo of Kyle, preferably one where he was exerting himself in a sport. "I will Photoshop him onto a kicker," Singer said, eliciting a chuckle from McGlashan.

OVER THE SUMMER, the federal government had intercepted more than nine thousand phone calls or text messages to or from Singer's phones. Plenty in the calls was ho-hum. Transcripts noted Singer bitching about traffic. Nearly six hours of calls deemed not pertinent were of Singer jawing with his family, and more than four hours chatting with women he dated.

Singer had no idea the feds were closing in, or so it seemed later to Cheryl Silver Levin, his childhood friend, who talked to him during that time with no idea that the government was after him. Decades had passed since chubby "Ricky" was trying to prove himself in Lincolnwood, Illinois. He heard Levin had been widowed and reached out over the summer, using her nickname and saying: "Silves, you're the strongest woman I know. You can handle this."

She spotted exaggerations in their banter—"the old Ricky is still there," she thought—but was happy that he sounded upbeat. He talked about his son, now a minister, and all his business ventures and successes. "He finally got what he wanted," she said. "He was on top of the world and he couldn't fall."

But the recordings left no doubt that prosecutors had uncovered an outrageous and widespread nationwide scheme to game college admissions. They knew millions of parents dealing with college anxiety would flip when they saw how these already privileged parents had acted on those anxieties. Lelling, the U.S. Attorney, was so struck by the extremes parents were going to that he doubled down, he later told *The Boston Globe*, on a message he had been giving his teenage daughter: Don't freak out. You are going to be all right whether or not you land at a prestigious university.

The case was the kind that boosts careers and gives a U.S. Attorney's Office a national presence; the kind of desirable investigation that prosecutors might want to keep for themselves.

Competition is strong for the sexiest cases. U.S. Attorneys are "ambitious publicity hounds," as Lelling called his peers, only partly joking. If a U.S. Attorney's Office gets the original tip, they may plant a flag, even if most of the dirty tricks are committed elsewhere, as in Singer's operation. Other districts can make a play for a case if they think it should be on their turf.

Boston investigators went to creative lengths to keep other districts from trying to lay claim to the James "Whitey" Bulger case, when the Boston mob boss was captured in Santa Monica in June 2011 after sixteen years on the lam. They instructed authorities flying Bulger back to Boston for his arraignment to stop for gas on an island, rather than in Florida, because a landing there could have allowed Miami to claim a piece of the case.

As the college admissions investigation secretly brewed in Boston, a person close to the case thought, "the Southern District is going to shit when they see this." That sentiment referred to the U.S. Attorney's Office for the Southern District of New York, which includes Manhattan and is known for being particularly aggressive in stepping on other districts' turf and taking cases for itself.

Some in the U.S. Attorney's Office for the Central District of California, which includes Los Angeles, jokingly called the Southern District "Fucking New York."

Arresting and flipping Singer in Boston would certainly help keep the case in Massachusetts.

. . .

ON SATURDAY MORNING, SEPTEMBER 15, Singer hopped on the phone with John Wilson, a client and private equity investor.

They discussed the outlook for his daughters, who Wilson said were eyeing extremely competitive schools. Everyone needed an edge for those places. "I'll make them a sailor or something," Singer told Wilson.

Wilson was a Harvard Business School alumnus and had given some money to the school. "Not a lot," as he put it. "A few hundred grand." Given his Harvard ties, what Singer said next must have sounded a bit impressive.

"I'm going to Harvard next Friday. The president wants to do a deal with me."

There was no such deal, no real meeting at Harvard. Singer had taken the bait.

The feds had Rudy Meredith, the Yale coach turned government cooperator, set Singer up. Meredith extended a made-up invitation to Singer to meet in Boston, saying he would introduce Singer to some contacts at Tufts and Harvard. Singer had apparently exaggerated, suggesting the Harvard president was on board, but clearly the sting was working. Singer was excited for the chance to meet insiders at top colleges.

By Friday, September 21, Singer was on his way to meet Meredith in Boston at the Long Wharf Marriott, the same big touristy harborside hotel where Meredith himself had been caught in a sting earlier that year.

In hindsight, the meeting spot might have been a giveaway that something was up. Harvard is across the Charles River, in Cambridge, where there are plenty of hotels.

But Singer walked into the trap totally unaware of what awaited. He entered the 1980s-style atrium, rode the escalator up to the main lobby, and then went to Meredith's hotel room, where he was confronted by three FBI agents and one agent from the IRS's criminal division. They were pros, having handled major fraud stings, and they meant business. They told Singer that they knew about his illegal scheme, and he initially pushed back, portraying his dark arts as legal. The conversation grew boisterous. His reaction, downplaying how crooked his actions were, was not uncommon. White-collar criminals often rationalize their misdeeds and have trouble thinking of themselves as lawbreakers. Singer would later say that while he knew asking families to make donations to college programs and paying coaches was wrong, as was fabricating athletic credentials, he didn't realize it was illegal.

Singer needed a lawyer, fast, and he got a message to his longtime friend Don Heller, who was in his office in Sacramento. Singer was still in the hotel, now being supervised by the FBI, when Heller called back. Singer sounded upset and scared; he realized he was in serious trouble. He quickly gave Heller a name to call: Assistant U.S. Attorney Eric Rosen. First Heller went on Google to look up Rosen. He wanted to know who he was up against. Heller was impressed with his credentials, noting a stint at the Manhattan District Attorney's Office, of which he was also a proud alum. He deduced right away that he would be talking with an experienced lawyer and a bright guy.

Over the phone, Rosen provided a cool summary of the case, enough to let Heller know that the government saw it as a big deal. Heller called Singer again, and quickly determined the government had likely been tapping his client's phones. The feds soon confirmed as much. Heller knew how strong that evidence could be.

Singer didn't become a formal cooperator right away, but he was now firmly tethered to the feds no matter which way he turned. Agents in Boston grilled him, equipped him with an old-school flip phone to communicate with them, and allowed him to head home to Newport Beach. Three days after his arrest, he was back in sunny Southern California, but his mind was lurching to a dark place. He called his half brother Cliff and filled him in on the FBI bust. He had a pressing question: What was prison like?

Rosen agreed to meet with Heller and Singer in Southern California later the following week. First, Heller wanted time with his client. "I was kind of shocked," Heller recalled. He'd known Singer as a successful, legitimate college counselor. Several people who knew Singer would come to think that somewhere along the way, his pathological need to win had caused him to go to the dark side.

In long meetings down in Newport Beach, including one over pasta at an

Italian restaurant where old mobster photos hung on the wall and Frank Sinatra music played, Singer described his elaborate and extraordinary scheme.

Heller listened, took copious notes, and got a handle on what he was dealing with: this, his experience told him, was a "sentencing case," as opposed to the kind of case a lawyer takes to trial. The focus would be on trying to minimize Singer's time spent in prison, by cutting him the best deal possible.

"What do I face?" Singer asked him.

Heller bluntly laid it out. Millions had gone through Singer's foundation for the bogus deals. That would bump the sentencing guidelines way up. If he didn't cooperate with the government, he was probably looking at fifteen or more years, even in Boston, which Heller considered a more lenient district.

"You have no priors; that's a good thing," Heller told him. "But you have huge exposure. So I think you should cooperate."

Singer agreed with Heller.

Within days, Singer and Heller were headed to the U.S. Attorney's Office in Santa Ana, in Orange County, to meet with a team of prosecutors and FBI agents who'd flown out from Boston. In a proffer meeting lasting three days, Singer, like Tobin, dished on what he knew in exchange for limited immunity. The government had come well prepared, bringing vast records showing Singer's illicit financial transactions around college admissions. Singer impressed them, Heller could tell, by being able to answer every question in detail without barely even looking at the spreadsheets.

They'd meet multiple times, over the next few months, in Santa Ana, Los Angeles, Sacramento, and Boston, and Singer would provide them with well over one hundred names of clients and others he said were involved in the scheme.

There were no headlines about the government's star witness. The plan was to get Singer to carry on as usual, just working as an undercover rat.

His other image, as a savvy businessman who dabbled in charity, seemed safe.

On September 26, just five days after Singer was nabbed in Boston, a "who's who of Oakland celebrities," including Golden State Warriors star Andre Iguodala, came to the grand reopening of a basketball training hub, which would now be called Soldiertown. Set in a small industrial strip next to a restaurant supply store and dog hotel, the place hummed. VIPs ogled the newly renovated courts as youngsters conducted basketball drills and a DJ spun music.

Mark Olivier, director of the nonprofit that had helped buy the four-year-old facility, addressed the crowd. His group ran the AAU youth basketball powerhouse Oakland Soldiers and had long been interested in taking over the facility for their activities. The sale had closed that summer.

Olivier told the crowd he and his business partner wanted to rethink youth sports, and identified his partner in this worthy venture: Rick Singer.

THE NEXT DAY, SEPTEMBER 27, Singer signed over explicit permission for the government to monitor his calls.

One phone pal the government would be very interested in: McGlashan, who'd been talking to Singer about getting his son into USC as a kicker or punter. Singer told agents that very day that he wasn't counting on McGlashan to do the side door.

But that afternoon, McGlashan texted Singer, asking, "How are you feeling on USC?"

On September 29, McGlashan texted again. "So when will we know definitively on USC?"

24

THE FINAL STRETCH

AFTER FLIPPING HIM LIKE a stack of pancakes, the feds sent Singer off with marching orders. His calls would be recorded. He'd wear a wire under his usual jogging suit as he made the rounds to clients. For the plan to work, Singer had to pretend things were business as usual, and not raise suspicions. No tipping anyone off, the FBI and prosecutors in Boston warned him.

On one of his early undercover operations, he arrived early at a client's home to see the mom drive away. And the student wasn't home yet.

He went in and told the dad, "You haven't done anything wrong yet, so please don't say anything that would be harmful to you guys."

Singer had flat-out confessed to the dad that he was wired.

The government's prime cooperating witness had just double-crossed them.

WHEN ROSEN, FRANK, AND the others in Boston found out what Singer had done they were angry—and nervous.

Singer, it turned out, had not leaked just to that one father, he'd tipped off a total of six families that October, during his first few weeks as a cooperator. He wasn't fully grasping how much trouble he was in, and he also felt bad for some of his clients. He'd alerted current and past clients to play dumb and deny, deny, deny if he called them and started rehashing old high jinks, because the feds might be eavesdropping. He'd managed to keep an unmonitored side phone, and in one case, he'd told Bill McGlashan they needed to talk face-to-face at the Santa Monica Airport because Singer thought his phone was wired. They never did meet up, though Singer did have an off-line conversation with another parent at a rental house on the beach near there, met another at a McDonald's, and spilled the beans to another in a car pulled over on the side of the road.

Singer, accompanied by his lawyer, had to explain his lapse to a team of prosecutors and federal agents. He told them he had disclosed the investigation to these families because he felt loyalty to them.

In Massachusetts, Steve Frank, chief of the economic crimes unit, braced himself to break the bad news to Lelling—who, as expected, was beside himself. He'd cautioned his team about this very outcome. Lelling wasn't taking any chances. Yank Singer back here and get him with us, he told prosecutors.

Cooperators can be tough to wrangle. After all, they're criminals.

Some are terrible actors and need to be coached on what to say and how to keep cool. Or they could have second thoughts about turning on others and decide to clue them in.

From the start, Singer made an unusual cooperator. Feds usually roll up, as the saying goes, not down. Pinching a lower-level guy allows investigators to work up the chain. An insider can provide evidence against another target and can buttress other witnesses and proof. The better the intel, the more likely it is that prosecutors will urge the judge to hand down a more lenient sentence.

Lelling had real concerns about flipping Singer, and the team debated before deciding he could be a valuable cooperator. Defense lawyers could argue all they wanted that Singer had hoodwinked their clients, but with parents on tape chatting up their own misdeeds, Singer's flaws would matter a lot less.

Yet the alliance between the feds and their key cooperator would still give some defense lawyers an opening to attack the investigation.

Just days after agreeing to work with the authorities, Singer, unbeknownst to his federal handlers, wrote notes in his iPhone about a "loud and abrasive call" with agents, in which "they continue to ask me to tell a fib" about where his clients' money was going. "It was a donation," he wrote, "and they want it to be a payment."

A judge would eventually call the notes, which came out a year later in a battle over evidence, "disturbing," and demand prosecutors to explain themselves.

The judge ultimately sided with prosecutors, who argued that Singer was initially a reluctant witness who wrote the notes in an isolated case of venting, before he was fully cooperating with the government. Singer later admitted that the early dispute was really just about terminology. He hadn't understood, until his lawyer explained it, that his quid pro quo deals with parents were in fact just the same as cold hard bribes—and very much illegal.

A FEW WEEKS AFTER his arrest, aiming to keep an eye on their key witness, authorities brought Singer back east for days at a time. He situated himself in a big leather chair in a harbor-view conference room at the U.S. Attorney's Office. He might be flanked at the table by three FBI agents and two prosecutors, including Rosen, and they left nothing to chance, noting the very minute they handed the calls over and listening in as he greeted his unknowing parents: "How are ya?" Someone even escorted Singer when he needed to use the restroom down the hall. He agreed to plead guilty to obstruction of justice, expanding his legal woes.

The babysitting, and the obstruction charge, did the trick. Singer, ferociously competitive, seemed to decide that if he was going to be a cooperator he would be the most prolific one the government had ever seen. He'd stride into the office, super tanned and wearing his swishy black tracksuit and visor; cordial and chatty, he'd get to work and bang out one call after another, often staying past 7:00 p.m.

His script couldn't have been simpler: Call a former client. Claim his foundation was being audited and ask for reassurance that the client wouldn't tell the IRS what their payments—er, donations—were used for.

The audit script is an oldie but goodie. No one wants to face scrutiny by the taxman, and the threat of some kind of government interview forces parties to try to get their stories straight. Inevitably someone says, "don't mention [X]," and blurts out the crime.

On each call, Singer would tell parents the IRS was poking into his foundation. That got their attention, since most of the clients had paid tens or hundreds of thousands of dollars for the test-cheating or "side door" schemes and then taken tax write-offs for those amounts.

Singer would explain that he had no plans to tell investigators what really went down, and urged parents to do the same—while deftly getting them to confirm the sordid details.

"I just want to give you a heads-up," Singer casually began one call with Huneeus, the Napa Valley wine magnate who had paid for Singer to rig his daughter's SAT score, now in talks to slide her into USC as a water polo recruit.

The government was asking all sorts of questions. Did Huneeus recall that $50,000 he sent to have someone fix Agustina's exam responses?

"Yeah, I remember," Huneeus responded.

"What I'm going to tell them is that you made a 50k donation to my foundation for underserved kids," Singer said, adding that *he* certainly would *not* mention the truth, how his corrupt proctor helped the teen take her test in West Hollywood.

Huneeus lost patience, as if offended that Singer didn't have faith in his ability to fool the IRS.

"Dude, dude, what do you think, I'm a moron?" Huneeus snapped.

Some were downright chatty. "So I'm in Boston now," Singer began in a call with Elizabeth Henriquez, a Silicon Valley client who'd engaged in his illegal scheme for two daughters.

She ribbed him playfully. He wasn't pronouncing the city's name right. Where was his New England accent? It should be Baahston.

Singer steered her back to business. His foundation was getting audited right now.

"Well, that sucks," she said.

But don't worry, he assured her. He wasn't going to tell the IRS Riddell had cheated on a college entrance exam for her older daughter.

"Right," she said.

Or how they'd paid "Gordie," Georgetown's tennis coach, to get the teen into that university.

She had a question: "So what's your story?"

Singer's script had a standard line about how parents had donated to Key Worldwide Foundation to "help underserved kids," "fund underserved kids," or "help fund underserved kids."

"Of course," Henriquez said. "Those kids have to go to school."

As the evidence mounted, Lelling was urging his prosecutors to wrap things up. It was his job to move cases along from investigation to criminal prosecution when they were ready. At some point you had to pull the trigger.

But Rosen and Frank were deeply invested now, and weren't ready to pack in the case. Workhorses with meticulous attention to detail, they were in the office day and night and weekends.

They were following hundreds of threads as they corroborated names and information provided by Singer and other cooperators. They found more witnesses, more conspirators, more evidence.

Lelling wanted frequent briefings, and the gatherings in the conference room next to his office could get tense. Lelling would hand down deadlines, only to have Rosen and Frank make a case about why they needed to continue digging, sometimes using PowerPoint presentations to highlight their evidence and where it would lead next.

Frank would go toe-to-toe with Lelling. Arguments could carry into the hall. He'd never been rattled by bosses; back at *The Wall Street Journal* years earlier, he'd deftly handled the super-competitive banking beat and demanding editors.

In the fall, Rosen and Frank gave a persuasive rationale for continuing the case: early-admission season was under way, when recruited athletes would be getting their offers. They knew Singer had pending deals with high-profile clients on both the sports and the testing fronts. Nobody wanted to take the case down half-assed.

Managers in the Boston office decided to put more lawyers on the fast-expanding case, which would be dubbed Operation Varsity Blues, though it took some work to convince Rosen and Frank they needed help or should parcel out pieces of the investigation. Rosen took seriously the idea that the best trial lawyers have to know every nuance of a case in order to be ready to handle any question a judge might throw at them. Lee Richards, a founding partner at New York firm Richards Kibbe & Orbe, marveled at Rosen's encyclopedic knowledge of cases when he worked there before moving to the government side. Rosen was used to handling every aspect of a case, having worked in smaller government offices where legal assistants might be busy. Back in Pittsburgh, he had served his own subpoenas.

The team carefully picked assistant U.S. attorneys who had the confidence to mesh with these forceful personalities. One, Justin O'Connell, was a rising star and Loyola University Maryland graduate whose witty, easygoing demeanor and penchant for wearing eye-catching socks belied his doggedness. He had been the lead prosecutor on a recent huge civil case in which the Royal Bank of Scotland had agreed to pay $4.9 billion for financial crisis–era misconduct, the largest fine of its kind imposed by the Justice Department. He'd joined the U.S. Attorney's Office in 2013 and on LinkedIn wryly described his job: "Do important stuff (most of which you'll never know about)." That sure was about to change.

Two lawyers who'd joined the Massachusetts U.S. Attorney's Office that November were also picked for the team. Trial attorney Leslie Wright had come up from the Miami office of the Justice Department's Criminal Division, and Kristen Kearney joined from a private law firm.

You could almost picture the slow-motion walk down the hallway as the opening credits rolled for some legal procedural TV show—except that this case was way too big to wrap in an hour with commercials.

AT LEAST ONE PARENT started to get nervous. Bruce Isackson, a Bay Area father, went along with an October call, saying "gotcha" and "okay" as Singer ran through the script.

After all, he'd recently asked Singer for a receipt so he could take a tax write-off on a $100,000 donation of Facebook stock for Singer's assistance in getting one of his daughters into college. (Isackson's two girls were slotted as soccer recruits to UCLA and USC, and his wife had started discussions about their son.)

The wife, Davina, also seemed fine when Singer gave her a buzz. He floated the line that the money was "a donation to our foundation for underserved kids." Was that all right with her?

"Okay. Yeah. Yeah."

Then all of a sudden, no. The phone line sounded clear, but Davina claimed it wasn't. "It's really hard to hear you," she told Singer. "Why don't we talk later tonight."

Singer, wearing a wire, went to their Hillsborough, California, house that evening to meet with Bruce. He asked if Davina wanted to join by phone, since she was traveling, but it wound up just being an uncomfortable conversation with a worried Bruce.

"You know, I am so paranoid about this fucking thing you were talking about," Bruce said. "I don't like talking about it on the phone, you know."

He was spinning out. He said he'd told Davina not to talk to Singer on the phone. "I mean, I can't imagine they'd go to the trouble of tapping my phone— but would they tap someone like your phones?"

SINGER WAS STILL LOCKING down some deals, in real time with fairly prominent parents, including Felicity Huffman. Huffman, who'd worked with Singer the previous year to rig the SAT score of her older daughter, Sophia, had been torn about doing the same for her younger daughter, Georgia. Georgia had been diagnosed with dyslexia as a child and attended a middle school specifically for kids with learning differences. Though she'd managed to flourish at the Westridge School, an academically demanding private school in Pasadena, Huffman was still anxious and leaning toward a backup strategy.

Her plan was to have her daughter take the test on her own first and then take it a second time under Singer's special assistance program: Riddell would clean up her answers.

"We're going to do like we did" with Sophia, Huffman confirmed in a November call.

Okay, Singer said. Riddell "will take it with her and for her."

"Yes," Huffman replied, with the FBI listening in.

Financier John Wilson was also continuing to give the feds rich material. Singer assured him on an October call that his twin daughters could land at top colleges as recruited athletes, but "don't have to play." Wilson ultimately plunked down a $500,000 deposit to get the ball rolling—after joking that he wished Singer had two-for-one pricing.

Was that all it takes? Wilson wanted to know, wowed at just how easy it was after Singer explained he'd gotten a guarantee from the Stanford coach. "No, no, no, no. That's not all it takes," Singer responded, seemingly miffed someone thought his dark magic was so easy. "This is not TJ Maxx or Marshall's or something like that."

And no, Wilson couldn't get two spots on Stanford's sailing team. "I asked him for a second spot in sailing and he said he can't do that because he has to actually recruit some real sailors," Singer explained. "So that Stanford doesn't catch on."

Wilson laughed. "Yeah, no. He's got to actually have some sailors. Yeah."

Wilson sent Singer's charity another $500,000 once promised a spot at Harvard, too. "We got both settled," he said of his girls. "I mean, life is good over at the Wilson house."

Life was also good for Jack Buckingham, whose mother choreographed an intricate plan with Singer to have the teen take a version of the ACT at home while Riddell sat for the exam on his behalf in Houston. Not realizing anything was amiss, Jack had apparently shared with at least one classmate how he had gotten sick and took his ACT at home in Beverly Hills, proctored by his mom.

News traveled fast in gossipy, competitive high school networks when a student seemed to have an unfair edge.

Rebecca Joseph, a professor and an independent college counselor for Westside Los Angeles families, picked up the scuttlebutt via a client who attended Brentwood with Jack.

She called around to others in the test prep business, and none had heard of such a crazy thing before.

She contacted the ACT in October 2018, first with a tweet. ACT responded by saying home tests weren't an option, but then clarified the person might have arranged testing accommodations. Joseph continued the chain, "But the mom was there in the room." ACT didn't reply. She then tried calling the ACT organization to report the irregularity, but couldn't make it past the first-line receptionist.

PROSECUTORS WERE STILL WATCHING to see if McGlashan would go through the side door for his son. There were flickers of hope, but Singer was doubtful, even telling his main USC contact he didn't think it was going to pan out.

The calls between him and McGlashan had gotten pretty weird as the fall progressed. Perhaps too much drama for McGlashan's taste. First, Singer had tipped him off that his phone might be bugged. Then, he'd told McGlashan the IRS was asking around.

McGlashan seemed to let him down politely. He was already working his contacts elsewhere at USC, a more traditional "back door" approach. He suggested to Singer they just table the whole conversation, "just till it's all cleared up exactly, you know, what the dynamic is of the foundation. I'd rather just sorta lay low."

"The fact is that side door is a lovely additional de-stresser, but if it doesn't—if it isn't possible, it isn't possible."

It wasn't possible anymore.

GORDON CAPLAN MAY HAVE been named a 2018 *American Lawyer* "Deal-maker of the Year," but he was on his way to making a terrible one with Singer.

Caplan had already said plenty on the calls with Singer when neither knew they were being recorded, but the feds were apparently looking to see if Caplan, a big name in the legal world, would actually bite and go through with the deal. Singer had written a note to his lawyer within a few days of agreeing to cooperate that it seemed like the government wanted to "nail Gordon at all costs."

The deal almost collapsed on its own. Initially, the ACT had denied the family's request for extra time on the daughter's test—twice. At the feds' request, the test company approved Caplan's daughter's accommodation on the third try.

In early November, Caplan asked for Singer's assurances his daughter's hands would remain clean. He needed to know that even though the proctor at the West Hollywood test center would fix up her answers later, she'd actually take the exam herself.

"Keep in mind I am a lawyer," he told Singer. "So I'm sort of rules oriented."

Singer provided the requisite confirmation, and Caplan wired $25,000 to an account under the Key Worldwide Foundation name. It was actually a Boston bank account that Singer had opened at the direction of law enforcement agents.

But Caplan still went back and forth, squirming over the details. How to work around his disapproving spouse. Whether his daughter's tutor, who didn't work with Singer, would find it weird if her ACT came back too high. How to explain traveling all the way to the West Coast for the test.

Bright and early on Saturday, December 8, law enforcement agents waited, secretly, outside West Hollywood College Preparatory School. There came Igor Dvorskiy, the school director, at 7:05 a.m.

Ten minutes later, agents saw Caplan and his daughter head in, followed by test proctor Mark Riddell at 7:21 a.m.

Caplan ducked out as his daughter began a stressful morning, fraught with the anxiety of taking a high-stakes test. Dad just worried about not getting caught. By noon, she was done, and they drove off. Deep breath. Any major mistakes on the test could now be wiped clean by Riddell.

Twelve days later, Caplan wired $50,000 more to what he thought was Singer's charity.

He'd tell Singer a few weeks after the test, "I never want to do anything that couldn't be on the front page of *The Wall Street Journal* but—we—we did what we did."

THE WEB OF CONSPIRATORS was growing almost absurdly messy. But there was another danger to letting the investigation go on too long: government cooperators can burn out. It takes a lot of mental energy to carry on as if all is normal, while moonlighting as a snitch.

Singer had the feds contacting him regularly to make sure he was staying in line. He had people listening to him every day. And he couldn't tell anyone.

He seemed a bit frayed by it.

For one of his countless side projects, he had invested around $1 million in USA-UES, a Los Angeles education technology startup aimed at serving Chinese students. He usually held productive and regular catch-up calls with Chris Li, the president and CEO, to talk patiently through goals and targets.

But Singer had grown short and snippy, for no apparent reason.

"Okay, maybe he just had a really shitty day," Li thought. But then the attitude kept up.

Singer was important to Li. He provided much-needed funding, as well as connections and a reputation. Testimonials on USA-UES's website were provided by Singer, copied from his own company site, the high praise intended to lure new customers to the not-yet-operating firm.

And Singer introduced Li and his team to top brass at the American Council on Education, a major higher education lobbying group. ACE was led by Ted Mitchell, a former Obama administration official who'd also sat on the board of Singer's early CollegeSource venture. With that entree, USA-UES had signed a deal in September 2018 to be a sponsor for ACE's national conference, scheduled for the following March.

But that fall Singer told Li he had to pull out of the venture, citing an audit—the ever-reliable IRS excuse—that was keeping him occupied and his money tied up. Singer stopped providing funding and sent Li and his partner scrambling. Li took a second mortgage on his house to keep the firm afloat, but the company ultimately folded.

Another cooperator also readied for the shit to hit the fan. In mid-November, current and former members of Yale's women's soccer team received a heads-up email from newbie athletic director Vicky Chun. "Please join me in thanking Rudy for his incredible dedication to the Yale Women's Soccer program for 24 years," she wrote. Longtime coach Rudy Meredith would be resigning. Soon Yale released the official press release, with glowing words from Chun and highlights of Meredith's career.

"It is time to explore new possibilities and begin a different chapter in my life," Meredith said. One day later, Yale received a federal grand jury subpoena.

ROSEN, FRANK, AND THE team in Boston had to wrap things up fast. Subpoenas had been sent out to schools. Lawyers were being called. Too many people knew.

They worked through the thirty-five-day federal government shutdown that began on December 22, due to a partisan impasse over funding for a wall on the U.S.-Mexico border.

Law enforcement agents had Singer continue to talk to clients over recorded lines in the early part of the year, and they also sent him to clients' houses in California with a new script.

Now, instead of claiming a looming IRS audit for his charity, Singer told parents that a college had launched an internal investigation. Or that authorities had subpoenaed the Houston test-site coordinator over out-of-state students who came to take their ACT or SAT there.

Los Angeles businessman Stephen Semprevivo seemed to know something was awry when Singer phoned March 3 with some news. He said Georgetown was conducting an internal investigation into why students who were not tennis players had been admitted through the tennis coach. Semprevivo's son had gotten to Georgetown through that exact channel. He asked a few questions, then the phone disconnected.

Semprevivo called back moments later. He said he didn't feel comfortable talking to Singer. "All I know is that we, you know, we used you for the charity stuff and we used you for the counseling," he stammered to Singer. "Your dealings are your dealings."

A day later, on the evening of March 4, Lori Loughlin called Singer, worried. She'd heard that the government had subpoenaed her daughter's records from Marymount. Did he know anything? "I wonder if it's that guy at Marymount again—is he trying to cause trouble?" Singer played ignorant.

The next day, Singer was on the phone with Felicity Huffman.

Would she go through with the testing scheme for her younger daughter, Georgia, as she had done for Sophia? Huffman and her husband, actor William

H. Macy, had been on a call with Singer months earlier to finalize plans for that next exam. And now they were nearing the final stretch ahead of Georgia's March SAT testing date. (Macy hadn't been involved in the machinations for Sophia. And while he'd engaged with Singer on some calls regarding Georgia's testing, Huffman was in the driver's seat.)

It had seemingly been a delightful time for the family. Macy had recently told *Parade* magazine, "Both Felicity and I, every once [in] a while, say, 'Good God, are we the luckiest people in the world?'"

In a *Men's Journal* piece published around the same time, he shared the best advice he'd ever gotten: "Never lie. It's the cheapest way to go. Lies cost you a lot, and they're never worth what they cost."

Ultimately, Huffman and Macy decided not to pursue the plan for Georgia. Huffman knew what she had done with Sophia was wrong. She didn't want to repeat her mistake.

The couple didn't know about the government's investigation or Singer's cooperation when Huffman told Singer on March 5 that they were out. "It just doesn't feel right," she said.

ONE MORNING IN EARLY FEBRUARY, Stanford sailing coach John Vandemoer was readying his kids for day care, still in pajamas himself, when he heard a knock at the door. Standing outside were two agents, one each from the FBI and the IRS.

He sat for two hours with the agents, answering their questions as best he could while still perplexed about what they were doing there, what he'd done wrong, how much trouble he was in.

One thing he did understand: he should find a lawyer.

Vandemoer didn't have a lawyer; he'd never needed one. An outdoorsy type, he barely ever needed a suit. His father, a retired ear, nose, and throat doctor on Cape Cod, contacted Nixon Peabody to help his son find counsel. Robert Fisher, a white-collar defense lawyer on his way to making partner at the Boston firm, got a new client.

Prosecutors had offered Vandemoer a plea deal, likely because he didn't fit neatly into the box of the college coaches the government was set to arrest.

Vandemoer was the only one who didn't pocket any of the bribe money for himself.

Fisher had the ideal background to help Vandemoer wade through the legalese and understand his options. A native of nearby blue-collar Revere, he'd spent nearly a decade as an assistant U.S. attorney in Boston before moving to private practice in 2016. Fisher had worked on some doozies, including one of the most puzzling ongoing mysteries in the art world: the Isabella Stewart Gardner Museum heist, in which thieves stole thirteen artworks worth an estimated $500 million.

And he'd been Rosen's mentor.

Fisher is plainspoken and friendly, not one to b.s. When he got the Vandemoer case, he made calls over to his former colleagues at the U.S. Attorney's Office and then quickly called Vandemoer in California.

"Okay, this is a big deal," Fisher told him.

Vandemoer hopped on a red-eye to the snowy city.

He spent eleven hours camped out in a glass-walled conference room at Nixon Peabody's offices on the thirty-first floor of Exchange Place, a modern skyscraper across the street from the site of the Boston Massacre.

As Vandemoer sat at a white marble table, with striking views out to the sailboats in Boston Harbor, Fisher and Nixon Peabody associate Scott Seitz scurried back and forth to federal court, a ten-minute walk away, to assess the evidence. It looked damning. Prosecutors had Singer and Vandemoer discussing deals on a recorded line. Emails fleshed out the proposed payment details.

Fisher and Seitz, a former lawyer for the National Security Agency who had worked for Fisher in law school and joined Nixon Peabody that January, saw Vandemoer as an unusual case. He'd flagged some applicants as recruits, even though they didn't sail. But he'd given all the money from Singer to the Stanford sailing program, to buy boats and supplies and pay for an assistant coach. Still, Fisher and Seitz explained, this was almost certainly a crime.

By Sunday night, March 3, the sailing coach's legal fate was set out in a six-page document in the case of United States v. John Vandemoer. On the last page was the statement: "I am entering into this Agreement freely and voluntarily, because I am in fact guilty of the offense."

Vandemoer signed his name.

He had one last weekend as a Stanford coach, leading his team at a regatta at St. Mary's College of Maryland. He'd had his first collegiate coaching job there, and he knew he'd now have his last. During breaks in the competition he took long walks alone to compose himself, having been warned by prosecutors not to speak about his legal case to anyone other than his lawyers and wife. He couldn't sleep at night, focused on the fact that "this massive thing is going to come down and that it's going to be so shameful," as he said later.

Stanford still won the regatta.

Riddell, the test taker, had signed a plea deal on February 22 and Meredith, the Yale coach, signed one on March 5. That was just the start.

25

——

TAKEDOWN

D AWN BEGAN TO BREAK March 12 upon another lovely L.A. day. The scent of citrus blossoms and jasmine burst across residential pockets of the city, a sweet sign of the approaching spring.

Marcus Buckingham's phone rang at 6:35 a.m. It was his son, Jack. Marcus was getting ready for work, but he answered right away.

Dad, could you come over?

Jack's voice sounded flat, disconnected from the bombshell he was about to deliver. "Mom has just been arrested by the FBI."

Just the Friday before, Jack had celebrated an acceptance letter from Southern Methodist University, where he now wanted to go. In typical low-key Jack fashion, he didn't want to make too big a deal about it since friends hadn't all heard back yet. His mom, Jane Buckingham, bought balloons and posted the good news on Instagram, but didn't go all out.

After their marriage broke up, Marcus had moved to the Hollywood Hills, fifteen minutes away from Beverly Hills, where Jane and the kids lived. The split had been acrimonious, but nothing about Jane being arrested computed even remotely for Marcus. Nobody had it more together than his ex-wife. He called her the "anti-flake."

He drove over, turning down a tree-lined street and pulling up to the stately home. Jack and Chloe were inside, sitting down and stunned. They told a story that sounded about as plausible as an alien invasion.

FBI agents banged on the door before sunrise and took their mom away.

Jack started scrolling through Twitter on his phone, looking for clues to what had happened, and as the morning went on, he started to see them. Lots of them. Marcus and Chloe hunched around him, peering over his shoulder at the tiny screen and the flurry of news popping out. Marcus didn't have his reading glasses and couldn't make out the words, but Jack and Chloe found a press release, something official, and began reading.

Almost in unison, they gasped.

INVESTIGATORS AND PROSECUTORS GATHERED early that morning at the FBI command post or at the U.S. Attorney's Office in Boston, where the cool air still felt a bit like winter. For roughly a year, they had kept their demanding investigation in stealth mode, limiting whom they told in other districts and at the DOJ headquarters to prevent leaks.

Spilled secrets tick off judges, thwart an investigation, and inspire suspects to do something rash, like hurt themselves or disappear to a place that doesn't have an extradition treaty with the United States. There had been a ton of work, and a ton of worry.

Now it was time to take down Operation Varsity Blues.

The government had already quietly secured plea deals with four targets: Singer; two coaches, Vandemoer and Meredith; and Riddell, the testing virtuoso. On this Tuesday morning, authorities would fan out to some of the toniest zip codes in the United States to apprehend more than forty other people, including celebrities, chief executives, and the cochairman of a global law firm. Some three hundred special agents from the FBI and the IRS's criminal division were carrying off the thunderbolt of surprise predawn arrests in six states across the country, as well as tracking down defendants who were traveling internationally.

Once the heavyweight scofflaws were taken into custody, they'd need to be booked, photographed, fingerprinted, and ushered into court for initial appearances.

Boston authorities were overseeing the whole takedown, coordinating a complex symphony where a single wrong note could turn into potential disaster.

. . .

JUST DAYS BEFORE THE TAKEDOWN, it appeared the lid might blow off early. Rosen, the lead prosecutor, sent out an urgent message. David Sidoo had bought a plane ticket to leave the country that coming Friday, March 8. The purchase set off an alert with federal investigators monitoring him.

Among the thirty-three parents the government aimed to arrest in just one week, Sidoo had star billing on a sealed indictment that had just been returned by the grand jury. The former Canadian pro football player turned business-man had paid Singer a total of $200,000 to have Mark Riddell take the SAT for his two sons.

Agents had planned to nab him in California Tuesday morning. Now he was gearing up to depart the United States for his waterfront Vancouver home (valued at about $24 million).

By this time, a growing number of sealed documents lurked in the court docket. The circle of those in the know included members of a Boston grand jury and lawyers and law enforcement officials in California and elsewhere.

Staffers in the Boston office had a predicament. If Sidoo decamped to Can-ada, it could be a headache to get him back. But his early arrest in the United States could alert other high-profile targets.

They took that risk, and the FBI snagged Sidoo that Friday at the San Jose Airport. He spent the weekend in custody while the Boston team called their counterparts in the Northern California district, begging them not to blab.

Authorities in Boston worked all weekend, preparing press releases and prewriting the website and social media language for Tuesday. They got word to the press teams in D.C. and L.A., sending a required "Urgent Report" to DOJ headquarters to put higher-ups on notice of an imminent high-impact, high-profile development in the Massachusetts district.

Sidoo's arrest didn't leak, even after he appeared in a San Jose federal court Monday and was released after agreeing to post a $1.5 million cash bond. That same day, in Massachusetts, Magistrate Judge M. Page Kelley signed thirty-two documents entitled "ARREST WARRANT" for the remaining parents at large, who were each being charged with one count of conspiracy to commit mail fraud and honest services mail fraud. She'd already signed warrants for coaches and other alleged Singer coconspirators days earlier.

The orders were clear:

"To: any authorized law enforcement officer," each warrant stated. "YOU ARE COMMANDED to arrest and bring before a United States magistrate judge without unnecessary delay . . ."

NEARLY TWENTY WARRANTS WENT to the FBI office in Los Angeles, which serves a sprawling area from Orange County up to the Central Coast, and inland to the Nevada border. Singer lived in this area, racked up clients here, and found his most fertile ground for bribing coaches at USC.

Agents based in a hulking white seventeen-story tower on Wilshire Boulevard, or some of the department's ten satellite offices, covertly worked on operational strategies, or "ops plans," for each home address where teams would need to deliver a warrant and take people into custody.

It's common for groups of law enforcement agents to make arrests in the wee hours, when targets will be home and caught off guard. But the raids can grab headlines and the optics are not pretty. Kids might be present. Agents bark commands, and may draw guns as a precaution because they don't know what's going to be on the other side of the doors they knock. People facing the prospect of public humiliation and prison time can get desperate and unpredictable.

Some seven weeks earlier, CNN had captured video of more than a dozen FBI agents moving up Roger Stone's Florida driveway before sunup with weapons and flashlights to arrest the Trump adviser. Critics blasted the operation as overkill, while others defended it.

A few eyebrows cocked in L.A. 's law enforcement community as March 12 approached. Were they really going to go arrest the likes of Huffman, rather than just summon her to appear? What were the odds the famous actress would grab her go-bag and become an international fugitive?

Yet authorities knew they also faced potential blowback if they appeared to be treating the wealthy defendants more gently. And the arrests would certainly send a message: cheat the system to get ahead of honest college applicants and you will be brought to justice—and it may happen before you've even taken a shower.

Boston prosecutors familiar with the controversy over the Roger Stone situation relayed their concerns to the FBI. No big scenes. No doors kicked in. And please, no "perp walks," or news footage of people with bedhead being led in cuffs to government vehicles.

The FBI teams, who would be joined by IRS agents, went over their meticulous plans and safety checklists, assigning a team leader, backup team, and FBI lawyer to call in case of legal trouble. Research revealed that several of the jet-setting targets would be out of town on March 12, requiring other districts to make the arrests.

They'd run recon at every home, scoping out routines and checking for fences, swinging gates, impenetrable hedges. Agents would have to figure out how to defeat home security systems or gain entry into gated communities.

The agents did a final check to confirm people were home, a process awkwardly called "bedding them down," and then the teams met well before dawn on March 12 in spots including Starbucks parking lots around the city.

These were the staging areas. The show was about to begin.

IN CALIFORNIA, THE ARRESTS unfolded in rapid succession from sleepy suburbs of the San Fernando Valley to glitzy beach towns. Around the same time in Beverly Hills, boisterous banging jolted a prominent developer out of bed and to the front door. It wasn't the Avon lady. "FBI!" the visitors shouted. He put his hands up.

Also at 6:00 a.m., different teams of agents nabbed a prep school director in Tarzana, a UCLA soccer coach in Century City, and in Fountain Valley, a former USC soccer coach whose wife answered the door in her bathrobe. At 6:05 a.m., the feds got a shipping executive in Newport Beach and a periodontist in Calabasas. Agents hit the North Hollywood condo of another onetime USC coach at 6:08 a.m. Seven minutes later, a team passed through the ornate black gates of a Bel Air manse to apprehend the business executive who lived there, while another unit moved up a private drive and busted Huffman at her home high in the hills above Sunset Boulevard. The feds collared a fashion designer at his Beverly Hills estate at 6:20 a.m., before banging on doors at a residence near the Beverly Hills Hotel.

Authorities hustled people into nondescript government-issue sedans and ferried them to downtown L.A.'s administrative core. Ads for bail bondsmen on benches appeared as the destination neared: a lockup facility inside the Edward R. Roybal Federal Building and U.S. Courthouse, a reddish granite twenty-two-floor tower.

Agents kept Boston apprised of each arrest, and back at the U.S. Attorney's Office, Steve Frank was sending out a stream of reassuring updates to the team with each person in custody. "No issues."

Up the coast, G-men took ten parents in the San Francisco vicinity into custody before breakfast; FBI special agents around New York City arrested a packaging-company owner at 6:00 a.m. and a prominent lawyer at 6:30 a.m. Other defendants were picked up in San Diego, Texas, and Colorado.

Parents had a range of surreal experiences. Jane Buckingham sat down on the floor, frozen, when the FBI descended on her lush Beverly Hills spread around 6:30 a.m. A kind female FBI agent helped her figure out whom to text— she tried her divorce lawyer—and had Buckingham's daughter get her mom an energy bar and her shoes. Huffman and Huneeus, the San Francisco vintner, described brash armed agents tramping through their homes and ordering the kids out of bed. In Menlo Park, Marjorie Klapper wore her pajamas when cuffed, before being allowed to change. At another home, a radiation oncologist and his wife were transported in separate cars to lockups.

Michael Center, the head men's tennis coach at the University of Texas, was carted off from his Austin home around 6:00 a.m. with a burnt orange T-shirt promoting a charity run by a longtime friend and Texas Longhorns sweatpants.

The famous UT slogan "hook 'em" took on a new meaning.

"When the FBI knocks on your door, pounds on your door," his attorney said, "it's never a good day."

THE NEWS ALERT HIT reporters' in-boxes at 10:09 a.m. eastern time: the U.S. Attorney's Office in Boston would hold a press conference in just over an hour to announce charges against "dozens of individuals involved in a nationwide college admissions cheating and recruitment scheme."

The FBI's National Press Office chimed in minutes later touting "a criminal matter out of the FBI Boston field office of broad interest."

This sounded big, and bigger still when an NBC News correspondent tweeted: "Breaking: Actress Felicity Huffman (Desperate Housewives) and Lori Loughlin (Full House) are defendants in the cheating probe coming out of Boston."

Reporters and cameras filled the ninth-floor press room of the federal courthouse, and stone-faced federal officials arrayed themselves on the gray-carpeted riser in front of a velvet curtain and the DOJ seal.

At the appointed time, Lelling stepped to the wooden podium.

"We're here today to announce charges in the largest college-admissions scam ever prosecuted by the Department of Justice," he said, before calmly launching into a startling recitation of the massive, country-crossing scandal.

Cameras whirred. Keyboards clacked as reporters typed and tweeted while he ran down the mind-boggling particulars: freshly unsealed charges naming three scam organizers, nine college coaches, a college administrator, a fixer, a proctor, two SAT/ACT administrators, and thirty-three parents who represented a "catalogue of wealth and privilege." In New York, a *Wall Street Journal* editor began printing out an FBI affidavit detailing the allegations, more than two hundred pages long, and others started reading to find boldfaced names.

The case had absurd doctored photos. Cooked SAT and ACT results. A racketeering conspiracy. Posh and well-known colleges: Yale. Georgetown. Stanford. Wake Forest. UCLA. The University of Southern California. The University of Texas. So esteemed was the group that one USC professor joked to a colleague that their admissions office was probably a little excited. "How great is that? We're being compared to Stanford and Harvard."

In the Boston press conference, Lelling laid out a fraud so extensive the U.S. Attorney's Office had diagrammed the scheme on a poster board. "There can be no separate college admissions system for the wealthy and, I'll add, there will not be a separate criminal justice system either," he warned.

Joseph Bonavolonta, the special agent in charge of the FBI's Boston field office, took the mic and gave an update on the mammoth takedown of the targets: more than three dozen people had been safely taken into custody that morning, while one was "actively being pursued" and seven were "working toward surrender."

Two defendants, Singer and Vandemoer, were set to cop to felonies in federal court in Boston that very afternoon, while two others would plead guilty in coming weeks.

Reporters jumped in with questions, including a burning one. Had the kids known?

In Beverly Hills, seventeen-year-old Jack Buckingham was just finding out. The U.S. Attorney's Office in Boston had blasted the voluminous charging documents onto the internet. Jack followed a Twitter thread to a lengthy legal document someone had posted: "Affidavit in Support of Criminal Complaint."

The introduction listed "defendants" in alphabetical order, along with the page on which they appeared.

"It says something about honest services fraud. Maybe she's a witness," Jack said, hope in his voice. His father, Marcus, and sister, Chloe, stood nearby as Jack narrated.

He landed on page 15 and began to read aloud, the optimism now drained.

"Mom paid Rick Singer $50,000 to cheat on my ACT," Jack said, "and she's planning to do the same thing" for Chloe. His face fell and he slumped. "What's going to happen now, Dad?" Jack asked.

Marcus grabbed him and hugged him tightly.

Sophia and Georgia Macy called their former nanny, comedy writer Ellen Etten, uncertain what to do after their mom was arrested. They spent the day at Etten's house, watching movies, eating Thai food, and crying.

In the community of Spring, Texas, a woman who had worked for Singer as a legitimate college counselor got a call from a friend who shouted: "Turn on the news!" The former employee spent the day wondering if the FBI was going to show up at her door.

In Florida, employees at IMG Academy were in a dither. Authorities had just revealed Mark Riddell, the school's popular head of test preparation, as the guy who'd rigged tests for Singer's clients. They initially hoped the government meant a different Mark Riddell. Then someone got to work erasing Riddell's bio from IMG's website.

Work slowed in offices across the United States as people scanned the government's 204-page affidavit with its tantalizing snippets of phone conversations, texts, and emails between Singer and the parents. Employees at Pimco's Newport Beach office circulated the salacious document, not least because it implicated Hodge, the firm's former CEO. Hodge was traveling internationally when the news broke and booked a red-eye home to surrender.

For the public, the scandal had it all. Loaded parents from Hollywood to Wall Street. Overprivileged kids. Greed. Corruption. Cash handoffs. Tapped phones. Wacky stunts. And confirmation, in the view of many, that the admissions system is not fair.

The internet lit up with memes about Aunt Becky's betrayal, a reference to Loughlin's character on *Full House*, and the scandal trended on every major news outlet. Late-night comedians readied their laugh lines for the day and *Saturday Night Live* writers made space for a new sketch, while politicians and academics rushed to opine.

Companies began quickly canning employees named in the scandal. Bill McGlashan submitted his letter of resignation to private equity firm TPG around 1:55 p.m., while the company sent him a note at 2:04 p.m. saying he was being terminated for cause and that they'd already been writing it when his resignation came through. Though the firm determined McGlashan hadn't had any misconduct related to TPG, he lost vested and unvested assets valued at upwards of $150 million.

Private schools rushed to oust parents as trustees.

USC axed Heinel, the administrator, and Vavic, the school's long-celebrated water polo coach. FBI agents had surprised Vavic at 6:30 a.m. at his hotel in Waikiki, where he'd been lodging ahead of an upcoming women's water polo match against the University of Hawai'i. He wore his cardinal red and gold USC windbreaker to court.

"People are ANGRY about the story," a KHON-TV Honolulu newscaster declared later during an on-air interview with a local law school professor who sported a Hawaiian shirt and jeans. "It's not funny," the professor said, his chuckles suggesting otherwise as he talked through the allegations against Lori Loughlin.

"It's a great story," the newsman observed, "in terms of just the juiciness value. It's also sad on many levels."

COURT PROCEEDINGS GOT UNDER WAY across the nation, nearly simultaneously. Known as detention hearings, the relatively perfunctory events kick the criminal process into motion. Judges make sure the accused understands the charge, then decide if the person will be released, and under what conditions.

No one was arguing in favor of keeping the accused white-collar felons in Operation Varsity Blues locked up, but prosecutors and defense lawyers quickly began sparring over how high bail needed to be to guarantee the parents would not flee, while the less wealthy coaches generally got lower bail.

"How do we ensure that we are providing enough incentive for people who have such significant resources that discarding $50,000 would be a drop in the bucket for them?" asked one California prosecutor. Defense lawyers pushed back, calling it preposterous to suggest that *these defendants* in particular were flight risks.

"They have children, which is the basis of the complaint," a defense lawyer astutely pointed out in San Francisco. The judge there imposed a $1 million bond each for a Kentucky bourbon distillery owner and the Napa Valley vintner.

A lot of people involved probably could have used a drink. In Las Vegas, longtime casino executive Gamal Abdelaziz pushed in a legal filing for his right to "be present in court without shackles" after being accused of paying a $300,000 bribe to get his daughter into college.

Texas coach Michael Center made his appearance in federal court in Austin alongside Adolfo Adam Rodriguez, a convicted felon facing a gun possession charge. He appeared before Judge Andrew W. Austin (yes, Austin is a judge in Austin).

"Interrupting, Judge," said Center's lawyer, in response to proposed travel restrictions for his client. "I assume you're aware that he's the coach at the University of Texas tennis team, and that requires extensive travel."

It didn't matter. The university put Center on leave, then fired him the next day.

In the elegant Italian Renaissance Revival–style federal courthouse in Grand Junction, Colorado, Magistrate Judge Gordon P. Gallagher greeted the room. "All right. Good morning, everybody. We're here in the matter of the United States vs. Marcia Abbott." Abbott was two hours from her Aspen home, a $16 million retreat on thirty acres in a community where neighbors have included hedge fund magnates and a Saudi prince.

She had an uptown pedigree: daughter of a former state senator in New York; onetime fashion editor at *Family Circle* magazine, and cum laude graduate from Duke. Her husband had expanded a major private-label pantyhose and underwear manufacturer, had founded another company, and was an early EarthLink investor.

Yet here she stood as an accused criminal.

Did she understand, the judge inquired, what the government claims she did?

"I—I—I don't know how I could have committed bribery," Abbott stammered. "I don't know what—I don't know what this is about."

BACK IN BOSTON, Rick Singer spent much of Tuesday milling around town, still an anonymous middle-aged college counselor at the edge of infamy.

Don Heller, Singer's longtime friend from Sacramento and now his lawyer, walked Singer over to the U.S. District Court that morning to get fingerprinted and photographed at the U.S. Marshals office. They then moseyed to Heller's hotel room near the courthouse to watch Lelling's televised press conference.

The room fell quiet. Singer had known it was a big case. But the enormity of it was just hitting him as authorities announced the massive numbers, and his name, to the world.

"The central defendant in the scheme, William Singer . . ."

"Wealthy parents paid Singer about $25 million in total."

"We identified Singer some time ago."

Singer went to get ready. Tanned and thin with a crown of gray hair, he changed from jeans into a dark suit, a very unusual wardrobe choice for him.

He topped it off with a navy Patagonia windbreaker and then walked with Heller to the courthouse.

Singer was due in court that afternoon, the main event on an already wild day. In legal jargon, this was a "Rule 11" hearing. In plain terms, the government had gotten Singer to plead guilty to the whole shebang.

He walked unrecognized by reporters camped outside, and then went into the courthouse, where the mastermind of the stunning nationwide college admissions scandal ate lunch from the cafeteria salad bar. Heller used the time to go over a few things.

Rule 11 hearings can be routine affairs, where the judge runs down standard questions, making sure defendants understand the powerful rights they are relinquishing. But the hearings are potential land mines, because they are the first time a defendant has direct communication with the judge who will eventually sentence him.

Heller knew that the most painful thing to watch is a defendant who minimizes his conduct, grumbles, or makes excuses. It makes a terrible impression on the judge and can affect sentencing. "Now remember what we talked about," Heller told Singer. "Don't sugarcoat it. Just tell the truth."

At 2:32 p.m. eastern time, onlookers packed into a courtroom to see Singer. No one from the U.S. Attorney's Office in Massachusetts wanted to miss their star witness. "You need four prosecutors here for this?" U.S. District Judge Rya W. Zobel asked drolly, glancing at the abundance of federal lawyers on hand.

The judge then directed her attention to the fifty-eight-year-old Singer.

"Understand, Mr. Singer, the government is accusing you of a number of felonies," Zobel said. "Under the Constitution, you have an absolute right to insist that if the government wants to accuse you of such felonies that it first go to a grand jury."

"Yes, ma'am. Yes, ma'am," Singer answered in a clear voice.

Rosen started detailing the four charges Singer would plead to: racketeering conspiracy, money-laundering conspiracy, conspiracy to defraud the United States, and obstruction of justice.

This was going to take a while. There was the lying. The cheating. The bribing. The falsifying.

"Finally, tax evasion," he concluded, referring to Singer's efforts to defraud his nation. After he finished the long soliloquy, a tense pause hung in the air.

The judge turned to Singer.

Singer spoke in a firm tone; he'd taken Heller's advice.

"Your Honor, everything that Mr. Rosen stated is exactly true. All of those things, plus many more things."

Singer laid out his whole illegal testing operation, going into even greater detail than the prosecutor.

"Now, how about the money laundering?" Zobel asked.

"So I am absolutely guilty of that as well, ma'am."

He explained how he was "essentially buying or bribing the coaches for a spot," and he did it "very frequently."

How about the tax fraud? she asked.

Check.

"Obstruction of justice?"

Yep. "I am totally wrong," Singer said. "And I did that kind of situation on multiple occasions to multiple families."

That was that. The judge accepted his guilty plea. She released him on a $500,000 bond secured by his brother's property until his sentencing, which was set for June but would get delayed.

Court adjourned at 3:26 p.m., and Singer left in a way much different from how he'd come in. TV cameras surrounded him and Heller, who made a few remarks and then ushered his client away.

Three thousand miles away, a group of wealthy parents would soon head into court themselves.

THE THIRTEEN PEOPLE ROUSED from their homes before dawn in the L.A. area were passing the day in a jail housed in the Roybal Federal Building downtown.

Life had shifted drastically. ("It is a radical change in circumstances that has been visited upon them," as a prosecutor in Southern California artfully put it that day.) The assortment of parents, college coaches, a school director, and a few others were ushered into two holding cells, one for men and one for women. A freakish L.A. reunion unfolded as some jailbirds recognized one another. Jane Buckingham, who'd been arrested in workout gear, was lying on a bench when in came her friend Felicity Huffman. They realized for the first time that they had both hired Rick Singer. Huffman at times would be overcome by emotion.

The lawyers started arriving by 11:30 a.m., advising their clients in small rooms off the holding cells. Everyone got a chance to read the affidavit and complaint, or at least the parts that related to them—it was a fat stack of papers, after all. Then they shuffled back into the bare-bones cells until detention hearings later that afternoon. They sat on hard benches eating bagged lunches. There were no clocks, no wicker baskets of magazines to browse, not even an ancient copy of *National Geographic* or *Time*.

Fashion designer Giannulli, wearing a baggy blue sweatshirt, tried to start a conversation in the men's cell. Laura Janke, the former USC soccer coach who'd crafted phony athletic profiles for Singer's clients, worried about being able to pump breast milk for her two-month-old.

What of all the life plans? Buckingham was scheduled to go to a wedding in Arizona. Flaxman, the developer, had a pregnant partner awaiting a promised trip to Hawaii. The periodontist usually kept a brisk schedule as a speaker at dental conferences and symposia, and had upcoming engagements as a keynote speaker in Barcelona, Taipei, Kuala Lumpur, and Vancouver.

The only calendar item certain now was the afternoon court hearing. The time had come to face the public, to let go of any hope that this was all going to blow over quietly or quickly.

PROSECUTORS IN L.A. joke that a seized oil tanker filled with cocaine wouldn't attract the same attention as a scandal involving sex, celebrities, or animals.

With only one of the three—rich people accused of doing fairly crazy things for their kids—this case seemed to top all of that.

In Courtroom 341 on the third floor of the Roybal Federal Building of the

Central District of California, the well-heeled defendants stared out from "the bullpen," an area separated by a clear glass window from the courtroom and guarded by muscled officers.

In a foyer outside the courtroom, before an ominous poster touting the U.S. Marshals Service's "Fifteen Most Wanted Fugitives," the crowd grew so thick that anyone stepping off the elevator had a hard time navigating the mosh pit. The entire press corps showed up. Local stations. National networks. Entertainment correspondents. Relatives of defendants. The blue-coated security officers delivered instructions about how to behave inside the court: do not try to communicate with those in custody in any way, or there could be a large fine.

The bullpen's glass partition came lower on one side, allowing the inmates to step up one by one to speak into a microphone propped on a podium, situated on the free side of the courtroom.

"You are charged with a criminal offense against the United States," Magistrate Judge Alexander F. MacKinnon told his captive audience.

As each defendant stepped to the mic, the federal judge went over the necessary housekeeping. Did they understand the charge? Did they know their rights?

Since the proceedings weren't televised, the chief public affairs officer for the U.S. Attorney's Office in L.A. was live-texting the developments back to the press office in Boston.

Then things got interesting. Many people dabble in "real estate porn," that guilty pleasure of ogling insane homes. Now courtroom spectators were treated to what could be best described as bank account porn. To argue for high bail, prosecutors reeled off jaw-dropping figures: Robert Flaxman's $15 million in cash and ten properties. Felicity Huffman's real estate assets in excess of $20 million, and $4 million in liquid securities in her stock account.

The zenith of this wallet-exposing exercise came when Judge MacKinnon called up Michelle Janavs, the forty-eight-year-old Newport Beach socialite and heiress to the fortune created in part by Hot Pockets, the tasty microwavable hangover snacks known for burning the roof of your mouth.

The public was about to learn just how popular those snacks were.

"In this case, the defendant here enjoys a trust fund with a monthly income of some $100,000," said Assistant U.S. Attorney Adam Schleifer, adding, "and by the way, a $14 million home." Schleifer asked for Janavs to be released only after posting a whopping $2 million bond. The judge settled on a $400,000 appearance bond—a promise to pay if she didn't show up—signed by her father.

The defendants were returned to their cells, processed, and then released into the evening, and the media still camped outside.

"We just got Felicity and Mossimo after posting bail," TMZ posted at 7:58 p.m. "And it was clear they didn't want to talk."

ANNOUNCEMENT OF OPERATION VARSITY BLUES generated even more buzz than anyone thought it would. Boston's press team would field two thousand media inquiries in the first forty-eight hours. L.A.'s public affairs office handled so many press calls that the Boston team sent a package of two lobsters, plus clam chowder, in gratitude. The L.A. press guy gave Boston tips on whom to trust among the tabloids and entertainment bloggers, and the U.S. Attorney's Office in Boston soon subscribed to *People* magazine to stay on top of the news coverage. This was a different kind of case from what they were used to.

The FBI was also pulled into the spectacle. At some point, tipsters complained to the tabloids about the FBI's arrest of Huffman. That set off such a flood of calls that the agency felt compelled to issue a statement saying the actress had been treated like other defendants.

In another pain in the neck for law enforcement personnel, Loughlin had to fly home from a film set in Vancouver. Court would be closed by the time she arrived, and the feds didn't want the PR nightmare of keeping Aunt Becky in lockup overnight. They prayed the paparazzi wouldn't show up at the airport to watch her waltz out.

At the end of the day, authorities around the country were relieved. Overall, the massive operation had gone smoothly. The action would soon turn to Boston, where defendants had been ordered to appear in late March.

But first, the parents headed home to face the children they had betrayed.

Matteo Sloane, on spring break from his freshman year at USC, was in the kitchen of his family's Spanish-style home in Bel Air when Devin Sloane walked through the door that night. Matteo knew the allegations against his father.

"Why didn't you believe in me?" Matteo implored. "Why didn't you trust me?"

"I never stopped believing in you, not even for one second," Devin told Matteo. "I lost sight of what was right, and I lost belief in myself."

Matteo was mad. Did his mom and dad saying they were proud of him really mean anything? But that anger quickly shifted. "It kind of transformed into me feeling sorry for him," Matteo later said.

26

THE PARADE

Bill McGlashan wore a sharp gray suit, crisp white shirt, royal blue tie, and an imperturbable expression, like the Bay Area dealmaker he was. Standing in a Boston courtroom on a chilly day in late March, he faced the possibility of prison time.

But first, he had a crucial fight to pick with the federal magistrate judge in front of him.

He wanted permission to go on a family vacation.

Two weeks after the government announced the charges in Operation Varsity Blues, the parade had begun for what may have been the flashiest, most influential group of defendants ever seen there. Mothers and fathers, including movie stars, trekked in from Greenwich, Bel Air, Aspen, Marin County, or other upper-crust enclaves, accompanied by their coteries of counselors. Some parents had crisis-communication teams on the payroll. All hired heavy-hitting white-collar defense attorneys from just about every major law firm in the country, including Ropes & Gray, Latham & Watkins, and Boies Schiller Flexner. Their lawyers were a who's who of former federal prosecutors, including those who'd handled the cases against Boston Marathon bomber Dzhokhar Tsarnaev and Enron executives.

Going through security at the courthouse, some of the lawyers from D.C.

and L.A. were flummoxed when the officers, mostly retired Boston cops, asked to see their "bah cahds."

What the hell was that? Oh, they learned after some repetition. Bar cards proving they were lawyers, which allowed them to bring their phones and other devices into court.

Along with the parents, coaches accused of taking bribes spilled into court with slightly less prominent lawyers but creds from some of the country's most prestigious university sports programs. The court got so busy that prosecutors one day had to dash from a hearing for a Yale soccer coach right over to one in a nearby courtroom for a University of Texas tennis coach.

USC had to endure not only the indignity of indicted former coaches and an administrator trekking into federal court at once, but also confusion from New Englanders about why anyone would possibly need to break the law to get in there.

"Can I stop you?" a Harvard-educated judge asked a prosecutor innocently one day as the hearings were under way. "I don't know USC very well. That's a private college, right? It's not a public one. UCLA is public, of course."

Almost none of the Varsity Blues defendants had "been in the system before," and they had "no priors," a prosecutor noted. But the well-heeled accused felons presented the judges in Massachusetts with a particular quandary: how to keep tabs on defendants with globe-trotting lifestyles, multiple homes, international business interests, money to burn, and an unfamiliarity with having to follow orders?

McGlashan, with a graying beard and salt-and-pepper hair, was in court in March for an initial appearance along with about fourteen other parents. These were perfunctory proceedings, with no requirement to enter a plea yet. Magistrate Judge M. Page Kelley would simply go over the rules of their new lives as accused felons.

She spoke to the defendants in a slow, firm, don't-make-me-tell-you-twice tone, probably the first person to speak to them like that since their middle school principals.

"Please listen carefully." And "You will surrender any passport. Has that been done?" To Mr. McGlashan, Judge Kelley said, "I know that you have a holiday trip planned. I am not inclined to allow people to travel for vacations because I'm just trying to be consistent, and I have allowed travel for business purposes, limited travel for business purposes. I'm happy to hear you but I'll just say I'm disinclined to allow that."

That seemed like the end of that discussion. The nation had seized on the parents as the very face of privilege run amok, and it might seem a good time to lie low and at least act humiliated. A good time for a staycation.

McGlashan's lawyer, Jack Pirozzolo, a former Boston federal prosecutor who'd become a partner at Sidley Austin, rose. "I would like to be heard on that, Your Honor."

THE PARENTS HAD DARTED past a line of reporters and news cameras that day to file into the redbrick courthouse.

Judge Kelley began calling parents up in groups of three to go over the myriad ways she would restrict their routines.

In came the scion of a Napa Valley wine dynasty renowned for its pinot noir and chardonnay. In came a Beverly Hills real estate magnate whose vast portfolio included a Moroccan-style luxury resort outside of Phoenix. And there was Greg Abbott, the preppy founder of International Dispensing Corporation, maker of the spout on ubiquitous soft box containers for soup broth and nonrefrigerated creamers. Life had unraveled quickly. Three months earlier, the company proudly announced it had won a global award "often referred to as the 'The Oscars of Packaging.'" (Abbott would later get a letter of support, filed to the court, from the retired chairman of the company that invented Bubble Wrap.)

A shipping industry executive from Newport Beach, California, charged with having his son's ACT rigged, was in the first group of three and hard to miss. The sixty-four-year-old wore a neon yellow vest and needed a Mandarin interpreter. The woman who accompanied him to court toted a giant Louis Vuitton bag.

Judge Kelley turned her attention to another defendant, Gamal Abdelaziz, a former high-level MGM and Wynn Resorts casino executive in Las Vegas and Macau whom the government had now accused of participating in a different sort of gaming: bribing his daughter's way into USC as a fake basketball recruit. She did play the sport, just not at the Division I level. Abdelaziz had a special request, too. He had filed a motion to take an international business trip.

Assistant U.S. Attorney Justin O'Connell rose in opposition. Abdelaziz had extensive foreign ties, he said, alluding to a flight risk.

Nonsense, replied the defendant's lawyer, Brian Kelly. Now a partner at Nixon Peabody, Kelly was a former assistant U.S. attorney who'd helped prosecute mob boss James "Whitey" Bulger. "He's not running from this case. He intends to fight this case. In fact, if the court looks at his complaint, it is not a strong case against him. It's a one-witness case, a witness named Singer who is deeply compromised."

Judge Kelley agreed to let Abdelaziz take his upcoming work-related trip to Mexico, but made clear she would permit these kinds of trips for business reasons only. He would need to turn in his passport after each trip.

Judge Kelley launched into the standard conditions for release for all the defendants. For instance, the parents were prohibited from speaking to other defendants. Well, that wouldn't quite fly here, since some were married to each other. She adjusted. Greg Abbott could speak with his wife, Marcia, who was also charged and was in the court. (They may not have wanted to, as they were separated.)

Some of the defense lawyers sought to make their extraordinary clients more relatable. Thomas H. Bienert Jr., a former federal prosecutor who'd assisted Kenneth Starr on the Whitewater investigation in Washington, D.C., now represented a Varsity Blues parent. He told Judge Kelley the government had incorrectly portrayed his client as an executive at a food company.

"My client has been a homemaker and a volunteer for the last 20 years," he said, motioning to Michelle Janavs, the Hot Pockets heiress.

THE LIMITS OF THE court's mercy were clear, but McGlashan's lawyer, Pirozzolo, argued his client should get an exception. McGlashan, fifty-five, wanted to proceed with a family spring-break vacation to Mexico.

Pirozzolo said it would be "punitive" to bar McGlashan, and in effect the entire family, from going on this long-planned trip. Please, he asked, don't "deprive" them of this opportunity.

Spectators and reporters in the gallery craned to see McGlashan, whose face didn't appear to register anything unusual here. Punitive? Deprive?

"Okay. Thank you," the judge said, betraying nothing with tone. "Anything from the government?"

Assistant U.S. Attorney Eric Rosen rose. "Yes, just a few things."

He had come prepared.

The government had accused McGlashan of paying $50,000 to rig a son's ACT test and of considering the fake-athlete plan.

Rosen launched into the evidence against McGlashan with great granularity, detailing plane travel, cell tower data, text messages, and phone calls caught by a court-ordered wiretap.

After the lacerating recitation of evidence, Rosen finally turned to McGlashan's request to take a holiday. He went in for the kill, glancing down at research he held in his hand.

"He has a home in Big Sky, Montana, that's worth $12 million he can use. He has a home in Truckee, California, that's worth a lot of money that he can also use," he said, referring to the mountain town near Lake Tahoe. "He's free to travel in the continental United States. He only wants to go to Mexico, which is something not granted to any other defendant."

The judge agreed. No vacation.

THE SAME WEEK PARENTS began appearing, Senior U.S. District Judge Mark L. Wolf leaned back in his seat at the bench in a different courtroom. The towering intellectual once wrote a 661-page opinion and held a ten-month hearing on FBI misconduct in the Whitey Bulger case.

Now, his desk piled with folders, he was ready to hold forth on the United States of America v. Rudolph "Rudy" Meredith, Criminal Action, No. 19-10075-MLW.

But before the hearing on the former Yale women's soccer coach who'd led prosecutors to Singer and taken hundreds of thousands in bribes himself, Wolf needed to unburden himself. The judge himself was a 1968 Yale graduate.

Potential conflicts quickly arose in the Varsity Blues legal case. Lawyers whose firms had in the past represented the elite schools named in the case as victims needed to determine whether they could also defend the parents who may have bribed employees at those institutions. Some prominent lawyers scooped up more than one parent as clients, forcing a judge to call special hearings on the possible divided loyalties should one defendant flip.

Wolf took several minutes to meander through his Yale bona fides. "I make what by Yale's standards is a modest contribution each year to the annual fund and pay dues. I made a somewhat larger contribution in connection with my 50th reunion last year."

Meredith, a trim fifty-one-year-old with an almost clean-shaven head and a royal blue shirt and dark suit, watched from the defendant's table.

The judge determined that he didn't have a bias, saying, "I'll decide matters in this case the way I would decide them if Mr. Meredith had coached someplace else." And then he got down to the question everyone was wondering about. Exactly who had bribed Meredith? The 204-page FBI affidavit filed in the case only cryptically referred to the parents of "Yale Applicant 1" and "Yale Applicant 2."

When Massachusetts U.S. Attorney Lelling announced the charges, he said the case had originated with a tip, out of an unrelated securities fraud case, but he wouldn't go any further.

An unexpected tip from a new source led *The Wall Street Journal* to a financial executive who told authorities that a former women's soccer coach at Yale University had sought a bribe. His name was Morrie Tobin.

It soon became clear that not only had he spilled about Meredith taking bribes, but he'd also given money to the coach to get his daughter into Yale. *The Wall Street Journal* broke the news that Tobin was the father of Yale Applicant 2.

But who was Yale 1? And would charges against this mystery person materialize? Judge Wolf wanted to know.

There hadn't been charges publicly revealed about the family of that Yale applicant, "if those charges were to exist," Rosen said, deepening the intrigue.

Before Meredith pleaded guilty, Wolf also wanted to make sure the former coach knew what he was giving up. If he contested the case, Meredith could have tried to argue he was entrapped and improperly lured to Massachusetts.

"I understand, your honor," Meredith said in a gravelly voice, leaning into the mic. "Nobody forced me to come to Massachusetts."

Meredith was probably never so glad to get out of the state. He had to fend off so many photographers outside the courthouse that his lawyer held up his hands and guided Meredith back inside, away from the scrum.

As PARENTS AND COACHES began to make court appearances, college students around the country were awaiting judgments of their own: could they stay in school?

Wake Forest quickly determined that the student who got in with help from a bribe didn't know about it, so could stay.

Jack Buckingham had to plead his case before administrators at Southern Methodist University, reiterating that he had no idea his ACT scores had been faked that third time. The earlier scores, taken on his own, were enough to keep him in school, SMU decided.

Others weren't so fortunate. USC put holds on the accounts of all students it determined may have been connected to Singer's dirty doings, meaning that while they could enroll for the next term if they cooperated with investigations, they still couldn't get their degrees or transcripts until things got sorted.

Georgetown and Northwestern kicked out students who got in with a lie. Yale and Stanford, too.

Federal privacy laws prevented schools from identifying just who was in, who was out. But the court documents and parents' names made it easy enough to figure out most of the students now facing discipline.

Yet the question remained: Who was Yale 1?

Tidbits in the affidavit and indictment against Meredith suggested she was from Southern California, had ties to China, and would be a college freshman now.

Wall Street Journal reporting, including checking a freshman student guide against the school's online directory, which was updated as people came and left, soon revealed a name had disappeared. Sherry Guo was gone.

That revelation led to a house hunt: Sherry's listed address was registered to an LLC, with no contact information for any of the company's officers. The accountant who signed the LLC's paperwork didn't return calls.

The morning of April 25, a young woman answered the door at a nondescript house to find a *Wall Street Journal* reporter standing on the stoop, a letter in her hand. The girl said she wasn't Sherry Guo and closed the door, but opened it again long enough to take the letter.

A few hours later Sherry's Los Angeles attorney, James Spertus, called *The Wall Street Journal*. He said Sherry learned English after arriving in the United States about five years earlier and had attended JSerra Catholic High School in San Juan Capistrano. She was an older student, around twenty-one at the time the scandal broke. And yes, her family had given Singer $1.2 million for a spot at Yale. He said it was understood to be a legitimate payment.

IN EARLY APRIL, outside the federal courthouse in Boston, Lori Loughlin emerged from a black van with tinted windows, looking remarkably chipper for an accused criminal. The fifty-four-year-old actress, outfitted in a chic camel pantsuit, smiled and waved as she maneuvered through a crowd of media and onlookers, including one who hollered, "Pay my tuition!"

The most famous figures in the admissions scandal had arrived. Helicopters hovered overhead, and satellite trucks flanked the courthouse as Loughlin and Huffman joined a second batch of parents making their initial appearances.

Local office workers on break, wearing lanyards and badges around their necks, came out to gawk and vent about the Varsity Blues parents. "Shame on them," said Jean Parker, a sixty-two-year-old executive assistant at a pharmaceutical company. "We worked very hard getting our kids into college." Others were fans of Aunt Becky. Two college students wore homemade masks of the actress.

Loughlin and her husband, Giannulli, had flown into Boston's Logan Airport on a private plane the day before. Looking stylish in mirrored sunglasses, her chestnut hair perfectly highlighted, she signed autographs and posed for pictures with fans outside her Copley Square hotel.

Her upbeat demeanor continued into the next day. Most parents, including

Huffman, maintained an appropriately businesslike affect as they entered the court. They appeared embarrassed. Loughlin seemed to think it would make more sense to act as if nothing was wrong.

"Hi, I'm Lori," Loughlin chirped, greeting courthouse employees, as she bounced down the hall. Inside the courtroom, she took the unusual step of going over to shake hands with prosecutors before facing the judge. "*That* was fucking embarrassing," muttered a lawyer who represented another parent and was sitting in the gallery.

The celebrities drew all the attention. But a motion filed in court just ahead of that day's hearing quietly indicated a big turn in the case. The filing came from a lawyer for P. J. Sartorio, the founder of a frozen Mexican food company known for its burritos. Sartorio, who was fifty-four, had paid $15,000 to have his daughter's ACT rigged.

He had just become the first Varsity Blues parent to go on the record saying he planned to plead guilty.

Other parents were also in plea talks. As one defense lawyer explained, some legal teams were looking at the government's evidence and telling their clients plainly, "They've gotcha." It wasn't always easy to get that across to this group of defendants. "These kinds of people don't want to say they did anything wrong," the lawyer said.

But the pressure to cut deals was building in large part because the legal situation was about to get a lot worse for parents. Prosecutors had kept another potential charge in their pocket: money-laundering conspiracy, related to payments parents made to Singer's charity. They were doled out as bribes. Some moms and dads had taken tax write-offs on the bribes.

It's a common tactic for federal prosecutors to threaten, and then add, more charges as defendants dig in, and as the government uncovers additional evidence or new witnesses. The feds were gearing up to add a money-laundering conspiracy charge in a superseding indictment. Some defense lawyers were eager to get ahead of that and possibly have their clients plead now, in part because that indictment would be joined into an existing one, against Canadian businessman David Sidoo. He'd been assigned to a judge known as one of the more conservative judges in the federal court in Massachusetts.

On April 8, thirteen parents and one college coach caved and agreed to plead guilty for their roles in the scandal. Some of the parents issued public statements, expressing their shame and regret.

They returned to the courthouse in Boston to formally plead guilty in groups of two or three at a time. The proceedings were awkward up-and-down dances, with defendants looking slightly confused about when to stand and sit, like someone who's never been to Catholic Mass before. The judge bopped between defendants as they rose to answer "yes, Your Honor" or "I do," and then sat.

They'd have to respond to a volley of prying queries, to demonstrate they were sober, of sound mind, and clear about what rights they would have had—and what burden prosecutors would have had to meet—if they took the case to trial.

Bruce and Davina Isackson were the first to formally plead guilty, and they appeared together before Chief U.S. District Judge Patti Saris on a morning in early May to face charges on a cheating bonanza. The couple lived in the up-scale San Francisco suburb of Hillsborough, their 6,400-square-foot mansion tucked safely behind a wrought-iron gate and tall shrubs. He was president of a real estate investment and development firm; she had a master's degree in biomedical engineering. The Isacksons had paid $600,000, including a large quantity of Facebook stock, to Singer's charity to get their daughters into UCLA and USC as pseudo soccer and rowing recruits. They'd also paid to rig one of the daughter's ACT scores and were in talks to "control the test room" for a third child.

Bruce had then written the fraud off on his taxes. When Singer, wearing a wire, met with Bruce to give his phony story that he was getting audited in December 2018, the father had a terrible thought about what would happen if the IRS discovered what his payments were for: "Oh my God," he told Singer. Was this going to be "the front page story"?

The national media were indeed in the courtroom gallery watching Bruce and Davina, who were seated at separate wooden tables, each set with gold-and-black pitchers of water.

The couple looked alternately shell-shocked and relieved. Bruce, sixty-two, sat next to his lawyer, William Weinreb, a former federal prosecutor who'd won a death penalty conviction against the Boston Marathon bomber.

Davina, fifty-five, had long brown wavy hair and was in all black, with her fashionable oversize leather bag beside her. She was next to her Boies Schiller lawyer David Willingham, the former deputy chief of the major frauds section of the U.S. Attorney's Office for the Central District of California.

As the moment approached for Judge Saris to arrive, the courtroom fell silent. Bruce sipped his water. Saris came in and after a few formalities, she began asking Bruce the standard questions posed to defendants who plead guilty. Bruce's affect grew very flat.

"Do you feel physically all right today?" the judge asked him. "I know it's a tough day, but do you feel physically and mentally all right?"

"Yes, your honor," he said.

Davina dabbed at her eyes with a tissue. Willingham patted her back.

27

DIGGING IN

BUSINESS DEALS AND PARTNERSHIP payouts were at stake. Professional reputations and licenses hung in the balance. Amy and Gregory Colburn, a Palo Alto couple accused of ponying up $25,000 to have Riddell fix their younger son's SAT a year earlier, were ready to do whatever it took.

Just weeks after the government announced Operation Varsity Blues in mid-March, the thirteen parents and a coach had pleaded guilty. But prosecutors were wrong if they thought these defendants would all fold easily.

The Colburns had just rejected a deal to plead guilty to a charge each of conspiring to commit fraud, and like the other parents who didn't plead, they were then indicted on the new money-laundering charge, related to their tax-deductible donation to Singer's charity.

Hiring white-shoe law firms to challenge the federal government's claims carried big risks. Going to trial could run upwards of $3 million in legal fees, and to some observers, the affluent parents had a particular liability in the public-relations department: regular people in the jury box wouldn't be able to relate to them.

The Colburns were maintaining their innocence—and they simply couldn't stomach a felony. Gregory Colburn was a radiation oncologist, explained his lawyer Patric Hooper, a former deputy attorney general of the state of California who represented health-care providers in disputes with the government.

No way someone of Colburn's stature was going from a doctor's coat to a prison jumpsuit.

"He *can't* have this," Hooper said in an interview the evening the second charge was filed. "The impact of criminal allegations against a physician is much greater than the average person."

Gregory, then sixty-one, and his wife, who was forty-nine, cut a dignified picture. She had been a curator of an art gallery in San Francisco and then, later, an interior decorator and "color advisor" for residential clients. He sported chunky horn-rimmed glasses, while she wore her hair in an elegant updo.

Gregory worked at a San Jose hospital and was respected by peers in the Bay Area's radiation oncology community. He felt the publicly announced charges had already pummeled his professional reputation. Now his practice, medical license, and six-figure salary were all on the line if he pleaded guilty or was convicted.

The government had the couple on an incriminating taped call, seeming to float along in agreement as Singer recounted how they'd had their son take the SAT hundreds of miles from home at a West Hollywood testing center, and how they had paid for Riddell to clean up the boy's test after he finished.

"Mm-hmm," Amy murmured at one point. "Right," said Gregory.

They weren't actually agreeing, their lawyer later said. Rather, they were doing what polite society does when trapped in tedious conversation—try to civilly wind it down with tacit agreement, anything to get the hell off the phone. Singer spoke in clipped sentences, interrupted himself, and brought up events from more than a year earlier. "There was something odd about the call," Hooper said. Amy, he said, wondered if Singer might have the Colburns confused with another family, while Gregory "thought he was high."

Hooper also told a version of events around the SAT that provided a possible early glimpse of his defense strategy. Yes, the Colburns were Singer clients and had agreed to send their son to Southern California in March 2018 to take the test. Hooper believed the couple had been under the impression that going to the West Hollywood test site was beneficial for students who needed special testing arrangements, such as extra time. He said their son had for years received such allowances for a legitimate medical issue. The couple traveled with the teen and even turned the visit into a fun family weekend, visiting Gregory Colburn's old stomping grounds of West Hollywood, where he lived while doing his medical residency at UCLA, Hooper said. The teen brought his pencils and packed his lunch like his peers.

But according to Hooper, the couple had no idea that Singer's corrupt proctor would be there, or that he would take the test from their son at the end and fix his answers.

The Colburns, Hooper said, "thought it was all legit."

To BE ONE DEFENSE LAWYER standing against the full power of the federal government takes more than skill. It takes extraordinary confidence and nerve, as well as a client willing to pay. In a spare home office stripped of most everything but the essential items needed for work, lawyer Stephen Larson kept a quote framed on the wall: "Fairy tales are more than true, not because they tell us that dragons exist, but because they tell us that dragons can be beaten."

The clock ticked past 5:00 p.m. on Saturday, April 13, and Larson was still working. He had a dragon to slay for his new client, who until the previous month had been the celebrated USC water polo coach.

Prosecutors had accused Jovan Vavic of funneling $250,000 in bribes into a USC bank account that funded the water polo team, in return for designating some of Singer's clients as phony water polo recruits.

Larson, a graduate of USC's law school, was a former judge and onetime chief of the organized crime section of the U.S. Attorney's Office in Los Angeles. Dressed in jeans and a T-shirt, in his home office in Upland, a small bedroom community thirty-five miles east of Los Angeles, Larson typed out an email at 5:01 p.m. to Eric Rosen, who was also working on a Saturday.

The two were tangling that day about what a protective order should look like for the voluminous evidence, from emails to recorded phone calls, in the case. Rosen worried about leaks of sensitive information, including material about numerous parents who hadn't been charged. He referenced controls put in place with discovery in cases involving MS-13, an international criminal gang.

Larson bristled at the comparison to a case where the lead defendant was "aka Psycho."

"To even use MS-13 in the same sentence as a case involving parents, coaches, and university administrators strains credulity," he wrote. This was, he hoped the prosecution realized, "a different ball game altogether."

To Larson, that reference was another example of the government's overzealous approach. Coaches of patrician sports like water polo were now akin to gangsters?

"My own feeling is that the government may have cast far too wide a net on this," Larson said in a May 2019 interview. "This seems to be a publicly driven spectacle."

His confidence was about to get another boost as a weak spot in the government's case was emerging.

NOMINATED TO THE BENCH in 1979 by then president Jimmy Carter, U.S. District Judge Rya Zobel had seen a lot. But the case before her gave her pause.

The government had charged more than a dozen of the defendants, including most of the coaches accused of taking bribes, under the RICO statute, or the Racketeer Influenced and Corrupt Organizations Act, aimed at organized crime since the 1970s.

"To combat the Cosa Nostra," Zobel specified from the bench in Courtroom 12 at the federal courthouse in Boston in June. "And now it's being used in this particular context, which—it's a heavy statute."

A hint of disapproval seemed to drip from the voice of the eighty-seven-year-old judge, a Holocaust survivor with an elegant bearing and a crisp accent from her native Germany.

The first sentencing hearing in the college admissions scandal wasn't going well for the government.

Prosecutors had by then gotten twenty-two people, including fourteen parents, to plead guilty or say they would, and all agreed to deals in which the government could recommend the judge impose prison.

Outside the courthouse, the harbor teemed with dozens of sailboats on the beautiful late spring day. Inside, John Vandemoer sat in Zobel's packed courtroom, dressed in a dark suit and nervously awaiting his punishment. He hadn't had a decent night's sleep in about four months. His parents, sister, and wife sat behind him in the front row of the gallery. Prosecutors wanted thirteen months for Vandemoer, the former Stanford sailing coach. His attorneys wanted one year of probation.

Vandemoer had pleaded guilty to racketeering conspiracy for taking bribes from Singer for Stanford's sailing program in return for flagging some of the college counselor's clients as recruited athletes.

"This was the biggest mistake of my life," Vandemoer told *The Wall Street Journal* a day earlier in an interview at his attorney's office, where he wore a button-down shirt and sneakers.

It was the government's bad luck that Vandemoer went first.

If prosecutors wanted to send a signal that Operation Varsity Blues swept up entitled bad actors, Vandemoer wasn't the best poster boy. He was probably the least culpable of all the coaches accused, as even the judge said, because unlike the other coaches, he hadn't pocketed any money for himself and none of the students he tagged as recruits ended up attending Stanford.

But the biggest problem for the government wasn't an unusually sympathetic defendant. It was the metastasizing question that the Vandemoer sentencing was igniting—exactly who was harmed by Singer's illegal shenanigans?

In a broad sense, of course, the real victims of the scheme were obvious. Every teen admitted through fraud had essentially grabbed an opportunity that might have gone to another one who played by the rules. But punishment guidelines in federal fraud cases aren't based on conceptual losses; they are calculated based on direct financial impact to identifiable victims.

That led the prosecutors to cast the universities and the SAT and ACT testing agencies as victims.

But the U.S. Probation and Pretrial Services System, which prepares influential presentencing reports with recommendations for judges, found no financial loss to Stanford in the Vandemoer case. After all, the bribes actually went to Stanford, which was now trying to unload the ill-gotten gains. Even Stanford, in its victim impact statement, hadn't put a dollar amount on its harm. (Though the school said it'd had financial fallout, like investing in an investigation of the situation, and fighting off a class action lawsuit from students who claimed they didn't get in because of Singer's and Vandemoer's subterfuge.)

Judge Zobel decided: no loss.

She sentenced Vandemoer to one day in prison, which he had already served, and two years of supervised release, including six months' home confinement.

A number of defense attorneys were at Vandemoer's sentencing, furiously taking notes and later sharing summaries.

They knew they had just witnessed a setback for the government. Prosecutors may have just been saddled with an unfavorable precedent that would lead to lighter sentences for the others.

No, no, no, argued the lawyer for USC, donations didn't play a role in admissions.

Magistrate Judge M. Page Kelley cocked her head, skeptical.

Then why, the federal judge demanded from him in a September court hearing in Boston, did USC designate some applicants as "VIPs"?

A handful of internal USC admissions documents had spilled into the public days earlier, from discovery in the case.

The university's own records described "VIP" applicants in spreadsheets with references like "given 2 million already," and "1 mil pledge."

"What does the designation VIP signify?" Kelley asked.

Douglas Fuchs, the lawyer representing USC, just didn't seem eager to say aloud that some young applicants were Very Important People.

He danced around the question with a nonresponse that touched on "22 colleges throughout USC," and the ability to "apply a special-interest tag."

"So I think you said that," Kelley sighed. "But what specifically does VIP signify?"

Fuchs kept parsing. There was really no "quote, unquote VIP tag" but rather "six different tags that, as a collective group, are thought to be special-interest tags," he said.

Kelley referenced USC's own documents again. "So why do you see VIP, VIP, VIP?"

"It's shorthand," Fuchs said.

Fuchs's verbal gymnastics hinted that defense lawyers, by summer, had seized on a compelling counterattack. In legal filings that teased their eventual trial strategies, they sought to subpoena university admissions records and began trying to turn the spotlight on the gray area, the odious yet legal ways colleges have long courted donations from wealthy families and given their kids special consideration.

They suggested that Singer's scheme was merely a creative face of an accepted practice. Their clients were just doing what persons of prosperity have forever done to give their kids an edge.

"It's unfortunately the way American colleges work," lawyer Martin Weinberg told Kelley from the wooden podium in the September hearing, noting the role of philanthropy in admissions decisions.

Weinberg was representing Robert Zangrillo, a Miami Beach father of three accused of paying $200,000 to Singer and $50,000 to an account controlled by Singer's USC contact to admit his daughter, Amber, as a transfer student and competitive rower, after the university initially rejected her.

Though Singer had referenced a plan to pitch Amber as a rower, she was ultimately flagged by the athletic department as a "special interest" applicant. See? Weinberg said, USC gave preferential treatment to some applicants with deep pockets; this was no different. And the girl didn't even get in as an athletic recruit, so this wasn't some bribery scheme.

Zangrillo, the chief executive of Dragon Global, a private investment firm, was in it to win. Like a few of the parent defendants, he wasn't slowing down his business travel. He'd even gotten court permission to attend a "corporate off-site" in Tonga.

Zangrillo had hired one of the most well-respected trial lawyers in Boston. Weinberg had done solely defense since graduating from Harvard Law almost fifty years earlier. Known as fiercely intelligent, he tackled tough white-collar and criminal cases, from political corruption to murder. He'd represented Jeffrey Epstein until the disgraced financier took his own life a few weeks before this hearing.

"He made a donation to the school," Weinberg argued. "That's not a crime."

Weinberg had already successfully roughed up USC by publicly releasing the collection of internal USC admissions records—including the embarrassing "VIP" list—obtained in discovery. The disclosure drew a slew of headlines and was raising questions about whether USC had at least tacitly sanctioned Singer's actions.

The records also included intricate spreadsheets color-coded by university officials to track the "special-interest applicants"—flagged for their connections to USC officials, trustees, donors, or other heavyweights—with direct references to past and prospective dollar amounts of gifts from their families.

In one boorish email exchange included in the records, admissions officials mocked an applicant's grammar but agreed he was "good enough to shag balls for the tennis team."

"Heheh, you said balls," the dean of admissions replied to one of his direct reports, making a *Beavis and Butt-Head* reference.

Of course, a few pesky details weakened the notion that parents merely made donations to improve their odds. Prosecutors laid out evidence suggesting parents went to Singer for a guarantee, often not paying up until the acceptance letter arrived. And then there were those doctored athletic profiles, often done with parents' help. ("That's going to take some clever lawyering," one prominent defense lawyer involved in the case acknowledged over coffee near the courthouse one day.)

When it came his time to speak, Assistant U.S. Attorney Rosen jumped up from his seat, holding Amber Zangrillo's college application in his right hand. He read from it.

"The *very first* activity is that Amber Zangrillo spent 44 hours a week doing crew at the L.A. Rowing Club, which is patently false!" he said.

Rosen steered away from the debate over USC's records and claims that parents were just making legitimate donations. "It's ridiculous," he said. "This is a complete side show, completely unrelated to the issues at hand."

Weinberg jumped in to speak for his client, who was not present. "The evidence from the audiotapes will demonstrate Mr. Singer, the government's pivotal witness, to be mendacious, to be extortive, to lie to parents, to fill out applications like the one that Mr. Rosen just read," Weinberg said. "Mr. Zangrillo or his daughter didn't fill out that application." He was hinting at another defense strategy—to claim the larger trove of evidence in the case would reveal Singer as a duplicitous bully who took control of submitting college applications and inserted false information.

THE GOVERNMENT MAINTAINED open case files against dozens of parents and coaches, and continued to try to get even more defendants to cut deals. Prosecutors sent "target letters" to some of the young adults who'd benefited from the scheme, informing—or perhaps warning—them that they could be implicated as well. It wasn't an accident that no students were charged initially: the government clearly saw parents and other adults as the prime movers. Yet, prosecutors hadn't ruled out going after the kids, some of whom knew all about the machinations—copied on emails, posing for photos, joining in phone conversations.

The target letters didn't mean charges were coming, but they could push parents to plead in hopes of protecting their kids.

The U.S. Attorney's Office in Massachusetts also continued to investigate new leads coming from the defendants who had pleaded guilty and were cooperating, like the Isacksons and Laura Janke. Singer himself had handed over his entire Rolodex, offering names of many more possible violators beyond the thirty-three initially charged.

Prosecutors interviewed new witnesses and targets in Los Angeles and elsewhere. Some past Singer clients lawyered up, terrified they would be entangled in the case. Indeed, the government would add three more parents to the pack before the year was out, including San Diego surf company executive Jeffrey Bizzack; Newport Beach, California, mother Karen Littlefair; and Xiaoning Sui, a Chinese mother who was arrested in Spain.

AT THE SAME TIME, the structural crack in the case widened. It had the potential to massively embarrass the government.

Rosen arrived at another federal court hearing in mid-September with hat in hand. He needed to make a good impression on Judge Indira Talwani, who had just become the most powerful figure in the college admissions case.

"We come in peace to the hearing, your honor," Rosen told her in a halting voice, "and I want to make sure that the court understands that."

Something had gone terribly wrong for Rosen and the other prosecutors, and he needed to get the case back on course—fast.

Probation department officials, preparing presentencing reports for a group of eleven parents who pleaded guilty, were coming back with conclusions that stunned prosecutors: just as in the Vandemoer case, they said, the parents' conduct had caused no clear pecuniary damage. After all, the parents still paid tuition and gave bribes that wound up in the coffers of college programs. Some even made additional donations once their kids enrolled.

To correspond with that "no loss" finding, the probation department was recommending the judge use sentencing guidelines of zero to six months for each parent. Their guidelines aren't mandatory, but carry great weight. For first-time offenders in white-collar cases, that low category often means probation.

Prosecutors knew it would be a defeat to have a group of defendants leaving court to pad around their mansions under terms of home confinement. That outcome would send a message to the public that the wealthy and well connected really don't have to play by the same rules as everyone else.

It's unusual for disputes between prosecutors and the probation department to be aired publicly. But Massachusetts U.S. Attorney Lelling took an opportunity to do just that. Talwani had asked prosecutors to weigh in if they objected to her conferring privately with the probation department, a practice that varies among judges. Lelling did mind, and he wrote a strongly worded letter, filed in the court docket, essentially saying that probation had gotten the sentencing guidelines wrong.

When Talwani called a special hearing to discuss the rift over sentencing guidelines, some defense lawyers excitedly called it the biggest event yet in the case. They were predicting victory, which for them now came down entirely to one thing: keeping their prominent clients out of prison.

They had reason to feel positive. The judge, a graduate of UC Berkeley School of Law who was appointed to the bench by Barack Obama, was considered friendly to defendants. Some people from the prosecution side sensed Talwani just didn't like the case.

Parents who had pleaded guilty and faced sentencing in the coming days felt hopeful for the first time in months about avoiding prison. Attorneys were drafting formal memos to the judge asking for sentences no harsher than probation, leaning heavily on that "no loss" finding.

On the day of the hearing, so many defense lawyers showed up that they filled the gallery of Courtroom 9 and spilled into seats in the empty jury box, resembling a jury of your whitest and best-dressed male peers. They exchanged handshakes and confident smiles. Other lawyers called in via a conference line.

The parents themselves weren't in court, but they were abundantly and expensively represented. Some had two lawyers there. Buckingham, always the overachiever, had three.

As usual, a number of high-powered former federal prosecutors were in the mix, including Daniel Stein, a former chief of the Criminal Division for the U.S. Attorney's Office for the Southern District of New York. He was representing Greg Abbott, the food and beverage packaging executive who had pleaded guilty to a charge of having his daughter's ACT and SAT subject test scores fudged.

Abbott's wife had also pleaded guilty for her role, and the couple, with homes in Manhattan and Aspen, wasn't looking to take a meals-included getaway courtesy of the feds.

The lawyers would be allowed to address the court, and it seemed likely the hearing could last for hours. Judge Talwani eyed them. "Please don't feel that everyone is obligated to speak," she said, eliciting a chuckle.

An official from the probation department was also in the courtroom, and Rosen directed some of his first comments to her. "I realize some sharp elbows have been thrown throughout the recent proceedings," Rosen opened gently. "We come in peace." Some of Rosen's colleagues listening to the hearing worried his usual oratorical skills seemed muted from the stress, as if his endurance was flagging and he was just fighting to keep the case alive. Which he was.

This was a massive fraud that caused real loss, he told the judge, running down the damage: colleges had to fire corrupt coaches, fight lawsuits, investigate students connected to the scheme, and revamp administrative and athletics policies.

The SAT and ACT organizations were particularly victimized, he argued, with Singer and his conspirators corrupting testing sites and spitting out fraudulent scores.

But could the loss, the judge asked, be broken down among the defendants?

It's "impossible to break down the costs," Rosen admitted. But he made a last-ditch effort, saying the guidelines allowed the government to use gain as a proxy for loss—in this case the gain to the entire conspiracy, led by Singer, measured by the size of the bribes parents had paid.

"You're saying we have a loss," the judge said.

"Correct," Rosen replied.

"We can't differentiate the different parts of the loss."

"Correct."

"So as a substitute for that, we're looking at the gain."

"Correct."

Talwani asked if anyone in the courtroom wished to speak. Not one of the defense lawyers piped up. "Silence," she said, sounding surprised. "Okay."

Why speak when you're ahead?

After the hearing, defense lawyers huddled in the hall. Rosen walked past them to the elevator, loaded down with law books, none of which seemed to be coming to his rescue.

Judge Talwani's ruling came three days later, filed in the federal court system just hours before her first sentencing. She was adopting the guidelines of zero to six months and the finding of no financial loss to victims in the parents' cases. She said she would consider each parent individually, but she rejected the government's proposal to tie sentences to the size of bribes paid by parents.

It appeared a string of parents could quite possibly dodge jail.

But there was one thing about Talwani that defense lawyers hadn't counted on. She was thinking more broadly than they realized. She believed college admissions were already rigged in favor of the wealthy, and that many of these parents had exploited those advantages to a notable degree.

28

SENTENCED

PRESIDING OVER A PACKED courtroom on Friday, the thirteenth of September, Judge Talwani held her eyeglasses between her thumb and index finger and peered out at the solemn defendant before her.

The judge had been reflecting on why there was a sense of moral outrage in the college admissions case. It wasn't because the public had suddenly discovered that it's not a true meritocracy out there. It wasn't about the financial harm to the colleges, or the testing agencies that had generated the technical infighting at the courthouse in recent days.

"The outrage," she said from the bench, "is a system that is already so distorted by money and privilege in the first place."

And the outrage, the judge continued, looking directly at actress Felicity Huffman, was "that you took the step of obtaining one more advantage to put your child ahead of theirs."

The musical score for the courtroom scene was subtle, punctuated by the shifting in seats, the clicking keyboards of reporters, the occasional cough or audible gasp. It crescendoed as the judge, known for being more lenient, revealed her cards for the first time. What had seemed very doubtful just that morning, when her opinion on the matter of financial loss and sentencing guidelines came through, now seemed to be a real likelihood. Was she actually sending Huffman to prison?

Almost exactly six months after the U.S. Attorney's Office announced charges in Operation Varsity Blues, the punishment phase for parents was under way.

It quickly took on the feel of a ritual, with camera crews stationed outside. Defendants walked, lips pursed and eyes straight ahead, down a sunlit hallway of freshly polished marble to the courtroom. Rosen or the other assistant U.S. attorneys opened their three-ring binders and leafed through documents, highlighting and circling and preparing their pitches until the last minute. Over at the defense table, the opposing lawyers would be doing the same as their clients sat, staring straight ahead.

After months of strategizing, it was go time. The defendants' lawyers were filing long memos for Talwani's review, painting pictures of the parents' law-abiding lives and unrelenting selflessness—until they joined up with Singer. In a bid for leniency, these affluent families were desperately hurling every scintilla of hardship that they had ever known in what became an almost amusing bid to earn the sympathy of the court. One dad told of being so poor as a child that his family cooked hot dogs over an open flame. Another had a stepmother younger than the defendant himself. Others struck a different note, like a divorce that made a defendant a single mom, albeit with a nanny and a nearly $9 million Beverly Hills mansion. Not exactly Charles Dickens–level horror.

Some of the high-priced attorneys would smartly present their clients as relatable, or as relatable as multimillionaires could be, while others just didn't know how to read the room.

One suggested the court should go easy on his client because the feds had interrupted the crime before the kid could get into the college, like a thief who gets caught while the bank teller is filling the bag with cash and claims he didn't actually rob anyone. One called his client, who lived in a home valued at more than $3 million, "middle-class."

Legal teams submitted letters of support to the court that included plaudits from people on the parents' payroll. A ballet instructor wrote that she went to Jane Buckingham's house and witnessed Buckingham's parenting style on an intimate level "as I instructed her daughter on arabesques and pirouettes."

Marcia and Greg Abbott, who'd paid $125,000 for falsified SAT subject test and ACT scores for their daughter, received letters of support from their two housekeepers, as well as from their French-trained architect and interior decorator. "They were kind enough to ask me to build and decorate their home in Aspen, and later their apartment in New York," he wrote.

A friend noted Marcia's earthiness, writing to the court how, "on more than one occasion, I saw her covered in grease from having delved into the engine of a Cessna as she learned to fly."

Other letter writers described the Abbotts' more charitable acts, and their daughter recalled in a letter to the judge how her family held barbecues and benefits for underprivileged children, and on Christmas Day served meals to the homeless. The Abbotts themselves wrote that they had entered Singer's testing scheme not for status, but out of a misguided desire to help a child struggling with Lyme disease.

The lawyers were leaving nothing on the cutting room floor when it came to keeping their clients out of prison. David Kenner, once dubbed the legal consigliere to Marion "Suge" Knight and his gangsta rap label Death Row Records, was representing Semprevivo, the Los Angeles father who'd bribed his son's way into Georgetown. Kenner asked for leniency in part due to Semprevivo's draconian economic suffering. Among the losses? The $400,000 Semprevivo had paid and the taxes he now owed on that bribe after he'd fraudulently deducted it a few years earlier.

And to bolster the case that "Mr. Singer pierced through Mr. Semprevivo's existing psychological defenses," Kenner submitted a thirty-four-page assessment from a criminologist who had also worked with Mike Tyson and Tupac Shakur.

Talwani chafed. This wasn't going to be Court TV.

"I don't feel I need an expert report from a criminologist to tell me how to rule here," she said. "Particularly where it's the same criminologist that's going to be probably presenting for everybody in LA."

Huffman was the first parent up, after two others were rescheduled for the pivotal hearing on the sentencing guidelines. Outside the waterfront courthouse, police directed traffic to keep the lookie-loos moving, and a gauntlet of media thronged behind a barricade waiting to glimpse Huffman.

A reporter from *Inside Edition* scoped out his rival from *Extra*, the celebrity-news TV show. The *Extra* reporter, sunglasses on a cord around her neck, held a mic and a notepad with her list of very important questions: "Have you spoken to Lori? What are her plans?"

Every slowing black SUV set off the same murmur in the crowd: "Is that them?"

THE GOVERNMENT CONSIDERED HUFFMAN'S conduct less egregious than most of the other parents'. She had paid $15,000 to have Sophia's test fixed—partly because Singer simply charged parents different rates—and had abandoned plans in early 2019 to repeat the fraud for her younger daughter, Georgia. She'd owned up to her crime and was the model of contrition. A major concern for her was making sure the public knew her daughter wasn't involved in the scheme.

Huffman's legal team, headed by Martin Murphy, a Harvard Law grad who previously ran the U.S. Attorney's Office's major crimes division in Massachusetts and was now a partner at Foley Hoag, had pressed themes they hoped would keep her out of prison, requesting twelve months' probation instead. They commissioned a lengthy statistical analysis of federal sentencing data for similar defendants to bolster their argument that prison would be overkill. They filed twenty-seven letters of support. Many of the notes, from longtime friends like actress Eva Longoria, siblings, nephews, and former colleagues from her early New York theater days, extolled Huffman's work ethic and warmth, and several harkened the same image of the easily influenced and overanxious mom that Huffman herself advanced. "Her brain is a bit like Swiss cheese," one friend wrote.

Such letters are common, and can be meaningful. But strike the wrong note—especially in the letter the defendant writes directly to the judge—and they carry a risk. There is a fine line between providing context for illegal conduct and providing an excuse.

Rosen didn't doubt Huffman's sincerity when she described herself as feeling insecure as a mother. Yet Rosen, a father of three, and his boss Frank, a father of four, considered every other parent out there who felt stressed and exhausted, terrified of making mistakes. They didn't become cheats or felons. "Welcome to parenthood," the team wrote into the remarks for the sentencing.

Prosecutors had asked for one month's imprisonment for Huffman, calling incarceration "the great leveler" between rich and poor. The parents were in this mess not because of need or desperation, they said, but because of a "sense of entitlement, or at least moral cluelessness, facilitated by wealth and insularity." What better place than prison, where everyone is subject to the same rules, to serve as an antidote?

The morning of the sentencing, staffers on the government's team were bracing for Talwani to side with the defense. And they feared it would kick off a string of other disappointments, with prominent parents landing light punishments—yet another instance of the powerful acting with impunity.

FINALLY, ABOUT FORTY-FIVE MINUTES before the 2:30 p.m. sentencing, a black SUV stopped outside the courthouse.

Huffman and her husband, William H. Macy, stepped out, wearing stoic expressions. Rail thin and dressed in a conservative navy dress and simple beige heels, Huffman clutched her purse with her right hand and Macy's hand with her left. Macy, sporting a rakish chin-scruff, looked shell-shocked, his deep blue eyes slightly watery. A local police officer and one from Homeland Security hovered nearby.

To some mothers watching that widely publicized entrance, it seemed a little unfair. Once again, it was all Mom's fault. "Huffman's next wardrobe call will be a fitting for a prison uniform," *The Boston Globe* wrote, "while Macy is awaiting the November premiere of the 10th season of his hit show *Shameless*."

The room was teeming with reporters, curious locals, and defense lawyers for other parents, as well as Huffman's friends and family. Latecomers were ushered into an overflow room to watch via video. Macy slid into a bench in the gallery, while Huffman took her spot at a wooden table with a placard atop it that said DEFENDANT.

The hearing didn't reveal any great surprises—at first.

Rosen, who hadn't even known who Felicity Huffman was when the investigation began, presented the government's case for imprisonment. He made his points about all the frazzled parents out there who didn't resort to fraud as Huffman had. And he noted that the actress had deliberated about her crime. "The defendant didn't just go into Walmart one day, pick up a fake SAT score off the shelf and check out," he said.

He mentioned Kelly Williams-Bolar, an Akron, Ohio, teacher's aide at a high school for students with disabilities. In 2011, she served ten days in jail for falsifying her daughters' home address so they could attend a better school than the one in their inner-city neighborhood.

"Ten days in prison for conduct far less egregious than that of the defendant here," Rosen said. "If a poor single mom from Akron, who is actually trying to provide a better education for her kids, goes to jail, there is no reason that a wealthy, privileged mother with all the legal means available to her should avoid that same fate."

Murphy on Huffman's team voiced a concern that had been rumbling through the community of defense lawyers in the case. They worried the parents were being judged more harshly because of their affluence. In other words, it was fun to skewer the rich and powerful.

"I count 27 references to Ms. Huffman's wealth and fame from the government," he said of the prosecutors' sentencing memo. Just as rich people shouldn't get off easy if they commit crimes, he argued, nor should they face unduly harsh punishment because of their wealth.

Huffman stood to address the court. She apologized to the judge, to the students, parents, and colleges she said had been affected by her actions, and to her family.

"One of the hardest things I've had to face after my arrest is when my daughter found out what I had done, and she said to me, 'I don't know who you are anymore, mom,'" Huffman said, her voice wavering. "And then she asked me, 'Why didn't you believe in me? Why didn't you think I could do it on my own?' I had no adequate answer for her."

Talwani lauded Huffman's quick acceptance of responsibility. Her comments meandered to community service, and how it would be an integral part of Huffman's rehabilitation. Staffers from the U.S. Attorney's Office observing from the gallery assumed they had their answer. Here we go, one thought. No prison.

That sense only deepened when Talwani said she would take a few arguments by the government off the table, in particular their statements that the parents had undermined confidence in the college admissions process. The playing field had cracks in it with or without these parents' actions, the judge said, listing legal donations, the preference for legacy students, and the high percentage of spots that go to the nation's wealthiest families.

But then the judge's mood shifted.

The cracks, she said, "give the context of where this all happened." Talwani ticked off all the ways children from well-heeled families already wielded an immense edge, including access to top high schools, pricey tutoring, private counselors, and a family network that allowed them to land the best summer internships.

In her view, that made it even worse that parents who benefited from that flawed system took yet one more liberty. They were already on third base, yet they still cheated to score a run.

She imposed fourteen days of prison on the actress, setting off whispers in the courtroom as everyone craned to get a look at Huffman.

With the clerk's announcement of "all rise," the court was in recess, and the whole tone of the college admissions case had just shifted. To casual observers, a fourteen-day sentence seemed light. But in reality, the government had landed an unexpected victory. Huffman, one of the least culpable of all the parents, got prison.

Outside, the defense lawyers huddled again, freaking out. They knew their clients, some of whom had paid Singer more than twenty times the amount Huffman did, were going to be serving time. One said, stunned, he'd have to rewrite his client's sentencing memo so as not to seem tone-deaf by asking just for probation.

Prosecutors left the courtroom and walked toward the elevator, faces neutral. But their relief was palpable. They had pulled the case back from the brink.

. . .

ELEVEN DAYS LATER, ROSEN set a folder on the podium in Courtroom 9 and unspooled a story he said began back in June 2017.

He recounted in withering detail how Devin Sloane, a Los Angeles dad, had his teenage son don a newly purchased Speedo and swim cap, pantomiming water polo poses in the backyard swimming pool.

"Imagine the conversation that ensued," Rosen told Talwani. "Imagine the direction that defendant provided to his own son."

The judge listened intently, chin in hand.

As defendants would learn in the coming weeks, she had a special distaste for the cheating parents who roped sometimes-unsuspecting teens into playing roles in the scheme.

"Sloane's participation in the crime did not stop on the edges of his infinity pool," Rosen continued. "Over the course of the next year, Sloane continued to actively and deliberately complete the crime and secure that admission slot at USC. And he developed a particular aptitude for lying."

Over at the defendant's table, Sloane's lawyer handed him a glass of water.

Huffman's sentencing made it obvious Talwani likely planned to give some term of prison to each parent, but the looming question was whether she would impose short symbolic sentences, as the fourteen days for Huffman had arguably been, or more meaningful stints of incarceration.

If Huffman seemed to be one of the more sympathetic parents in the case, Sloane came off as less likeable.

He had entered the courtroom wearing a fitted navy suit and stylishly bookish glasses, and gripping a brown leather briefcase with his left hand. A young-looking fifty-three years old, with a full head of hair, he might have been a chief executive headed into a meeting to discuss investments in the water treatment industry rather than someone who'd pleaded guilty to paying $250,000 to get his son into USC as a phony water polo recruit.

To highlight the better parts of his résumé, Sloane and his lawyers submitted to the court a polished video detailing his charitable work with the Special

Olympics, as well as dozens of letters of support, including from a Buckley School football coach who said Sloane was one of the few parents there who stopped to ask how he was doing.

Yet while Sloane and his lawyers said he accepted responsibility, the long sentencing memo his team submitted appeared to be an exercise in deflection. They sprayed around the blame: Counselors at his son's $45,000-per-year high school were "overburdened" so he'd had to hire Singer. Singer had duped this savvy successful businessman. He'd had a tough childhood. The memo from Sloane's lawyers even grumbled that USC had never returned Sloane's illicit payment for the ill-gotten admission spot.

"Well, let this be a lesson learned," Rosen said in court. "When you bribe someone to commit a crime, you don't get your money back."

Rosen said that Sloane had so taken the ten-foot pole to his own conduct that the probation department questioned whether he should be entitled to the sentencing advantages given to defendants who accept responsibility. The judge did give him credit.

Also poorly received was Sloane's proposal to avoid prison by instead volunteering for a community service project that would "create a bridge program that basically brings the values of inclusion, anti-bullying, and diversity, directly to the independent school children, who are the focus of this case," explained Sloane's lawyer, Nathan Hochman.

"I don't think the independent school children are the focus of this case," Talwani said. "That's about as tone-deaf as I've heard."

She stared out at him. "And who are the victims of this case, because it certainly is not the independent school children, is it?" she said, noting that the term was a euphemism for those in private schools.

It was obvious that Talwani wanted Hochman to plainly say the victims were the kids that didn't have the opportunity to go to USC because spots were obtained by bribes and trickery.

After a stumble, Hochman hit on the answer she wanted—but then proceeded to water it down, describing "the level of victim."

He was losing the judge. Defense lawyers for other parents who had pleaded guilty were in the courtroom. "He just didn't get it," one said later. "It was painful to watch."

"I keep hearing these words, 'facilitate, in connection with,'" Talwani continued. "The one word that is not, I don't think anywhere in your papers, is 'bribe.'"

Hochman again split hairs, saying "the quibble we've always had with the government" is that Sloane didn't know exactly who at USC would be getting his money.

More cringes from defense lawyers watching from the gallery. "Of course it was a fucking bribe," one said later. "I wanted to hit him in the back of the head with a piece of paper."

Talwani was determined to set the record straight in court.

"So you're saying your client didn't know how the messy details were worked out, but he understood that he was paying a bribe to get a spot for his son?"

"Yes, your Honor."

It didn't feel like the day was going Sloane's way when he stood to give his statement and said he took full responsibility, with no excuses or justifications.

"Some people see this as a case of privilege and arrogance," he said. "I think about this a lot, and it repulses me. In my heart and soul I only wanted what is best for my son. I realize now that my actions were the antithesis of that."

He had ended on a sincere-sounding note, one echoed by many parents in the case who said they tried, in a misguided way, they now knew, to help their children.

The judge, however, wanted them to consider whom they were really trying to help.

"I am going to start with a point that permeates a lot of the statements from parents here, 'I wanted to do what was best for my child,'" she began, repeating Sloane's words slowly, and pausing for effect.

There was more to it than that, she suggested.

"The crime that is at issue in all of these cases is not basic caretaking for your child," she said. "It is not getting your child food or clothing. It is not even getting your child a college education. It is getting your child into a college that might be called 'exclusive.'

"It is something maybe parents should be thinking about, which is, are they doing that for their children?" She paused. "Or are they doing it for their own status or for their own other goals that do not have anything to do with their children?"

Sloane would have time to think about it. She sentenced him to four months in prison.

BY LATE OCTOBER, TALWANI had sentenced eleven parents. She sent all but one to prison, from two weeks for Huffman to five months for Napa Valley vintner Agustin Huneeus. No one was getting near the incarceration prosecutors asked for, but white-collar first-time offenders who'd banked on probation were preparing to spend the holiday season at USP Lompoc or FCI Loretto or one of a number of other minimum-security correctional institutions.

A few themes had emerged. Talwani viewed the testing scheme as less awful than the "side door" bribes to coaches, which she saw as outright buying a spot at a university. She added a premium penalty for people who'd dragged their teens into the scam. Huneeus fell into that category and got five months in prison.

A key reason she was sending these parents to prison reverberated clearly when Marcia and Greg Abbott arrived to be sentenced together.

The hearing was unusual from the start, since their three-decade marriage was on the rocks. Before their lawyers arrived to sit between them, Marcia settled in at one end of the long defense table, Greg at the other, like a movie scene where a disunified couple occupies opposite ends of a formal dining table. Greg's counsel portrayed the couple's breakdown in communication as a root cause of his client's illegal entanglement with Singer.

Greg stopped to kiss Marcia on the head as he walked to the podium to give his statement. He had shaggy white hair and clear-framed glasses, and was already sniffling as he gripped the sides of the dais and spoke.

"Believe me, your honor, I have seen it all in Manhattan, from nursery school to college," he said. "I myself have been offended by the sense of entitlement and the dizzying lengths parents go to promote their agendas for their children, concoct resumes, buy board seats, and pony up to schools that marginalize those families who can barely afford to pay their tuition."

He stopped, took a deep breath, and tried to compose himself.

Then he said something that only reinforced to the judge why prison was needed.

"Your honor, many dear friends have tried to console me that the system is terribly flawed and that I, in my particular situation, did what many parents would have done to help their child," he said. Abbott went on to make clear that he certainly disagreed with these pals, and had let them know he had made a terrible mistake.

Yet judges don't sentence only for the defendant before them. They sentence to send a message to the people in the defendant's orbit who might be inclined to pull the same stunt. Again and again, Talwani would essentially tell parents that while she thought they'd learned their lesson, she wasn't sure about their peers.

She imposed a month in prison each for both him and Marcia, meant to be punitive to them and a warning shot to those sympathetic friends.

Throughout the fall, the lawyers pushed to keep their clients out of prison, citing a host of calamities as mitigating factors.

"We had death, we had illness, and everything in between," Justin O'Connell, the assistant U.S. attorney, mused at one point.

The lawyers also worked hard to portray their clients as, if not good, at least less awful than other defendants:

"There was no Photoshopping."

"Our case is not like the parent who hired a lawyer to fight the ACT."

"Our case is not like the folks who actually did a second fraudulent test."

The best approach seemed to entail just an unvarnished unloading of the truth.

That tactic was on display one October morning when Gordon Caplan put on his reading glasses and rose to make his statement. Caplan wore a dark gray suit with a white shirt and maroon tie, standard garb for a corporate lawyer. Now, though, he was a defendant, about to be sentenced for paying $75,000 to fudge his daughter's ACT score. Family, professional associates, and police officer friends from home in Greenwich, Connecticut, were in the court. Current and former Willkie Farr partners had written in support.

"This is hard, but I've come to the painful realization that this whole episode was, at least in large part, my own ambition for where my daughter went to school," Caplan said to the judge. "I lost sight of what it means to be a good father, as I obviously did not act in the best interest of my daughter."

Caplan's attorney asked for fourteen days in prison at most, considering Caplan was on his way to losing his law license, a substantial punishment already. The judge gave Caplan a month.

What would it take to avoid prison?

The courtroom crowd had thinned eight days later when P. J. Sartorio arrived to get his punishment for paying $15,000 to Singer to falsify his daughter's ACT score. Sartorio had something in his favor: he seemed like a regular-guy crook. He'd paid Singer in cash to avoid creating a paper trail. He'd even structured bank withdrawals over several days.

He piqued Judge Talwani's interest. She had clearly been irked throughout the proceedings by parents who sugarcoated their fraud by mingling it with proclaimed good deeds. "He is the only one in front of me who didn't try to convince himself, let alone his tax accountant, let alone the U.S. government, that what he was doing was legitimate." He got probation.

OTHER PARENTS WERE CALCULATING: stay and fight or cut bait. In late October, the expectation that prosecutors were about to file new charges, related to bribing people at colleges that receive federal funding, pushed some over the edge.

Four high-profile parents reversed themselves and entered guilty pleas, including Doug Hodge, his fellow former Sage Hill trustee Michelle Janavs, and former Hercules Capital leader Manuel Henriquez and his wife, Elizabeth.

Hodge appeared cool and composed in court, while Henriquez removed his glasses to wipe away tears.

The government took some criticism for bringing new bribery charges, classified as a crime under the ominous-sounding Title 18, section 666 of the

United States Code, against the holdouts. The move could be seen as trying to pressure people to plead, and to run up prison time for those who got sentenced.

"This is a case in search of a bribe or kickback," U.S. District Judge Douglas P. Woodlock told an assistant U.S. attorney at the end of October. Woodlock was sentencing Jeffrey Bizzack, a California surfing executive who admitted to paying $250,000 to have Singer get his son into USC as a false volleyball recruit.

Woodlock, a soft-spoken, erudite Reagan appointee, launched into his many questions about the case. He referenced the Greek mythological figure Procrustes, a 1930s *New Yorker* cartoon, and the economist and sociologist Thorstein Veblen. The sentencing went three hours and six minutes and for a while didn't appear to be going the government's way.

But when a prosecutor argued why probation wouldn't be appropriate, Woodlock waved his hand to cut her short.

"It's a jail case for me," he assured her. "This is a rich person's crime, that's what it is."

Bizzack was sentenced to two months.

Arguably, the most important sentencing after Huffman's came on an unusually frigid day in mid-November, when San Diego–area title insurance executive Toby Macfarlane arrived to be sentenced by U.S. District Judge Nathaniel M. Gorton.

Gorton was assigned to most of the parents remaining in the case, including those who might go to trial; this would provide a valuable preview into his take on their culpability and the egregiousness of the crimes. One camp thought he'd emphasize the families' wealth less, given that he was part of a fish stick dynasty as a descendant of the founders of the Gorton's Seafood empire.

But others viewed Gorton, a U.S. Navy veteran appointed by former president George H. W. Bush and considered one of the more conservative Boston judges, as the best draw for prosecutors. Lawyers for other defendants packed the courtroom, as did a now-familiar contingent of reporters. The final moments never got any less suspenseful.

Macfarlane, who pleaded guilty to paying $450,000 to have two kids pushed into USC as fake athletic recruits, appeared shaken when he stood and apologized "for the worst set of decisions I've made and worst actions I've taken in my entire life."

Gorton accepted his apology but said the blatant misuse of his good fortune "will be no more tolerated than the conduct of a common thief, because that's what you are, a thief of the respected values of decency and fair play that is a fundamental concept of our way of life."

Three months later, Gorton had similarly choice words for Doug Hodge, who'd admitted to working with Singer for five kids over more than a decade.

"Mr. Hodge, your conduct in this whole sordid affair is appalling and mind-boggling," he said in front of a packed courtroom. "There is no term in the English language that describes your conduct as well as the Yiddish term of chutzpah."

Gorton sentenced Hodge to nine months, the longest sentence thus far, and ordered him to pay a $750,000 fine.

Two days after his sentencing, Hodge would author an op-ed in *The Wall Street Journal*, saying he was still perplexed by "how I allowed myself to be taken in" by Singer.

He believed he was providing financial support to universities, while also helping his children, he wrote. (No mention of the fact that the payments went straight to Ernst, not to any university accounts.)

Chutzpah indeed.

29

***

A SYSTEM REFORMED?

IN LATE SEPTEMBER 2019, more than 6,600 college counselors, admissions officers, and people in the enrollment management consulting business descended on Louisville, Kentucky, for the annual conference of the National Association for College Admission Counseling.

The three-block radius around the Kentucky International Convention Center was buzzing with talk of yield management and recruiting tactics, recommendation letters, and application-fee waivers. School-branded stress balls, pens, and notebooks abounded. Collegewise, a college counseling firm, passed out what was by far the best swag: buttons that read "I said no to Aunt Becky," a snarky nod to Lori Loughlin's *Full House* character.

There were panels and break-out sessions on using social media to drum up interest in a college, the pros and cons of early decision, and the realities of college counseling at enormous high schools. There were concerned updates about a Justice Department antitrust investigation into the trade group, which represents around 1,720 colleges and universities, more than 2,460 secondary schools, and 730 independent college counselors.

And in the library-themed bar of the Omni Hotel, hallways of the convention center, and restaurants around the city, a common refrain: Varsity Blues wasn't an admissions scandal.

It was about bribery. Athletics. Testing. But remember, no admissions officers were charged in the scheme. They were the heroes, with Julie Taylor-Vaz at Buckley and PJ Petrone from Marymount trying valiantly to flag suspicious activity. At least that was what they kept telling themselves.

Bright and early at 8:30 on the first full day of the conference, Stefanie Niles, then the president of NACAC, took to the microphone in an enormous ballroom at the convention center. Behind her were nine of her peers, seated on two levels of risers, looking like they were on the stage of some throwback celebrity-studded game show. In the audience were a college counselor from a tony high school with multiple students connected to the scandal, and a private counselor who'd turned down a request to work with a student now looking to transfer to another college, their current academic career on hold because of ties to Singer.

Here was an opportunity for college counselors at high schools to own the fact that they didn't really know what their students were submitting to colleges, that they had turned a blind eye to the outsize role of outsiders. For independent consultants to say there was a quality control problem in their corner of the profession. For admissions officers to admit they may have trusted applicants a bit too much, given coaches too much autonomy, and too heavily favored applicants whose families might donate.

"If you are like me, you may have mixed feelings about the scandal," Niles said as the din died down. "On one hand I am relieved that no admission professionals have been implicated in the alleged illegal activity. On the other hand, of course, it's been dismaying to hear, in the wake of the scandal, that a significant portion of the general public believes that the U.S. college admission process is unfair, or even corrupt."

And so began the most formal acknowledgment of the Varsity Blues scandal and the havoc it played across the industry.

"The scandal has raised some legitimate questions about the influence of wealth and privilege in the admission process," Niles said. And, she added, it had also revealed a serious lack of understanding about how recruiting and college admissions worked.

But the panel pivoted to a hodgepodge discussion of everything the public believes to be wrong with the admissions process: schools rely too much on standardized tests; they ignore low-income students or those from rural high schools without a track record at the college. And their lack of transparency breeds mistrust. The insiders said again and again, "This was not an admissions scandal."

Jim Rawlins, the admissions director at the University of Oregon, lamented at one session about the harm done to people with such privileges as those involved in the Varsity Blues case, but also wrote the scandal off to "a couple of bad actors," leading to laughs about the double entendre and dig at Huffman and Loughlin.

The case was at once omnipresent and somehow absent. Among the thousands of registered attendees were representatives from Sage Hill in Newport Beach; Buckley, Brentwood, and Marymount in Los Angeles; Marin Academy, Woodside Priory, and La Jolla Country Day—a near-full roster of high schools attended by the kids of parents charged in the case, not to mention admissions officers from UCLA and USC.

Yet a session on "top need-to-know legal issues in college admissions" started with a disclaimer that the scandal was *not* on the agenda. The elephant in the room was often evicted with a joke. After Tulane admissions director Jeff Schiffman told a story at one panel about how someone had forged their college counselor's signature to apply early decision, USC admissions director Kirk Brennan feigned horror that someone would send in fake documents—as if USC, at the epicenter of the scandal, would have no idea what it was like to be fooled. It got a hearty chuckle from the packed room.

Emboldened by the convivial atmosphere and bourbon at a dessert reception for engineering schools one evening, a reporter approached two Sage Hill counselors to offer her business card and request a casual chat. After all, two trustees from the school—Doug Hodge and Michelle Janavs—were charged, and at least one other family from there had ties to Singer.

"We can't comment," they sputtered out in unison, standing in front of a spread with vanilla ice cream cooled by liquid nitrogen and bourbon-infused toppings. She had only said, "Hi, there." The yellow name tag with the label PRESS gave her away.

Arms stiffly to their sides, the counselors stared at the business card. After multiple requests, a plea for mercy, and an uncomfortably long stare, one accepted it. The card likely ended up in the garbage, along with soiled cocktail napkins and giveaways from Syracuse and Georgia Tech.

So if the national association governing admissions wasn't going to own the scandal, who would?

Schools offered early glimmers of hope, suggesting they would examine and reform the apparatus that allowed Singer to thrive. Soon after prosecutors announced charges in March 2019, Stanford and Dartmouth—the latter not even named in the criminal case—said additional administrators would now need to review the athletic credentials of those flagged by coaches as possible recruits. Yale said it would check on anyone who didn't show up after being recruited for a roster spot, and unveiled plans to randomly audit applicants' and admitted students' records, extracurricular accomplishments, and awards.

UT Austin had already made changes back in 2015, in response to the Kroll report on its admissions practices, in an effort to weed out unqualified candidates and eliminate undue influence by lawmakers or major donors. The reforms didn't address athletic recruiting, but after this scandal the school said it would now require written assessments of prospects' athletic abilities, and a review by someone in the athletic department's leadership confirming the veracity of the coach's claims. They'd also scrutinize anyone who dropped a sport right after getting to campus.

Notre Dame High School in Belmont, where Manuel and Elizabeth Henriquez had sent one daughter, said in March that it, too, would add another verification step when students' college applications claimed participation in outside club sports. The school would ask the club team coach to sign a letter confirming the student's involvement, the dates of participation, and even the teen's skill level and what tournaments she'd played in. The school already had a similar process in place for students who listed external volunteer or internship activities.

Marlborough School struck a sober tone, acknowledging in searing terms that community's role in helping to create such a scandal. Head of School Priscilla Sands wrote that the scandal was, "in some ways, the end result we knew was coming and probably deserve. No one was shocked, but we are all complicit, and it bears holding a mirror and gazing unflinchingly at our reflection."

She continued: "In this setting of high stakes and inflated expectations, college admissions has become increasingly transactional and parents who judge their own self-worth by the vanity bumper sticker on the family cars send a message to their children that they cannot be trusted with their first independent decision—the beginning of their entrance into adulthood. Cocktail parties are awash with conversations about early decision, early action, how respective schools are doing vis-a-vis one another, forcing us into a competition that obscures our missions and one we did not ask for. Parenting is not graded on where your child goes to college."

But scroll down the main Marlborough website, and those destinations still clearly matter: "85 percent acceptance rate to highly selective colleges," the page reads as it lists one of the selling points for the school, "highly selective" italicized and in yellow font popping off the purple background.

At the time Sands wrote her heartfelt letter, Morrie Tobin, father of Marlborough senior Sydney, hadn't yet been named as the tipster who'd brought the whole case down. Nor had he been identified as one of the parents who'd paid a bribe.

Still, Sands wrote, "We are all tainted by this scandal."

IN OCTOBER 2019, California governor Gavin Newsom signed into law three bills drafted in direct response to Varsity Blues, perhaps the most serious effort to reform the system in the state that was ground zero for the scandal.

One requires California's public and private four-year colleges to disclose whether they give any admissions preference to applicants with ties to donors or alums; another bars those found guilty in the case from taking tax deductions for donations they made to the state's schools in connection with the scheme; and the third requires three administrators to sign off on any admission of a student who falls short of the school's academic requirements (mainly, athletes or others with particular unique talents).

"We must strive for a level playing field in the college admissions process, so there can be equal opportunity for all," said Assemblymember Phil Ting, who authored one of the bills.

But there isn't equal opportunity for all.

Because if colleges post figures on who got in because of a rich dad or grandmother, or even stopped giving extra weight to candidates with the "recruited athlete" tag, privilege would still course through the admissions system.

Wealthy students would still have more opportunities to burnish their résumés with volunteer trips and unpaid internships, and they'd still have influential family connections who can put in a good word at a particular university. They can continue to afford SAT or ACT tutoring, private coaches to brainstorm and polish essays. They can pay private school tuition to attend schools like Buckley and Brentwood.

And as long as admissions offices leave open the gaping holes in their verification processes for regular applicants, little incentive will exist for high school seniors—or whoever's filling out their applications—to think twice before signing an affirmation on the Common Application that submitted material "is my own work, factually true, and honestly presented."

WHILE SINGER WAS NOW facing years in prison, he wasn't the only one out there.

There were still elaborate, international test fraud rings with hired guns and fake IDs and stolen exams shared overseas. Advising schemes thrived, too, technically legal but certainly shady. In summer 2019 *The Wall Street Journal* and *ProPublica* both wrote about a Chicago-area college counselor, Lora Georgieva, who advised affluent families in recent years to relinquish guardianship of their own kids so they stood a better shot at getting need-based financial aid. She was doing it—for a fee of $5,000—because she saw clients dipping into retirement accounts to pay for college, she told *The Journal*. "I don't think I figured out a loophole," she said, explaining that the criteria for being considered an independent student were easily found on the federal financial aid website. "It's all right there."

And coaches outside Singer's network were on the take, too. Who knows how many.

In 2013, around the time Singer was solidifying his relationship with USC coaches, Jerome Allen, then the men's basketball coach at Penn, began meeting with Florida businessman Philip Esformes in the lobby of the swanky Fontainebleau Hotel in Miami Beach.

At each meeting Esformes would hand Allen $10,000 in cash, stuffed in a brown envelope inside a plastic bag. It was a more direct tack than he'd taken for his older daughter a year earlier. Esformes had used Singer to pitch her to USC as a soccer recruit, along with the daughters of Doug Hodge and Toby Macfarlane. Allen had agreed to flag Esformes's son as one of five basketball recruits in 2014, to help grease his way into Wharton, even though Allen had assessed his talent as underwhelming.

In total, Allen earned $85,000 in cash and bribes and another $220,000 in wire transfers over two years.

The teen got into Wharton, but didn't join the varsity basketball team. Allen was sentenced in July 2019 to house arrest, probation, and community service.

PARENTS ARE ALSO VERY much at fault for feeding the frenzy that allowed someone like Singer to thrive.

At the start of 2019, the head of Sidwell Friends in Washington, D.C., urged families to be, well, a little friendlier. A little less conniving and backstabbing and petty.

The college counseling office had declared just before winter break that it wouldn't consider anonymous allegations about student behavior. In other words: please stop calling us and claiming that some other kid who also applied to your son's top-choice school is actually a bad apple with a drug habit or history of cheating.

"If a parent ever feels the need to inform me or my colleagues regarding the actions of a child that is not their own—I will ask you to leave my office or end the phone conversation," wrote Patrick Gallagher, director of college counseling.

A second letter, this one from the head of school, put the regulations in context by noting a handful of "unfortunate and uninformed interactions."

Head of School Bryan Garman knew this madness well, having just watched his daughter apply to college the prior year: "I know firsthand that it can stir deep emotions and elicit insecurities."

Sidwell's counselors "understand that we parents love our children, and they demonstrate tremendous patience when that love blurs our vision."

Still, Gallagher and Garman said: No more verbal assaults or disrespectful outbursts. Misguided passion is no excuse.

THE PARENTS WHO WERE criminally charged in the college admissions scandal learned all too well where the madness could lead. Their downfalls were swift and stunning: careers gone, licenses yanked, social standing obliterated.

Elizabeth Henriquez was mostly ostracized by her friends and neighbors in Silicon Valley, while Bruce and Davina Isackson, who agreed to cooperate with the government, were shunned because people felt they were selling out their friends. Morrie Tobin, whose entirely unrelated stock-fraud charge led investigators to the corrupted Yale coach and then to Rick Singer, was similarly derided as a snitch by some in his Los Angeles community.

They had to try to repair bonds with their children. Devin Sloane said that even worse than going to prison was knowing how he'd hurt Matteo.

Some parents who participated in the scheme still seemed in denial, framing themselves as victims and unable to admit a flaw even after pleading guilty in court. One father spent most of an interview talking about his own good deeds and how Singer lied to him, but refused to answer questions about the months in which he went along with the illicit plan and participated in falsely branding his child as an athletic recruit. A mother who pleaded guilty to paying Singer to rig college entrance exams for her child declined to talk except to say someone needed to get the "real story" of Rick Singer.

Still, other defendants seemed somehow transformed by the experience. They grew emotional in interviews, tearful when discussing the harm they'd caused their kids.

After leaving court the day of his March 12, 2019, arrest, Beverly Hills developer Robert Flaxman shielded his face with a dark hoodie sweatshirt from news cameras. He quickly pleaded guilty to paying Singer to fix his daughter's ACT score, and retreated inward for a long stretch.

"Certainly I went through a period of self-loathing," Flaxman said. "You're really disappointed in yourself. You've hurt other people." But, he said, he eventually found meaning in it all and recognized the unfairness in using wealth, power, and connections to gain an advantage, even when done legally. "It just made me realize that there is a softer way of doing things."

He served one month at a federal prison in Arizona, and enjoyed a visit from his daughter. He hoped that by pleading guilty, he was teaching her that the right way to handle a mistake is to own up to it. His big takeaway from the ordeal was to have a little more faith in his children, he said, and "trust they find their own path."

Gordon Caplan, once a high-flying corporate lawyer, also looked himself squarely in the mirror after pleading guilty to having Singer rig his daughter's college entrance test. The contrition and shame he displayed at court when he pleaded guilty, and at his sentencing, seemed genuine. "I blame no one but myself. I am only angry at myself, I am not even angry at Rick Singer," Caplan said months later. "He was selling something which I should never have bought."

The admissions case also resonated with people who weren't involved, but who watched the legal drama unfold. There was a greater appreciation for people and institutions who were doing things right. Tens of thousands of dollars in donations poured into Occidental College, including from donors who had no connection to the school, after *The Wall Street Journal* highlighted how the college had years earlier refused a request from Singer to reconsider an application from an academically challenged daughter of a wealthy family.

Other parents recognized they personally could have been the ones to cross the line if the opportunity was there. It had been that group Judge Talwani was trying to reach when she decided to send the defendants to prison.

At the Muttontown Club, a Long Island golf club that advertises its ability to offer "a sense of gracious civility," about seventy parents of seniors at another Quaker high school gathered one gray day in November 2019 to hear reassurances about how their kids, and they as well, would survive life after high school.

The mothers and fathers had already invested tens of thousands of dollars each year to enroll their kids at Friends Academy in Locust Valley, New York. Some had been paying tuition since preschool, and the price tag for the upper school was $37,000. The wife of a venture capitalist sat across the table from the head of Brooks Brothers, whose father founded the Luxottica eyewear conglomerate. Gucci scarves and Prada purses abounded.

And yet, over a luncheon of salad and choice of chicken or salmon, red or white wine, they fretted. Most of their kids applied early to some school or another, and now were waiting. Would the daughter get into the University of Chicago? Was the University of Southern California a long shot for the aspiring actress? Was it a mistake not to have started the Advanced Placement calculus sequence last year?

They hugged the head of college counseling, known for giving thoughtful and practical advice and writing heartfelt recommendations for students since the early 2000s. They traded upbeat words and well-wishes, even though some had sons and daughters essentially vying for the same spots. They spoke about the Varsity Blues scandal, the crazy scheme, those ridiculous parents. And yet, some shrugged, wouldn't you do almost anything for your kid if you had the means?

Matteo Sloane might have cautioned those parents to listen to their beloved children.

Ten months after his father, Devin, was arrested for cheating the system to land the young man a spot at USC, Matteo was still sorting out how his life had taken this turn. He was twenty years old, still enrolled in college, and now visiting his father at a federal prison in Lompoc, 150 miles away.

He had worked so hard in high school, but his father's illegal interference diminished the value of what he had accomplished.

In the beginning, after his family became national news, he had a constant pit in his stomach. Some friends disappeared. Yet Matteo forgave his father, and gained a new maturity and perspective. He said the college admissions scandal had just exposed a larger problem of parents being too invested in their kids' lives—and in the ability to tout those children's accomplishments as their own. He also realized that he hadn't spoken up enough or pushed back against the pressure-cooker environment that he and his peers were in.

He didn't plan to stay silent anymore when it came to decisions about his own future. What Matteo now worked toward was what he thought all kids should have. Breathing room, and agency to shape their life's path, whether it's charmed or twisted.

ACKNOWLEDGMENTS

This book arose out of our work breaking news developments in and covering the Varsity Blues college-admissions case for *The Wall Street Journal* and would not have been possible without the guidance and encouragement of *Journal* editors including Matt Murray, Emily Nelson, Kate Linebaugh, Ashby Jones, Joe Barrett, Tedra Meyer, and Christine Glancey.

We also had support from fellow *Journal* reporters and researchers coast to coast, whose own work helped us shed light on every corner of this sprawling and complex story. These colleagues include Melanie Grayce West, Sara Randazzo, Alicia Caldwell, Jim Oberman, and Maya Sweedler, with particular gratitude to reporter Doug Belkin, whose big ideas and deep digging made us all smarter.

Of course, we would have never launched on this endeavor at all if not for our agent Eric Lupfer, of Fletcher & Company, who gave us the confidence that we could write a book and cheered us along as we put together a proposal in one weekend. Throughout the process, he has been a wonderful writing coach, a deft editor, and a source of sage counsel.

We are so fortunate that this project found a home with the team at Portfolio, particularly our skillful editor Trish Daly, whose enthusiasm inspired us from the start. Thanks also to Nina Rodriguez-Marty, Niki Papadopoulos,

Adrian Zackheim, Tara Gilbride, Amanda Lang, Mary Kate Skehan, Lavina Lee, Megan Gerrity, Meighan Cavanaugh, and Jennifer Heuer.

We wrote this book over the course of just over a year. There were many early mornings, late nights, weekend road trips, and marathon editing sessions. We can't give enough thanks to the family and friends, too numerous to mention, who boosted our spirits and believed in us.

FROM JENNIFER: BOSTON BUREAU colleagues Jon Kamp, Mark Maremont, and Brett Arends provided almost daily advice and laughs, and Amanda Milkovits was a constant source of wisdom. Thanks to my West Coast family and friends, including Kathryn, Fred, Sidney, Jessica, and Marcelle, for hosting me during research trips, and to my mom for even hopping in the car with me at times. I am grateful to the Arsenault clan, and most of all to Mark, who read my drafts, delivered well-timed craft beers to my desk, and cheered me on every day.

FROM MELISSA: MY *WSJ* family has kept me motivated, grounded, inspired, and always striving to produce better journalism. Thanks to Dan Hughes for his legal-eagle eye, to Dan Korn for telling me he believes in me even during the toughest stretches, and to my dad for providing speedy, brilliant edits on the first full draft. My eternal gratitude to Abby for putting up with a mom-under-pressure for the past year.

NOTES

Many details of charged families' involvement with Rick Singer, including exact payment amounts, test scores teens received, and information listed on their college applications, come from an FBI affidavit filed in Boston federal court in March 2019 in connection with the criminal cases, and are not cited individually here.

PREFACE

designed to replicate the medieval hill towns: Draft Environmental Impact Report, Brentwood School Education Master Plan, filed December 2015.

She strode the stage: UATJLCenter, "Global Retailing Conference 2016—Jane Buckingham, Founder and CEO, Trendera," YouTube video, April 27, 2016, https://www.youtube.com/watch?v=9gnXWEYkq1Y.

"She felt she had to be": Descriptions of Jane Buckingham's parenting style and personality, and details of her childhood, are drawn in part from letters written by family and friends to U.S. District Judge Indira Talwani. Document 559, Exhibit B, filed October 16, 2019, in USA v. Buckingham, case no. 19-cr-10117-IT.

About a decade earlier, Buckingham had spoken: Rachel Abramowitz, "The X/Y factor," *Los Angeles Times*, December 30, 2007, https://www.latimes.com/archives/la-xpm-2007-dec-30-ca-trend30-story.html.

School fundraisers featured performances: Rebecca Ford, "Victoria Beckham Worked a Snack Bar at Her Kids' School," *The Hollywood Reporter*, August 18, 2017, https://www.hollywoodreporter.com/news/victoria-beckham-worked-a-snack-bar-at-her-kids-school-1029876.

At circle time for a toddler gym class: The circle time anecdote comes in part from letter from Daniel and Ben Barnz to U.S. District Judge Indira Talwani. Document 425-5, Tab 16, filed September 6, 2019, in USA v. Huffman, case no. 19-cr-10117-IT.

In 2010, celebrities and socialites: Sara Wilson, "A New How-To," *Los Angeles Magazine*, May 26, 2010, https://www.lamag.com/culturefiles/a-new-how-to1/.

"One of your parents has done something": Jane Buckingham, *The Modern Girl's Guide to Sticky Situations*. New York: HarperCollins, 2010.

"try to take joy in who my kids ARE": September 27, 2012, tweet by @JaneBuckingham.

"When your friends tell you to lie": Job or No Job, season 1, episode 2, https://freeform.go.com/shows/job-or-no-job/episodes/season-1/2-los-angeles-fashion.

CHAPTER 1: FUTURE STARS

had Singer the next year in Santa Monica: Details of Singer's place of birth, his son's birth, and his marriage and divorce come from: Divorce resolution plan for Singer, William & Allison, Sacramento Superior Court case no. 11 FL 07072.

He smiles in his senior yearbook photo: Lexi Lee and Violet Gilbert, "Face of College Admissions Scandal is a Niles West Alum," *The Niles West News*, March 14, 2019, https://nileswestnews.org/71029/news/face-of-college-admissions-scandal-is-niles-west-alum/.

"I would most like to be remembered": Image of yearbook quote printed in Matthew Hendrickson and Nader Issa, "How Rick Singer went from Niles West grad to face of college bribery scandal," *Chicago Sun-Times*, March 15, 2019, https://chicago.suntimes.com/2019/3/15/18482523/how-rick-singer-went-from-niles-west-grad-to-face-of-college-bribery-scandal.

Singer later said he moved: Deposition of Rick Singer, October 14, 2016, in Dayo Adetu, et al. v. Sidwell Friends School, case no. 15-CA-009948-B.

he was featured in the school newspaper: John C. McClanahan, "Alumnus pleads guilty in bribery scandal," *The Brookhaven Courier*, April 8, 2019, https://brookhavencourier.com/104999/campus-news/alumnus-pleads-guilty-in-bribery-scandal/#.

Years later, in a deposition: Rick Singer, at Sidwell Friends deposition.

Singer was looking for a new job: Some details of Singer's move to Sierra and his schedule while there come from Jeff Caraska, "Just Look Who's Undefeated in BVC," *Auburn Journal*, January 17, 1988.

After college, Singer taught English and PE: Marina Starleaf Riker, "Man at the center of college admissions scandal has ties to San Antonio," *San Antonio Express-News*, March 13, 2019, https://www.expressnews.com/news/local/article/Man-at-the-center-of-college-admissions-scandal-13686943.php.

Ever blunt, he told The Sacramento Bee: Ron Kroichick, "The all-overlooked team. Sometimes you have to look hard to see the talent," *The Sacramento Bee*, February 11, 1988.

Within days, the district fired: Bee Sports Staff, "Singer out as Encina's basketball coach," *The Sacramento Bee*, February 18, 1988.

the players liked Singer: Bee Sports Staff, "Encina boys vote to boycott game," *The Sacramento Bee*, February 19, 1988.

traveling around California and other states: Jim Van Vliet, "Morris gives Hornets an inside force," *The Sacramento Bee*, January 9, 1992.

"He was the kind of guy who'd": Dale Kasler, Michael McGough, and Joe Davidson, "Who is William Rick Singer, Sacramento man accused in college admissions scam?" *The Sacramento Bee*, March 12, 2019, https://www.sacbee.com/news/local/article227458949.html.

A 1992 budget shortfall: Ricci R. Graham, "Hoop dreams at Kennedy High School," *The Sacramento Bee*, February 20, 1995.

a more nuanced admissions review: "Undergraduate Access to the University of California After the Elimination of Race-Conscious Policies," University of California Office of the President, March 2003, https://www.ucop.edu/student-affairs/_files/aa_final2.pdf.

would charge a flat fee: Michael McGough, "Massive college admission scam led by Sacramento man, indictment says; 2 from Folsom charged," *The Sacramento Bee*, March 12, 2019. References prices listed in a 1994 *Sacramento Bee* article, https://www.sacbee.com/news/local/article227457069.html.

He wrote the 1978 initiative: Patt Morrison, "Patt Morrison Asks: Donald Heller, death-penalty advocate no more," *Los Angeles Times*, July 16, 2011, https://www.latimes.com/opinion/la-xpm-2011-jul-16-la-oe-morrison-donald-heller-071611-story.html.

A law clerk once said: Ibid.

He and Allison hewed to: Normal D. Williams, "The first step whether you want to save for retirement or simply live within your means: A budget is the way to start," *The Sacramento Bee*, November 9, 1995.

Singer landed the position after: Kathy Robertson, "Thousands turn to college-prep coach," *Sacramento Business Journal*, February 6, 2005, https://www.bizjournals.com/sacramento/stories/2005/02/07/story7.html.

CHAPTER 2: TIMING IS EVERYTHING

On February 1, 2002, the front page: The Jewish Press, February 1, 2002, https://issuu.com/jewishpress7/docs/2002-02-01.

also touted an upcoming evening event: Diane Axler Baum, "Program to Outline '25 Steps to College,'" ibid.

After the Money Store folded in Sacramento: "Business People," *Omaha World-Herald*, November 5, 2000.

five-year-old son, Bradley: Baum, "Program to Outline '25 Steps to College.'"

end up at DePaul University: Rick Singer, at Sidwell Friends deposition.

Singer had indeed enrolled: PhD program referenced in ibid.

hard data on everything: Robert Daly, Anne Machung, and Gina Roque, "Running to Stay in Place: The Stability of U.S. News' Ranking System," published October 2006, https://files.eric.ed.gov/fulltext/ED493830.pdf.

"Children do not become strong": A portion of Jonathan Haidt's quote initially appeared in Melissa Korn, "Failure 101: Colleges Teach Students How to Cope with Setbacks," *The Wall Street Journal*, December 19, 2018, https://www.wsj.com/articles/failure-101-colleges-teach-students-how-to-cope-with-setbacks-11545129000.

"CEO and master coach": See, for example, "Students planning U.S. degree need brand-building exercise," *The Economic Times*, June 21, 2004, and "About The Key" section of Key Worldwide archived website, https://web.archive.org/web/20190312154013/http://www.thekeyworldwide.com/about-the-key/.

Mitchell saw his unpaid role: Douglas Belkin and Melanie Grayce West, "From High School Basketball Coach to Ringleader of the Nation's Largest College Admissions Scandal," *The Wall Street Journal*, March 14, 2019, https://www.wsj.com/articles/from-high-school-basketball-coach-to-ringleader-of-the-nations-largest-college-admissions-scam-11552591369.

he had a dozen coaches: Kathy Robertson, "Thousands turn to college-prep coach," *Sacramento Business Journal*, February 6, 2005.

Come hear "nationally acclaimed college advisor": Advertisement from April 10, 2005, *South Florida Sun-Sentinel*.

Singer was charging $2,500: Robertson, "Thousands turn to college-prep coach."

Between 1994 and 2002, admit rates: "Undergraduate Access to the University of California After the Elimination of Race-Conscious Policies," University of California Office of the President, March 2003, https://www.ucop.edu/student-affairs/_files/aa_final2.pdf.

CHAPTER 3: ROAD TO RICHES

He was living in Tokyo: Some details of Doug Hodge's time in Tokyo, comments on his children's educational achievements, and travel activity come from Harvard Business School alumni bulletins, including December 2005, June 2006, June 2007, March 2008, December 2009, and September 2013.

An only child himself: Some descriptions of Doug Hodge's childhood, charitable endeavors, and aim to please his children come from Hodge's sentencing memo, filed January 31, 2020, in USA v. Hodge, case no. 19-cr-10080-NMG.

He mentioned Peyton's impending college search: Brien O'Connor at Rule 44(c) hearing for Douglas Hodge, July 22, 2019, USA v. Hodge, case no. 19-cr-10080-NMG.

"Why don't you meet Rick Singer?": Ibid.

Peyton wanted Georgetown: Hodge sentencing memo.

Singer told Hodge his daughter: February 4, 2008, email from Rick Singer to Doug Hodge and Kylie Schuyler, in affidavit of FBI Special Agent Laura Smith in Support of Criminal Complaint, filed March 11, 2019, in USA v. Abbott et al., case no. 19-mj-06087-MPK. Subsequently referred to as "affidavit," https://www.justice.gov/file/1142876/download.

also poor judgment: Letter from Doug Hodge to U.S. District Judge Nathaniel Gorton. Document 810, Exhibit A, filed January 31, 2020, in USA v. Hodge, case no. 19-cr-10080-NMG. ("I have made serious mistakes in judgment.")

In June 2008, Powers had urged: Justin Baer, Melissa Korn, and Gregory Zuckerman, "Pimco's Ties to Architect of College Admissions Scam Ran Deep," *The Wall Street Journal*, May 20, 2019, https://www.wsj.com/articles/pimcos-ties-to-architect-of-college-admissions-scam-ran-deep-11558344603.

Soon after, Singer sought: Ibid.

"It's kind of like the difference between": Kelsey Knorp, "Using Every Advantage," *The Granite Bay Gazette*, October 14, 2011, https://issuu.com/granitebaygazette/docs/october_2011_issue_for_web_posting.

in Sacramento, where the recession: Dale Kasler and Phillip Reese, "Sacramento's economy is booming. But is a recession on the horizon?" *The Sacramento Bee*, August 2, 2018, https://www.sacbee.com/news/business/article215187860.html.

When house prices plummeted: Moritz Kuhn, Moritz Schularick, Ulrike I. Steins, "Income and Wealth Inequality in America, 1949–2016," Opportunity & Inclusive Growth Institute, Federal Reserve Bank of Minneapolis, June 2018, https://www.minneapolisfed.org/institute/working-papers-institute/iwp9.pdf.

connected to Singer through: Jennifer Levitz and Melissa Korn, "Coaches Played Crucial Role in College Admissions Cheating Network," *The Wall Street Journal*, November 14, 2019, https://www.wsj.com/articles/coaches-played-crucial-role-in-college-admissions-cheating-network-11573727401.

Hodge paid Ernst $150,000: Government's consolidated sentencing memo for Elizabeth and Manuel Henriquez, Douglas Hodge, and Michelle Janavs, filed February 3, 2020, case no. 19-cr-10080-NMG.

spoke openly in interviews: Theresa Walker, "How a froyo shop in France is helping girls overcome the odds in Santa Ana, Africa, and Asia," *The Orange County Register*, May 18, 2016, https://www.ocregister.com /2016/05/18/how-a-froyo-shop-in-france-is-helping-girls-overcome-the-odds-in-santa-ana-africa-and -asia/.

She founded the nonprofit: Jodie Tillman, "My OC: Kylie Schuyler of Global G.L.O.W.," *The Orange County Register*, June 30, 2016, https://www.ocregister.com/2016/06/30/my-oc-kylie-schuyler-of-global-glow/.

This one cost him $175,000: Government's consolidated sentencing memo for Elizabeth and Manuel Henriquez, Douglas Hodge, and Michelle Janavs.

O.C. heavy hitters, including: Robin Fields, "Wired into the curriculum," *Los Angeles Times*, October 9, 2000, https://www.latimes.com/archives/la-xpm-2000-oct-09-fi-33820-story.html.

school administrators even did away with: Fermin Leal, "Sage Hill aims to shape 'whole student,'" *The Orange County Register*, November 26, 2008, https://www.ocregister.com/2008/11/26/sage-hill-aims-to-shape -whole-student/.

Marketing material used in 2012: Randy Krum, "The Sage Hill Difference marketing infographic & interview," *Cool Infographics*, October 22, 2012, https://coolinfographics.com/blog/2012/10/22/the-sage-hill-difference -marketing-infographic-interview.html.

a spot as a featured mentor: thekeyworldwide100, "Clarkson Quarterback Camp," YouTube video, January 10, 2012, https://www.youtube.com/watch?v=u81dUyVAdig.

The quarterback academy brought seven: Tom Luginbill, "Rettig Shines as Super Seven Concludes," ESPN.com, July 3, 2009, https://www.espn.com/college-sports/recruiting/football/news/story?id=4309596.

Montana would become a client: March 14, 2019, tweet by @JoeMontana, https://twitter.com/JoeMontana /status/1106352364703879168?ref_src=twsrc%5Etfw.

Singer also wrote a column: Rick Singer, "Working College Entrance in Your Favor," *Westlake Malibu Lifestyle*, May/June 2010, http://www.wmlifestyle.com/wp-content/uploads/2015/01/Westlake_Malibu_Lifestyle _MAY_JUNE_2010.pdf.

A video advertisement for the Key: thekeyworldwide100, "The Key Worldwide Overview," YouTube video, January 10, 2012, https://www.youtube.com/watch?v=0wq6yHlCznI.

Singer even tried his hand at reality TV: Descriptions of Singer's audition reel are drawn from TMZ, "Bribery Ringleader Rick Singer Reality Show Audition on College Admissions," YouTube video, March 13, 2019, https://www.youtube.com/watch?v=FK3HIGT6g5Y.

By late 2011, Singer and his wife: Singer divorce resolution.

CHAPTER 4: GOLDEN BOY

On December 2, 2011: Some details of Riddell's trip to Vancouver to take the SAT on behalf of Jake Sidoo come from: Third superseding indictment. Document 610, filed October 22, 2019, in USA v. Sidoo et al., case no. 19-cr-10080-NMG.

grappling with a brazen cheating scheme: "Students, Educators Say SAT Cheating Is Rare," *All Things Considered*, December 6, 2011, https://www.npr.org/2011/12/06/143224366/students-educators-say-sat-cheating -is-rare.

By late November 2011: Greg Cergol and Pei-Sze Cheng, "13 More Arrested in SAT Cheating Scandal," NBC New York, November 22, 2011, https://www.nbcnewyork.com/news/local/sat-cheating-scandal-students -surrender-long-island-probe-arrest/1933338/.

The main "academic gun for hire": Some details of the scam come from televised remarks by prosecutor Kathleen Rice on "The Perfect Score: Cheating on the SAT," *60 Minutes*, January 1, 2012, https://www.cbsnews .com/news/the-perfect-score-cheating-on-the-sat/.

By 2006, he was back: Some details of Singer's involvement with IMG first appeared in Jennifer Levitz, "A Core of the College Admissions Scandal Was Built at Elite Florida Sports Academy," *The Wall Street Journal*, July 1, 2019, https://www.wsj.com/articles/a-core-of-the-college-admissions-scandal-was-built-at-img -11561973402.

David Sidoo had a heartwarming origin story: Douglas Quan, "How a B.C. philanthropist who 'hit the motherlode' got caught up in the U.S. college admissions scandal," *National Post*, December 6, 2019, https:// nationalpost.com/news/canada/how-a-self-made-b-c-multimillionaire-became-ensnared-in-the -u-s-college-admissions-scandal.

earned a mediocre 1460 out of 2400: Third superseding indictment.

costing Sidoo a cool $100,000: Ibid.

That December day in Vancouver: Assistant U.S. Attorney Eric Rosen, at Rule 11 hearing for Mark Riddell, April 12, 2019, USA v. Riddell, case no. 19-cr-10074-NMG.

A year later, he'd take a test: Third superseding indictment.

CHAPTER 5: NEWPORT BEACH

An academic tutor, Timothy Lance Lai: Hannah Fry, "Effort to alter Corona del Mar grades detailed," *Los Angeles Times*, January 29, 2015, https://www.latimes.com/socal/daily-pilot/news/tn-dpt-me-0201-cdm-lai -20150129-story.html.

The whole story had a comical resemblance: "Rebel with a Cause" episode, originally aired November 11, 1992, recap on *Television of Yore*, https://www.televisionofyore.com/recaps-of-beverly-hills-90210/beverly-hills -90210-season-3-episode-13.

In the real-life case at Corona del Mar: Fry, "Effort to alter Corona del Mar grades detailed."

The tutor, Lai, eventually pleaded guilty: Orange County Criminal Court case no. 14HF2720.

He described the Key: "While College Admissions Become More Competitive, The Key Helps Students Stand Out Amongst Their Peers," April 6, 2011, press release, https://www.yahoo.com/news/While-College -Admissions-iw-1340938016.html.

At one point, he said he'd life-coached: Defendants' reply to the government's opposition to their motion for production of exculpatory evidence regarding Title III interceptions and consensual recordings and for other appropriate relief. Document 773, filed January 23, 2020, in USA v. Sidoo et al., case no. 19-cr-10080.

Phil Mickelson: March 14, 2019, tweet by @PhilMickelson, https://twitter.com/PhilMickelson/status /1106271208692244481.

Singer met with the then president: August 27, 2019, email from Jamie Ceman, vice president of strategic marketing and communications at Chapman University.

The college shifted the girl: Ibid.

Singer had been pitching: "While College Admissions Become More Competitive, The Key Helps Students Stand Out Amongst Their Peers," April 6, 2011, press release.

his mom gobbled up: Jennifer Levitz and Melissa Korn, "'Nope, You're Not Special.' How the College Scam Mastermind Recruited Families," *The Wall Street Journal*, September 6, 2019, https://www.wsj.com/articles /nope-youre-not-special-how-corrupt-college-counselor-recruited-families-11567782077.

"Tweak your narrative": Ibid.

The following year, Singer posted: "The Key Summer Intensive Program Announced for 2014," Key Athletics Club blog, May 29, 2014. Website now inactive.

"may help to provide placement": Key Worldwide Foundation 2013 Form 990.

Neighbor Daniel Darrow said: Gangster Capitalism, season 1, episode 4, "Ricky," June 4, 2019, https://www .stitcher.com/podcast/cadence13/gangster-capitalism/e/61652930.

"Oxy" had made the decision: Jennifer Levitz and Douglas Belkin, "When Admissions Adviser Rick Singer Called, This School Said, 'No, Thanks,'" *The Wall Street Journal*, November 6, 2019, https://www.wsj.com /articles/when-admissions-adviser-rick-singer-called-this-school-said-no-thanks-11573036202.

"Are you kidding?": January 2012 email from Rick Singer to Vince Cuseo.

sentenced to prison after: Appeal from the United States District Court for the Northern District of Texas, USA v. Clifford Singer. Opinion filed August 21, 1992, in U.S. Court of Appeals for the Fifth Circuit, case no. 91-7367.

Alternative schools weren't always as rigorous: Jennifer Levitz and Melissa Korn, "The Trick High-Schoolers Are Using to Boost Their Grades," *The Wall Street Journal*, June 18, 2019, https://www.wsj.com /articles/a-way-for-high-school-students-to-boost-their-gpas-take-classes-at-other-high-schools -11560850201.

He was pitched as: "Halstrom Academy Open House," Manhattan Beach, CA, *Patch*, April 24, 2013, https:// patch.com/california/manhattanbeach/ev—halstrom-academy-open-house-ef90a2b0, and "Halstrom Academy Speaking Event," West Valley Warner Center Chamber of Commerce, May 8, 2013, https:// www.woodlandhillscc.net/readpost.php?news_id=6607.

CHAPTER 6: FIERCE

Rebekah Hendershot sat stunned: Gregory Korte, "'So that's what he was up to': Rick Singer, architect of the scam, peddled a 'side door' to college admissions," *USA Today*, March 12, 2019, https://www.usatoday

.com/story/news/education/2019/03/12/college-scam-rick-singer-william-singer-felicity-huffman-lori
    -loughlin/3142687002/.

In fall 2013, he drafted an essay: Third superseding indictment.

"Can we lessen the interaction with the gangs": Ibid.

Thang Diep, for instance, understood he had: Student amici opening statement, October 15, 2018, in Students for
    Fair Admissions v. President & Fellows of Harvard College et al., case no. 2014-cv-14176-ADB. https://
    www.advancingjustice-la.org/sites/default/files/Harvard-Student-Amici-Opening-Statement.pdf.

Singer and his team helped fill out: Attorney Jonathan McDougall at sentencing hearing for Marjorie Klapper,
    October 16, 2019, USA v. Klapper, case no. 19-cr-10117-IT.

marking the boxes for "African-American" and "Mexican": Marjorie Klapper's sentencing memo. Document
    541, filed October 11, 2019, in USA v. Klapper, case no. 19-cr-10117-IT.

indicated the parents had no: Government's sentencing memo for Marjorie Klapper. Document 529, filed Oc-
    tober 9, 2019, in USA v. Klapper, case no. 19-cr-10117-IT.

Marjorie Klapper waffled a bit: Ibid.

Northeastern University in Boston: Melissa Korn and Rachel Louise Ensign, "Colleges Rise as They Reject," *The
    Wall Street Journal,* December 25, 2012, https://www.wsj.com/articles/SB100014241278873247313045781
    89282282976640.

Parents in this bubble brought: U.S. District Judge Douglas P. Woodlock at sentencing hearing for Jeffrey Bizzack,
    October 30, 2019, USA v. Bizzack, case no. 19-cr-10222-DPW. ("How do they socialize their kids to think
    that there are only a couple of schools worth going to when this country is filled with terrific colleges.")

As one mother's lawyer put it: Michelle Janavs's sentencing memo. Document 862, filed February 20, 2020, in
    USA v. Janavs, case no. 19-cr-10080-NMG.

Singer self-published a book: Rick Singer, *Getting In: Gaining Admission to Your College of Choice.* Newport
    Beach, CA: Key Worldwide, 2014.

Some families turned to outside experts: Melissa Korn, "Whose Advice Are You Taking? The Fight Over Col-
    lege Counseling at Elite High Schools," *The Wall Street Journal,* October 26, 2019, https://www.wsj.com
    /articles/whose-advice-are-you-taking-the-fight-over-college-counseling-at-elite-high-schools
    -11572082200.

a little under 600 members: Trends in Independent Educational Consulting 2016, https://www.iecaonline.com
    /wp-content/uploads/2017/02/IECA_State-of-Profession-2016.pdf.

their average all-in fee in 2015: Ibid.

In the late 2000s, two-thirds: December 17, 2019, emailed comments from Mark Sklarow, CEO of Independent
    Educational Consultants Association.

Stuyvesant High School in New York City: Robert Kolker, "Cheating Upwards," *New York Magazine,* September
    14, 2012, http://nymag.com/news/features/cheating-2012-9/.

A cluster of suicides shook: Hanna Rosin, "The Silicon Valley Suicides," *The Atlantic,* December 2015, https://
    www.theatlantic.com/magazine/archive/2015/12/the-silicon-valley-suicides/413140/, and "Epi-Aid 2016
    -2018: Undetermined risk factors for suicide among youth, ages 10-24—Santa Clara County, CA, 2016,"
    https://www.sccgov.org/sites/phd/hi/hd/epi-aid/Documents/epi-aid-report.pdf.

a vivid, searing description: Carolyn Walworth, "Paly school board rep: 'The sorrows of young Palo Altans,'"
    Palo Alto Online, March 25, 2015, https://paloaltoonline.com/news/2015/03/25/guest-opinion-the
    -sorrows-of-young-palo-altans.

"Remember, colleges are looking for": Singer, *Getting In.*

About one-third of public: College Board press release, "10 Years of Advanced Placement Exam Data Show
    Significant Gains in Access and Success; Areas for Improvement," February 11, 2014, https://www
    .collegeboard.org/releases/2014/class-2013-advanced-placement-results-announced.

Meanwhile, the Common Application offered: Jacques Steinberg, "When Listing Extracurricular Activities, No
    Need to Fill All Blanks," *The New York Times,* November 4, 2010, https://thechoice.blogs.nytimes.com
    /2010/11/04/activities/.

Heck, families whose kids lost: Shalini Shankar, "At the Spelling Bee, a New Word Is M-O-N-E-Y," *The Wall
    Street Journal,* May 24, 2019, https://www.wsj.com/articles/at-the-spelling-bee-a-new-word-is-m-o-n-e-y
    -11558702800.

One analysis of applications: Jennifer Giancola and Richard D. Kahlenberg, "True Merit: Ensuring Our Bright-
    est Students Have Access to Our Best Colleges and Universities," Jack Kent Cooke Foundation, January
    2016, https://www.jkcf.org/wp-content/uploads/2018/06/JKCF_True_Merit_FULLReport.pdf.

Dartmouth, Vanderbilt, and Northwestern fill: Melissa Korn, "The Decision That Hurts Your Chances of Getting Into Harvard," *The Wall Street Journal*, March 28, 2018, https://www.wsj.com/articles/the-decision-that-hurts-your-chances-of-getting-into-harvard-1522229400.

CHAPTER 7: THE GRAY AREA

In November 2013, Alessandra Bouchard: November 14, 2013, and November 15, 2013, email exchange among Alessandra Bouchard, Roger Cheever, and others. Plaintiff's exhibit 106 in Students for Fair Admissions v. President & Fellows of Harvard College et al.

"There is a front door getting in": William Rick Singer, at his Rule 11 hearing, March 12, 2019, USA v. Singer, case no. 19-cr-10078-RWZ.

As he said in a 2014 email: February 6, 2014, email from Rick Singer to John Wilson. In John Wilson's supplemental motion to compel production of exculpatory evidence. Document 699, Exhibit 7, filed December 18, 2019, case no. in USA v. Wilson, case no. 19-cr-10080-NMG.

He told one father the side door: September 15, 2018, call between Rick Singer and John Wilson, in ibid., Exhibit 4.

Jared Kushner is perhaps: The circumstances surrounding Jared Kushner's admission to Harvard are detailed in Daniel Golden, *The Price of Admission.* New York: Crown, 2006.

A spokeswoman for Kushner Companies: Daniel Golden, "The Story Behind Jared Kushner's Curious Acceptance Into Harvard," *ProPublica*, November 18, 2016, https://www.propublica.org/article/the-story-behind-jared-kushners-curious-acceptance-into-harvard.

In June 2013 David Ellwood: June 11, 2013, email from David Ellwood to William Fitzsimmons. Plaintiff's exhibit 104 in Students for Fair Admissions v. President & Fellows of Harvard College et al.

A Duke economist's statistical analysis: Expert Report of Peter S. Arcidiacono, Table A.2. Document 415, Exhibit 1 in Students for Fair Admissions v. President & Fellows of Harvard College et al.

"not so much a message": Plaintiff's opening statement, October 15, 2018, in Students for Fair Admissions v. President & Fellows of Harvard College et al.

Legacies—the children of alumni—stood a nearly 34 percent chance: Expert Report of Peter S. Arcidiacono, Table A.2.

Harvard men's tennis coach: October 2014 email exchange between David Fish, William Fitzsimmons, and others. Plaintiff's exhibit 111 in Students for Fair Admissions v. President & Fellows of Harvard College et al.

In May 2014, a worried mother called: Accounts of the track, women's water polo, and men's tennis admissions to UCLA, including exchanges between Singer and prospective students and their families, come from William H. Cormier, "Student-Athlete Admissions: Compliance Investigation Report," July 1, 2014, https://assets.documentcloud.org/documents/6393344/2014-UCLA-Compliance-Investigation-Report.pdf. Billy Martin's name was redacted from the report, but he was identified in Nathan Fenno, "Could UCLA have stopped Rick Singer and the admissions scandal 5 years ago?" *Los Angeles Times*, September 12, 2019, https://www.latimes.com/california/story/2019-09-11/ucla-rick-singer-college-admissions-scandal. That article also noted who else at UCLA was apprised of the matter.

Martin was even the point person: June 24, 2014, email from Mick Deluca to William Cormier.

After issuing its report, the school instituted: UCLA statement on 2014 Athletics Admissions Compliance Report, April 13, 2019.

"so bad for so many reasons": Details of UT Austin's admissions practices, "holds" for students, and the investigation come from "University of Texas at Austin—Investigation of Admissions Practices and Allegations of Undue Influence: Summary of Key Findings," February 6, 2015, https://www.utsystem.edu/sites/default/files/news/assets/kroll-investigation-admissions-practices.pdf.

In late October 2018, a seventy-something: Testimony of Ruth Simmons, October 30, 2018, in Students for Fair Admissions v. President & Fellows of Harvard College et al.

"Without lineage, there would be": Scott Jaschik, "How Harvard Can Legally Favor Alumni Children and Athletes," *Inside Higher Ed*, August 6, 2018, https://www.insidehighered.com/admissions/article/2018/08/06/education-department-once-investigated-harvards-preferences-alumni.

"Not a great profile but": Ibid.

"only preserves the status quo": William C. Dudley, "The Monetary Policy Outlook and the Importance of Higher Education for Economic Mobility," October 6, 2017, speech, https://www.newyorkfed.org/newsevents/speeches/2017/dud171006.

In recent years the admit rate: Melissa Korn, "How Much Does Being a Legacy Help Your College Admissions Odds?" *The Wall Street Journal,* July 9, 2018, https://www.wsj.com/articles/legacy-preferences-complicate-colleges-diversity-push-1531128601.

Applicants with strong but: Plaintiff's opening statement, October 15, 2018, in Students for Fair Admissions v. President & Fellows of Harvard College et al.

According to statements from: Student amici opening statement, October 15, 2018, in Students for Fair Admissions v. President & Fellows of Harvard College et al., https://www.advancingjustice-la.org/sites/default/files/Harvard-Student-Amici-Opening-Statement.pdf.

CHAPTER 8: PLAY BALL

"On the soccer or lacrosse field": September 17, 2013, email from Rick Singer to Toby and Madison Macfarlane, in affidavit.

her college list including: Toby Macfarlane's sentencing memo. Document 335, filed November 8, 2019, in USA v. Macfarlane, case no. 19-cr-10131-NMG.

She played soccer, but she wasn't good enough: Government's sentencing memo for Toby Macfarlane. Document 334, filed November 8, 2019, in USA v. Macfarlane, case no. 19-cr-10131-NMG.

a well-regarded senior executive: See, for example, letters from Robert Farrior, Vincent Martin, and Art Wadlund to U.S. District Judge Nathaniel M. Gorton. Document 335-1, Exhibit C, filed November 8, 2019, in USA v. Macfarlane, case no. 19-cr-10131-NMG.

unsuccessful round of couples counseling: Details of Toby Macfarlane's childhood, marriage troubles, and mindset as he engaged with Singer come from personal statement of Toby Macfarlane. Document 335-1, Exhibit A, filed November 8, 2019, in USA v. Macfarlane, case no. 19-cr-10131.

He also liked the idea: Toby Macfarlane's sentencing memo. Document 335, filed November 8, 2019, in USA v. Macfarlane, case no. 19-cr-10131-NMG.

"Our sports teams engender pride": March 15, 2019, email to Yale community from President Peter Salovey.

Critics say the practice only serves: Saahil Desai, "College Sports Are Affirmative Action for Rich White Students," *The Atlantic,* October 23, 2018, https://www.theatlantic.com/education/archive/2018/10/college-sports-benefits-white-students/573688/.

About 65 percent of all students: NCAA Demographics Search, 2018, Search by Gender and Diversity, http://www.ncaa.org/about/resources/research/ncaa-demographics-search.

higher than the overall: Digest of Education Statistics 2018, Table 306.10. Integrated Postsecondary Education Data System, U.S. Department of Education's National Center for Education Statistics, https://nces.ed.gov/programs/coe/pdf/coe_cha.pdf.

For skiing, lacrosse, and field hockey: NCAA Demographics Database, 2018, Coach and Student-Athlete Demographics by Sport and Title, http://www.ncaa.org/about/resources/research/ncaa-demographics-database.

A 2016 review at Amherst College: "The Place of Athletics at Amherst College," May 2016, https://www.amherst.edu/system/files/media/PlaceOfAthleticsAtAmherst_Secure_1.pdf.

thirteen for Division I men's basketball: ScholarshipStats.com, edited by Patrick O'Rourke, www.scholarshipstats.com.

The NCAA has fairly low standards: "Academic Standards for Initial-Eligibility," NCAA, http://www.ncaa.org/student-athletes/future/academic-standards-initial-eligibility.

In the Ivy League, student-athletes must: February 14, 2020, email from Matt Panto, associate executive director of strategic communications and external relations for the league.

review applicants in under eight minutes: Melissa Korn, "Some Elite Colleges Review an Application in 8 Minutes (or Less)," *The Wall Street Journal,* January 31, 2018, https://www.wsj.com/articles/some-elite-colleges-review-an-application-in-8-minutes-or-less-1517400001.

"I'm not a volleyball expert": Brian Costa, Melissa Korn, and Rachel Bachman, "Colleges Rethink Athletic Special Admissions in Wake of Indictments," *The Wall Street Journal,* March 17, 2019, https://www.wsj.com/articles/colleges-rethink-athletic-special-admissions-in-wake-of-indictments-11552820400.

now another administrator is expected: Message from Stanford President Marc Tessier-Lavigne and Provost Persis Drill, on Stanford's Notes from the Quad website, March 21, 2019, https://quadblog.stanford.edu/2019/03/21/an-update-on-the-admissions-fraud-scheme/.

Julia's SAT subject tests and SAT: Government's consolidated sentencing memo for Elizabeth and Manuel Henriquez, Douglas Hodge, and Michelle Janavs.

They also recommended his services: See, for example, Assistant U.S. Attorney Leslie Wright at waiver of indictment and plea to information of Bruce and Davina Isackson, May 1, 2019, USA v. Isackson, case no. 19-cr-10115-PBS.

CHAPTER 9: "ISN'T IT A GREAT DAY TO BE A TROJAN!"

"Isn't it a great day to be a Trojan!": Sue Vogl and Lynn Lipinski, "In Memoriam: USC President Emeritus Steven B. Sample, 72," *USC News*, March 29, 2016, https://news.usc.edu/97360/in-memoriam-usc-president-emeritus-steven-b-sample-75/.

"Good morning, everyone!" He beamed: C. L. Max Nikias inaugural speech, "The Destined Reign of Troy," October 15, 2010, https://presidentemeritus.usc.edu/the-destined-reign-of-troy-2010/.

Stanford's marching band snidely spelled: Kenneth R. Weiss, "Steven Sample transforms USC from a chronic academic underachiever into a rising star," *Los Angeles Times Magazine*, September 17, 2000, https://www.latimes.com/local/education/la-me-steven-sample-usc-rising-star-20000917-story.html.

pushing past skeptics: "LA 500: C. L. Max Nikias," *Los Angeles Business Journal*, August 10, 2017, https://labusinessjournal.com/news/2017/aug/10/la-500-cl-max-nikias/, and Jason McGahan, "How USC Became the Most Scandal-Plagued Campus in America," *Los Angeles Magazine*, April 24, 2019, https://www.lamag.com/citythinkblog/usc-scandals-cover/.

Fas Regna Trojae: Lynn Lipinski, "The Campaign for USC Hits $6 Billion and Keeps on Going," *USC News*, Summer 2017, https://news.usc.edu/trojan-family/the-campaign-for-usc-hits-6-billion-and-keeps-on-going/.

nicknamed the "$6 billion man": Matt Lemas, "The six billion dollar man: How Nikias is engineering the future of USC," *Daily Trojan*, December 1, 2016, http://dailytrojan.com/2016/12/01/six-billion-dollar-man-nikias-engineering-future-usc/.

To the north of the school: Tiffany Kelly, "It's a Trojan kind of town: Deep, long connection ties USC to La Cañada," *Los Angeles Times*, October 10, 2013, https://www.latimes.com/socal/la-canada-valley-sun/news/tsn-vsl-its-a-trojan-kind-of-town-deep-long-connection-ties-usc-to-la-cantildeada-20131010-story.html.

USC even surpassed UCLA: Larry Gordon, "USC beats UCLA in U.S. News & World Report rankings," *Los Angeles Times*, August 27, 2010, https://www.latimes.com/archives/la-xpm-2010-aug-27-la-me-rankings-20100827-story.html.

"would go there in a heartbeat!!": December 20, 2014, email from Doug Hodge to Rick Singer, in affidavit.

steering a golf cart: Karen Crouse, "Man of Many Fields and a Singular Mission," *The New York Times*, August 22, 2010, https://www.nytimes.com/2010/08/23/sports/23haden.html.

illicit payments to football star: Billy Witz, "U.S.C. President-Elect Cleans House," *The New York Times*, July 20, 2010, https://www.nytimes.com/2010/07/21/sports/21usc.html.

The NCAA sanctioned the university: "University of Southern California Public Infractions Report," June 10, 2010, https://web3.ncaa.org/lsdbi/search/miCaseView/report?id=102369.

USC offered up its own sanctions: "USC Announces Sanctions on Men's Basketball Team," *USC News*, January 3, 2010, https://news.usc.edu/26528/usc-announces-sanctions-on-men-s-basketball-team/.

USC doubled its athletic compliance staff: February 27, 2020, email from Lauren Bartlett, senior director of communications at USC.

he didn't want that "compliance culture": Whitney Blaine, "Faces of a new era: Pat Haden," *Daily Trojan*, August 17, 2010, http://dailytrojan.com/2010/08/17/faces-of-a-new-era-pat-haden/.

The university was an early adopter: Linda Kosten, "Outcomes-Based Funding and Responsibility Center Management: Combining the Best of State and Institutional Budget Models to Achieve Shared Goals," Lumina Foundation, June 2016, https://www.luminafoundation.org/files/resources/obf-and-responsibility-center-management-full.pdf, and "USC's Revenue Center Management System: How The Money Flows," USC Academic Senate, May 2019 newsletter, https://academicsenate.usc.edu/uscs-revenue-center-management-system-how-the-money-flows/.

At that point only football and basketball: USC, "A Conversation on Athletics Fundraising with Al Checcio and Pat Haden," YouTube video, August 5, 2011, https://www.youtube.com/watch?v=kYQCERusQIQ.

"You need to always be out": Ibid.

One of Haden's major goals: Ibid.

In 2012 he announced: "USC Athletics Announces $300 Million Fundraising Initiative," *USC News*, August 21, 2012, https://news.usc.edu/40434/usc-athletics-announces-300-million-fundraising-initiative/.

more than eighty projects: Peter Kiefer, "Can C. L. Max Nikias Turn USC into the Stanford of Southern California?" *Los Angeles Magazine*, October 27, 2014, https://www.lamag.com/citythinkblog/six-billion-dollar-man/.

People joked that cranes: "USC 2015: New Buildings on the Rise," *USC News*, December 28, 2015, https://news.usc.edu/90127/usc-2015-new-buildings-on-the-rise/.

In the most ambitious project: Diane Krieger, "A Strong Foundation for USC Village," *USC News*, Autumn 2014, https://news.usc.edu/trojan-family/the-rise-of-troy/.

USC also broke ground: Christopher Hawthorne, "Review: Disneyland meets Hogwarts at $700-million USC Village," *Los Angeles Times*, August 21, 2017, https://www.latimes.com/entertainment/arts/la-et-cm-usc-village-review-20170820-story.html.

"A fantasia of just-add-water": Ibid.

The "slow creep" of Collegiate Gothic: Ibid.

Fourteen percent of students: Data available at "Economic Diversity and Student Outcomes at America's Colleges and Universities," *The New York Times*, January 18, 2017, based on research by Raj Chetty et al., https://www.nytimes.com/interactive/projects/college-mobility/.

The off-campus Lorenzo student housing complex: "Lorenzo Luxury Student Housing for USC Students Grand Opening," May 29, 2013, press release, https://www.prweb.com/releases/2013/5/prweb10774901.htm, and "Palmer 'Re-Gentrified' Downtown LA, Despite Doubters and Design Criticism," *The Planning Report*, October 30, 2015, https://www.planningreport.com/2015/10/30/palmer-re-gentrified-downtown-la-despite-doubters-and-design-criticism.

various members of USC's administration: Douglas Fuchs, at September 18, 2019, hearing before U.S. Magistrate Judge M. Page Kelley in USA v. Zangrillo, case no. 19-cr-10080-NMG. ("anyone from 22 colleges throughout USC and other departments within USC can apply a special-interest tag").

Athletic officials sent wish lists: Jennifer Levitz and Melissa Korn, "'Father Is Surgeon,' '1 Mil Pledge': The Role of Money in USC Admissions," *The Wall Street Journal*, September 3, 2019, https://www.wsj.com/articles/father-is-surgeon-1-mil-pledge-the-role-of-money-in-usc-admissions-11567548124.

reps from USC's business school and athletics: February 21, 2014, emails among USC's Liz Frank, Ron Orr, Sarah Peyron Murphy, Donna Heinel, and Scott Jacobson, in opposition by Robert Zangrillo re: third-party motion to quash subpoena. Document 546, Exhibit 13, filed September 3, 2019, in USA v. Zangrillo, case no. 19-cr-10080-NMG.

"It is so, um, commercial": October 24, 2018, phone call between Bill McGlashan and Rick Singer, in government's consolidated response in opposition to defendants' motions to compel. Document 736-1, Exhibit SS, filed January 14, 2020, in USA v. Sidoo et al., case no. 19-cr-10080-NMG. Subsequently referred to as "government's opposition filing."

Loaded and high-profile moms and dads: See, for example, September 27, 2016, emails between USC official (name redacted) and Mossimo Giannulli, in government's opposition filing, Exhibit F.

After Doug Hodge made: Hodge sentencing memo.

"both tuition and philanthropy": February 27, 2020, email from Lauren Bartlett, senior director of communications at USC.

The school had other competing interests: See, for example, March 13, 2015, email from admissions dean Timothy Brunold to Donna Heinel, in opposition by Robert Zangrillo, Exhibit 8. ("I really need to protect the SAT.")

ass-kissing lines like: March 15, 2018, and March 9, 2016, emails from Donna Heinel to Timothy Brunold, in ibid., Exhibits 11 and 9.

CHAPTER 10: TAG, YOU'RE IN

Wilson's résumé, later posted: Callum Borchers, "Mass. Businessman Charged in College Admissions Case Has a Resume on LinkedIn. So We Fact-Checked It," WBUR, March 14, 2019, https://www.wbur.org/bostonomix/2019/03/14/mass-businessman-charged-in-college-admissions-case-posted-his-resume-on-linkedin-so-we-fact-checked-it.

whether a neighbor's tennis court: May 3, 2010, meeting minutes from Architecture and Design Review Board for Town of Hillsborough, https://www.hillsborough.net/AgendaCenter/ViewFile/Minutes/539.

his dad emailed Singer about options: February 10, 2013, email exchange between John Wilson and Rick Singer, in affidavit.

He'd even managed to set up a 2007 meeting: September 21, 2007, email to Rick Singer, subject line "meeting with USC President Steve Sample," in opposition by Robert Zangrillo, Exhibit 16.

Singer had connected in late 2007: February 3, 2020, email from Stephen Larson, attorney for Jovan Vavic.

"my guy": August 30, 2018, phone call between Rick Singer and Agustin Huneeus, in government's opposition filing, Exhibit LLL.

Originally, all the "side door": Report of government meeting with Rick Singer, September 21, 2019, in Defendants' Memorandum of Law in Support of Their Motion to Dismiss Indictment with Prejudice or, in the Alternative, for Suppression of Evidence Based on Governmental Misconduct and for Discovery and an Evidentiary Hearing. Document 972, Exhibit BB, filed March 25, 2020, in USA v. Sidoo et al., case no. 19-cr-10080-NMG. Subsequently referred to as "defendants' March 25, 2020, memorandum."

Vavic's lawyer later said there was pressure: February 3, 2020, email from Stephen Larson.

Singer told John Wilson the good news: October 13, 2013, email from Rick Singer to John Wilson, in government's opposition filing, Exhibit UU.

Vavic wanted him to "embellish": Government's opposition filing, Exhibit UU.

"needs to be a good résumé": Affidavit.

Vavic never requested anyone falsify: February 3, 2020, email from Stephen Larson.

Among the fibs was that: Government's opposition filing, Exhibit VV.

Vavic's wildly positive endorsement: February 26, 2014, email from Jovan Vavic, in government's opposition filing, Exhibit XX.

"Thanks again for making this happen!": March 1, 2014, email from John Wilson to Rick Singer, in government's opposition filing, Exhibit YY.

Would teammates know his son: March 26, 2013, email from John Wilson to Rick Singer, in affidavit.

to at least be able to scrimmage: October 23, 2013, email exchange between John Wilson and Rick Singer, in government's opposition filing, Exhibit WW.

"frankly after the 1st semester": March 27, 2013, email from Rick Singer to John Wilson, in affidavit.

his grades had suffered: January 12, 2015, email from Sam Wilson to Jovan Vavic, in John Wilson's consolidated memorandum of law in support of his motion to sever, to dismiss, and to strike. Document 995, Exhibit 12, filed March 31, 2020, in USA v. Wilson, case no. 19-cr-10080-NMG.

"mysterious $100,000 cashier check": July 22, 2014, email from USC official, in government's opposition filing, Exhibit DDD.

Vavic's water polo program would get: Superseding indictment, filed October 22, 2019, in USA v. Ernst et al., case no. 19-cr-10081-IT.

Vavic also received money for: Ibid.

Singer's charity listed a 2015 donation: Key Worldwide Foundation 2015 Form 990.

the charity gave water polo scholarships: February 3, 2020, email from Stephen Larson.

Khosroshahin agreed to designate: Assistant U.S. Attorney Justin O'Connell, at Rule 11 hearing for Ali Khosroshahin, June 27, 2019, USA v. Khosroshahin, case no. 19-10081-IT.

Singer gave a total of $350,000: Ibid.

in exchange for tagging four teens: Assistant U.S. Attorney Eric Rosen, at Rule 11 hearing for Laura Janke, May 14, 2019, USA v. Janke, case no. 19-10081-IT.

acting as a broker: Jennifer Levitz and Melissa Korn, "Coaches Played Crucial Role in College Admissions Cheating Network," *The Wall Street Journal,* November 14, 2019.

Khosroshahin would admit to: Plea hearing for Ali Khosroshahin, June 27, 2019, USA v. Khosroshahin, case no. 19-cr-10081-IT.

including introducing Singer to coaches: Levitz and Korn, "Coaches Played Crucial Role in College Admissions Cheating Network."

"Would you be willing to": July 14, 2017, and July 16, 2017, email exchange between Rick Singer and Laura Janke, in affidavit.

Janke earned more than $134,000: Assistant U.S. Attorney Eric Rosen, at Janke Rule 11 hearing.

In 2015, the USC athletics department hit: Susan L. Wampler, "USC Athletics Hits Its Highest Fundraising Total Ever," *USC News,* April 1, 2015, https://news.usc.edu/79117/usc-athletics-hits-its-highest-fundraising-total-ever/.

"significant milestone": Ibid.

That $300 million number would grow: March 6, 2019, tweet by @USC_Athletics, https://twitter.com/USC_Athletics/status/1103390097473331200.

Haden promoted her: Dave Dulberg, "A Trojan Promotion," USCTrojans.com, July 1, 2011, https://usctrojans.com/sports/2017/6/15/blog-2011-07-a-trojan-promotion-html.asp.

by 2008: J. Brady McCollough, "USC athletic administrator arrested for bribery in admissions scandal 'knew her stuff,'" *Los Angeles Times*, March 13, 2019, https://www.latimes.com/sports/usc/la-sp-usc-heinel-admissions-corruption-20190313-story.html.

at one point cost $100: Some details of Clear the Clearinghouse's services and prices come from Kaidi Yuan and Ashley Zhang, "Indicted USC Administrator Involved Colleagues in Her Private Dealings," *LAist*, December 5, 2019, https://laist.com/2019/12/05/indicted_usc_administrator_involved_colleagues_in_her_private_dealings.php.

USC officials were aware: February 27, 2020, email from Lauren Bartlett, senior director of communications at USC.

Heinel would admit she had: USCAnnenberg, "Sports & the Collegiate LGBT Experience," YouTube video, November 1, 2013, https://youtu.be/q6wV98L0Q1Q.

a proud father of a gay son: March 31, 2015, tweet by @ADHadenUSC, https://twitter.com/ADHadenUSC/status/582939268730867712.

he'd invited Heinel and her partner: "Sports & the Collegiate LGBT Experience."

The emailed introduction was enthusiastic: May 25, 2015, email to Pat Haden, in John Wilson's consolidated memorandum of law in support of his motion to sever, to dismiss, and to strike. Document 995, Exhibit 10, filed March 31, 2020, in USA v. Wilson, case no. 19-cr-10080-NMG.

he had a "red flag" up: July 4, 2015, email from Pat Haden to Donna Heinel, in ibid., Exhibit 4.

"I don't know anything about": July 6, 2015, email from Tim Brunold to Donna Heinel, in government's opposition filing, Exhibit UUU.

"Everybody has to go through her": August 30, 2018, phone call between Rick Singer and Agustin Huneeus, in affidavit.

Singer talked about meeting: July 14, 2017, email from Rick Singer to Laura Janke, in ibid.

At times, Heinel would weigh in: Ibid.

She successfully sold a teen: Examples of Singer's clients who Heinel pitched as athletes come from the affidavit.

a form of institutionalized fundraising: Brian Costa, "At USC, Admissions Cheating Scandal Runs Deeper," *The Wall Street Journal*, March 13, 2019, https://www.wsj.com/articles/at-usc-admissions-cheating-scandal-runs-deeper-11552505533.

Singer's clients would pay: Indictment. Document 1, filed March 5, 2019, in USA v. Ernst et al., case no. 19-cr-10081-IT.

She, in turn, facilitated: Ibid.

Heinel's lawyer later said: September 3, 2019, statement from Nina Marino, attorney for Donna Heinel.

Singer later said he hid the alliance: Footnote 6, government's consolidated sur-reply in opposition to defendants' motions to compel. Document 834, filed February 7, 2020, in USA v. Sidoo et al., case no. 19-cr-10080-NMG.

Heinel or someone who reported to her: February 27, 2020, email from Lauren Bartlett, senior director of communications at USC.

"Admissions just needs something": 2015 email from Rick Singer to Douglas Hodge, in affidavit.

"When there is an ethos": November 2019 interview with William Tierney.

"no quid pro quos": February 2020 interview with John "J. K." McKay.

continued to give Heinel great power: Arash Markazi, "Lynn Swann says USC was 'blindsided' by alleged actions of administrator in college admissions scandal," *Los Angeles Times*, March 15, 2019, https://www.latimes.com/sports/usc/la-sp-lynn-swann-usc-20190315-story.html. ("We had one person in charge," he says in the article, and "there's trust that this one person is doing the right thing.")

Heinel's financial relationship with Singer: Indictment in document 1, filed March 5, 2019, in USA v. Ernst et al., case no. 19-cr-10081-IT.

USC officials would get someone: Government's opposition filing.

CHAPTER 11: THE COACH

The night of June 22: Date from affidavit in support of criminal complaint against Michael Center. Document 4-1 in USA v. Center, case no. 19-mj-06065-MPK.

UT Austin had razed: Danny Davis, "Home at last: Texas finally debuts its new tennis center," *Austin American-Statesman*, January 28, 2018.

Center arrived at the airport: Assistant U.S. Attorney Eric Rosen, at plea hearing for Michael Center, April 24, 2019, USA v. Center, case no. 19-10116-RGS.

the tennis courts were demolished: Davis, "Home at last: Texas finally debuts its new tennis center."

UT Austin had just paid another university: Alex Sims, "Texas Releases Charlie Strong's Contract Details, Including Incentives," *Bleacher Report*, January 13, 2014, https://bleacherreport.com/articles/1922073-texas-releases-charlie-strongs-contract-details-including-incentives.

the team hopped around: Davis, "Home at last: Texas finally debuts its new tennis center," and Ralph K. M. Haurwitz, "UT East Campus plan wins praise from neighbors," *Austin American-Statesman*, April 30, 2015.

"alumni support, student support": Job description from Michael Center's personnel file.

His performance evaluations: Ibid.

The major athletic conferences report: Barrett Salee, "SEC generates $651 million in revenue, distributes over $44.6 million per school in 2018–19," CBSsports.com, January 30, 2020, https://www.cbssports.com/college-football/news/sec-generates-651-million-in-revenue-distributes-over-44-6-million-per-school-in-2018-19/.

the athletic department stared down: Brian Davis, "Horns operating in the red," *Austin American-Statesman*, January 11, 2015.

he earned just about $65,000: Jennifer Levitz and Melissa Korn, "Coaches Played Crucial Role in College Admissions Cheating Network," *The Wall Street Journal*, November 14, 2019.

He gave tennis lessons to Michelle Obama: Jennifer Steinhauer, "A First Lady at 50, Finding Her Own Path," *The New York Times*, January 16, 2014, https://www.nytimes.com/2014/01/17/us/a-first-lady-at-50-finding-her-own-path.html.

and to her daughters: Chris Almeida and Joe Pollicino, "Break Point: The Murky Future of Tennis on Georgetown's Campus," *The Georgetown Voice*, October 8, 2015, https://georgetownvoice.com/2015/10/08/break-point-the-murky-future-of-tennis-on-georgetowns-campus/.

He taught children of ambassadors: Ibid.

When tennis pro Anna Kournikova came: "Gordie Ernst and Adam Gross Take Part in Anna Kournikova Tennis Clinic," GUHoyas.com, July 24, 2009, https://guhoyas.com/news/2009/7/24/gordie_ernst_and_adam_gross_take_part_in_anna_kournikova_tennis_clinic.aspx.

He grew up in middle-class Cranston: Bill Reynolds, "Charges against Gordie Ernst a sad chapter in a R.I. story," *Providence Journal*, March 16, 2019, https://www.providencejournal.com/sports/20190316/bill-reynolds-charges-against-gordie-ernst-sad-chapter-in-ri-story.

"the golden boy of Rhode Island": Ibid.

he played on the pro tennis circuit: Jessica Tuchinsky, "Ernst has followed an unlikely path," *The Daily Pennsylvanian*, October 6, 1999, https://www.thedp.com/article/1999/10/ernst_has_followed_an_unlikely_path.

"We need these dollars": Justin Berman, President's Page column in *Hoya Netters Club News*, Winter 2006–07, https://docplayer.net/17008044-Hoya-netters-club-news.html.

At least as early as 2007: Levitz and Korn, "Coaches Played Crucial Role in College Admissions Cheating Network."

Ernst started taking payments: Assistant U.S. Attorney Eric Rosen, Rule 44(c) hearing, September 5, 2019, USA v. Ernst, case no. 19-cr-10081-IT.

he would be listed at times: See, for example, Key Worldwide Foundation 2015 and 2016 Forms 990.

In exchange, Ernst tagged: Superseding indictment in USA v. Ernst et al., case no. 19-cr-10081-IT.

The government would say he also: Ibid.

They had a membership: United States' memorandum in support of application for post-indictment restraining order, filed March 14, 2019. Document 25 in USA v. Ernst, case no. 19-cr-10081-IT.

"Queen of Clubs": Chevy Chase Club website, https://www.chevychaseclub.org/.

A Las Vegas businessman was visiting: Many details of the father's interactions with Rick Singer and Gordon Ernst were first reported in Jennifer Levitz and Melissa Korn, "'Nope, You're Not Special.' How the College Scam Mastermind Recruited Families," *The Wall Street Journal*, September 6, 2019.

Ernst would earn more than $2.7 million: Indictment. Document 1, filed March 5, 2019, in USA v. Ernst et al., case no. 19-cr-10081-IT.

gained a perch as a power broker: Matt Malatestas, "The Basketball Powerbrokers," *Vype High School Sports Magazine*, November 2011, http://www.ourdigitalmags.com/publication/?m=11820&i=88552&p=26.

"Martin is the man who knew": A portion of Sonny Vaccaro's quote first appeared in Jennifer Levitz, Douglas Belkin, and Melissa Korn, "'He Had the Magic Elixir:' How the College Cheating Scandal Spread," *The*

Wall Street Journal, March 25, 2019, https://www.wsj.com/articles/it-was-like-he-had-the-magic-elixir
-how-a-consulting-business-spawned-the-college-cheating-scandal-11553539186.

North Carolina native: Defendant details on summary page for Harris County, Texas, court records, case no.
102494001010-3.

Fox was a slender six feet: Ibid.

He was enthusiastically photographed: Pat Forde, Pete Thamel, and Dan Wetzel, "Meet Martin Fox, the mysterious Houston sports fixture caught up in the college bribery scandal," *Yahoo Sports*, March 13, 2019,
https://sports.yahoo.com/a-whole-new-world-of-corruption-how-houston-middleman-martin-fox
-fit-into-operation-varsity-blues-011841886.html.

accused of working with: Details of the crime come from United States Postal Inspection Service Investigative
Report, case no. 598-1317365-FB(1).

and was given a deferred adjudication: Order of Deferred Adjudication in Texas v. Martin Fox, case no.
1024940.

And his name came up: Trial testimony of T. J. Gassnola, October 11, 2018, in USA v. Gatto, case no. 17-cr-
00686-LAK.

Pump and his brother ran: Double Pump website, http://doublepump.com/about/.

Singer came calling in fall 2014: Center affidavit.

though he played tennis his freshman year: Ibid.

Singer sent the boy's transcript: Assistant U.S. Attorney Kristen Kearney, at change of plea hearing for Martin
Fox, November 15, 2019, USA v. Fox, case no. 19-10081-IT.

Two days later, Fox passed it on: Ibid.

"looks like he goes to": Details of Center's receipt of Schaepe's application material, response to Fox and for-
warding information onward within UT Austin, as well as the paperwork associated with the teen's scholarship, come from Center affidavit.

UT Austin admitted the teen: Assistant U.S. Attorney Eric Rosen, at plea hearing for Michael Center, April 24,
2019, USA v. Center, case no. 19-10116-RGS.

They also donated stock: Assistant U.S. Attorney Kristen Kearney, at Rule 11 hearing for Martin Fox, November 15, 2019, USA v. Fox, case no. 19-cr-10081-IT.

the boy returned the scholarship money: Assistant U.S. Attorney Eric Rosen, at Center plea hearing.

Singer sent Fox $100,000: Assistant U.S. Attorney Kristen Kearney, at Fox Rule 11 hearing.

In April and June, Singer gave Center: Center affidavit.

That spring, Singer withdrew $60,000: Ibid.

By 5:30 the next morning: Ibid.

CHAPTER 12: TEST DAY

had gone through hell in high school but: William Weinreb, at sentencing hearing for Robert Flaxman, October
18, 2019, USA. v. Flaxman, case no. 19-cr-10117-IT.

a divorced dad raising two teenagers: Sentencing memo for Robert Flaxman. Document 544, filed October 11,
2019, in USA v. Flaxman, case no. 19-cr-10117-IT.

He employed relatives and provided: Ibid. Flaxman's sentencing memo references exhibits B-2 and B-5, letters
filed under seal from Norah Groat and Kristine Flaxman to U.S. District Judge Indira Talwani.

Her treatment team at school voiced optimism: William Weinreb, at Flaxman sentencing hearing.

more than a little discouraging: Flaxman sentencing memo. ("Nowhere.")

Singer referenced Emily's unattractive academic history: Ibid.

She'd taken the test earlier: Supplemental sentencing memo for Robert Flaxman. Document 560, filed October
17, 2019, in USA v. Flaxman, case no. 19-cr-10117-IT.

had become so anxious: Flaxman sentencing memo.

She scored a 20: Ibid.

used fake IDs to stand in: Assistant U.S. Attorney Eric Rosen, at Riddell Rule 11 hearing.

"We have closed the loopholes": "L.I. Cheating Scandal Prompts Sweeping Security Changes for SAT, ACT," CBS
New York, March 27, 2012, https://newyork.cbslocal.com/2012/03/27/l-i-sat-act-cheating-scandal-prompts
-sweeping-test-security-changes/.

a group of Chinese nationals participated: US v. Han Tong et al., indictment unsealed May 28, 2015, case no.
15-cr-00111-JFC.

Chinese and South Korean test-prep companies exploited: "Cheat Sheet" series from Reuters, 2016, https://www
.reuters.com/investigates/section/cheat-sheet/.

"the only way that the scheme could work": Rick Singer, at his Rule 11 hearing.

Jack Yates High School elicited immense pride: Jose de Jesus Ortiz, "Third Ward proud of high-scoring Yates basketball team," *Houston Chronicle,* January 30, 2010, https://www.chron.com/sports/high-school/article /Third-Ward-proud-of-high-scoring-Yates-basketball-2014834.php.

The Yates boys' basketball team smashed: Doug Huff and Ronnie Flores, "Yates' blowout victories have people talking," ESPN.com, January 29, 2010, https://www.espn.com/highschool/rise/basketball/boys/news/story? id=4869093.

By 2015, Singer was paying Fox: Assistant U.S. Attorney Kristen Kearney, at Fox Rule 11 hearing.

paid Williams to allow Riddell: Superseding indictment in USA v. Ernst et al., case no. 19-cr-10081-IT.

"the outta-state kids": Rick Singer, at January 27, 2019, meeting with Manuel and Elizabeth Henriquez, in affidavit.

"I own two schools": June 15, 2018, phone call with Rick Singer, Scott Treibly, and Gordon Caplan, in government's opposition filing, Exhibit OOO.

it still sometimes operated: See, for example, Dvorskaya Alternative School 2012 and 2015 Forms 990, https:// projects.propublica.org/nonprofits/organizations/954829104.

began taking bribes from Singer: Assistant U.S. Attorney Leslie Wright, at Rule 11 hearing for Igor Dvorskiy, November 13, 2019, USA v. Dvorskiy, case no. 19-10081-IT.

a skyrocketing number of high school students: Douglas Belkin, Jennifer Levitz, and Melissa Korn, "Many More Students, Especially the Affluent, Get Extra Time to Take the SAT," *The Wall Street Journal,* May 21, 2019, https://www.wsj.com/articles/many-more-students-especially-the-affluent-get-extra-time-to-take-the -sat-11558450347.

"It's the right thing to do, but": Tamar Lewin, "Abuse Feared as SAT Test Changes Disability Policy," *The New York Times,* July 15, 2002, https://www.nytimes.com/2002/07/15/us/abuse-feared-as-sat-test-changes-disability -policy.html.

Requests to the College Board: Belkin, Levitz, and Korn, "Many More Students, Especially the Affluent, Get Extra Time to Take the SAT."

The exams could run $5,000 to $10,000: Ibid.

The College Board approved: Ibid.

He'd once crafted a phony tutoring invoice: Assistant U.S. Attorney Justin O'Connell at Klapper sentencing hearing. (O'Connell references a 2015 email from Singer that read, in part, "It is a fake invoice.")

"needs testing for 100 percent time": May 25, 2017, email from Rick Singer to Agustin Huneeus and psychologist, in affidavit.

"I'm gonna talk to our psychologist": June 15, 2018, phone call between Rick Singer and Gordon Caplan, in affidavit.

The kids often thought: Rick Singer, at his Rule 11 hearing.

would sign the paperwork: ACT Administration and Payment Report—Special Testing, in government's opposition filing, Exhibit GG.

"between 11 and 17 days later": Rick Singer, at his Rule 11 hearing.

Williams earned $5,000 directly: Indictment in document 1, filed March 5, 2019, in USA v. Ernst et al., case no. 19-cr-10081-IT.

through a middleman: Assistant U.S. Attorney Kristen Kearney, at Fox Rule 11 hearing.

Dvorskiy, at West Hollywood College Preparatory: Assistant U.S. Attorney Leslie Wright, at Dvorskiy Rule 11 hearing.

Riddell would go on to earn: Assistant U.S. Attorney Eric Rosen, at Riddell Rule 11 hearing.

"We got on the last flight out": October 5, 2018, phone call between Marcia Abbott and Rick Singer, in affidavit.

Riddell fudged enough tests: Assistant U.S. Attorney Leslie Wright, at Dvorskiy Rule 11 hearing.

Repeat customers requested Riddell: See, for example, August 3, 2018, phone call between Marcia Abbott and Rick Singer, in affidavit.

Singer hired a second corrupt proctor: Affidavit.

One mother mused with Singer: November 5, 2018, phone call between Elizabeth Henriquez and Rick Singer, in affidavit.

"Through connections there, we have been": September 13, 2016, emails between Elizabeth Henriquez and a high school counselor, in ibid.

later said he'd gloated with the girl: Government's consolidated sentencing memo for Elizabeth and Manuel Henriquez, Douglas Hodge, and Michelle Janavs.

He gave a phony story: Flaxman sentencing memo.
He would later get emotional: Robert Flaxman, at his sentencing hearing.
she'd taken the exam alongside: Assistant U.S. Attorney Justin O'Connell, at ibid.
encouraged them to get different ones: Government's consolidated sentencing memo for Elizabeth and Manuel Henriquez, Douglas Hodge, and Michelle Janavs.
Riddell had changed the plan: Flaxman sentencing memo.
Flaxman thought about calling Singer: Details of Flaxman's reaction to the new testing scheme come from attorney William Weinreb, at Flaxman sentencing hearing.
The rigged ACT got her a score of 28: Government's supplemental sentencing memo for Robert Flaxman. Document 542, filed October 11, 2019, in case no. 19-cr-10117-IT.
came back as a 24: William Weinreb, at Flaxman sentencing hearing.
She got into the University of San Francisco: Flaxman sentencing memo.

CHAPTER 13: THE ERG

throw on a gray pleated skirt: Details of Olivia Giannulli's morning routine come from her YouTube videos, including ones posted on June 19, 2017, August 28, 2017, and January 13, 2018.
who she'd want to play her: oliviajadebeauty, "being confident about youtube, making 3 wishes, etc. . . . ," YouTube video, June 13, 2015, https://www.youtube.com/watch?v=PBodSO9NZW8.
have her own makeup line: oliviajadebeauty, "lets talk & eat pizza," YouTube video, September 18, 2016, https://www.youtube.com/watch?v=e4CK2MSwiWw.
She sat down on an erg: July 28, 2017, email from Mossimo Giannulli to Rick Singer and Lori Loughlin, in government's response in opposition to defendants' motion to dismiss. Document 1066, Exhibit U, filed April 8, 2020, in USA v. Sidoo et al., case no. 19-cr-10080-NMG.
women's rosters have topped 100: Henry J. Cordes, "Football Schools Like Alabama, Clemson, Michigan Use Massive Women's Rowing Rosters for Gender Equity," *Omaha World-Herald*, August 1, 2019, https://www.omaha.com/sports/football-schools-like-alabama-clemson-michigan-use-massive-women-s/article_03d2e53d-1a19-5d2e-a752-5472a2532342.html#comments.
Giannulli told a story about: Bobby Hundreds, "The Man. The Myth. The Mossimo," *The Hundreds*, October 31, 2016, https://thehundreds.com/blogs/bobby-hundreds/the-man-the-myth-giannulli-mossimo-interview . Olivia Jade Giannulli also discussed it on a March 8, 2019, appearance on *Zach Sang Show*, https://www.youtube.com/watch?v=DY05-Uhcek0.
They wanted a more traditional path: Olivia Jade Giannulli's March 8, 2019, appearance on *Zach Sang Show*, https://www.youtube.com/watch?v=DY05-Uhcek0. ("My parents really wanted me to go.")
The family hired Singer in summer 2015: Government's opposition filing.
In April 2016, Giannulli wrote Singer: April 22, 2016, email exchange between Mossimo Giannulli and Rick Singer, in ibid., Exhibit A.
Bella's grades hovered: July 24, 2016, email from Rick Singer to Mossimo Giannulli, in affidavit.
"in workout clothes like a real athlete": August 18, 2016, email from Rick Singer to Lori Loughlin and Mossimo Giannulli, in government's opposition filing, Exhibit B. (Giannulli responded later that same day, "Will get all," and sent email September 7, 2016, with photos attached. Ibid., Exhibit C.)
Singer said he would pitch her: September 21, 2016, email from Rick Singer to Mossimo Giannulli and Lori Loughlin, in ibid., Exhibit E.
USC's development office had even contacted: September 27, 2016, email chain with Mossimo Giannulli, in ibid., Exhibit F.
He told his wife he blew them off: September 27, 2016, email from Mossimo Giannulli to Lori Loughlin, in ibid.
Singer, however, would later describe: Report of FBI meeting with Rick Singer, in defendants' March 25, 2020, memorandum, Exhibit U.
Sidwell had been sued: Melissa Korn, "Testimony Offers Different Side of Alleged Mastermind of College-Admissions Scam," *The Wall Street Journal*, June 3, 2019, https://www.wsj.com/articles/testimony-offers-different-side-of-alleged-mastermind-of-college-admissions-scam-11559579112.
"There are certain things": Rick Singer's comments and characterizations of the athletic recruiting process, and details of his expert report, come from his Sidwell Friends deposition.
Two weeks after: Bella Giannulli was presented at the October 27, 2016, subcommittee meeting, date listed in affidavit.

The photo of her on the erg: Details of Bella's athletic profile and application file come from government's opposition filing, Footnote 5, Exhibit D and Exhibit H.

two days later Singer emailed Giannulli: October 29, 2016, email from Rick Singer to Mossimo Giannulli, in government's opposition filing, Exhibit G.

Giannulli said he asked his business manager: November 1, 2016, email from Mossimo Giannulli to Rick Singer, in ibid.

she and Bella had spent much of June: Today, August 3, 2017.

"I wanted to show her the reality": Today, November 10, 2016.

grinding his way through high school: Some descriptions of Matteo Sloane's high school career, his family's interactions with Singer and Devin and Matteo Sloane's reflections on that period first appeared in Jennifer Levitz and Melissa Korn, "'Why Didn't You Believe in Me?' The Family Reckoning After the College Admissions Scandal," *The Wall Street Journal,* January 17, 2020, https://www.wsj.com/articles/why-didnt-you -believe-in-me-the-family-reckoning-after-the-college-admissions-scandal-11579276312.

He gave a presentation at a local conference: "Buckley's SDLC Reps Present at Student Voices 2017," Buckley School news story, January 25, 2017, https://www.buckley.org/news-detail?pk=864666.

Sloane saw himself in Matteo: Details of how Devin Sloane thought about helping his son through the college application process come from letter from Devin Sloane to U.S. District Judge Indira Talwani. Document 462, Exhibit B, filed September 19, 2019, in USA v. Sloane, case no. 19-cr-10117-IT, and from Devin Sloane's sentencing memo. Document 462, filed September 19, 2019, in USA v. Sloane, case no. 19-cr-10117-IT.

Sloane visited Amazon.com: Details of the online purchases, photo shoot and work with the graphic designer, and Matteo's athletic profile come from affidavit and government's sentencing memo for Devin Sloane. Document 455, filed September 17, 2019, in USA v. Sloane, case no. 19-cr-10117-IT.

Singer later posted on his website: Claudia Koerner, "Here's How a Life Coach Scammed the College Admissions System for Wealthy Families," *BuzzFeed News,* March 12, 2019, https://www.buzzfeednews.com /article/claudiakoerner/rick-singer-life-coach-college-admissions-scam.

"I wanted to thank you again": April 10, 2017, email from Mossimo Giannulli to Rick Singer, in government's opposition filing, Exhibit L.

"Good news," Bella was in at USC: April 10, 2017, email from Mossimo Giannulli, in ibid., Exhibit K.

"Yes Olivia as well": April 10, 2017, emails from Mossimo Giannulli and Lori Loughlin to Rick Singer, in ibid., Exhibit L.

ditched organized sports years earlier: oliviajadebeauty, "Get to Know Me Tag," YouTube video, December 24, 2016, https://www.youtube.com/watch?v=3G2gGdQT0l4.

"I'd be like, 'Where's my lipstick?!'": oliviajadebeauty, "Most Likely to Challenge ft. my sister," YouTube video, June 25, 2015, https://www.youtube.com/watch?v=ar9lcdDPEmk&t=4s.

Olivia's in-home cardio days: Details of Olivia Giannulli's workout activity come from YouTube videos. See, for example, "Vlog: Packing, Family Time, Organizing My Life," January 13, 2018, https://www.youtube.com /watch?v=9TQcv7oiZ7U, and "let's talk & eat pizza," September 18, 2016.

she had a personal trainer: February 6, 2018, tweet by @oliviajadee, https://twitter.com/oliviajadee/status /961077315424808960?lang=en, and testimonials on MichelleLovitt.com http://www.michellelovitt.com /testimonials/.

She hated physics: Comments about Olivia Giannulli's academic interests come from YouTube videos, including "Get to Know Me Tag," December 24, 2016, and "Snapchat Q&A w Bella," January 3, 2016, https://www .youtube.com/watch?v=O5lbyUoGErQ.

Singer asked Janke to craft: July 14, 2017, email from Rick Singer to Laura Janke, in affidavit.

He emailed Giannulli and Loughlin: July 16, 2017, email from Rick Singer to Mossimo Giannulli and Lori Loughlin, in ibid.

"If we want USC": July 20, 2017, email from Rick Singer to Mossimo Giannulli and Lori Loughlin, in government's opposition filing, Exhibit M.

"Moss will get this done": July 20, 2017, email from Lori Loughlin to Rick Singer and Mossimo Giannulli, in affidavit.

Her first day of senior year: oliviajadebeauty, "First day of Senior Year," YouTube video, August 28, 2017, https:// www.youtube.com/watch?v=GOjHBKh6M84.

The fabricated rowing résumé said: Government's consolidated sur-reply in opposition to defendants' motions to compel. Document 834-2, filed February 7, 2020, in USA v. Sidoo et al., case no. 19-cr-10080-NMG.

"CONGRATULATIONS!!!": November 16, 2017, emails between Rick Singer, Mossimo Giannulli, and Lori
    Loughlin, in government's opposition filing, Exhibit O.
Giannulli sent a $50,000 check: Ibid., Exhibit Q.
and agreed to send: Affidavit.

CHAPTER 14: DO IT ALL FOR THE KIDS

Brian Werdesheim sat on a stool: Banyan Foundation video, http://www.thebanyanfoundation.org/wp-content
    /uploads/2017/08/Banyan_Introv12_64.mp4.
members of the Young Presidents Organization: March 22, 2019 email from YPO spokeswoman Amy Reid,
    referencing events in San Diego and Bellevue, Wash. Client Eric Webb also saw him at a YPO event in
    Champaign, Ill.
And he addressed clients at: Jennifer Levitz, Douglas Belkin, and Melissa Korn, "'He Had the Magic Elixir:'
    How the College Cheating Scandal Spread," *The Wall Street Journal,* March 25, 2019.
That evening had a hefty title: Sloane sentencing memo.
Singer's illicit acts involved: March 11, 2020, email from Don Heller to prosecutors and other attorneys, in de-
    fendants' March 25, 2020, memorandum, Exhibit O.
Singer talked to a friend: Report of FBI meeting with Rick Singer, November 29, 2018, in ibid., Exhibit VV.
the purpose was to help: Ibid.
"Our contributions to major athletic university programs": Key Worldwide Foundation 2013 Form 990.
"I also knew that my daughter": Gregory Abbott at his sentencing hearing, October 8, 2019, USA v. Abbott, case
    no. 19-cr-10117-IT.
"Oh, even better!": July 12, 2018, phone call between Rick Singer and Jane Buckingham, in affidavit.
Singer told a father: Text message chain between Homayoun Zadeh and Rick Singer, beginning March 20, 2017,
    in affidavit.
"the last college 'donation'": February 5, 2018, email from Mossimo Giannulli, in government's opposition fil-
    ing, Exhibit S.
Dan Larson was initially intrigued: Portions of this anecdote first appeared in Jennifer Levitz and Melissa
    Korn, "'Nope, You're Not Special.' How the College Scam Mastermind Recruited Families," *The Wall
    Street Journal,* September 6, 2019.
"When you're dealing with": Dana Pump interview with David Meltzer, "How to Build and Leverage Rela-
    tionships with Successful People," *Entrepreneur,* May 11, 2019, https://www.entrepreneur.com/video
    /333346.
Philip Esformes, a Miami businessman: Assistant U.S. Attorney Eric Rosen, at Janke Rule 11 hearing.
Esformes was ultimately in legal trouble: Esformes was charged in 2016 with Medicare fraud conspiracy, taking
    illegal payments from federal health-care programs, money-laundering conspiracy, and other crimes, in
    USA v. Esformes, case no. 16-cr-20549-RNS. He was found guilty on a number of counts, though not on
    the main Medicare fraud allegation, and has since appealed his conviction.
a legitimate donation to his wife's charity: Key Worldwide Foundation 2013 Form 990, and report of FBI meet-
    ing with Rick Singer, November 29, 2018, in defendants' March 25, 2020, memorandum, Exhibit VV.
Banyan drew big-name donors including: Banyan Foundation 2017 Form 990.
Singer's company also gave money: Ibid.
Werdesheim served on that group's board: "Board of Directors," Fulfillment Fund website, https://fulfillment
    .org/about-us/board-of-directors/.
The organization went from recording: Details of Key Worldwide Foundation's finances, donations, and claims
    of charitable activity come from its IRS form 990s.
with whom Singer formed a short-lived company: Florida business records for the Opportunity Engine, http://
    search.sunbiz.org/Inquiry/CorporationSearch/SearchResultDetail?inquirytype=OfficerRegistered
    AgentName&directionType=Initial&searchNameOrder=ORENDERDONNA%20L120001012862
    &aggregateId=flal-l12000101286-f37ff773-8149-4620-b2c5-24abc92d7c36&searchTerm=orender
    %20donna&listNameOrder=ORENDERDONNA%20F9500000600425.
led by UCLA men's soccer coach: California business records, https://businesssearch.sos.ca.gov/Document
    /RetrievePDF?Id=02645368-11292517.
including a chain of Mexican restaurants: Racketeering forfeiture allegation in criminal information against
    Rick Singer. Document 1, filed March 5, 2019, in USA v. Singer, case no. 19-cr-10078-RWZ.
was for a time an executive: Gregory Korte, "Inside Rick Singer's college admissions network: An ex-con half
    brother, a Welsh soccer team, and a former NFL owner," *USA Today,* May 2, 2019, https://www.usatoday

.com/story/news/nation/2019/05/02/college-cheating-ring-rick-singer-half-brother-cliff-singer-swansea
-city/3631132002/.

parents gave to the charity knowing: William Rick Singer, at his Rule 11 hearing.

she was directed to the regular applicant pool: Assistant U.S. Attorney Leslie Wright at Isackson plea hearing.

"Per our discussion can you please": July 11, 2016, email exchange between Bruce Isackson and Rick Singer, in affidavit.

When his bookkeeper emailed to ask: October 17, 2018, email from John Wilson, in government's opposition filing, Exhibit HHH. Employee's title comes from main body of the filing.

CHAPTER 15: THE TARGET

"a new Jane": Letter from Kaye Kramer to U.S. District Judge Indira Talwani. Document 559, Exhibit B, filed October 16, 2019, in USA v. Buckingham, case no. 19-cr-10117-IT.

As a little girl, she ran: TheMomsView, "Ambition, Balance, and Training Bras!" YouTube video, June 6, 2012, https://www.youtube.com/watch?v=I3JTcfJjaJU.

spoke out on an airplane: Trombone Player Wanted, short-film series, released 2006 by the Marcus Buckingham Company.

got his name on the leaderboard: Records from City of Newport Beach; monthly pool schedule included "Punch Pass Leaders" list.

"I rented out Versailles": October 15, 2018, call between Rick Singer and John Wilson. In Wilson's December 18, 2019, filing, Exhibit 10.

"Well, Atlanta's not redneck": September 15, 2018, call between Rick Singer and John Wilson, in ibid., Exhibit 4.

The same client also struck down: Ibid.

A millionaire developer hired Singer's employee: Third superseding indictment.

including one called "Fitness Fundamentals 2": July 23, 2017, invoice from The Key for Robert Zangrillo. Document 851-1, Exhibit K, filed February 13, 2020, in USA v. Zangrillo, case no. 19-cr-10080.

if it wasn't "handled ASAP": June 12, 2018, email from Rick Singer to Robert Zangrillo. Ibid., Exhibit L.

she expected a discount: Criminal information against Karen Littlefair. Document 1, filed December 9, 2019, in USA v. Littlefair, case no. 19-cr-10463-ADB.

They hired Singer in 2014: Some details of the Semprevivo family's engagement with Singer, including Semprevivo's hopes for Adam's college path and the teen's high school career, come from: Report from criminologist Sheila Balkan. Document 467, Exhibit 1, filed September 19, 2019, in USA v. Semprevivo, case no. 19-cr-10117-IT.

after meeting the college counselor through: Letter from Mark and Renee Paul to U.S. District Judge Indira Talwani, ibid.

He coached baseball, basketball, and soccer: Details of Semprevivo's parenting style, childhood, work ethic, and career come from criminologist report and letters from friends and family to U.S. District Judge Indira Talwani. Document 467, Exhibit 1, filed September 19, 2019, in USA v. Semprevivo, case no. 19-cr-10117-IT.

Singer talked about building a Google Doc: Details of Singer's game plan for Adam Semprevivo, including college lists and discussions with the teen about his top choices, come from emails included in Document 467, Exhibit 3, filed September 19, 2019, in USA v. Semprevivo, case no. 19-cr-10117-IT.

Singer sent Semprevivo, his wife, and his son: August 19, 2015, email from Rick Singer to Stephen, Rita, and Adam Semprevivo, in affidavit.

"I have played very well": Details of the message Adam Semprevivo sent to Gordon Ernst, the material Singer drafted for his college essay for Georgetown, and information in his applications to other schools come from government's supplemental sentencing memo for Stephen Semprevivo. Document 466, filed September 19, 2019, in USA v. Semprevivo, case no. 19-cr-10117-IT.

"looks fine": Affidavit.

Singer made the following notation: Ibid.

"I just lost confidence": Criminologist report.

"worked me over": Letter from Stephen Semprevivo to U.S. District Judge Indira Talwani. Document 467, Exhibit 1, filed September 19, 2019, in USA v. Semprevivo, case no. 19-cr-10117-IT.

a "target" for Singer: Stephen Semprevivo's sentencing memo. Document 467, filed September 19, 2019, in USA v. Semprevivo, case no. 19-cr-10117-IT.

His GPA topped 3.0: Criminologist report.

CHAPTER 16: SEDUCTION

Huffman typed notes: Sentencing memo for Felicity Huffman. Document 425, filed September 6, 2019, in USA v. Huffman, case no. 19-cr-10117-IT.

"Control the outcome": Ibid.

humble, kind, well-adjusted children: Characterizations of the Huffman girls, details of Felicity Huffman's parenting activities, and the family's involvement with LACHSA come in part from letters from family and friends to U.S. District Judge Indira Talwani. Document 425-5, filed September 6, 2019, in USA v. Huffman, case no. 19-cr-10117-IT.

Yet motherhood bewildered Huffman: Letter from Felicity Huffman to U.S. District Judge Indira Talwani. Document 425-2, Exhibit A, filed September 6, 2019, in USA v. Huffman, case no. 19-cr-10117-IT.

"I found mothering my two children": "Felicitations," WhatTheFlicka.com, March 2016, https://web.archive .org/web/20190309050329/http://whattheflicka.com/felicitations/2016/.

Forbes *described it as:* Meghan Casserly, "The 100 Best Websites for Women, 2013," *Forbes,* August 20, 2013, https://www.forbes.com/sites/meghancasserly/2013/08/20/the-100-best-websites-for-women-2013 /#7cb25f7e57c8.

"It's hard to let them fail": "What Kind of Life Skills Are You Teaching Your Children?" episode of *Jen and Barb Mom Life,* http://jenandbarb.com/what-kind-of-life-skills-are-you-teaching-your-children/.

For six years starting in 2012: Some details of the family's engagement with Wendy Mogel come from a letter she wrote to U.S. District Judge Indira Talwani. Document 425-5, Tab 18, filed September 6, 2019, in USA v. Huffman, case no. 19-cr-10117-IT.

"I sat down in her office": "Felicitations for August: Surviving Summer," WhatTheFlicka.com, August 2013, https://web.archive.org/web/20170915125229/http://whattheflicka.com/felicitations/2013/.

"She's struggled to find the balance": Letter from William H. Macy to U.S. District Judge Indira Talwani. Document 426, Tab 1, filed September 6, 2019, in USA v. Huffman, case no. 19-cr-10117-IT.

Yet Huffman felt justified after: Letter from Felicity Huffman to U.S. District Judge Indira Talwani.

She started getting extra time on tests: Felicity Huffman, at her plea hearing, May 13, 2019, in USA v. Huffman, case no. 19-10117-IT.

mothers of previous graduates warned: Letter from Felicity Huffman to U.S. District Judge Indira Talwani.

Huffman hired the counselor in 2016: Details of Singer's work with Huffman's daughters come from Huffman sentencing memo.

Singer warned it wasn't enough: Letter from Felicity Huffman to U.S. District Judge Indira Talwani.

He might grow curt and dismissive: Some characterizations of how Rick Singer approached families were first detailed in Jennifer Levitz and Melissa Korn, "'Nope, You're Not Special.' How the College Scam Mastermind Recruited Families," *The Wall Street Journal,* September 6, 2019.

a score of 1250, or ideally 1350: Huffman sentencing memo.

Several of Sophia's classmates: Ibid.

But Huffman had come to rely: Ibid.

"I felt an urgency": Letter from Felicity Huffman to U.S. District Judge Indira Talwani.

regular (for Hollywood) events: See, for example, People.com Star Tracks listings for September 19 and September 20, 2017, https://people.com/celebrity/star-tracks-tuesday-september-19-2017/?slide=5919003 #5919003 and https://people.com/celebrity/star-tracks-wednesday-september-20-2017/?slide=5921104 #5921104.

She adopted Singer's legal recommendation: Huffman sentencing memo.

The clinician had reassessed Sophia: Ibid.

Macy's episode of Finding Your Roots: October 17, 2017, tweet by @WilliamHMacy, https://twitter.com /WilliamHMacy/status/920391624701616129?s=20.

"Are we doing this on her own": Exchange between Huffman and Singer was detailed in Huffman sentencing memo.

Sophia asked if they could have a treat: Felicity Huffman at her sentencing hearing, September 13, 2019, USA v. Huffman, case no. 19-cr-10117-IT

"Turn around, turn around": Ibid.

On December 4, promoting merchandise: December 4, 2017, tweet by @WilliamHMacy, https://twitter.com /WilliamHMacy/status/937827053054828545?s=20.

"If you would please stop asking": "5 Things Brentwood Students Are Sick of Hearing," *The Flyer,* February 15, 2018, http://www.bwsflyer.com/stories/2018/2/15/5-things-brentwood-students-are-sick-of-hearing.

Singer provided legitimate services: Jane Buckingham's sentencing memo. Document 559, filed October 16, 2019, in USA v. Buckingham, case no. 19-cr-10117-IT.

He took the ACT twice on his own: Government's sentencing memo for Jane Buckingham. Document 558, filed October 16, 2019, in USA v. Buckingham, case no. 19-cr-10117-IT.

Singer had indicated that wasn't enough: Letter from Jane Buckingham to U.S. District Judge Indira Talwani. Document 559-1, Exhibit A in USA v. Buckingham, case no. 19-cr-10117-IT.

"I needed to make myself feel": Ibid.

"Hello everyone! Welcome to": July 12, 2018, tweet from @TBasketpod, https://twitter.com/TBasketpod/status/1017270359094059009.

Buckingham spoke twice on the phone: Details of the test-cheating plan, including having Mark Riddell take the test in Houston while Jack stayed in Los Angeles, the desired score, and a request for Jack's handwriting, come in part from July 12, 2018, and July 13, 2018, phone calls between Rick Singer and Jane Buckingham, in affidavit.

"To whom it may concern": July 13, 2018, email from Jane Buckingham to Rick Singer, in ibid.

"I just found out what you did": Government's sentencing memo for Jane Buckingham.

"the only kind of shady thing": November 15, 2018, phone call between Rick Singer and Jane Buckingham, in ibid.

Marcus had thought Jane blocked him: Michael Proctor, at sentencing hearing for Jane Buckingham, October 31, 2019, USA v. Buckingham, case no. 19-cr-10117-IT.

Singer reassured her: Details of Huffman's thought process as she assessed whether to engage Singer's illicit services for Georgia come from Huffman sentencing memo.

CHAPTER 17: NAME YOUR PRICE

Guo wasn't a Summa client: Jennifer Levitz and Melissa Korn, "Oppenheimer Financial Adviser Connected to College Admissions Cheating Scandal," *The Wall Street Journal,* April 30, 2019, https://www.wsj.com/articles/oppenheimer-financial-adviser-connected-to-college-admissions-cheating-scandal-11556638212.

Yang emailed Rick Singer: Criminal information against Rudy Meredith. Document 1, filed February 28, 2019, in USA v. Meredith, case no. 19-cr-10075-MLW.

Sherry Guo had moved to the United States: Melissa Korn and Jennifer Levitz, "In College Admissions Scandal, Families from China Paid the Most," *The Wall Street Journal,* April 26, 2019, https://www.wsj.com/articles/the-biggest-clients-in-the-college-admissions-scandal-were-from-china-11556301872.

At another school, teachers surrounded: Barbara Demick, "For Chinese, getting into Harvard is a class act," *Los Angeles Times,* June 4, 2010, https://www.latimes.com/archives/la-xpm-2010-jun-04-la-fg-china-college-20100605-story.html.

Countless businesses and secondary schools: Ibid.

Some observers traced the obsession: See, for example, Tracy Jan, "Chinese Aim for the Ivy League," *The New York Times,* January 4, 2009, https://www.nytimes.com/2009/01/04/world/asia/04iht-ivy.1.19063547.html.

Among the character-building exercises: "In China, Not All Practice Tough Love," *The Wall Street Journal,* January 8, 2011, https://www.wsj.com/articles/SB10001424052748704111504576059720804985228.

"Reading it during middle school": Zara Zhang, "When Harvard Becomes 'Ha Fu,'" *Harvard Magazine,* July 20, 2015, https://harvardmagazine.com/2015/07/harvard-in-china.

China had more than a million millionaires: Robert Frank, "China Creates 40,000 New Millionaires," CNBC, September 12, 2014, https://www.cnbc.com/2014/09/12/chinas-millionaire-machine-is-slowing-40000-added-last-year.html.

The number of students from China: "Leading Places of Origin," Institute of International Education Open Doors Report, https://www.iie.org/Research-and-Insights/Open-Doors/Data/International-Students/Places-of-Origin.

Terms like "liberal arts": Zhang, "When Harvard Becomes 'Ha Fu.'"

Dr. Gerald Chow took the witness stand: Many details of Chow's testimony, his family's hiring of Mark Zimny, Zimny's written plan for engagement, and allegations against Zimny come from USA v. Zimny, case no. 13-cr-10024-RWZ, filed January 24, 2013, and Chow et al v. Zimny et al., case no. 10-cv-10572, filed April 5, 2010.

One of the people who wrote: Mark Zimny's sentencing memo. Document 295, filed September 15, 2015, in USA v. Zimny, case no. 13-cr-10024-RWZ

an official referral list for Morgan Stanley: Many details of Rick Singer's inroads at financial services firms, including Freestone Capital, were first reported in Jennifer Levitz, Douglas Belkin, and Melissa Korn, "'He Had the Magic Elixir': How the College Cheating Scandal Spread," *The Wall Street Journal*, March 25, 2019.

Though Singer had been on a referral list: Melissa Korn and Jennifer Levitz, "In College Admissions Scandal, Family Paid $6.5 Million to Get Their Daughter Into Stanford," *The Wall Street Journal*, May 2, 2019, https://www.wsj.com/articles/in-college-admissions-scandal-family-paid-6-5-million-to-get-their-daughter-into-stanford-11556729011.

So when one client: Melissa Korn and Jennifer Levitz, "Chinese Mother Who Paid $6.5 Million for a Shot at Stanford Says She Was Misled," *The Wall Street Journal*, May 2, 2019, https://www.wsj.com/articles/chinese-mother-who-paid-6-5-million-for-a-shot-at-stanford-says-she-was-misled-11556833560.

attended boarding school in the U.K.: Details about Zhao family come from Kate Taylor, Jennifer Medina, Chris Buckley, and Alexandra Stevenson, "Admissions Scandal: When 'Hard Work' (Plus $6.5 Million) Helps Get You Into Stanford," *The New York Times*, May 2, 2019, https://www.nytimes.com/2019/05/02/us/yusi-molly-zhao-china-stanford.html, and Korn and Levitz, "Chinese Mother Who Paid $6.5 Million for a Shot at Stanford Says She Was Misled."

Stanford still admitted Yusi: Assistant U.S. Attorney Eric Rosen, at Rule 11 hearing for John Vandemoer, March 21, 2019, USA v. Vandemoer, case no. 19-cr-10079-RWZ.

The Zhao family sent Singer's foundation: Korn and Levitz, "Chinese Mother Who Paid $6.5 Million for a Shot at Stanford Says She Was Misled."

he was tricked, too: Ibid.

Yang from Summa Group emailed: Details about Sherry Guo's application material being sent to Rudy Meredith come from criminal information against Rudy Meredith.

She actually didn't play competitive soccer: Details about Rudy Meredith flagging Sherry Guo as a recruit come from Assistant U.S. Attorney Eric Rosen, at Singer Rule 11 hearing.

Sherry's family paid Singer and his charity: Criminal information against Rudy Meredith.

they felt comfortable making the donation: February 12, 2020, email from Jim Spertus, attorney for Sherry Guo.

Columbia or Oxford: Korn and Levitz, "In College Admissions Scandal, Families from China Paid the Most."

Sherry faked an injury: Assistant U.S. Attorney Eric Rosen, at Singer Rule 11 hearing.

CHAPTER 18: "ONE TEAM, ONE PLAN, ONE GOAL, ONE STANFORD"

The twenty-minute drive: Description of Vandemoer's commute from the boathouse and early interactions with Singer come from interviews with John Vandemoer. Some details were first reported in Melissa Korn and Jennifer Levitz, "A Stanford Coach Ensnared by the College Admissions Scandal: 'The Biggest Mistake of My Life,'" *The Wall Street Journal*, June 12, 2019, https://www.wsj.com/articles/a-stanford-coach-ensnared-by-the-college-admissions-scandal-the-biggest-mistake-of-my-life-11560368211.

Under Vandemoer, Stanford sailing had rocketed: Many details about Vandemoer's sailing career, reputation, and involvement with his kids come from letters from friends and family to U.S. District Judge Rya Zobel. Document 22, Exhibit 1, filed June 7, 2019, in USA v. Vandemoer, case no. 19-cr-10079-RWZ.

Stanford says fundraising is: June 11, 2019, email from Brad Hayward, associate vice president of university communications.

"some ability to tolerate misery": Korn and Levitz, "A Stanford Coach Ensnared by the College Admissions Scandal: 'The Biggest Mistake of My Life.'"

Singer also approached six other: Melissa Korn, "College Admissions Mastermind Tried to Recruit Seven Stanford Coaches, School Says," *The Wall Street Journal*, December 3, 2019, https://www.wsj.com/articles/college-admissions-mastermind-tried-to-recruit-seven-stanford-coaches-school-says-11575390744.

"If I could take the development piece": Korn and Levitz, "A Stanford Coach Ensnared by the College Admissions Scandal: 'The Biggest Mistake of My Life.'"

Singer's team built the girl: Government's sentencing memo for John Vandemoer. Document 21, filed June 7, 2019, in USA v. Vandemoer, case no. 19-cr-10079-RWZ.

Vandemoer couldn't help: Assistant U.S Attorney Eric Rosen, at Vandemoer Rule 11 hearing.

Her stellar sailing record helped: Ibid.

Singer's charity sent Stanford $500,000: Government's sentencing memo for John Vandemoer.

paying for an assistant coach's salary: John Vandemoer's sentencing memo. Document 22, filed June 7, 2019, in USA v. Vandemoer, case no. 19-cr-10079-RWZ.

a teen boy with another fabricated athletic profile: Criminal information against John Vandemoer. Document 1, filed March 5, 2019, in USA v. Vandemoer, case no. 19-cr-10079-RWZ.

"same outcome for both sides": Details of the two other prospects Singer asked Vandemoer to pitch as sailors come from government's sentencing memo for John Vandemoer.

The following May: Criminal information against Rick Singer.

minimal sailing experience: Assistant U.S. Attorney Eric Rosen, at Vandemoer Rule 11 hearing.

CHAPTER 19: THE SECRET'S OUT

"Is Bill McGlashan doin' any of this shit?": Details of Agustin Huneeus's concerns about Bill McGlashan come from August 30, 2018, phone call between Rick Singer and Agustin Huneeus, in government's opposition filing, Exhibit LLL.

had been a high-maintenance client: Government's sentencing memo for Agustin Huneeus. Document 495, filed September 27, 2019, in USA v. Huneeus, case no. 19-cr-10017-IT. ("He chastised Singer for not giving the scheme enough attention.")

the same year that Atherton mom: Assistant U.S. Attorney Leslie Wright at Isackson plea hearing.

And Marjorie Klapper introduced Singer: Assistant U.S. Attorney Leslie Wright at plea hearing for Marjorie Klapper, May 24, 2019, USA v. Klapper, case no. 19-cr-10017-IT.

an ordinary water polo player: Government's sentencing memo for Agustin Huneeus.

McGlashan was a regular at Davos: See, for example, interview with Erik Schatzker, "McGlashan Seeing Deals That Have Dimensions of Blockchain," Bloomberg, January 23, 2018, https://www.bloomberg.com/news /videos/2018-01-23/mcglashan-seeing-deals-that-have-dimensions-of-blockchain-video.

after hiring Singer in spring 2017: Government's opposition filing.

He'd met Singer through a college friend: Letter from Agustin Huneeus to U.S. District Judge Indira Talwani. Document 494, Exhibit A, Tab 1, filed September 27, 2019, in USA v. Huneeus, case no. 19-cr-10117-IT.

driven there, he would later admit: Ibid.

Huneeus was a devoted dad: Details of Agustin Huneeus's family activities come from letter from Macarena Huneeus to U.S. District Judge Indira Talwani. Document 494, Exhibit A, Tab 19, filed September 27, 2019, in USA v. Huneeus, case no. 19-cr-10117-IT.

drafted behind with the privilege: Letter from Agustin Huneeus to U.S. District Judge Indira Talwani.

"I became brilliant later in life": August 30, 2018, phone call between Rick Singer and Agustin Huneeus, in government's opposition filing, Exhibit LLL.

He told a Marin Academy counselor: Government's sentencing memo for Agustin Huneeus.

"long standing commitment": Ibid.

She got a score of 1380: Ibid.

Huneeus complained that it wasn't high enough: August 30, 2018, phone call between Rick Singer and Agustin Huneeus, in government's opposition filing, Exhibit LLL.

was in talks with Singer to spend: Government's sentencing memo for Agustin Huneeus.

Singer had told him the daughter stood no shot: August 30, 2018, phone call between Agustin Huneeus and Rick Singer, in government's opposition filing, Exhibit LLL.

traditional college counseling: See, for example, Exhibit XXX in government's opposition filing.

"double time": September 7, 2017, email from Kyle McGlashan, in government's opposition filing, Exhibit W.

McGlashan's legal team would say it was moved: Memorandum in support of defendant William McGlashan Jr.'s motion to compel the production of materials. Document 697, filed December 18, 2019, in USA v. McGlashan, case no. 19-cr-10080-NMG.

The two flew down in a private plane: Passenger manifest and reservation details for flights December 8, 2017, and December 9, 2017, in government's opposition filing, Exhibits EE and FF.

McGlashan had asked his assistant to book: December 4, 2017, emails from Bill McGlashan, in ibid., Exhibits CC and DD.

Dvorskiy even wrote into his file: ACT Administration and Payment Report—Special Testing, in ibid., Exhibit GG.

McGlashan's flight home left: December 9, 2017, flight status notification email, in ibid., Exhibit FF.

Riddell later admitted to correcting: Assistant U.S. Attorney Eric Rosen, at Riddell Rule 11 hearing.

"He was pushing hard, like": Quotes from this conversation, and the description of what Huneeus was telling another family, come from September 1, 2018, phone call between Bill McGlashan and Rick Singer, in affidavit.

He attended an early orientation session: Details of Spencer's encounter with the USC counselor were related to Rick Singer by Elisabeth Kimmel and her husband, Greg Kimmel, in a July 26, 2018, phone call, in affidavit.

Spencer wasn't a pole vaulter: Affidavit.

Midwest Television sold the stations: "TEGNA to Acquire Midwest Television Inc.'s Broadcasting Stations in San Diego, CA" press release, December 18, 2017, https://www.tegna.com/tegna-to-acquire-midwest -television-inc-s-broadcasting-stations-in-san-diego-ca/. (The deal closed February 15, 2018.)

as a purported tennis player: According to the affidavit, the girl's Georgetown application said she was a ranked player, and she was flagged by Georgetown tennis coach Gordon Ernst as a recruit. However, prosecutors say, she didn't join the team upon her arrival.

Spencer continued to get messages: August 2, 2018, email from Elisabeth Kimmel to Rick Singer, in affidavit.

"I will take care of tmw": Affidavit.

The ex told a Yale administrator: Details of the Akash Maharaj case come in part from Isaac Arnsdorf, "The man who duped the Ivy League," *Yale Daily News*, September 10, 2008, https://yaledailynews.com/blog/ 2008/09/10/the-man-who-duped-the-ivy-league/, and Karen W. Arenson, "Yale Student Is Accused of Lying on Application," *The New York Times*, April 10, 2008, https://www.nytimes.com/2008/04/10/education /10yale.html.

He said he was a sophomore transfer: Details of Adam Wheeler's scheme are drawn largely from Julie Zauzmer, *Conning Harvard: The True Story of the Con Artist Who Faked His Way Into the Ivy League.* Guilford, CT: Lyons Press, 2013. See also *Harvard Crimson* stories written by Zauzmer.

He took a plea: Mike Vilensky, "Former Harvard Student Pleads Guilty to Lying His Way Into (and Then Through) College," *New York Magazine*, December 16, 2010, https://nymag.com/intelligencer/2010/12 /adam_wheeler.html.

violated his probation: "Harvard Con Man Accused of Citing University on Resume," Associated Press, November 9, 2011, https://www.wbur.org/news/2011/11/09/harvard-fraud-2.

He had been on a routine call: March 10, 2017, account of counselor call, in government's opposition filing, Exhibit J.

Those who used private counselors: Melissa Korn, "Whose Advice Are You Taking? The Fight Over College Counseling at Elite High Schools," *The Wall Street Journal*, October 26, 2019, https://www.wsj.com/articles /whose-advice-are-you-taking-the-fight-over-college-counseling-at-elite-high-schools-11572082200.

Again he had questions: Affidavit.

"our little friend" at Marymount: December 12, 2017, email from Lori Loughlin to Rick Singer and Olivia Giannulli, in affidavit.

His team submitted the applications: Affidavit.

parents didn't hesitate to go over: Letter from Mike Hamilton to U.S. District Judge Indira Talwani. Document 462, Exhibit D, filed September 19, 2019, in USA v. Sloane, case no. 19-cr-10117-IT.

Taylor-Vaz confronted a strange situation: Details of Buckley's discovery of Lizzie Bass's application and some information about the material in them first appeared in Evgenia Peretz, "To Cheat and Lie in L.A.: How the College-Admissions Scandal Ensnared the Richest Families in Southern California," *Vanity Fair*, July 31, 2019, https://www.vanityfair.com/style/2019/07/to-cheat-and-lie-in-la-college-admissions -scandal.

The Bass family blamed: Statement from Bass family, provided via a spokesman on July 31, 2019.

they only learned of the lies: Ibid.

prosecutors say Ernst took bribes: Superseding indictment in USA v. Ernst et al.

at the University of Rhode Island: "University statements on Gordon Ernst," March 14, 2019, https://www.gorhody .com/sports/w-tennis/2018-19/releases/20190312mmvbnz.

On April 12, Petrone got a call: Details of the meeting between Giannulli and Petrone come from note written by PJ Petrone in Olivia Giannulli's file, in government's April 8, 2020, response, Exhibit AA.

"First and foremost": April 12, 2018, email from PJ Petrone to Mossimo Giannulli, in affidavit.

reached out to USC: Note written by PJ Petrone in Olivia Giannulli's file, in government's April 8, 2020, response, Exhibit AA.

accused of having raised marks: Some details of the grade-changing incident, and resultant investigation, come from Peretz, "To Cheat and Lie in L.A.: How the College-Admissions Scandal Ensnared the Richest Families in Southern California."

for five students over five years: Lindsay Weinberg, "From Grade Inflation to Lawsuits: Inside 5 L.A. Private School Debacles," *The Hollywood Reporter,* August 24, 2018, https://www.hollywoodreporter.com/news/a-breakdown-5-la-private-school-debacles-1136207.

including for some without board ties: Sofia Heller, Kaitlin Musante, and Alex Goldstein, "Sculpted by students: Students discuss the way they shape their own grades," *The Chronicle,* March 21, 2018, http://hwchronicle.com/sculpted-by-students-students-discuss-the-way-they-shape-their-own-grades/.

On April Fool's Day 2018: Details of the exchange between Singer and Sloane regarding Buckley's inquiries come from affidavit.

She told the admissions director: April 11, 2018, emails between Donna Heinel and USC admissions director, and others, in ibid.

"the parents getting angry": April 12, 2018, voicemail left by Donna Heinel for Rick Singer, in ibid.

Sloane also had to face: Devin Sloane relayed the interaction with USC development to Rick Singer in an August 30, 2018, phone call with Rick Singer, in ibid.

CHAPTER 20: ON THIRD BASE

When Laura Janke crafted: Affidavit.

A picture of him clearing the bar: Amy McDaniel, "Water Valley boys in position to defend team title," *San Angelo Standard-Times,* May 13, 2016, photo by Adam Sauceda, http://archive.gosanangelo.com/sports/local/hs-track-field-water-valley-boys-in-position-to-defend-team-title-32c0116a-70a4-07b5-e053-0100007fl-379471921.html.

"When will I know about USC": October 8, 2018, meeting with Agustin Huneeus, Agustina Huneeus, and Rick Singer, referenced in sentencing hearing for Agustin Huneeus, September 27, 2018, in USA v. Huneeus, case no. 19-cr-10117-IT

"We're not going to say this to anyone": Ibid.

She likely would have fared well: U.S. District Judge Indira Talwani at Huneeus sentencing.

spent a semester of high school: Asha Khanna, "Sophomore travels to Spain for semester-long exchange," *The Broadview,* September 8, 2015, https://broadview.sacredsf.org/8755/news/sophomore-travels-to-barcelona-for-exchange-program/.

Her family's Tahoe-area ski retreat: "A Family Ski Retreat That's a World Away from Cars," *Dwell,* February 22, 2015, https://www.dwell.com/article/a-family-ski-retreat-thats-a-world-away-from-cars-744df6ec.

Her father had been in talks: August 30, 2018, phone call between Agustin Huneeus and Rick Singer, in government's opposition filing, Exhibit LLL.

And Agustina's grandfather had recently pledged: Ibid.

wasn't a real college prospect: Government's sentencing memo for Agustin Huneeus.

"You understand that [my daughter]": August 30, 2018, phone call between Agustin Huneeus and Rick Singer, in government's opposition filing, Exhibit LLL.

In the same academic year: Assistant U.S. Attorney Justin O'Connell, at Huneeus sentencing hearing.

"You can't tell it's not her": Call between Rick Singer and Agustin Huneeus, September 22, 2018, in affidavit.

Shannon played water polo for Santa Rosa: Phil Barber, "How Ukiah's Shannon Whetzel got pulled into celebrity college admissions scandal," *The Press Democrat,* April 11, 2019. https://www.pressdemocrat.com/sports/9491101-181/barber-how-ukiahs-shannon-whetzel?sba=AAS.

The Ukiah High water polo star: Ibid.

Shannon's long, light brown hair: Lexie Garrett, "Ukiah High caught up in college cheating scandal," *Ukiah Daily Journal,* April 10, 2019, https://www.ukiahdailyjournal.com/2019/04/10/ukiah-high-caught-up-in-college-cheating-scandal/.

CHAPTER 21: USE THE ODDS TO YOUR ADVANTAGE

Meredith had been exposed for: Some details of the alleged academic deceit were first reported in Bill Gallagher and Skakel McCooey, "Meredith allegedly used players to write his grad school papers," *Yale Daily News,* March 16, 2019, https://yaledailynews.com/blog/2019/03/16/meredith-allegedly-used-players-to-write-his-grad-school-papers/.

the winningest coach in the school's history: Bio for Rudy Meredith, Yale University, https://yalebulldogs
   .com/sports/womens-soccer/roster/coaches/rudy-meredith/509.
diagnosed with learning disabilities: Jake Schaller, "Bichy Says Goodbye to the Job of a Lifetime," *The Washing-ton Post,* December 30, 2004.
An anonymous complaint was also sent: Gallagher and McCooey, "Meredith allegedly used players to write his grad school papers."
He coached local youth teams: See, for example, "Ridgefield Team Wins U.S. Youth Title," *The Hartford Cou-rant,* August 4, 1997.
after meeting her at a match: Jerry Trecker, "Rivals on Field, Partners at Home," *The Hartford Courant,* September 5, 2013.
earned his one hundredth career win: Ryan Hartnett, "Meredith snags 100th career win," *Yale Daily News,* October 19, 2004, https://yaledailynews.com/blog/2004/10/19/meredith-snags-100th-career-win/.
"If you had asked any CFC player": Randall Beach, "The 'Coach Rudy' news shocks my daughters," *New Haven Register,* March 22, 2019, https://www.nhregister.com/news/article/Randall-Beach-The-Coach-Rudy-news -shocks-13707188.php.
By 2015, though he hit his two hundredth win: André Monteiro, "Yale secures HC Meredith's 200th victory," *Yale Daily News,* October 12, 2015, https://yaledailynews.com/blog/2015/10/12/womens-soccer-yale-secures-hc -merediths-200th-victory/.
As of 2013, the university handed out: Rishabh Bhandari, "Future of athletic recruitment remains uncertain," *Yale Daily News,* October 18, 2013, https://yaledailynews.com/blog/2013/10/18/future-of-athletic -recruitment-remains-uncertain/.
he had between five and seven: Daniela Brighenti, "New colleges bring potential for growth in athletics," *Yale Daily News,* November 6, 2015, https://yaledailynews.com/blog/2015/11/06/new-colleges-bring-potential -for-growth-in-athletics/.
"If I have seven spots": Ibid.
Meredith had connected to Rick Singer: Jennifer Levitz and Melissa Korn, "Coaches Played Crucial Role in College Admissions Cheating Network," *The Wall Street Journal,* November 14, 2019.
By spring 2015, Meredith had begun taking payments: Assistant U.S. Attorney Eric Rosen, at Rule 11 hearing for Rudolph Meredith, March 28, 2019, USA v. Meredith, case no. 19-cr-10075-MLW.
in exchange for flagging applicants: Criminal information against Rudy Meredith.
Singer directed $250,000: Key Worldwide Foundation 2015 Form 990.
Meredith approached the Los Angeles father: Assistant U.S. Attorney Eric Rosen, at Meredith Rule 11 hearing.
the shocking death of his longtime friend: Jane Miller, "Former assistant coach passes," *Yale Daily News,* September 28, 2017, https://yaledailynews.com/blog/2017/09/28/former-assistant-coach-passes/.
"He was the one that tried": Ibid.

CHAPTER 22: QUEEN FOR A DAY

In February 2018: Boston initial appearance for Michelle Janavs, Stephen Semprevivo, and William McGlashan Jr., March 29, 2019, case no. 19-mj-06087-MPK.
Tobin was a hockey star: Bill Brownstein, "Montrealer was tipster in U.S. college bribery scandal—and has kids at Yale," *Montreal Gazette,* March 22, 2019, https://montrealgazette.com/opinion/columnists/brownstein -montrealer-was-tipster-in-u-s-college-bribery-scandal.
"Every guy wanted to be": Ibid.
he actually left Yale: Jennifer Levitz and Melissa Korn, "The Yale Dad Who Set Off the College Admissions Scandal," *The Wall Street Journal,* March 14, 2019, https://www.wsj.com/articles/the-yale-dad-who-set -off-the-college-admissions-scandal-11552588402.
Tobin didn't see himself as image conscious: Comments from Morrie Tobin, relayed through his attorney on March 17, 2020.
Tobin grew up in Côte-Saint-Luc: Brownstein, "Montrealer was tipster in U.S. college bribery scandal—and has kids at Yale."
attended the Northwood School: Northwood School Annual Report 2014/15, https://issuu.com/issuuns/docs /annualreport2015.
He and Gale initially settled: Katherine Laidlaw, "Rosedale is not amused," *Globe and Mail,* October 18, 2008, https://www.theglobeandmail.com/news/national/rosedale-is-not-amused/article661861/.
"A shocking disregard for history and taste": Ibid.

"The feeling was that he had burned": Brownstein, "Montrealer was tipster in U.S. college bribery scandal—and has kids at Yale."

Tobin disputed that assessment: Tobin comments, via his attorney.

probing a classic pump-and-dump: Details of the charges and fraud scheme come largely from SEC complaint against Morrie Tobin et al. Filed November 27, 2018, https://www.sec.gov/litigation/complaints/2018/comp24361.pdf, and "Founder of Swiss Brokerage Firm Pleads Guilty in Connection with Global Securities Fraud Scheme," press release, January 13, 2020, https://www.justice.gov/usao-ma/pr/founder-swiss-brokerage-firm-pleads-guilty-connection-global-securities-fraud-scheme.

For years, the group had coordinated: Assistant U.S. Attorney Eric Rosen, at Rule 11 hearing for Morrie Tobin, February 27, 2019, USA v. Tobin, case no. 18-cr-10444-NMG.

Tobin said she used to come home: Tobin comments, via his attorney.

Several times in 2017 and 2018: Evgenia Peretz, "To Cheat and Lie in L.A.: How the College-Admissions Scandal Ensnared the Richest Families in Southern California," *Vanity Fair*, July 31, 2019.

"most likely to get a PhD": Yearbook superlative for Sydney Tobin.

Tobin denied the account: Tobin comments, via his attorney.

Meredith had recruited one of her older sisters: Ibid.

Tobin met with Meredith: Ibid.

"So excited to say": September 5, 2017, Instagram post.

Tobin was on a flight: Details of Tobin's meetings with investigators come from Assistant U.S. Attorney Eric Rosen, at Meredith Rule 11 hearing.

serving fresh-squeezed orange juice: Terzah Ewing, "Queen for Day: Martha Stewart Earns Initial Public Offering Crown," *The Wall Street Journal*, October 20, 1999, https://www.wsj.com/articles/SB940365459655529718.

By the end of the day: "Stewart: Billionaire homemaker," *CNNMoney*, October 19, 1999, https://money.cnn.com/1999/10/19/companies/ipos/.

"who has some questions": Liz Claman and Steve Frank, "Market Watch: Martha Stewart Living Omnimedia Inc. CEO Interview," CNBC/Dow Jones Business Video, October 19, 1999.

Frank married his best friend: Kathryn Shattuck, "Adam Berger and Stephen Frank," *The New York Times*, September 17, 2006, https://www.nytimes.com/2006/09/17/fashion/weddings/17vows.html.

"Hi Donna," they wrote: March 28, 2018, email to Donna Heinel, in government's opposition filing, Exhibit VVV.

There was an explanation for everyone: Email from Donna Heinel, in ibid.

In a series of phone calls: Details of Meredith's work as a cooperator and the Boston meeting between Meredith and Tobin come from Assistant U.S. Attorney Eric Rosen, at Meredith Rule 11 hearing.

Who? Rosen and the team: Ibid. (The Court: "Is that the first you had heard of Mr. Singer?" Mr. Rosen: "Indeed it was.")

Six days after the Boston meeting: Criminal information against Rudy Meredith.

he agreed to cooperate: Assistant U.S. Attorney Eric Rosen, at Meredith Rule 11 hearing.

then went down to Naples, Fla.: Tournament records for Minto U.S. Open Pickleball Championships, April 21–28, 2018.

CHAPTER 23: THE WIRE

"Rudy commissioner": July 28, 2018, phone call between Rudy Meredith and Rick Singer, in Wilson's December 18, 2019, filing, Exhibit 12.

son of a Bronx dentist: Neil Swidey, "Meet the 2019 Bostonians of the year: Andrew Lelling and Rachael Rollins," *Boston Globe*, December 11, 2019, https://www.bostonglobe.com/2019/12/11/magazine/meet-2019-bostonians-year-andrew-lelling-rachael-rollins/.

A glimpse of the USS Constitution: Shelley Murphy, "Andrew Lelling fills his office with meaning," *Boston Globe*, October 14, 2019, https://www.bostonglobe.com/business/2019/10/14/lelling-fills-his-office-with-meaning/KPyVLJ9ofjM6RQ817qBpQN/story.html.

Meredith began making recorded calls: Assistant U.S. Attorney Eric Rosen, at Meredith Rule 11 hearing.

Singer sought Meredith's help: May 4, 2018, phone call between Rudy Meredith and Rick Singer, in affidavit.

By June 5, prosecutors had enough: Government's opposition to defendants' motion for production. Document 734, filed January 14, 2020, in USA v. Sidoo et al., case no. 19-cr-10080-NMG.

Late morning June 15: June 15, 2018, phone call with Rick Singer, Gordon Caplan, and Scott Treibly, in government's opposition filing, Exhibit OOO.

whose Hamptons estate sold for $35 million: Candace Taylor, "A Big Sagaponack Estate Sells Fast," *The Wall Street Journal*, October 23, 2014, https://www.wsj.com/articles/a-big-sagaponack-estate-sells-fast-1414086394?mod=WSJ_3Up_RealEstate.

Dozens of family photos adorned: Details of Gordon Caplan's family devotion and reputation within Willkie Farr come from letters from family and friends to U.S. District Judge Indira Talwani. Document 490, filed September 26, 2019, in USA v. Caplan, case no. 19-cr-10117-IT.

But for all his strengths: Gordon Caplan at his sentencing hearing, October 3, 2019, USA v. Caplan, case no. 19-cr-10117-IT.

The Caplans had already been approached: Details of the Caplans' interactions with college counselors come from letter from Amy Caplan to U.S. District Judge Indira Talwani. Document 490, Tab 1, filed September 26, 2019, in USA v. Caplan, case no. 19-cr-10117-IT.

a $290 million company: June 15, 2018, phone call with Rick Singer, Scott Treibly, and Gordon Caplan, in government's opposition filing, Exhibit OOO.

"What we do is we help": Ibid.

having endowed scholarships: Gordon Caplan's sentencing memo. Document 490, filed September 26, 2019, in USA v. Caplan, case no. 19-cr-10017-IT.

Singer called the $750,000 gift: June 15, 2018, phone call with Rick Singer, Scott Treibly, and Gordon Caplan, in government's opposition filing, Exhibit OOO.

Whoa, whoa, whoa: Attorney Joshua Levy at sentencing hearing for Gordon Caplan, October 3, 2019, USA v. Caplan, case no. 19-cr-10117-IT.

"So, most of these kids don't even have issues": June 15, 2018, phone call between Rick Singer and Gordon Caplan, in affidavit.

if he could rig SAT subject tests: August 3, 2018, phone call between Marcia Abbott and Rick Singer, in ibid.

"Kid doesn't have to play the sport": September 19, 2018, phone call between John Wilson and Rick Singer, in government's opposition filing, Exhibit PPP.

On the phone with Miami real estate investor: June 11, 2018, phone call with Rick Singer, Mikaela Sanford, and Robert and Amber Zangrillo, in government's opposition filing, Exhibit MMM.

His employees took at least some portion: Invoices dated July 18, 2017, April 24, 2018, November 20, 2018, and December 4, 2018, from The Key for Robert Zangrillo. Document 851-1, Exhibits K, L, and P, filed February 13, 2020, in USA v. Zangrillo, case no. 19-cr-10080.

How about that biology class?: June 11, 2018, phone call with Rick Singer, Mikaela Sanford, and Robert and Amber Zangrillo, in government's opposition filing, Exhibit MMM.

"I know how this works": August 10, 2018, phone call between Rick Singer and Doug Hodge, in affidavit.

"So we're now the largest education investor": July 30, 2018, phone call between Bill McGlashan and Rick Singer, in government's opposition filing, Exhibit KK.

discussing testing accommodations: Ibid.

the end goal for the oldest son: Ibid.

"It's amazing how he's changing": August 22, 2018, phone call between Bill McGlashan and Rick Singer, in government's opposition filing, Exhibit MM.

He'd already arranged a lunch: Details of McGlashan's considerations regarding whether to pull strings for Kyle at USC, and how his son might feel about that, as well as initial discussions about pitching the teen as a football player, come from July 30, 2018, phone call between Bill McGlashan and Rick Singer, in government's opposition filing, Exhibit KK.

"I'm gonna make him a kicker/punter": August 22, 2018, voicemail from Rick Singer for Bill McGlashan, in government's opposition filing, Exhibit LL.

"I will Photoshop him onto a kicker": August 22, 2018, phone call between Bill McGlashan and Rick Singer, in government's opposition filing, Exhibit MM.

intercepted more than nine thousand: Defendants' motion for production of exculpatory evidence regarding Title III interceptions and consensual recordings, and for other appropriate relief. Document 681, filed December 9, 2019, in USA. v. Sidoo et al., case no. 19-cr-10080-NMG.

bitching about traffic: September 19, 2018, phone call between John Wilson and Rick Singer, in government's opposition filing, Exhibit PPP.

Nearly six hours of calls: Government's opposition to defendants' motion for production.

Singer had no idea the feds were closing in: Interview with Cheryl Silver Levin.

so struck by the extremes: Swidey, "Meet the 2019 Bostonians of the year: Andrew Lelling and Rachael Rollins."

"ambitious publicity hounds": Ibid.

They discussed the outlook: September 15, 2018, phone call between Rick Singer and John Wilson, in Wilson's December 18, 2019, filing, Exhibit 4.

"Not a lot," as he put it: September 29, 2018, phone call between John Wilson and Rick Singer, in government's opposition filing, Exhibit EEE.

"I'm going to Harvard": Wilson's December 18, 2019, filing, Exhibit 4.

three FBI agents and: Report of September 21, 2018, FBI meeting with Rick Singer, in defendants' March 25, 2020, memorandum, Exhibit BB.

he initially pushed back: Declaration of Elizabeth Keating, in government's sur-reply in opposition to defendants' motion to dismiss. Document 1104, Exhibit 1, filed April 24, 2020, in USA v. Sidoo et al., case no. 19-cr-10080-NMG.

The conversation grew boisterous: FBI's April 22, 2020, interview of Rick Singer, in government's sur-reply in opposition to defendants' motion to dismiss. Ibid, Exhibit 4.

while he knew asking families: Ibid.

equipped him with an old-school flip phone: Ibid., Exhibit GG.

He called his half brother Cliff: Report of October 23, 2018, FBI meeting with Rick Singer, in ibid., Exhibit HH

the U.S. Attorney's Office in Santa Ana: Report of September 26, 2018, FBI meeting with Rick Singer, in defendants' March 25, 2020, memorandum, Exhibit V.

In a proffer meeting lasting three days: Government's April 8, 2020, response in opposition to defendants' motion to dismiss.

"a who's who of Oakland": "Oakland Soldiers' Soldiertown Grand Opening," Murray Athletic Development, https://www.madtraining.org/post/oakland-soldiers-soldiertown-grand-opening.

Olivier told the crowd: Ibid.

The next day, September 27: Government's opposition filing.

Singer told agents that very day: Ibid.

But that afternoon, McGlashan texted Singer: Government's opposition filing, Exhibit QQ.

CHAPTER 24: THE FINAL STRETCH

On one of his early undercover operations: Rick Singer, at his Rule 11 hearing.

"You haven't done anything wrong yet": Ibid.

Singer had flat-out confessed: Ibid.

tipped off a total of six families: Assistant U.S. Attorney Eric Rosen, at Singer Rule 11 hearing.

He'd managed to keep an unmonitored side phone: Government's opposition filing.

they needed to talk face-to-face: Affidavit.

They never did meet up: Ibid.

Singer did have an off-line conversation: Report of FBI meeting with Rick Singer, October 23, 2018, in defendants' March 25, 2020, memorandum, Exhibit HH.

because he felt loyalty to them: Ibid.

Just days after agreeing to work: Mossimo Giannulli and Lori Loughlin's supplemental memorandum regarding trial groupings and motion to postpone setting of trial date. Document 875, Exhibit A, filed February 26, 2020, in USA v. Sidoo et al., case no. 19-cr-10080-NMG.

A judge would eventually call the notes: Memorandum and order by U.S. District Judge Nathaniel M. Gorton. Document 1085, filed April 17, 2020, in USA v. Sidoo et al., case no. 19-cr-10080-NMG.

the early dispute was really just about terminology: FBI's April 22, 2020, interview of Rick Singer, in government's sur-reply in opposition to defendants' motion to dismiss. Document 1104, Exhibit 4, filed April 24, 2020, in USA v. Sidoo et al., case no. 19-cr-10080-NMG.

He might be flanked: Report of government meeting with Rick Singer, October 24, 2018, in ibid., Exhibit X.

"I just want to give you a heads-up": November 29, 2018, phone call between Rick Singer and Agustin Huneeus, in affidavit.

"So I'm in Boston now": October 24, 2018, phone call between Rick Singer and Elizabeth Henriquez, in ibid.

saying "gotcha" and "okay": October 24, 2018, phone call between Rick Singer and Bruce Isackson, in ibid.

he'd recently asked Singer for a receipt: September 26, 2018, phone call between Rick Singer and Bruce Isackson, in ibid.

discussions about their son: August 23, 2018, phone call between Rick Singer and Davina Isackson, in ibid.

"a donation to our foundation": December 3, 2018, phone call between Rick Singer and Davina Isackson, in ibid.

"You know, I am so paranoid": December 3, 2018, meeting between Rick Singer and Bruce Isackson, in ibid.

Georgia had been diagnosed with dyslexia: Letter from William H. Macy to U.S. District Judge Indira Talwani.

attended a middle school: Letter from Douglas Phelps to U.S. District Judge Indira Talwani. Document 425-5, Tab 27, filed September 6, 2019, in USA v. Huffman, case no. 19-cr-10117-IT.

Her plan was to have: November 12, 2018, phone call between Rick Singer and Felicity Huffman, in affidavit.

"We're going to do like we did": Ibid.

"don't have to play": October 15, 2018, phone call between Rick Singer and John Wilson, in government's opposition filing, Exhibit FFF.

he wished Singer had two-for-one pricing: September 15, 2018, phone call between Rick Singer and John Wilson, in Wilson's December 18, 2019, filing, Exhibit 4.

"No, no, no, no": October 27, 2018, phone call between John Wilson and Rick Singer, in government's opposition filing, Exhibit III.

"I asked him for a second spot": Ibid.

"Yeah, no. He's got to actually have": Ibid.

"We got both settled": November 29, 2018, phone call between John Wilson and Rick Singer, in government's opposition filing, Exhibit JJJ.

She contacted the ACT: Tweet by @getmetocollege, October 3, 2018, https://twitter.com/getmetocollege/status/1047607580623687680?s=20.

even telling his main USC contact: Reply in support of McGlashan's motion. (Referencing October 16, 2018, communication between Rick Singer and Donna Heinel, in which Singer said McGlashan had "family ties with Jimmy Lovine [sic] and various board members and is going that route.")

Singer had tipped him off: Affidavit.

he'd told McGlashan the IRS: October 24, 2018, phone call between Rick Singer and Bill McGlashan, in affidavit.

"just till it's all cleared up": October 24, 2018, phone call between Bill McGlashan and Rick Singer, in government's opposition filing, Exhibit SS.

Gordon Caplan may have been named: "The 2018 Dealmakers of the Year," *The American Lawyer*, April 2018, https://www.willkie.com/~/media/Files/News/2018/04/ALM%20Dealmaker%20of%20the%20Year%20Willkie_Caplan%20reprint%202018.PDF.

It seemed like the government: FBI's April 22, 2020, interview of Rick Singer, in government's sur-reply in opposition to defendants' motion to dismiss. Document 1104, Exhibit 4, filed April 24, 2020, in USA v. Sidoo et al., case no. 19-cr-10080-NMG.

"nail Gordon at all costs": Mossimo Giannulli and Lori Loughlin's supplemental memorandum regarding trial groupings and motion to postpone setting of trial date. Document 875, Exhibit A, filed February 26, 2020, in USA v. Sidoo et al., case no. 19-cr-10080-NMG.

"Keep in mind I am a lawyer": Gordon Caplan ran through a list of concerns in November 8, 2018, and November 15, 2018, phone calls with Rick Singer, in affidavit.

There came Igor Dvorskiy: Arrival and departure times to and from the testing site are from affidavit.

"I never want to do anything": January 24, 2019, phone call between Rick Singer and Gordon Caplan, in government's sentencing memo for Gordon Caplan. Document 489, filed September 26, 2019, in USA v. Caplan, case no. 19-cr-10117-IT.

"It is time to explore": "Meredith Resigns as Head Coach," November 15, 2018, press release, https://web.archive.org/web/20190316091513/http://www.yalebulldogs.com/sports/w-soccer/2018-19/releases/20181115i01t60.

One day later: Melissa Korn, "Yale Was Subpoenaed in November Related to Admissions Cheating Scandal," *The Wall Street Journal*, March 15, 2019, https://www.wsj.com/articles/yale-was-subpoenaed-in-november-related-to-admissions-cheating-scandal-11552692608.

"All I know is that we": March 3, 2019, phone call between Rick Singer and Stephen Semprevivo, in affidavit.

Lori Loughlin called Singer, worried: March 4, 2019, phone call between Rick Singer and Lori Loughlin, in defendants' March 25, 2020, memorandum, Exhibit U.

to finalize plans for that next exam: December 12, 2018, phone call with Rick Singer, Felicity Huffman, and William H. Macy, in affidavit.

"Both Felicity and I": Walter Scott, "William H. Macy on His Favorite Frank Moments from *Shameless* and Working with Wife Felicity Huffman," *Parade*, January 18, 2019, https://parade.com/732550/walterscott

/william-h-macy-on-his-favorite-frank-moment-from-shameless-and-working-with-wife-felicity -huffman/.

"Never lie. It's the cheapest": Larry Kanter, "William H. Macy on Astronauts, Abraham Lincoln, and the Adventure That Most Changed his Life," *Men's Journal*, February 1, 2019, https://www.mensjournal.com /entertainment/william-h-macy-on-astronauts-abraham-lincoln-and-the-adventure-that-changed-his -life/ and to see date: https://www.pressreader.com/usa/mens-journal/20190201/282570199284742.

Huffman knew what she had done: Letter from Felicity Huffman to U.S. District Judge Indira Talwani.

The couple didn't know about: Huffman sentencing memo.

"It just doesn't feel right": March 5, 2019, phone call between Rick Singer and Felicity Huffman, in ibid.

"I am entering into this Agreement": Plea agreement for John Vandemoer, signed March 3, 2019. Document 3, filed March 5, 2019, in USA v. Vandemoer, case no. 19-cr-10079-RWZ.

"this massive thing is going to": Melissa Korn and Jennifer Levitz, "A Stanford Coach Ensnared by the College Admissions Scandal: 'The Biggest Mistake of My Life,'" *The Wall Street Journal*, June 12, 2019.

Riddell, the test-taker, had signed: Plea agreement for Mark Riddell, signed February 22, 2019. Document 14, filed March 23, 2019, in USA v. Riddell, case no. 19-cr-10074-NMG.

Meredith, the Yale coach: Plea agreement for Rudolph Meredith, signed March 5, 2019. Document 17, filed March 14, 2019, in USA v. Meredith, case no. 19-cr-10075-MLW.

CHAPTER 25: TAKEDOWN

Marcus Buckingham's phone rang: Marcus Buckingham provided an account of that morning in "The Speech I Never Intended to Give," posted on his website, https://www.marcusbuckingham.com/rwtb/the-speech i never intended/. Some details also appeared in Jennifer Levitz and Melissa Korn, "'Why Didn't You Believe in Me?' The Family Reckoning After the College Admissions Scandal," *The Wall Street Journal*, January 17, 2020.

paid Singer a total of $200,000: Second superseding indictment against David Sidoo et al. Document 314, filed April 9, 2019, in USA v. Sidoo et al., case no. 19-cr-10080-NMG.

Sidoo's arrest didn't leak: Initial appearance for David Sidoo, March 11, 2019, in USA v. Sidoo, case no. 19-mj-70367-MAG. (The attorneys and judge discuss that the indictment remained under seal.)

post a $1.5 million cash bond: Ibid.

Magistrate Judge M. Page Kelley signed: See, for example, USA v. Abbott et al., Document 4, filed March 11, 2019, in case no. 19-cr-10117-IT.

She'd already signed warrants: See, for example, USA v. Ernst et al., Document 3, filed March 5, 2019, in case no. 19-cr-10117-IT.

"To: any authorized law enforcement": Ibid.

Some seven weeks earlier: "Video shows FBI at Roger Stone's house," CNN, January 25, 2019, https://www.cnn .com/videos/politics/2019/01/25/roger-stone-fbi-arrest-vo.cnn.

more than a dozen FBI agents: Miles Parks, "Fact Check: Did the FBI Use Unusual Force When It Arrested Roger Stone?" NPR.org, February 1, 2019, https://www.npr.org/2019/02/01/690305364/fact-check-did-the -fbi-use-unusual-force-when-it-arrested-roger-stone.

Also at 6:00 a.m., different teams of agents: Arrest times come from Report Commencing Criminal Action, Central District of California. See, for example, Document 2 in 2:2019-mj-00996, USA v. Michelle Janavs.

brash armed agents tramping: Huffman sentencing memo; also, letter from Macarena Huneeus to U.S. District Judge Indira Talwani.

In Menlo Park, Marjorie Klapper: Marjorie Klapper's sentencing memo.

carted off from his home: Casey Claiborne, "UT Tennis Coach Michael Center appears before federal judge," *Fox 7 Austin*, March 12, 2019, https://www.fox4news.com/news/ut-tennis-coach-michael-center -appears-before-federal-judge.

"When the FBI knocks on your door": Ibid.

The news alert hit reporters' inboxes: March 12, 2019, email from U.S. Attorney for the District of Massachusetts, "Media Advisory—For Planning Purposes Only."

"a criminal matter out of": March 12, 2019, email from FBI National Press Office, time stamp 10:31 A.M.

an NBC News correspondent tweeted: Tweet by @JuliaEAinsley, March 12, 2019, https://twitter.com /JuliaEAinsley/status/1105477620743966720.

"We're here today to announce": U.S. Attorney Andrew Lelling, at March 12, 2019, press conference, https:// www.youtube.com/watch?v=KJUOGKvyRPE.

Jack followed a Twitter thread: Marcus Buckingham provided an account of that morning in "The Speech I Never Intended to Give," posted on his website.

Sophia and Georgia Macy called: Letter from Ellen Etten to U.S. District Judge Indira Talwani.

FBI agents had surprised Vavic: "USC water polo coach arrested in Waikiki," KITV, March 12, 2019, https://www.kitv.com/story/40113933/usc-water-polo-coach-arrested-in-waikiki-amid-massive-college-cheating-scheme.

"People are ANGRY about the story": "Ken Lawson on college bribery scheme," KHON2, March 12, 2019, https://www.khon2.com/news/usc-water-polo-coach-arrested-in-waikiki-in-connection-with-college-bribery-scheme/.

"How do we ensure": Assistant U.S. Attorney Alex Wyman, at March 12, 2019, Los Angeles detention hearing, case no. 19-mj-981 to 19-mj-996.

"They have children, which is the basis": Jodi Linker, at detention hearing for Diane and Todd Blake, March 12, 2019, case no. 19-mj-70373-JCS.

"be present in court without shackles": Assertion of right to be present in court unshackled and preservation of appellate rights. Document 6, filed March 12, 2019, in U.S. v. Abdelaziz, case no. 19-mj-00180-VCF.

accused of paying a $300,000 bribe: Second superseding indictment against David Sidoo et al. Document 314, filed April 9, 2019, in USA v. Sidoo et al., case no. 19-cr-10080-NMG.

"Interrupting, Judge": Attorney Dan Cogdell, at initial appearance for Michael Center, March 12, 2019, case no. 19-mj-160.

"All right. Good morning, everybody": U.S. Magistrate Judge Gordon P. Gallagher, at initial appearance for Marcia Abbott, March 12, 2019, case no. 19-mj-6087.

She had an uptown pedigree: "Marcia Meighan Wed to Gregory B. Abbott," *The New York Times*, May 2, 1987, https://www.nytimes.com/1987/05/02/style/marcia-meighan-wed-to-gregory-b-abbott.html.

Her husband had expanded: "International Dispensing Company Names Greg Abbott CEO," November 27, 2006, press release, https://www.businesswire.com/news/home/20061127005660/en/International-Dispensing-Company-Names-Greg-Abbott-CEO.

"I—I—I don't know how": Marcia Abbott, at her initial appearance, March 12, 2019, USA v. Abbott, case no. 19-mj-6087.

"The central defendant": These quotes come from U.S. Attorney Andrew Lelling, at March 12, 2019, press conference.

"You need four prosecutors": U.S. District Judge Rya Zobel, at Singer Rule 11 hearing.

"It is a radical change": Assistant U.S. Attorney Adam Schleifer, at March 12, 2019, Los Angeles detention hearing, case nos. 19-mj-981 to 19-mj-996.

worried about being able to pump: Attorneys conveyed clients' concerns, including about impending travel, at ibid.

Robert Flaxman's $15 million: Defendants' assets were detailed at March 12, 2019, Los Angeles detention hearing.

"We just got Felicity and Mossimo": "Felicity Huffman Released After FBI Arrest with Guns Drawn," TMZ.com, https://www.tmz.com/2019/03/12/felicity-huffman-arrest-guns-drawn-fbi-college-bribery/.

Matteo Sloane, on spring break: Letter from Devin Sloane to U.S. District Judge Indira Talwani. Some details of the reunion between Devin and Matteo Sloane were first reported in Levitz and Korn, "'Why Didn't You Believe in Me?' The Family Reckoning After the College Admissions Scandal."

CHAPTER 26: THE PARADE

He wanted permission to go: Boston initial appearance for Michelle Janavs, Stephen Semprevivo, and William McGlashan Jr., March 29, 2019, case no. 19-mj-06087-MPK.

"Can I stop you?": U.S. Chief District Judge Patti Saris at Isackson plea hearing.

"been in the system": Assistant U.S. Attorney Justin O'Connell, at Boston initial appearance for Gregory and Marcia Abbott, Gamal Abdelaziz, I-Hsin Chen, Robert Flaxman, Agustin Huneeus, and Elisabeth Kimmel, March 29, 2019, case no. 19-mj-06087-MPK.

Three months earlier, the company proudly announced: "IDC's The Answer Wins 2019 WorldStar Award," December 10, 2018, press release, https://www.idcinnovation.com/idcs-the-answer-wins-2019-worldstar-award/.

He had filed a motion: Memorandum in support of defendant Gamal Abdelaziz's motion to modify pretrial conditions to allow international business travel. Document 217, filed March 28, 2019, in USA v. Abdelaziz, case no. 19-mj-06087-MPK.

taken hundreds of thousands: Assistant U.S. Attorney Eric Rosen, at Meredith Rule 11 hearing.

An unexpected tip: Jennifer Levitz and Melissa Korn, "The Yale Dad Who Set Off the College-Admissions Scandal," *The Wall Street Journal*, March 14, 2019.

Tobin was the father: Jennifer Levitz and Melissa Korn, "Alleged Tipster in College Cheating Scandal Bribed a Coach, Source Says," *The Wall Street Journal*, March 19, 2019, https://www.wsj.com/articles/alleged -tipster-in-college-cheating-scandal-bribed-a-coach-source-says-11553005101.

USC put holds: "USC Information on College Admissions Issue," *USC News*, April 24, 2019, https://web .archive.org/web/20190502070108/https://news.usc.edu/155225/usc-information-on-college-admissions -issue/.

He said Sherry learned English: Melissa Korn and Jennifer Levitz, "In College Admissions Scandal, Families from China Paid the Most," *The Wall Street Journal*, April 26, 2019.

smiled and waved as she maneuvered: Scenes from outside the courthouse were first detailed in Jennifer Levitz, Jon Kamp, and Melissa Korn, "Lori Loughlin, Felicity Huffman Appear in Court for College-Admissions Case," *The Wall Street Journal*, April 3, 2019, https://www.wsj.com/articles/actresses-felicity-huffman -lori-loughlin-to-appear-in-court-for-college-admissions-case-11554315522.

Loughlin and her husband, Giannulli, had flown: Megan Johnson, "'Chatty' Lori Loughlin Signs Autographs for Fans Ahead of Hearing in College Admissions Scandal," *People*, April 2, 2019, https://people .com/tv/lori-loughlin-signs-autographs-chats-fans-college-admissions-scandal-court-hearing/.

The filing came from a lawyer: Defendant Peter Sartorio's motion to continue, filed April 3, 2019, Document 288 in USA v. Sartorio, case no. 19-cr-10117-IT.

paid $15,000 to have: Plea hearing for P. J. Sartorio, May 22, 2019, USA v. Sartorio, case no. 19-cr-10117-IT.

On April 8, thirteen parents and: Melissa Korn, "Prosecutors Net 14 New Guilty Plea Agreements in College Cheating Probe," *The Wall Street Journal*, April 8, 2019, https://www.wsj.com/articles/two-more-parents -to-plead-guilty-in-college-admissions-case-11554741856.

she had a master's degree in: Davina Isackson, at Isackson plea hearing.

"control the test room": Rick Singer, in August 23, 2018, phone call with Davina Isackson, in affidavit.

Bruce had then written the fraud off: Assistant U.S. Attorney Leslie Wright at Isackson plea hearing.

"Oh my God": Bruce Isackson, at December 3, 2018, meeting with Rick Singer, in affidavit.

CHAPTER 27: DIGGING IN

accused of ponying up $25,000: Affidavit.

indicted on the new money-laundering charge: Second superseding indictment against Sidoo et al.

"He can't have this": March 26, 2019, interview with attorney Patric Hooper.

"color advisor": January 2, 2020, email from attorney Patric Hooper.

Singer recounted how they'd: October 24, 2018, phone call with Rick Singer and Amy and Greg Colburn, in affidavit.

They weren't actually agreeing: Jennifer Levitz and Melissa Korn, "Two Parents in College-Admissions Scheme Indicted on New Charge," *The Wall Street Journal*, March 26, 2019, https://www.wsj.com/articles /two-parents-in-college-admissions-scheme-indicted-on-new-charge-11553642532.

"There was something odd": Hooper interview.

Larson typed out an email at 5:01 p.m.: April 13, 2019, email exchange between Stephen Larson and Eric Rosen, in Jovan Vavic's opposition to the government's motion for a protective order. Document 155, Exhibit F, filed October 18, 2019, in USA v. Vavic, case no. 19-cr-10081-IT.

"My own feeling is that": May 3, 2019, interview with Stephen Larson.

a Holocaust survivor: "Rya Zobel: A Child of Nazi Germany Says 'I've Been Incredibly Fortunate,'" August 28, 2019, U.S. Courts, https://www.uscourts.gov/news/2019/08/28/rya-zobel-child-nazi-germany-says-ive-been -incredibly-fortunate.

Prosecutors had by then gotten: Melissa Korn and Jennifer Levitz, "A Stanford Coach Ensnared by the College Admissions Scandal: 'The Biggest Mistake of My Life,'" *The Wall Street Journal*, June 12, 2019.

"This was the biggest mistake": Ibid.

He was probably the least culpable: See, for example, U.S. District Judge Rya Zobel, at sentencing hearing for John Vandemoer, June 12, 2019, USA v. Vandemoer, case no. 19-cr-10079-RWZ.

A handful of internal USC admissions documents: Jennifer Levitz and Melissa Korn, "'Father Is Surgeon,' '1 Mil Pledge': The Role of Money in USC Admissions," *The Wall Street Journal*, September 3, 2019.

"What does the designation VIP signify?": Discussion of the VIP designation took place at September 18, 2019, hearing in USA v. Zangrillo.

after the university initially rejected her: April 20, 2017, email from USC account, name redacted. Document 851-1, Exhibit J, in USA v. Zangrillo, case no. 19-cr-10080-NMG.

Though Singer had referenced a plan: Affidavit.

she was ultimately flagged: Email from Donna Heinel to Rick Singer, June 26, 2018, Document 851-1, Exhibit R, in USA v. Zangrillo, case no. 19-cr-10080-NMG.

collection of internal USC admissions records: Levitz and Korn, "'Father Is Surgeon,' '1 Mil Pledge': The Role of Money in USC Admissions."

In one boorish email exchange: Emails between USC's Tim Brunold and Kirk Brennan, in opposition by Robert Zangrillo. Document 546, Exhibit 17, filed September 3, 2019, in USA v. Zangrillo, case no. 19-cr-10080-NMG.

Prosecutors sent "target letters": Melissa Korn and Jennifer Levitz, "Students, Graduates May Be Next Targets of College-Admissions Scandal Investigation," *The Wall Street Journal*, April 14, 2019, https://www.wsj .com/articles/students-graduates-may-be-next-targets-of-college-admissions-scandal -investigation-11555272625.

"We come in peace": Assistant U.S. Attorney Eric Rosen at September 10, 2019, hearing in USA v. Abbott et al., case no. 19-cr-10117-IT.

Probation department officials, preparing presentencing reports: Jennifer Levitz and Melissa Korn, "Why Parents in the College-Admissions Scandal May Get Light Sentences," *The Wall Street Journal*, September 4, 2019, https://www.wsj.com/articles/in-college-admissions-scandal-the-legal-fight-to-set-sentences-for-the -parents-11567589400.

he wrote a strongly worded letter: Letter from U.S. Attorney Andrew Lelling to U.S. District Judge Indira Talwani. Document 411, filed August 23, 2019, in USA v. Abbott et al., case no. 19-cr-10117-IT.

She was adopting the guidelines: Memorandum and Order of U.S. District Judge Indira Talwani. Document 443, filed September 13, 2019, in USA v. Abbott et al., case no. 19-cr-10117-IT.

She believed college admissions were already rigged: U.S. District Judge Indira Talwani at Huffman sentencing hearing.

CHAPTER 28: SENTENCED

had been reflecting on: U.S. District Judge Indira Talwani at Huffman sentencing hearing.

One dad told of being so poor: Sloane sentencing memo.

Another had a stepmother: Letter from Aliza Avital-Caplan to U.S. District Judge Indira Talwani, dated May 15, 2019. Document 490, Tab 5, in USA v. Caplan, case no. 19-cr-10117-IT.

a divorce that made a defendant: Michael Proctor, at Buckingham sentencing hearing.

One suggested the court should go easy: Agustin Huneeus's sentencing memo. Document 494, filed September 27, 2019, in USA v. Huneeus, case no. 19-cr-10117-IT.

"middle-class": Peter Jan Sartorio's sentencing memo. Document 512, filed October 4, 2019, in USA v. Sartorio, case no. 19-cr-10117-IT.

once dubbed the legal consigliere: Matt Diehl, "The Endless Fall of Suge Knight," *Rolling Stone*, July 6, 2015, https://www.rollingstone.com/music/music-news/the-endless-fall-of-suge-knight-73346/.

Among the losses? The $400,000: Semprevivo sentencing memo.

"Mr. Singer pierced through": Ibid.

"I don't feel I need an expert": U.S. District Judge Indira Talwani, at sentencing hearing for Stephen Semprevivo, September 26, 2019, in USA v. Semprevivo, case no. 19-cr-10117-IT.

The government considered Huffman's conduct: Prosecutors' requested sentence for Huffman was among the lowest of any parents in the initial wave of sentencings.

"Her brain is a bit like Swiss cheese": Letter from Laura Bauer to U.S. District Judge Indira Talwani. Document 425-5, Tab 4, filed September 6, 2019, in USA v. Huffman, case no. 19-cr-10117-IT.

"Welcome to parenthood": Assistant U.S. Attorney Eric Rosen at Huffman sentencing hearing.

calling incarceration "the great leveler": Ibid.

"sense of entitlement": Government's supplemental sentencing memo for Felicity Huffman. Document 424, filed September 6, 2019, in USA v. Huffman, case no. 19-cr-10117-IT.

"Huffman's next wardrobe call": Beth Teitell, "Husband of the year? Moms say it's not William H. Macy," *Boston Globe*, October 3, 2019, https://www.bostonglobe.com/metro/2019/10/03/husband-year-moms-say -not-william-macy/xbU2n6vmXf8eUU6NoXcXdJ/story.html.

the probation department questioned whether: Assistant U.S. Attorney Eric Rosen, at sentencing hearing for Devin Sloane, September 24, 2019, in USA v. Sloane, case no. 19-cr-10117-IT.

their three-decade marriage was on the rocks: Joint sentencing memo for Gregory and Marcia Abbott. Document 521, filed October 8, 2019, in USA v. Abbott, case no. 19-cr-10117-IT.

Greg's counsel portrayed the couple's breakdown: Daniel Stein, at sentencing hearing for Gregory and Marcia Abbott, October 8, 2019, in USA v. Abbott, case no. 19-10117-IT.

"We had death, we had illness": Assistant U.S. Attorney Justin O'Connell at Buckingham sentencing hearing.

"There was no Photoshopping": Attorney Daniel Stein, at Abbott sentencing hearing.

"Our case is not like the parent": Attorney Michael Proctor at Buckingham sentencing hearing.

"Our case is not like the folks": Ibid.

Current and former Willkie Farr partners: See, for example, letters from Gregory Bruch (Tab 22), Steven Gartner (Tab 35), Matthew Guercio (Tab 40), Matthew Haddad (Tab 41) to U.S. District Judge Indira Talwani. Document 490-1, filed September 26, 2019, in USA v. Caplan, case no. 19-cr-10117-IT.

"He is the only one": U.S. District Judge Indira Talwani at sentencing hearing for P. J. Sartorio, October 11, 2019, in USA v. Sartorio, case no. 19-cr-10117-IT.

In late October, the expectation that: Jennifer Levitz, "More Parents Enter Guilty Pleas in College Admissions Cheating Case," *The Wall Street Journal,* October 21, 2019, https://www.wsj.com/articles/new-wave-of -parents-begin-entering-guilty-pleas-in-college-admissions-cheating-case-11571673455.

"This is a case in search of a bribe or kickback": U.S. District Judge Douglas P. Woodlock at Bizzack sentencing hearing.

Jeffrey Bizzack, a California surfing executive: Melissa Korn, "New Parent Is Charged in College-Admissions Scandal," *The Wall Street Journal,* June 28, 2019, https://www.wsj.com/articles/new-parent-is-charged -in-college-admissions-scandal-11561743391.

he was part of a fish stick dynasty: Milton J. Valencia, "Meet the judge who will hear the Boston legal challenge of Trump's ban," *Boston Globe,* February 2, 2017, https://www.bostonglobe.com/metro/2017/02/02/gorton -takes-nonsense-approach/ZzCCYgdTDT0cdQnfHFrY7O/story.html.

"for the worst set of decisions": Toby Macfarlane, at his sentencing hearing, November 13, 2019, in USA v. Macfarlane, case no. 19-cr-10131.

"Mr. Hodge, your conduct": Jennifer Levitz and Melissa Korn, "Former Pimco CEO Sentenced to Nine Months in Prison in College Admissions Case," *The Wall Street Journal,* February 7, 2020, https://www.wsj.com /articles/former-pimco-ceo-to-be-sentenced-in-college-admissions-scandal-11581089874.

Hodge would author an op-ed: Doug Hodge, "I Wish I'd Never Met Rick Singer," *The Wall Street Journal,* February 9, 2020, https://www.wsj.com/articles/i-wish-id-never-met-rick-singer-11581278199.

the payments straight to Ernst: Hodge sentencing memo.

CHAPTER 29: A SYSTEM REFORMED?

additional administrators would now need: Statement from Dartmouth spokeswoman Diana Lawrence; Marc Tessier-Lavigne, and Persis Drell, "An update on the admissions fraud scheme," *Notes from the Quad,* March 21, 2019. https://quadblog.stanford.edu/2019/03/21/an-update-on-the-admissions-fraud -scheme/.

Yale said it would check: Letter from President Peter Salovey to the Yale community, "Update—Actions to strengthen our ability to detect and prevent admissions fraud," August 28, 2019, https://president.yale .edu/speeches-writings/statements/update-actions-strengthen-our-ability-detect-and-prevent -admissions.

require written assessments: Legal Review of Athletics Admissions at the University of Texas at Austin, September 9, 2019, https://utexas.app.box.com/v/athletics-admissions-review.

add another verification step: March 20, 2019, email from spokesman George Retelas.

In October 2019, California governor Gavin Newsom: Sarah Ruiz-Grossman, "California Reforms College Admissions Following Bribery Scandal," *HuffPost,* October 4, 2019, https://www.huffpost.com/entry/california -legislation-college-scandal-admissions_n_5d719c19e4b03aabe359bc2e.

"We must strive for": Assemblymember Phil Ting, "California's First College Admissions Reform Bill Sent to the Governor Is Signed," October 4, 2019, press release, https://a19.asmdc.org/press-releases/20191004 -californias-first-college-admissions-reform-bill-sent-governor-signed.

The Wall Street Journal *and* ProPublica *both wrote:* Douglas Belkin, "College Financial-Aid Loophole: Wealthy Parents Transfer Guardianship of Their Teens to Get Aid," *The Wall Street Journal,* July 29, 2019, https:// www.wsj.com/articles/the-college-financial-aid-guardianship-loophole-and-the-woman-who -thought-it-up-11564595984, and Jodi S. Cohen and Melissa Sanchez, "Parents Are Giving Up Custody of

Their Kids to Get Need-Based College Financial Aid," *ProPublica Illinois*, July 29, 2019, https://www
.propublica.org/article/university-of-illinois-financial-aid-fafsa-parents-guardianship-children
-students.

"I don't think I figured out": Belkin, "The College Financial-Aid Guardianship Loophole and the Woman Who
Thought It Up."

Jerome Allen, then the men's basketball coach: Details of Allen's involvement with Esformes come in part from Jay
Weaver, "NBA Coach Jerome Allen gets probation for taking bribes to get student into Penn," *Miami Herald*,
July 1, 2019, https://www.miamiherald.com/news/local/article232137317.html#storylink=cpy.

Esformes had used Singer to pitch: Assistant U.S. Attorney Eric Rosen, at Janke Rule 11 hearing.

"If a parent ever feels the need": Letter quoted in Caitlin Gibson, "When Parents Are So Desperate to Get Their
Kids Into College That They Sabotage Other Students," *The Washington Post*, April 3, 2019, https://www
.washingtonpost.com/lifestyle/on-parenting/when-parents-are-so-desperate-to-get-their-kids
-into-college-that-they-sabotage-other-students/2019/04/02/decc6b9e-5159-11e9-88a1-ed346f0ec94f
_story.html.

Elizabeth Henriquez was mostly ostracized: Elizabeth Henriquez's sentencing memo. Document 978, filed
March 26, 2020, in USA v. Henriquez, case no. 19-cr-10080-NMG.

"I blame no one but myself": February 4, 2020, statement from Gordon Caplan.

Tens of thousands of dollars: Amount confirmed on April 3, 2020, by Vince Cuseo, vice president of enrollment
and dean of admission at Occidental.

"a sense of gracious civility": Muttontown Club website, https://www.themuttontownclub.com/.

to hear reassurances about how their kids: Melissa Korn spoke at the event for Friends Academy senior parents.
She is an alumna of the school.

Ten months after his father: Details of Matteo's life after his father's arrest come from a January 9, 2020, interview with him.